TEACHING VISUALLY IMPAIRED CHILDREN

ABOUT THE AUTHOR

Dr. Virginia E. Bishop was an itinerant teacher of visually impaired students in Pennsylvania for 30 years before moving to Texas to pursue a doctoral degree at The University of Texas at Austin. After earning that degree, she taught courses to prepare teachers of visually impaired students (TVIs) at a number of universities (The University of Texas at Austin, University of Arkansas at Little Rock, University of Nebraska at Lincoln, Georgia State University at Atlanta, and Texas Tech University in Lubbock). Dr. Bishop has also supervised teacher interns for The University of Texas at Austin, Texas Tech University, University of Arkansas at Little Rock, and Peabody College of Vanderbilt University.

Within the last 20 years, Dr. Bishop has written a number of journal articles, conducted a wide variety of training workshops for teachers throughout the state of Texas, and has presented professional papers in Germany, Scotland, the Netherlands, Australia, Thailand, Spain, and Brazil. Although officially "retired," Dr. Bishop still conducts in-service courses as needed, and continues to remain active in professional organizations.

Third Edition

TEACHING VISUALLY IMPAIRED CHILDREN

By

VIRGINIA E. BISHOP, PH.D.

Private Consultant
Austin, Texas

With a Foreword by

Natalie C. Barraga, ED.D.

Professor Emerita
The University of Texas Austin
Austin, Texas

Drawings by

Charles Denzler and **Virginia Bishop**

Computer Graphics and Charts by

Liz Broussard

CHARLES C THOMAS • PUBLISHER, LTD.
Springfield • Illinois • U.S.A.

Published and Distributed Throughout the World by

CHARLES C THOMAS • PUBLISHER, LTD.
2600 South First Street
Springfield, Illinois 62704

ISBN 0-398-07476-3 (hard)
ISBN 0-398-07477-1 (paper)

Library of Congress Catalog Card Number: 2003063440

With THOMAS BOOKS *careful attention is given to all details of manufacturing and design. It is the Publisher's desire to present books that are satisfactory as to their physical qualities and artistic possibilities and appropriate for their particular use.* THOMAS BOOKS *will be true to those laws of quality that assure a good name and good will.*

Printed in the United States of America
MM-R-3

Library of Congress Cataloging in Publication Data

Bishop, Virginia E.
Teaching visually impaired children / by Virginia E. Bishop ; with a foreword by Natalie C. Barraga; drawings by Charles Denzler and Virginia Bishop ; computer graphics and charts by Liz Broussard.–3rd ed.
p. cm.
Includes bibliographical references and index.
ISBN 0-398-07476-3 (hard) – ISBN 0-398-07477-1 (paper)
1. Children with visual disabilities–Education. I. Title.

HV1643.B56 2004
371.91'1–dc22

2003063440

This book is dedicated to
teachers of students with visual impairments (TVIs)
everywhere.
They make a difference!

FOREWORD

When students with visual impairments are placed in a variety of settings with regular classroom teachers, teacher aides, and specially-trained teachers, no one publication may be available that will address most of the critical issues facing these practitioners. The revised edition of this book is so comprehensive in scope and complete in detail that it would be the most likely one I could recommend for all of them, regardless of the setting or of their training or lack thereof.

The addition of a new chapter to focus on recent evidence of prenatal and early postnatal development of the visual system provides information not included in textbooks usually available. Also, little attention has been given to children who are gifted although visually impaired, and the content in that chapter is a valuable summary of the limited research findings. Other important inclusions are numerous factors related to assessment and evaluation as well as the appropriate learning environments for instruction in supplement skill development.

One of the most outstanding new sections is the discussion of the complexity of brain function as the basis for learning, and the impact of any neurological dysfunction on all aspects of development, especially that of visual learning. The impact of prematurity and cortical damage, as a result of lifesaving measures, on the early development of the visual system is fully explained. The vast majority of students today exhibit some degree of neurological impairment from mild to severe, and it is imperative that parents, teachers, and specialists understand the impact of this on behavioral function and on all academic learning tasks. Dr. Bishop has explained very sophisticated information in language understandable by any lay person, making it useful to everyone.

Some material formerly included in the Appendices has been included as chapters in the book itself, and rightfully so, since the present situations indicate the importance of such things as goal-based instructional planning, functional vision evaluation, and learning media assessment.

If this book were utilized daily by every parent and service provider involved with infants, preschoolers, students, and adults with visual impairments, there is no doubt that the quality of interaction and teaching would be enhanced to a marked degree. The content and how it is presented is reflective of the breadth of experiences of Dr. Bishop and her ability to convey to others so clearly what they need to know and practice. She is to be commended for providing a valuable up-to-date contribution to the literature.

NATALIE C. BARRAGA, ED.D.
Professor Emerita
The University of Texas at Austin

PREFACE

The first edition of this book was published in 1971–before federally mandated special education existed, and before there were any "how to" texts available in the field of visual impairment. It must have met a need since people all over the world have written or thanked me in person for providing a valuable resource.

Twenty-five years later (1996) the second edition of the book was published, and it was an almost completely new collection of information. It, too, has found a place in schools, colleges, and universities, and on professional bookshelves all over the world. Teachers, in particular, have reported that the content of the book is useful, informative, and relative. It was based on professional experience, practical common sense, and a deep respect for the uniqueness of the learning process for visually impaired students.

This third edition of the book retains much of the practical "how to" approach of the last edition, but adds depth in two dimensions: learning theory (emphasizing the eye-brain connection, and the importance of early childhood in the learning experience) and the educational process (from assessment, through the program-planning process, and using outcome-based thinking to direct programming). This edition also offers a chapter that the author believes is unique and has not been adequately addressed in any other known text: the student who is both visually impaired and gifted. Perhaps this chapter will challenge educators and researchers to take another look at this small but extremely unique group of special students.

The reader will notice that some terminology has been changed. The title "VI Teacher" has become "TVI," and O&M instructors may now be called COMS (certified Orientation and Mobility specialists). Most recent amendments to IDEA have been cited as support for procedures, and instructional areas such as "technology" have been updated. Many of the original references have been retained, but more current texts have also been cited. It is hoped that the reader will find a practical balance between the ageless old and the innovative new.

This third edition has retained the general format of the second edition with new materials added. Part One still focuses on "Vision" but has added more details on prenatal visual development, the role of vision in early development, some notes on cortical visual impairment and retinopathy of prematurity, and a look at the future of visual enhancement.

Part Two discusses "Learning" again, with some newer information on brain function, a review of recent research on the early development of visually impaired infants and toddlers, a concentrated discussion of the expanded core curriculum (ECC), suggestions for what role the TVI might have with students who have multiple disabilities, an entire chapter on giftedness and visual impairment, and some thought-provoking guidelines on the placement process for visually impaired students. Part Three still focuses on "Testing and Transitions" but adds more detail on disability-related evaluations.

The Appendix now contains a set of sequenced "listening games," lessons for teaching "touch typing," a guide for using the braille cell as a reference when teaching print writing to a blind child, a list of indicators for evaluating gifted programs, lists of assessment instruments and resources, and an updated time line of major events in the history of education for visually impaired students. A Glossary of Terms completes the third edition.

It may be a reflection of the times (and perhaps an indication of the increasing rate of change in society) that there has only been eight years between the second and third editions of this book, yet there is so much new information to add. Are we learning more, faster? Or are we just recognizing more easily what we *need* to know? Whichever answer the reader chooses, it has implications for educating visually impaired students. Compensatory skills and adapted equipment have gone beyond "important;" they are now *crucial* if visually impaired students are to take their places in an ever-changing society. We need to teach these students well, prepare them for lifetime learning, and help them realize as much of their potential as possible. Therein lies a very big challenge. I hope this book helps each reader to meet that challenge.

V.E.B.

CONTENTS

TEACHING VISUALLY IMPAIRED CHILDREN

Part One

VISION

Chapter One

WHAT IS VISION AND HOW DOES IT WORK?

There is an underlying premise to this book, and it is the assumption that the brain is the primary organ in the human body. Its capabilities are what distinguishes people from animals, and its ability to control all other body systems may compare it to a "master computer" within each human being. Damage to any part of that "master computer" interferes with the functioning of one or more body systems; total lack of brain function can cause death of the human organism. It is the brain that runs the person, not each sense or each body system. This concept should form the basis of any study of the sensory system and should be the foundation of learning theory. This book draws heavily on that concept.

INTRODUCTION

Vision has been compared to the working of a camera: light enters an aperture (opening), controlled in size to allow more or less light to enter, passes through a lens that bends (refracts) the light rays so that they focus clearly on the film at the back of a dark chamber. That much of the explanation appears to describe vision in simple terms, but most cameras are unable to develop the film into its end product: a photograph. The camera does not comprehend what it "sees"; it still requires a human brain to understand, or attach meaning to, the picture. Therefore, the comparison of vision to a camera is incomplete and simplistic.

A better simile might be the periscope of a submarine. An underwater vehicle can only sense what its sonar (hearing), periscope (vision), or impact (touch) tells it. It is otherwise sensorily isolated. The control center inside (the captain) cannot orient the submarine, or direct its activities without a knowledge of what is outside it. The sonar and periscope are information-collecting systems for the captain. Similarly, hearing, vision, and touch are the primary information-gathering systems of the human organism. Touch supplies immediate (within arm's reach) information (texture, size, shape, temperature, moisture); hearing provides data on a more distant area but is limited to sound-producing sources only; vision collects and integrates both near and distant information that includes shape, size, color, texture, form, movement, spatial location, and relationships. Notice the word "integrates." Neither touch nor hearing have the same ability to perceive and understand multiple qualities simultaneously. Touch is sequential; you can only touch one thing or spot at a time. Hearing is largely sequential; you select one sound from a background of noise and focus on that sound; speech is a sequence of meaningful sounds. Only vision is capable of perceiving a large number of bits of information, all at once. In one glance, you see an object's shape, its color, its size, its texture, its location in relation to objects around it, and possibly whether it is wet or dry, hot, or cold, and the material from which it is made. Only vision gives the brain this wide variety of information instantly and at one time.

Since vision, of all the senses, provides the most information to the brain, it is considered the primary sense. Even the *combined* senses of hearing, touch, taste, and smell do not provide the rich variety of information that vision does. If the sense of vision is impaired or lost, it is difficult to compensate for that reduction in information through the other senses. (Other parts of this book describe how a vision loss impacts development and learning, and the compensatory processes needed in order to substitute other less capable sensory channels for vision.)

THE VISUAL SYSTEM

The visual system is made up of an optical system and a perceptual system. Each without the other is ineffectual. The optical system collects and transmits the information that the perceptual system sorts, organizes, categorizes, compares, stores, and uses in decision-making activities. The optical system does not understand what it sees, and the perceptual system is totally dependent on what it receives to make sense of the external environment. Defects in either end of the visual system cause problems, either in the information-gathering process or the comprehension process. In order for the visual system to function as it was intended, all parts of both the optical system and the perceptual system must be mature, intact, and fully functional.

To understand the visual system, it is simplest to examine the optical system and the perceptual system separately, and then to relate them by describing the coordinated process of vision.

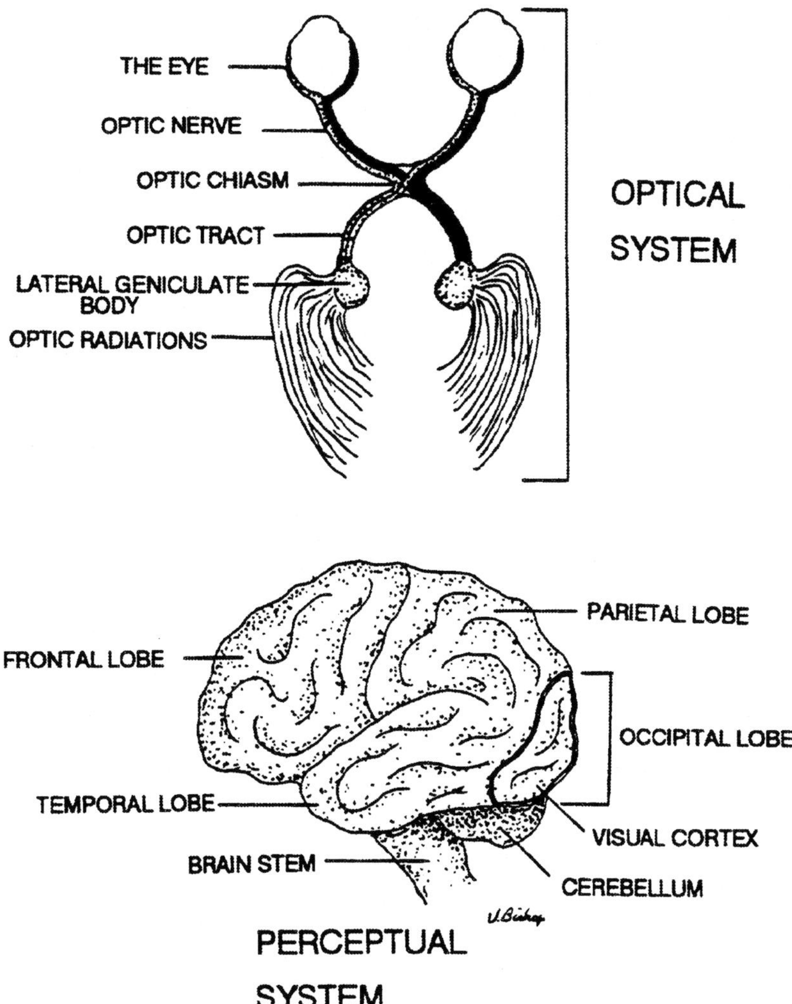

Figure 1.

THE OPTICAL SYSTEM

The optical system is composed of the eye and its external parts (eyelids, extraocular muscles, bony orbit), and optic nerve, optic chiasm, and optic tract. (The perceptual system is the brain.)

The eye is set into an indented cavity in the skull. This cavity has an opening in the deepest part, through which the optic nerve passes on its way to the brain. The cavity is called the bony orbit; it is lined with layers of fatty tissue to cushion the eyeball against possible impact. The bones of the cheek, nose, and forehead also provide protection for the eye against impact from

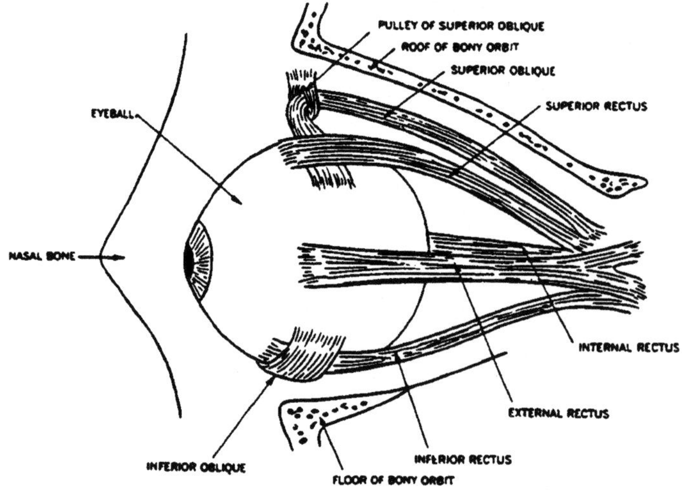

EXTERNAL EYE MUSCLES (left eye)

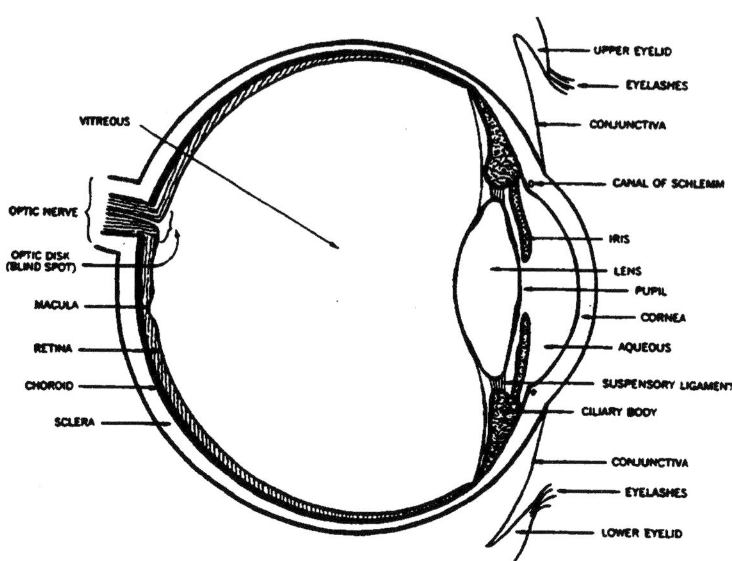

HORIZONTAL SECTION OF A RIGHT EYEBALL

Figure 2.

any large, blunt object.

The eye muscles (extraocular muscles) are attached to the outside of the eye, just behind the visible portion of the eyeball. There are six muscles for each eye–two at each side, and two at the top and bottom, called superior (top) rectus and inferior (bottom) rectus. These four muscles, a separate set attached to each eye, allow the eyes to move horizontally, right or left, and vertically, up or down. Each eye also has a muscle above and one below, attached in such a way as to allow the eyes to rotate slightly inward or outward. These two muscles are called the superior (upper) oblique and inferior (lower) oblique. The coordinated movements in these six muscles of each eye, and of the two eyes together, allow the eyes to move in every and all direction (including diagonally up or down). A specific part of the brain is responsible for coordinating and directing the movement of the eyes.

The eye lids are thin, muscular tissues whose major function is to protect the outer, exposed area of the eye by blinking or closing. They also help to control how much light enters the eyes, and distribute tears over the outer layer of the eye. The tears are generated by a gland (lacrimal gland) located among the fatty tissues above to the outer side of the eyeball. Tears are secreted by this gland and are distributed over the eye surface by the blinking of the eyelids; excess tears are drained into small openings (puncta) at the nasal side of the eyelid opening, pass into a collecting sac (the lacrimal sac), and ultimately drain into the nose. A very thin tissue (conjunctiva) covers the inner surface of the eyelids and the outer surface of the white part of the eye (sclera). The eye lashes, which normally curve upward on the upper eyelid and downward on the lower lid, serve as further protection from foreign objects entering the eye. A number of small sweat glands are located around each eyelash, and oil glands (which secrete a thin layer of oil on the tear surface to keep it from evaporating too quickly) are located just behind the eyelashes. Muscles in the eyelids can be consciously controlled (as in a "wink," or when trying to go to sleep), or react reflexively (as during a sneeze, or at the rapid approach of a foreign object); eyelid movement can also be unconsciously moderated by the brain when unusual conditions exist (excessively dry air which causes extra blinking to keep the eye moist, emotional reactions that cause excess tearing and frequent blinking, or a foreign object in the eye which causes both tearing and blinking).

The eye itself can be described as having three layers and two inner fluids. The outer layer consists of a tough, white tissue (sclera) which becomes transparent at the front (cornea). The sclera's main function is to protect the inner contents of the eye, while the cornea's curved surface serves to bend light rays as they enter the eye, helping to direct them through the pupil.

The middle layer of the eye is called the uveal tract and consists of the choroid layer (just inside the sclera), the ciliary body, and the iris. The choroid contains the blood vessels that nourish the eye. (When an eye doctor looks inside the eye, the blood vessels can be seen through the transparent retina, and their condition can represent both eye health and general body system health.) The ciliary body contains a portion (ciliary process) that generates one of the eye fluids (aqueous) and the ciliary muscle (which controls the ligaments that change the lens shape). The aqueous is secreted behind the iris but in front of the lens (posterior chamber), circulates through the pupil and into the area behind the cornea but in front of the iris (anterior chamber). Aqueous fluid nourishes the inner surface of the cornea and then is drained through a mesh-like tissue (trabecular meshwork) at the circular junction of the iris and cornea, and into a circular canal (Canal of Schlemm); from there, it is drained into the venous system and is absorbed. The iris (the visible, colored portion of the eye) is a circular muscle that opens wider (dilates) or becomes smaller (constricts) to control the amount of light entering the eye through a hole in the center of the iris (the pupil). Dilation and construction are controlled by the brain.

Although the lens is attached to the ciliary muscle by a ring of fine ligaments (zonules, or suspensory ligaments), the lens is not usually considered part of the uveal tract. The lens is a small, round, transparent structure that is capable of changing its shape from round to oval, and back to round, depending on whether the eye is looking at distant objects or near objects. this shape adjustment is controlled by the brain, and is called accommodation.

The innermost layer of the wall of the eye is the sensory layer (the retina). Although it is transparent, it is multilayered and contains the photoreceptor cells (rods and cones). The cones are concentrated in a small area of the retina (macula), with a center of nothing but cones (fovea). Cones are responsible for color perception and clearest vision; they need adequate light for best function. In order for normal vision to occur, light rays must focus on the macula. The remainder of the retina contains primarily rods, which provide peripheral vision. Rods perceive shape and movement, but not sharp vision. They respond under minimal lighting conditions, and do not perceive color.

The innermost area of the eye is filled with a jelly-like substance (vitreous), which maintains the shape of the eyeball. It fills the area behind the lens and helps to hold the retina in place against the inner-eye wall.

At the point where retinal tissue becomes the optic nerve and leaves the back of the eye, there is a small circle called the optic disk. This is also the normal "blind spot" in each eye, and is visible to the eye specialist when looking inside the eye; it appears as a lighter circle of a specific size and color.

The optic nerve exits from the back of each eye, and is composed of bundles of nerves, each surrounded by an insulation called myelin. The visual signals follow specific routes, from bundle to bundle, between the eye and the optic chiasm. Here, the nasal half of the signals from each eye cross over to the opposite side and join with the opposite eye's lateral signals; they then proceed onward along the optic tract towards a sorting and relay site (lateral geniculate body) on each side. The signals progress through specialized areas of the brain (optic radiations) and end up in the occipital lobe (visual cortex), where "visual processing" takes place.

In summary, light (electromagnetic signals) enters the eye through the cornea and is bent by the curved surface, passes through the clear aqueous fluid, goes through the pupillary opening, is further refracted as it passes through the lens, and proceeds through the vitreous to the retina. The photoreceptor cells of the retina are activated by the light-energy signals and send electrical impulses along the optic nerve and optic tract to the brain.

THE PERCEPTUAL SYSTEM

Not all visual signals are transmitted all the way to the visual cortex. Some nerve fibers carry signals that control the size of the pupil; these signals are diverted around the lateral geniculate body and are directed to the midbrain. Thus, pupil size is a reflex controlled by a lower level of the brain. A small number of nerve fibers continue through the lateral geniculate body to other portions of the brain (superior colliculi) which are thought to control reflex ocular movements (as when the eye automatically looks toward a moving target in the periphery); some nerve fibers may also be routed to the hypothalmus, for reasons that are as yet unclear.

Most visual signals terminate in the visual cortex, however, and this is where understanding takes place. In general terms, perception is the conversion of images into symbolic patterns which are encoded in the neurons of the visual cortex. Specifically, light impulses are received by the retinal photoreceptor cells (rods and cones), are sorted initially within the retina itself, and are transmitted along the optic nerve; they are separated at the optic chiasm, sent along the optic tract, sorted again at the lateral geniculate body, and passed into the visual portion of the occipital lobe (visual cortex). This visual area of the brain is made up of six layers of cells which are specialized to respond to different information ("dots" of light, lines, edges, movement, shapes, and colors). These cells are interconnected within and between layers, and are organized in columns a fraction of a millimeter in diameter. Each column is binocular (receives bits of information from each eye), and contains groupings of common orientors (color, movement, shapes, etc.). The electrical impulses enter the fourth layer of cells and are disseminated through chemical neurotransmitters to other related cells which convert the impulses to patterns. Connections between brain cells are enhanced by experience (repeated activity), and combinations of cell groups create patterns. The quantity of neurotransmitter chemical released varies according to whether the connection is novel or repetitive. Thus, the actual characteristics of the neurons may be altered through experience (learning).

The smallest area of the retina (macula) activates the largest portion of the visual cortex. Therefore, clearest vision and color perception utilize more neurons. Conversely, the largest area of the retina (the peripheral area) activates fewer neurons and is less acute in clarity but is more receptive to shape and movement. A small part of the temporal lobe of the cerebral cortex is believed to respond to complex visual patterns, although the mechanism is still somewhat unclear. It is generally accepted that over half of the human brain is involved in some way in processing visual information.

The perceptual system, therefore, takes the components of an image in the form of electrical impulses and converts them into patterns of neuronal connections in the brain. How and where these patterns are stored in memory and are retrieved for later use in decision-making is still largely unknown. It is beyond the scope of this book to present the various theories of memory and data retrieval. There may even be new information by the time this book is in print. The reader is encouraged to follow the rapidly advancing frontiers in neuroscience to gain a more thorough understanding of brain function.

SUMMARY

The visual system is a complicated, finely-tuned, minutely controlled information-intake system. When one considers the number of adjustments required for each glance to produce a clear visual image, the process is truly a miracle.

In order for images to be transmitted by the optical system to the brain, a number of conditions must be met *for every glance:*

1. The eyes must be in alignment.
2. The shape of the eyeball and the cornea must be correct, allowing focusing of the image precisely on the macula.
3. The pupil size must be adjusted for lighting conditions.
4. The lens must adjust its shape to provide the proper refractive curve for light passing through it.
5. The transparent parts of the eye must be clear (cornea, aqueous, lens, vitreous).
6. The retina must be functional (i.e., the photoreceptor cells must be working).

7. The optic nerve and visual pathways must be capable of transmitting the image to the visual cortex.
8. The brian must be capable of monitoring the fine adjustments (eye alignment, pupil size, lens shape) and it must be capable of receiving and processing the received impulses.

Any defect or malfunction at any stage of the visual process can result in impaired vision.

Chapter Two

DEVELOPMENT OF THE VISUAL SYSTEM: PRENATALLY, AT BIRTH, AND POSTNATALLY

It is helpful to have a basic understanding of the prenatal development of the optical system and its status at birth because so many optical system defects begin during the prenatal period. A general understanding of *normal* embryology, particularly as it relates to the visual system, will provide a basis for discussing abnormalities related to vision. Also, since the visual system is not totally mature at birth, some understanding of early maturation is necessary to place early visual behaviors in their proper context. One must first understand what is *normal* before attempting to recognize what is *abnormal.*

EMBRYOLOGICAL ORIGINS

To gain the best understanding of the eye-brain connection, one must go back to the embryonic beginning. Immediately following conception, cells begin to multiply and differentiate. The first recognizable structure is a three-layered embryo, with an outer, middle, and inner layer of cells. Each layer has already been encoded to produce different parts of the body. The innermost layer (endoderm) will produce tissue linings for the lungs, alimentary system, urinary tract, and several internal organs (liver, pancreas, and gall bladder). The middle layer of cells (mesoderm) will form muscle tissue and cartilage, bones, blood, kidneys, reproductive organs, and connective tissue. The outer layer (ectoderm) will specialize to produce the nervous system, sense organs, teeth, skin, hair, nails, and lining of the mouth. Notice that the inner layer develops into inner tissues, the middle layer forms "middle organs" or body parts, and the outer layer targets outer tissues. (The sense organs are outer collectors for the brain, which is the master processor of "what's outside" the body.)

The ectoderm (outer layer) further differentiates during early gestation. In the case of the ocular system, the surface ectoderm specializes in "outer" tissues (cornea, lens, eyelids, eyelashes, lacrimal gland, etc.), while the neural ectoderm focuses on the sensory receiving aspects of vision (brain, retina, iris muscles, ciliary body, and optic nerve). Neural crest cells put the "finishing touches"–the "fine tuning"–on parts of the optical system (see Figure 3). It is all a very remarkable, organized developmental process, and it creates all the necessary mechanisms for the brain to "run" the body (whether voluntarily or involuntarily). Moreover, an analysis of the developmental process reveals the direct connections between eye and brain–from the very beginning. The reader should utilize this observation when developing learning theory or designing instructional approaches. Teach to the brain.

PRENATAL VISUAL DEVELOPMENT

The first tissue to form in the fetus is neural, and will form the basis of the brain. At three weeks after conception, optical folds have formed from the neural tissue. These folds will elongate to form "eye stalks," and optical structures (eyes) will develop at the ends of these extensions of the brain. This is an important concept (the eye-brain connection), and will serve to explain why vision becomes the primary information-gatherer for the brain.

During the next several weeks, many parts of the eyes have begun to differentiate. By six weeks, an ocular cornea has begun to form, and at nine weeks there is a rudimentary cornea; at ten weeks, eyelids have formed and fused over the orb. An alternative nourishing mechanism (the hyaloid system) is at its maximum level of development at ten weeks.

By three months, there is a lens and cornea, and the vitreous is forming. The optic nerve has begun to develop and has maintained its connection to the brain. Around four months, the Canal of Schlemm develops from venous tissue, and suspensory ligaments of the lens begin to form. Eyelids are still fused but contain glands and lashes.

At five months of gestation, the retina is beginning to develop, and photoreceptors (rods and cones) begin to form. Blood vessels in the choroid have begun to be recognizable, and the iris can be identified. The eyelids begin to separate and open. The sclera is formed, and intraocular muscles are nearly complete.

Between six and eight months, parts of the ocular structures develop further and refine. The iris muscles form, basic retinal tissue and lens are nearly complete, and the macula begins to differentiate from the rest of the retina. Iris color is present, and myelinization of the optic nerve begins at the optic chiasm. The primitive vascular nourishing system (hyaloid system) will have disappeared by the eighth month, as the ocular blood vessels continue

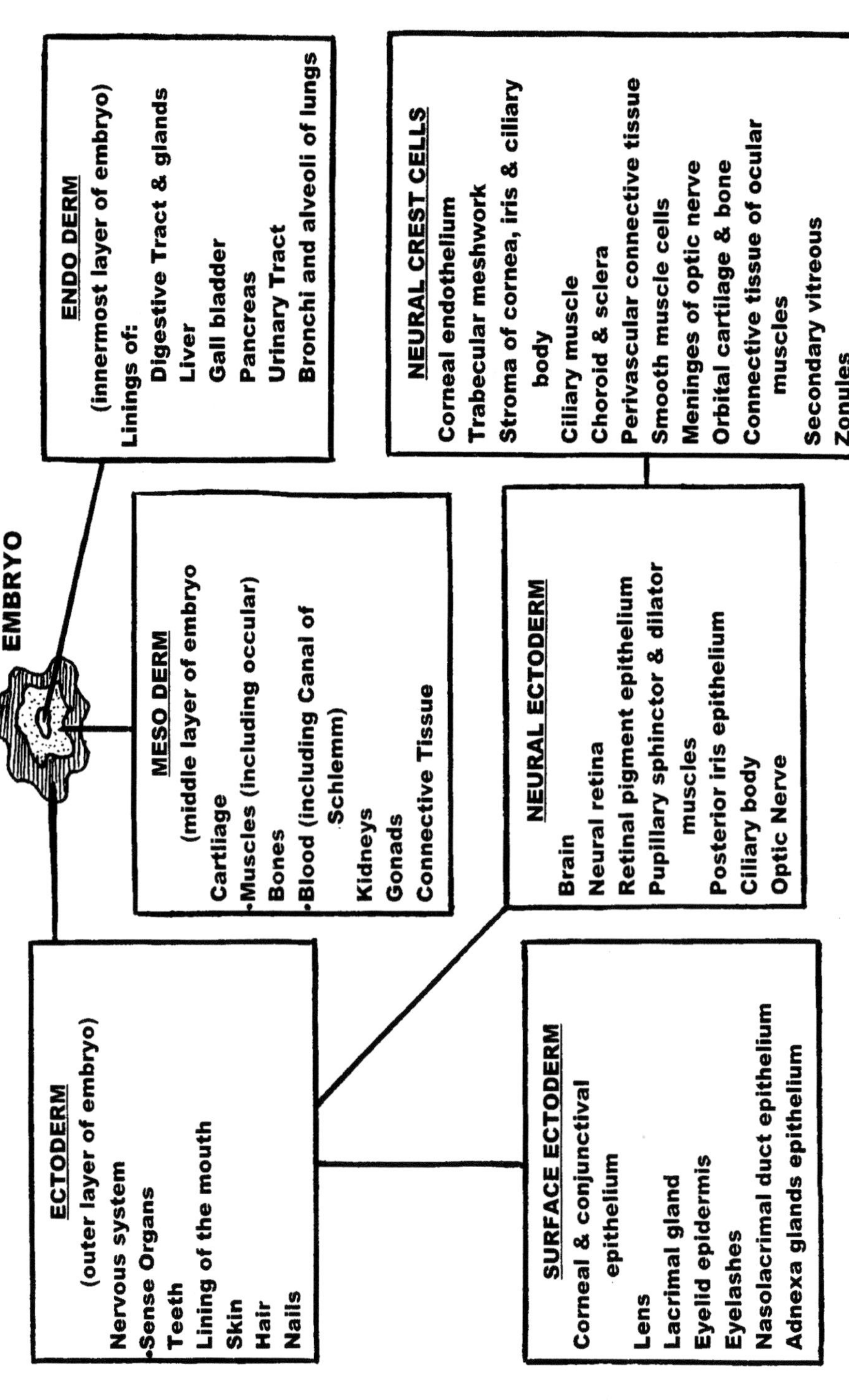

Figure 3. Embryological Origins of the Ocular System. Source: Cook, C., Sulik, K., & Wright, K. (2003). Embryology. In Wright, K. & Spiegel, P., *Pediatric ophthalmology and strabisumus.* New York: Springer.

to develop.

By nine months (full gestation), all of the eye parts are present, though some are still immature. The last to develop are the blood vessels, and they will have reached the nasal periphery of the retina by birth. Optic nerve fibers will have begun the myelinization process, but it will not be complete at birth (see Figure 4).

THE VISUAL SYSTEM AT BIRTH

Despite nine months of development, the optical system is still not fully mature at birth. The eyeball is still small (only about two-thirds of its adult size), the cornea is about 80 percent of its final diameter, and a number of eye parts are not fully functional. The iris muscles are not quite ready to control pupil size, and the suspensory ligaments cannot fully regulate lens shape until several months later. The macula is not rod-free until 15 months of age, and the optic nerve still needs some additional myelinization; the ocular muscles may not yet be well coordinated. The tear system is not fully functional, and eye color is not definitively established.

In terms of functional vision, a newborn has acuity in the range of 20/400; the infant may not be able to follow a moving target very well and is unable to shift gaze easily. The newborn may have a slow pupillary response, and probably won't have a blink reflex to a visual threat.

VISUAL DEVELOPMENT DURING THE FIRST TWO YEARS

Within the first month, pupillary response will develop, and by two months, the infant can usually fixate on an object or person of interest. By three months, the baby can follow a slowly moving object or person. Between three and six months, the macular area of the retina develops and eye muscle control is gained. Before this time, black and white visual stimuli were more interesting visual targets, but now color begins to be a factor in visual stimulation. By six months of age, the infant's eye should exhibit coordinated ocular movement.

The eye-brain connection is not fully myelinized until between seven months and two years of age. Not coincidently, 20/20 visual acuity occurs sometimes around two years of age. Therefore, in spite of a well-functioning optical system, the perceptual part of the visual system (the brain) may still need time to develop. The eyes may *see* but the brain may not yet *understand* what is being seen. This is why the period between one and two years of age may need to be focused on the hands-on experience it takes to attach mean-

NORMAL OCULAR DEVELOPMENT DURING A FULL NINE MONTHS GESTATION

CONCEPTION

3 Weeks: First signs of beginning eyes are "optic pits"
3.5 Weeks: "Eye stalks" form from neural tissue
1 mo. 4 Weeks: Lens begins to form
6 Weeks: Lens has developed

2 mos. 8 Weeks: Optic nerve fibers reach the brain
9 Weeks: Cornea is forming
10 Weeks: Eyelids cover developing orb and fuse; hyaloid system's maximum development

3 mos. 12 Weeks to 14 Weeks: Glands in eyelids forming; Ocular muscles begin; Vitreous forming

4 mos. Lashes form in eyelids (still closed); suspensory ligaments of lens develop
Aqueous forming; Canal of Schlemm present; hyaloid system begins to regress

5 mos. Iris is recognizable; rods and cones differentiate; eyelids open; choroid layers complete; Choroidal blood vessels begin to form; sclera and intraocular muscles complete

6 mo. Iris muscles formed.

7 mo. Retinal tissue and lens are completely formed; iris color is present.
Myelinization of optic nerve begins at the chiasm and proceeds forward towards eyes.

8 mo. Macula begins to differentiate; hyaloid system has disappeared.

9 mo. Retinal vessels have reached the nasal periphery but not the temporal.

BIRTH

Figure 4.

ing to objects and people. The young brain accumulates knowledge through interaction with what the senses experience (see Figure 5).

The status of the visual system at birth, and during the first several years of life, has implications for teachers or other personnel who do vision screening, functional vision evaluations, or learning media assessments. In vision screening, the examiner is only looking for clues that suggest visual functioning outside the expected normal range. That is, are there any reasons to pursue further visual evaluation by a pediatric eye specialist? Vision screening is, therefore, not diagnostic, but directive. A knowledge of early visual development will help the examiner to be alert to deviations from normal visual behaviors. A list of normal behaviors follows, with indications of when they might be expected in a young child with normal vision (see Table 1).

It should be noted that age two is the earliest time visual acuity can be established with any degree of confidence (see Chapter 6). It will not be until

VISUAL DEVELOPMENT

	AT BIRTH	< 2 MOS.	2-4 MOS.	4-6 MOS.	6 MOS- 1 YR	1-3 YRS	3-5 YRS	5-10 YRS	10+ YRS
BRAIN	INCOMPLETE MYELINIZATION	PERIOD OF BRAIN'S GREATEST GROWTH →				CONTINUES THE MYELLINIZATION PROCESS →		MYELINIZATION ESSENTIALLY COMPLETE AT 10 YRS	MAXIMUM BRAIN DEVELOPMENT AT 14 YRS
EYEBALL	SHORT... EXTREMELY HYPEROPIC	BUT HIGH REFRACTIVE POWER OF LENS COMPENSATES						REACHES FULL SIZE AT 7-8 YRS	
CORNEA	RELATIVELY LARGE; SOMEWHAT FLAT					REACHES ADULT SIZE AT 2 YRS			
IRIS	BLUISH TINT			FINAL COLOR ACHIEVED					
PUPIL	SMALL (DILATOR MUSCLE NOT FULLY DEVELOPED						DILATOR MUSCLE AT FULL POWER AT 5 YRS		
LENS	SOFT - ALMOST SPHERICAL	CONTINUES TO BECOME HARDER THROUGHOUT LIFE →							
CILIARY BODY	NOT FUNCTIONING WELL AT BIRTH					NORMAL ACCOMMODATIVE POWER AT 5 YRS			
MACULA	NOT FULLY DEVELOPED			FULLY DEVELOPED					
OPTIC NERVE	NOT FULLY MYELINIZED	MYELINIZATION PROCEEDS FROM OUTER TO INNER							
TEAR SYSTEM	NOT YET FUNCTIONAL		TEAR SYSTEM FUNCTIONAL AT 3 MOS.						
EYE MUSCLES	NOT WELL COORDINATED			EYES COORD. BY 6 MOS.					

Figure 5.

TABLE 1.

Age	Expected (Normal) Visual Behaviors
By one month:	Momentary fixation on a familiar person or object (Remember: • Acuity is still poor and eye movements may be uncoordinated. • Pupillary response may be absent or sluggish. • Blink reflex is usually absent.)
By three-four months:	Pupillary response is present. Eyes are coordinated and aligned most of the time. Child looks at/is interested in: own hands caregiver(s) face interesting toys B&W designs Child can follow (track) a slowly moving target. Child may attempt to reach for objects (bats at or swipes at).
By six months:	Child's eyes are coordinated and aligned when looking or tracking. Colorful targets are usually more interesting than B&W. Child reacts differently to strangers than to familiar persons. Child tries to reach for/grasp desired objects. Child is able to recognize/show interest in both near and distant (at least 6′ away) objects and people.
By 1 year:	Child looks for dropped objects. Child spots and tries to pick up small objects (raisins, Cheerios, lint). Child tries to grab at caregiver's glasses or jewelry. Child reacts to facial expressions (smile, frown, "funny face"). Child indicates desire to have an object seen at least 6′ away. Child shows interest in books or pictures. Child reaches into a container to remove an object.

several years later that vision screening techniques that utilize matching ability can be used reliably. The first few years of life are spent in the maturational process for the visual system, and some portions of the brain may not be totally mature until sometime between 10 and 14 years of age. (See Figure 6 for a graphic representation of this developmental process.)

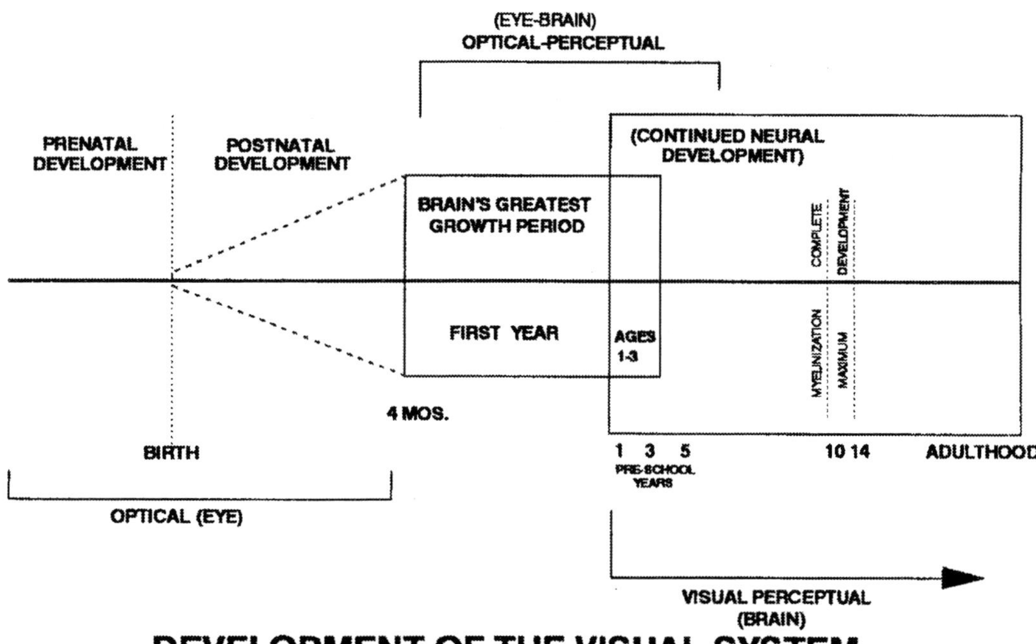

Figure 6. Modified and redrawn, with permission, from Barraga, N. & Erin, J. (2001). *Visual Impairments and Learning* (4th Ed.). Austin, TX: Pro-Ed.

Chapter Three

WHAT CAN GO WRONG WITH THE VISUAL SYSTEM

Because of the complexity of the visual system, the possibilities for defects, diseases, and injuries are almost endless. This chapter will describe only a few of the many ways the visual system can be impaired, particularly in young children and those of school age. The information presented in this chapter is not intended to be a comprehensive discussion of eye diseases/defects, since many textbooks have been written about this topic. The reader is directed to the list of texts at the end of this section for more information.

STRUCTURAL ANOMALIES

There are a number of ocular malformations or defects that occur during the prenatal period and can be identified at birth or shortly thereafter. Among these are **anopthalmia** (absence of eyes), **microphthalmia** (abnormally small eyes), **aniridia** (absence of, or a minimal iris), **dislocated lens** (the lens is not located directly behind the pupil), and **colobomas** (clefts in one or more eye parts, commonly the iris, retina, and choroid). There are also many **chromosomal abnormalities and syndromes** that have ocular components, and they begin in the prenatal period. It is beyond the scope of this book to discuss the many syndromes and chromosomal aberrations, since there are so many types and varieties. The reader is directed to the Corn and Koenig text or other medical books for further information.

EXTRAOCULAR MUSCLE IMBALANCES

Strabismus is a term that includes any muscle imbalances of the eyes.

Esotropia is one or both eyes that turn inward toward the nose; **exotropia** is one or both eyes that turn outward toward the ears; **hypertropia** is an eye that turns upward, and **hypotropia** is an eye that turns downward. If any of these conditions are evident in a child older than 6 months of age, it should be treated by an eye specialist before vision begins to decrease in the deviating eye. A child does not "outgrow" strabismus. If left untreated, the decrease or loss of vision (amblyopia) can be permanent. Treatment can include surgical realignment of the eyes and/or "patching" (covering the better eye to force the deviating eye to function). Treatment is best done before age 2. Which treatment (or both) is the decision of the eye specialist (an ophthalmologist, if surgery is an option). Strabismus can be an accompanying condition to other eye problems as well; the eye specialist will recommend best treatment options. (Children with cerebral palsy often have ocular muscle imbalances that are generally untreatable.)

Nystagmus is an involuntary, usually "jerky" movement of the eyes. It may be minor (as in eyes that "wiggle" or "waver") or serious (the eyes make noticeable and repeated rhythmic movements, usually together). Nystagmus can be horizontal (left-right) or pendular (undulating) and may have a "null point" (position of minimal movement). The eye specialist can determine whether treatment might be helpful, although nystagmus is rarely "cured," only minimized. The child with nystagmus may *appear* worse than he/she actually sees; it is believed that the brain adjusts to whatever information it receives, and learns to perceive a stationary world. Nystagmus can be a symptom of or may accompany other eye disorders, and the *lack* of nystagmus can differentiate among defects (e.g., children with cortical visual impairment do *not* have nystagmus). The eye specialist should be the one to evaluate causes and possible treatment.

REFRACTIVE ERRORS

The length (from the front to the back) of the eyeball is a critical factor in the most common eye disorders: **nearsightedness (myopia)** and **farsightedness (hyperopia)**. When an eyeball is too long, the natural focal point is somewhere in front of the retina, and corrective lenses are needed to compensate for that difference. Similarly, if the eyeball is too short, the natural focal points is theoretically behind the retina, again, corrective lenses can compensate for the error by bringing the focal point nearer. A longer-than-normal eye is myopic (nearsighted), while a shorter-than-normal eye is hyperopic (farsighted).

If the curvature of the cornea is incorrect (in very simple terms, there is a "bump" or "dent" in it somewhere), a different kind of corrective lens can compensate for that refractive error. An improperly shaped cornea is called **astigmatism**.

When the lens of the eye becomes cloudy (**cataract**), it may be surgically removed. (**Aphakia** is the term used to describe a missing lens.) Special bifocal lenses may also be worn to correct visual defects due to the absence of the natural lens. Congenital cataracts are now being surgically removed shortly after birth (except in the case of maternal rubella) and contact lenses are prescribed for the infant.

These three defects, which are related to the shape of the eyeball or cornea, or the transparency of the eye's lens, are the common refractive errors usually corrected with glasses. Most other eye defects cannot be corrected through the use of regular glasses, although special optical devices may help to enhance vision (see Chapter 5).

DISEASES OR DEFECTS

Probably the most common eye-related disease is **conjunctivitis**; it is an infection of the tissue which lines the eyelids and covers the visible portion of the sclera (white part of the eye). It can be viral, bacterial, fungal, allergic, parasitic, toxic, chemical, or mechanical. Careful differential diagnosis by an eye specialist is essential, since treatments vary according to the causes.

A **sty** (hordeolum) is an infection of an eyelash follicle. Hot compresses applied for 10 minute periods, four to five times daily, can help resolve the infection, but a topical ocular antibiotic may be suggested by the eye specialist. Cleanliness is important, since the infection can be spread from one eyelash to another, or from one eye to the other.

Neither conjunctivitis nor a sty usually causes impaired vision, except for the period of medication. If untreated, however, either could spread infection to other parts of the eye (e.g., the cornea), which *may* result in impaired vision. All eye infections, regardless of how minor they may seem, should be checked by an eye specialist.

Corneal diseases or injury can cause the cornea to become cloudy or elongated (cone-shaped instead of rounded). When the cornea loses its transparency because of scar tissue being formed, or when the corneal shape cannot be corrected with a compensating lens, a corneal transplant may be indicated. A disc-shaped piece of health donor cornea is surgically transplanted into the center of the defective cornea after a corresponding slice of nonfunctional cornea has been removed.

An imbalance between aqueous production and drainage is called **glaucoma**. When too much aqueous is produced, or when the drainage system does not work properly, intraocular pressure builds behind the cornea. If left untreated, the pressure transfers to the back of the eye and can damage the optic nerve. Treatment depends on the cause and can range from eye drops to surgical opening of the drainage system. Glaucoma is rarely "cured," and is almost always "controlled."

Cataracts (a clouding of the eye's natural lens) can be congenital (usually genetically determined), rubella-caused, associated with other eye diseases/ defects, caused by trauma, or can be the natural consequence of the aging process. Rubella-caused cataracts are left untreated if present at birth, since the live rubella virus is still present and may cause additional infection within the eye if the cataract is disturbed. Congenital cataracts (other than rubella-caused) are usually surgically removed within days or weeks of birth to allow normal eye development during the critical first several months and years. If removed too late, acuity may never reach normal levels. Cataracts that occur as a result of the aging process are usually left untreated until their presence interferes with the person's life style. The natural risks that accompany cataract removal (retinal detachment, and/or glaucoma) have been minimized but still exist, even with the most careful surgical treatment.

Retinal diseases are usually serious, are often painless, and result in impaired vision of some extent. Any infection that causes scar tissue in the retina also results in an unseeing areas at the site of the scar tissue. Depending on the location of the scar tissue, some part of the peripheral vision will be lost, or part/all of the central acuity may be lost. **Retinitis pigmentosa**, a group of degenerative retinal diseases, usually results in a gradual loss of peripheral vision (until only central, or "tunnel" vision is left), but may also include a decrease in central acuity. **Macular degeneration** is a deterioration of only central acuity, leaving peripheral vision intact. The individual has a "blind spot" in the center of the visual field, and must use "eccentric viewing" (appearing to look to the side and usually slightly upward or downward) to utilize a portion of the less efficient peripheral retina.

RLF/ROP (former name: retrolental fibroplasia; current name: retinopathy of prematurity) is a disease not uncommon in premature babies (but also occurs occasionally in full-term infants). Although the actual cause is still unknown, it may be oxygen-related or a characteristic of an immature choroid. Blood vessels halt growth and then grow rapidly but weakly to "catch up." The retina sometimes detaches, causing blindness. Functional vision can range from nearly normal to total blindness. For more information, see page 28.

Retinoblastoma is a genetically determined tumor of the eye. It is usually congenital and is discovered shortly after birth. Chemotherapy is nearly always tried initially, but many children with retinoblastoma end up having one or both eyes surgically removed by the time they are two years old. If left untreated, it is lethal, since the optic nerve will carry the tumor directly to the brain.

Albinism is a hereditary defect that may affect only the eyes (ocular albinism) or is evident in the eyes, hair, and skin (oculocutaneous albinism). In the ocular type, only the pigment of the retina is affected; photophobia and nystagmus are usually present, and visual acuity is usually affected to some degree. In the oculocutaneous type, the individual is usually very fair-skinned, has white-blonde hair, has pale colored irises, is light sensitive (photophobic), and usually has reduced acuity.

Colorblindness is a genetically determined disorder of the retinal cone cells. It occurs mostly in males (is carried by females), and occurs in females only when it is associated with other macular disease (e.g., achromatopsia). Total colorblindness is rare in humans; most people called "colorblind" have color deficiencies (cannot identify, or confuse, only certain colors). There is no treatment.

OPTIC NERVE DEFECTS

Optic atrophy is a malfunction of the optic nerve. It causes reduced central or peripheral vision, depending on which nerve fibers have been damaged. Optic atrophy is caused by disease or trauma to the nerve fibers and can be identified by an optic disk that is lighter in color than normal (a "pale disk"). Since it is difficult to examine any part of the optic nerve directly, the extent of function or nonfunction is often evaluated by observing and assessing functional vision. Acuities can range from near-normal to blindness.

Optic nerve hypoplasia is characterized by a smaller than normal optic disk, with a "halo" around it. It is a small optic nerve which regressed during the prenatal period because of an insult to the central nervous system (often drug or alcohol related). It can occur in one or both eyes, and vision is usually diminished. There may be other ocular defects as well: malformation of the iris, an abnormally small eyeball (microphthalmia), clefts in other ocular tissues, and facial abnormalities. **Septo-optic dysplasia** is an extreme form of optic nerve hypoplasia, in which there is a high incidence of brain malformation (absence of the septum pellucidum and/or corpus callosum) and endocrine abnormalities. Many of these children have multiple disabilities in addition to their visual impairment.

Damage to other portions of the visual pathway usually results in **visual fields defects**. The type and extent of visual loss is related to the site of damage or pressure. Damage to either optic nerve before it reaches the optic chiasm results in reduced vision in only one eye, whereas damage at the optic chiasm itself can cause either a half field loss in one eye or opposite (inner or outer) half field losses in both eyes. Damage to the optic tract produces same-half field losses in both eyes. Careful clinical fields testing is needed to identify both the extent of the fields losses and the sites.

Brain damage, whether from anoxia, hemorrhaging, or cortical malformation, can cause a wide range of visual impairments, from perceptual problems to apparent blindness (cortical visual impairment). The optical system may be intact, but if the perceptual system is nonfunctional or impaired, vision will also be impaired or nonfunctional. Children with **cortical visual impairment** (CVI) have unique behavioral and learning characteristics; the special teacher of visually impaired students will be able to assist in the interpretation of visually impaired students will be able to assist in the interpretation of behaviors and in the modifications needed for instruction. (For more information see page 29.)

INJURIES

Despite nature's precautions (placing the eyes within cushioned cavities surrounded by bony protection and covering them with protective lids), human beings manage to injure their eyes with frightening frequency. Most common of these injuries are abrasions, lacerating or penetrating wounds, physical and/or chemical burns, and blunt trauma.

Abrasions are usually caused by foreign bodies that scratch the sclera or cornea. Surface abrasions, while painful, heal quickly if cleaned thoroughly, but scratches that penetrate the surface layers of the cornea can cause scar tissue to form in the healing process. Infection is the greatest danger and an eye specialist should always check any scratches or abrasions to the eye for damage to corneal tissue.

Lacerations of the lids can be sutured and treated medically, while lacerations and penetrating wounds of the eye itself (caused by arrows, glass, metal fragments, BBs, etc.) may require more involved medical care. The risk of infection may depend on the lacerating/penetrating material (wood slivers nearly always cause some level of infection). Immediate medical attention is required; vision may or not be affected.

Chemical burns of the eye often cause severe corneal scarring and are difficult to treat. Vision is usually lost or badly impaired. Physical burns (fire/heat related) are not as common but equally serious. Radiant energy burns (ultraviolet and infrared light) are not as well-known but do occur. Ultraviolet light is absorbed by the cornea and/or lens, but is accumulative and can cause burn-type damage. Sun lamps, germicidal lamps, arc welders, and extended exposure to snowfields ("snow blindness") are examples of sources of ultraviolet damage. Infrared light (e.g., looking at a solar eclipse without protection) can burn the retina or cause a cataract. Electromagnetic energy of long wave lengths (e.g., radar) is known to cause cataracts, and there is some speculation that electromagnetic energy from video display terminals (TV screens and computer screens) may also cause cataracts.

Blunt trauma (a blow to the head, in the ocular area) can cause hemorrhages, ruptures in the eyeball itself, corneal abrasions, iris rupture, lens dislocation, or vitreous rupture. Child abuse is a common cause of blunt trauma damage in children. Treatment depends on the type and extent of injury, as does the potential for visual treatment.

"Shaken Baby Syndrome" deserves mention here, since it is a growing concern among pediatric ophthalmologists. There is often a lack of any external symptoms, but the ophthalmologist can identify a unique pattern to the retinal hemorrhaging; cortical hemorrhaging also occurs. A third of the babies die, and 75 percent have neurological damage; of these 80 percent end up with visual problems. (Dr. Paul Rychwalski, Pediatric Ophthalmologist; presentation at the Blind Children's Seminar, November 2002, Berea, KY.)

THE EFFECTS OF PREMATURITY AND DYSMATURITY ON THE VISUAL SYSTEM

Prematurity ("born too soon") and dysmaturity ("born too small") both have implications for visual functioning. Since the invention of the incubator, more babies who are born before 36 weeks of gestation are surviving. There has been a price for survival, however, since many of these infants end up with significant neurodevelopmental problems (cerebral palsy, mental retardation, hearing and/or vision abnormalities, or a combination of these). In 2001, nearly 12 percent of all births were premature (as compared to 7% in 1965) (*Wall Street Journal,* January 30, 2003, p. D2) and some of these infants were born as early as 23 weeks, with birthweights of less than 3.5 pounds (*U.S. News and World Report,* May 27, 2002, p. 52–53). Causes of early births include advanced maternal age, improved reproductive technologies, drugs/alcohol, diabetes, stress, and hypertension.

The danger to visual function is a condition called retinopathy of prematurity, or ROP (formerly called retrolental fibroplasia, or RLF). Because the baby is born early–before the optical system has had a chance to complete its growth sequence–the incomplete portions of the optical system are affected. During the last few months of normal gestation, the choroidal blood vessels are forming and spreading into the periphery of the fundus. Their function is to provide oxygen (nourishment) to the inner eye. When supplemental oxygen is provided (to aid the respiratory difficulties most premature infants experience), the ocular blood vessels arrest growth; when oxygen therapy is no longer needed, the ocular blood vessels proliferate to make up for lost time, may leak or hemorrhage, and, in worst cases, result in a detached retina.

Focus has been on the oxygen factor from the beginning (when RLF was first identified in 1942), but the causative mechanism has eluded researchers. Attempts at regulating both concentrations of oxygen and the length of time administered have not resulted in the elimination of the disease, and alternative factors have even been explored (Vitamin E supplements; illumination levels). Therapies currently include both laser and cryo treatments of retinal areas not yet served by blood vessels (essentially telling the vessels not to grow there). The most current theory involves a genetic protein (vascular endothelial growth factor, or VEGF) that responds to oxygen levels and regulates vessel growth. Genetic therapy (regulating VEGF) may hold promise, but has not yet been tried with humans (at the time this text revision was being written).

Some full term, but low birth weight babies (especially those under 3 1/2 pounds) and a few full-term/normal birth weight babies have developed ROP. The mechanism of acquisition is still unclear; it may be related to an immature retinal vascular system, or to the quantity of VEGF present. The low birth weight babies are often born to teen-age mothers, women who weigh less than 100 pounds, or mothers who had poor prenatal care, used cocaine, or smoked cigarettes. Identification of ROP should follow the same timelines as for premature infants: pediatric ophthalmological exams at 4–6 weeks, 8–10 weeks, and 12–26 weeks.

ROP continues to be one of the leading causes of visual impairment in young children, and should be suspected when visual impairment is present in a child born prematurely. Although there is a wide range of visual functioning, from no significant impairment to total blindness, the presence or absence of ROP should be confirmed in all premature babies, and any accompanying defects (myopia, strabismus) treated early.

CVI: A SPECIAL CASE

Brain damage, whether from anoxia (oxygen deprivation), hemorrhaging, or cortical malformation can cause a wide range of visual impairments, from perceptual problems to apparent blindness. The optical system may be intact, but if the perceptual system (brain) is impaired or non-functional, vision will also be impaired or non-functional. Children with brain-based visual problems are said to be "cortically visually impaired" (also called "cerebral visual impairment," or CVI), and have both unique visual behaviors and unique diagnostic characteristics. There is no observable nystagmus (which often accompanies other ocular anomalies) and a pupillary response is usually present; color perception is usually preserved, although visual functioning may vary from day-to-day and hour-to-hour. There is no "eye pressing," and the eyes "look normal." However–the child seems visually inattentive, tends to look away from people or objects, may not recognize faces, and has an inaccurate reach; the child may hold objects closer, not because of poor acuity, but to reduce distracting surroundings. Children with CVI are likely to have other neurological problems, and may have multiple disabilities. CVI continues, at this writing, to be the leading cause of visual impairment among young children, and reflects the rising numbers of multiple disabilities among children with visual impairments (see Chapter Ten).

Chapter Four

HOW IS THE VISUAL SYSTEM EVALUATED/TESTED?

The status of the visual system is difficult to evaluate in children less than three or four years old and is largely a clinical procedure. Usually, the younger the child, the less cooperative he/she is. Testing methods for preverbal children fall into one of two categories: clinical or informal. For the purposes of this book, "clinical" will be defined as procedures that may only be done by a specially trained person (usually an ophthalmologist or medical technician) and cannot be performed outside of the clinical setting (hospital or laboratory). There are a number of these procedures, some more invasive than others, and nearly all require some level of sedation. The three most well-known of these procedures are the "CAT Scan" (Computerized Axial Tomography) or CT (Computerized Tomography), the electroretinogram (ERG), and the Visually Evoked Potential (VEP) or Visually Evoked Response (VER). The "CAT Scan" uses low dosage X-rays to examine layers of tissue. It can identify brain or optic nerve/optic tract abnormalities and tumors of the eye (retinoblastoma). The ERG uses light flashes to determine whether the retina is functioning, but cannot measure macular ability precisely. The VEP/VER also uses light flashes but measures whether the visual signal from each eye is reaching the visual cortex. It can identify deficits in optical nerve/optic tract function, but usually not their precise locations. The ERG and VEP/VER are often used to identify cortical visual impairment but the results may not be totally reliable. The CAT Scan is often used to verify brain malformation when optic nerve hypoplasia or septo-optic dysplasia have been diagnosed. All of the above clinical tests are valid for the time of testing, and may not reflect later tissue maturation; thus, they may not be predictive.

Informal procedures may be performed in a clinic or doctor's office, and some procedures may even be used by specially trained technicians or teachers as a part of a functional vision evaluation. These procedures include: retinoscopy, ophthalmoscopy, use of the optokinetic drum, preferential viewing, pupillary response, fixation, following, and reaching. The first two procedures (retinoscopy and ophthalmoscopy) are only done by eye specialists; the optokinetic drum procedure and preferential viewing are usually performed by specially trained persons (usually eye specialists, but occasionally technicians or teachers). The remaining procedures are used by both eye specialists and special teachers.

Ophthalmoscopy is the examination of the retina with a special instrument (ophthalmoscope). The retina (including optic disk, blood vessels, and macula) is viewed by directing light into an eye which has a dilated pupil. Retinoscopy also uses a lighted instrument (retinoscope) but measures the refractive error of each eye. It is a way of estimating the refractive error in young or nonverbal children.

The optokinetic drum is a "cylinder on a stick." The cylinder is about 10″ in diameter and has vertical black and white stripes on the sides. The examiner rotates the cylinder slowly, about a foot from the child's face. If the child can see the stripes, his/her eyes will automatically follow them (i.e., fixate, follow, refixate, follow, etc.), resulting in a purposely induced but temporary nystagmus. By changing the width of the stripes, a rough measure of acuity is possible, but it is not always reliable. The many variables in this test (distance, speed, stripe width, ability of the child to fixate) make it only a gross screening instrument.

Preferential looking, performed correctly, requires a clinical setting. A variety of patterns (varying widths of black and white stripes on cards) are shown randomly through "windows" on either side of a large screen; the examiner (who is behind the screen) watches the child's head and eye movements through a "peephole" and records which width of stripe was attended by the child. When the child no longer looks at one or the other pattern presented, the width of the stripe is presumed to be no longer interesting (able to be seen). Because this test takes about an hour if all stimuli are presented, the age and attentiveness of the child are decisive factors in its reliability. Shorter and less complicated versions of this procedure (e.g., the Teller Acuity Cards) have been used with varying degrees of success, but the 50-50 chance of correct responses, the varying levels of experience and expertise in examiners, and the imprecise equivalency with Snellen acuities make this a general screening device. The information obtained should be combined with other observational data if more accurate functional vision measures are to be collected.

Pupillary response, corneal light reflex, blink reflex, fixation, following (tracking), and reaching are procedures utilized by both pediatric eye specialists and special teachers, especially with infants. They are all observational procedures, subject to individual interpretation. Pupillary response is the automatic constriction of the pupil when light is presented suddenly; however, since pupillary functions are controlled by the lower brain, they may be present in a child with cortical visual impairment. Pupillary response may be difficult to observe in a child with dark irises; also, if the child is receiving medications that affect muscles (e.g., seizure medications or tranquilizers), the pupillary response may be absent or sluggish.

Corneal light reflex measures (grossly) the alignment of the eyes. Between the ages of one month and six months, coordinated eye movements may not be totally consistent, but after six months, ocular alignment should be well established. A way of identifying possible misalignment is to shine a light from about one foot away and from a position below the child's nose. The position of the light reflection in the two eyes should be the same (i.e., both in the center, or, using the eye as a clock dial, both at 3 o'clock position, 7 o'clock position, etc.). Using a toys as an attention/fixation eliciting device near the flashlight can ease the examiner's task, allowing sufficient time to note the positions of the reflections. If the reflections are not in the same relative positions in the two eyes, the child should be seen by an eye specialist for further evaluation. Treatment of ocular muscle imbalances (lack of eye alignment) should begin early, preferably before age two, and before amblyopia has had a chance to begin. If left untreated until school age, the chances are lessened for successful retention or regaining of equal vision in both eyes.

Blink reflex is the automatic closing of the eyelids when a visual threat approaches suddenly. The most common procedure used to test blink reflex is to bring an open hand (fingers apart) rapidly and suddenly towards the child's face (without actually touching the face). Reaction will be sluggish or absent if there is brain damage, and may be inconsistent before the age of five months (by which time it is normally acquired). It may not be present in premature infants.

Fixation is the ability of the eyes to maintain a gaze on an interesting target, and following (tracking) is the ability to move the eyes in such a way as to keep the object in central fixation while the object moves. Fixation is present in rudimentary form at birth, but is related to coordinated eye movements; by six months, a child should be able to fixate on a target for at least one or two seconds. Following is also possible in children younger than six months, but should be a consistent ability from six months on. Eye specialists often measure gross visual abilities in very young or nonverbal children by the ability to "fix and follow." This means only that the child has sufficient vision to locate a target of interest and track its movement; it reveals little about actual acuity or perception. It is a gross measure of visual function. Reaching, on the other hand, can give added information about both vision and perception. How large a target, how far away, the need for contrasting background, the motor ability to coordinate eye and hand movements, and the accuracy with which the reaching hand attains its target are all bits of information that suggest acuteness of vision and perception. The number of variables for the target (size, color, background, contrast, distance when perceived) suggests the need to experiment when evaluating, and the observational ability of the examiner (judging eye-hand coordination and accuracy of reach) places this technique in the hands of specialists (medical or educational).

As soon as a child is able to match objects (understands sameness/differences), more structured vision testing can begin. There are a great many tests for central acuity testing (STYCAR toys, House-Apple-Umbrella chart, Lighthouse cards, HOTV charts, Snellen E charts, Snellen letter charts) and at least one useful procedure for gross fields testing (confrontation). (Clinical fields testing is more precise and involves the use of more sophisicated instruments, such as perimeters, tangent screens, Amsler grid.) Color perception can be evaluated using the Ishihara or Dvorine Plates, or by using colored construction paper squares to match. Perceptual evaluation and/or visual efficiency testing can be done with the Diagnostic Assessment Procedure (DAP), Motor-Free Visual Perception Test (MVPT), or informal tasks. Adult-oriented vision testing includes contrast sensitivity, clinical tonometry (measuring intraocular pressure as an indicator of glaucoma), and other highly specialized procedures (such as angiography to identify ocular blood vessel abnormalities, or ultrasonography to diagnose lesions and tumors).

Some of the same procedures used with infants and young children are also useful with older children, especially those with suspected visual problems and those with multiple disabilities. These include pupillary response, corneal light reflex, fixation, tracking, and reaching. These procedures are usually the initial tests used with severely multiple disabled children, and may be the only tests possible with students who have very low vision. If it can be established that the child can reach accurately, and track reasonably well (preschool and primary grade children may have discontinuous or poorly developed tracking skills–important prerequisites for reading), then a higher level of vision testing may be possible.

Most of the structured acuity tests are measures of central vision (clearest vision) only, and require a child to match objects or symbols. In the STYCAR toys test (performed at 10′ to maintain attention more easily), the child selects a toy or utensil (small fork, spoon, or knife) from "his" set to match the one held up by the examiner. In the Lighthouse cards (symbols of different sizes on individual cards), the House-Apple-Umbrella chart, and the HOTV chart, the child can use a hand-held "cue card" (card containing all possible choices, in the same size) to point to the same symbol indicated by the examiner on a chart 10′ or 20′ away. The Snellen E chart is used at 20′ and requires the ability to differentiate direction (directionality); it is simplest if the child has a large, sturdy (heavy cardboard or masonite) E in his/her hand, which can be rotated to "match" the orientation of the E indicated on the chart by the examiner. Snellen letter charts are used only with students who can identify letters. Whenever possible (depending on the age and cooperation of the child), each eye should be tested separately, as well as both eyes together; an occluder of some type is placed in front of the eye not being tested. If the student is *known* to have poor vision and may have trouble seeing even the largest symbol or letter on the chart, there are other test charts available with larger symbols, letters, or numbers (e.g., the Feinbloom chart), but these are specialized charts not commonly available.

Near vision is tested at reading distance (14″ to 16″) with "nearpoint cards" which have pictures, symbols, letters, numbers, or printed material to be read. It is important to measure nearpoint vision, since this is the vision used in most school activities (reading, writing, math, etc.). Unfortunately, more educators than eye specialists include this measure in evaluating visual function. Reading, writing, and math utilize nearpoint central acuity, and success in school may depend on having useful vision at that distance, whether natural, corrected with lenses, or enhanced with optical devices.

Peripheral fields testing is often overlooked in testing children's visual abilities, since it is a visual "supplement" for most children; it usually provides orientational and background visual information for persons with normal central acuity. When central acuity is diminished or missing, however, peripheral vision becomes vitally important and may be the primary source of visual information. Many multiply disabled children have peripheral fields losses caused by brain damage or central nervous system defects (e.g., optic nerve malfunction) and even a gross measure of peripheral fields can provide useful information for educational programming (what head or body position will permit best use of available vision, or how materials should be positioned to utilize functional visual fields). Confrontation fields testing consists of presenting a target (usually a white ball on a black wand, or a small, brightly colored toy) at the outermost point of the periphery above, below, to the right or left, and from diagonal points in between; then the object or ball is moved slowly in an arc toward the central midpoint. If a child perceives the target in the periphery, he/she will automatically look or turn toward it. If there is no shift of gaze, the assumption is that the target has not been noticed. In this manner, the peripheral fields can be grossly plotted. It is not precise, and any questionable responses should be checked by an eye specialist.

Color perception may be evaluated by several methods. Older children can respond to the Ishihara or Dvorine plates. (Numbers or "paths" are imbedded in distracting backgrounds of colors other than those used in the figures; the child must identify the number or trace the "road" with a finger.) An equally effective and simpler procedure (and one that can be used with younger children) is the matching of brightly colored construction paper squares. The names of the colors can be avoided with younger children (who may not understand the labels yet but can recognize the colors). The examiner asks the child to match one set of squares to the other, without naming the colors (unless the child does it on his/her own). Children who have color deficiencies often confuse shades (blue, purple, brown, green; red, orange); any hesitation in matching suggests uncertainty.

Visual perceptual evaluation should include some measures of visual discrimination (the ability to tell one shape or form from another), visual memory (the ability to remember something seen), form constancy (that a large dark square is still a square, even if it is small and white), visual closure (the ability to mentally "finish" an incomplete drawing by anticipating the rest of it), position in space (that a form can be turned upside down or rotated and still remain the same form), and figure-ground (the ability to select a visual target from a distracting background). The Motor-Free Visual Perception Test (MVPT) is a simple, enjoyable test that can be used with students who have sufficient nearpoint acuity to see line drawings. The Diagnostic Assessment Procedure (DAP) is actually a test of visual efficiency, but it can also be used to test many aspects of visual perception. It can be used with students with too little vision to see the drawings on the MVPT, but who have a mental age of at least three. There are a number of perceptual items in this procedure. The creative examiner can also accumulate a series of pictures and/or tasks to evaluate visual perception, but they will not be a standardized set of procedures; only the student's performance on each particular task can be observed and reported.

There is a difference between evaluating visual acuities, visual fields, visual perception, and functional vision. Eye specialists focus largely on optical system capabilities, while low vision specialists are more concerned with functional, task-oriented vision use. Educators are also concerned with the perceptual part of the visual system, since learning involves "making sense out of" visual images. A good functional vision evaluation (usually performed by the special teacher of students with visual impairments) includes the assessment of visual acuities, visual fields, visual perception, and the way vision is used in functional tasks in a variety of environments. The accumulation of this kind of information about a child's visual functioning provides the basis for recommending necessary modifications in learning environments, materials, and instructional methodology.

DEFINITIONS OF VISUAL IMPAIRMENT

When both clinical and functional visual assessments have been completed, some kind of descriptive label is usually assigned. These definitions form a continuum of descriptors that ranges from normal vision to total blindness. Categories are assigned after best corrections (glasses) have been given.

The continuum begins with the familiar label of "20/20" vision; however, this is only a description of central acuity at a distance of 20 feet. Each ensuing fractional label with a numerator of 20 (e.g., 20/70, 20/50, 20/200) also refers to a 20 foot distance acuity, but is qualified by the lower numeral. That is, a person with 20/70 acuity must be at 20′ to see what a normally sighted person can see at 70′; 20/200 means that a person sees at 20′ what most people see at 200′. These fractions are not percentage equivalents, but measures based on a calibrated eye chart, which is used at a specified distance, and measures only distance vision. There are many gradations of fractional descriptors between "20/20" and the next major qualifier.

"Legal blindness" is a relatively useless definition for educational purposes, since it uses a distance measure. The definition states: "20/200 or worse, in the better eye, corrected if applicable, or restricted fields of 20° or less." A 20° field means little or no peripheral vision, or "tunnel vision," although the central vision *could* be 20/20, and the individual would still qualify for economic purposes as "legally blind." Notice that the definition says "or" not "and," and says nothing about nearpoint, or reading distance, vision. Therefore, it is not really an appropriate definition to use in qualifying a student for special educational services. Most states' educational laws have agreed, and have made their eligibility requirements dependent on functional vision rather than on a numerical definition.

"Low vision" as a category is less easy to define, since two persons can have the same numerical descriptor and function very differently. The best definition is probably "a severe impairment after correction, but the potential exists for the use of available vision, with or without optical or nonoptical low vision devices and modifications" (Corn, 1983).

When the limits of numerical descriptors have been reached (that is, the individual cannot identify letters or symbols on any chart at any distance), the next category is "counts fingers." This means that the person can tell how many fingers the examiner is holding up, and is usually followed by a distance (e.g., CF @ 3′). It is a gross measure of acuity, and, again, has very little relationship to education beyond the probability that the person may be unable to read print. The next categorical label is not much better; it is "hand movements" and follows the same procedure; the individual indicates when a moving hand can be seen as the hand approaches; results are recorded in distances, as "HM @ 3′."

"Object perception" and "shadow perception" are also gross measures. Object perception means that the person is able to avoid large objects when walking around a room; shadow perception means the individual is able to discriminate (the ability to see) shadows. Both measures are only useful for mobility purposes.

The remaining two labels for visual capability are "LP" and "LProj." These mean "light perception" and "light projection." In "light projection," the individual can point in the direction of a light source, but in "light perception," the person can only tell the presence or absence of light. Having "light projection" has the advantage of being able to use a light source as a mobility clue. Totally blind persons are labeled "NIL," and they are a very small percentage of the visually impaired population.

For educational purposes, a definition of blindness implies the use of tactual and/or auditory channels for learning. Some educationally blind students will have useful vision for mobility purposes (e.g., can move toward or around objects, shadows, light, etc.) and some students can even see faces or outlines but optical devices are not helpful or useful. The student cannot read print of any size and will be a tactual/auditory learner.

This chapter has described the ways in which vision can be evaluated before assigning a qualifying descriptor label. In some cases, glasses or contact lenses have been prescribed before applying the descriptor, and often, the corrective lenses give the individual normal vision. When corrective lenses are not possible (i.e., when the visual defect is not a refractive error) or when it is impossible to give a strong enough prescription and the individual still has impaired vision even with glasses, a "low vision evaluation" may be recommended. This is a specialized assessment, done by a low vision specialist (usually an optometrist or ophthalmologist who has had advanced training in low vision and the use of optical devices). The assessment is usually task-oriented (i.e., the individual's particular task-needs are addressed in exploring visual enhancement options). The next chapter will discuss what kinds of optical devices are available and how they can enhance visual functioning.

Chapter Five

HOW CAN A VISUAL SYSTEM BE IMPROVED OR ENHANCED WHEN IMPAIRED?

Visual functioning can be enhanced through optical and/or nonoptical means. Each individual's specific needs depend on a number of factors: specific eye condition, acuities at near and far (both corrected and uncorrected), peripheral fields, need for contrast, lighting requirements, head and body position, fatigue factor, literacy media, personality, motivation, cognitive ability, and physical coordination. The functional vision evaluation, medical records (including the eye report), educational history, and low vision evaluation should collectively provide the information needed to make appropriate recommendations for modifications in materials, methods, and learning environments. This chapter will discuss the optical and nonoptical means of vision enhancement that can be used in instructional settings for students who have useful vision for learning purposes.

OPTICAL DEVICES

Some students will receive corrective lenses that give normal or near-normal vision. If they were found to be nearsighted (myopic), their lenses will be concave (or minus) lenses in the power needed to correct the refractive error. If the student was farsighted (hyperopic), those corrective lenses will be convex (or plus) lenses. Both "plus" and "minus" lenses are spherical. Any lens with no power (neither "plus" nor "minus"); flat on both sides) is called a "plano" lens and is used either as a protective lens or to fill the glasses frame when one eye has a normal refractive power and the other eye needs a prescriptive correction. When a refractive error involves astigmatism, a cylindrical lens (a "slice" of a cylinder) is ground into the normal spherical lens, placed in such a way as to correct only the improper corneal curvature. Since astigmatism can be myopic or hyperopic (depending on whether the corneal defect is a "bump" or a "dent"), the astigmatic correction can be a "plus" or a "minus." Corrections for astigmatism are in addition to any prescriptions for myopia or hyperopia; therefore, the innumerable possible combinations of prescriptions make each pair of glasses an individualized prescription. It is highly unlikely that any two people would have exactly the same prescription, so individuals should not exchange eyeglasses.

In the case of bifocal lenses, the top portion will contain any correction needed for distance vision, and the lower part will provide any necessary correction for near vision. When an individual has had his/her natural lenses removed (as in cataract surgery), the eye is called "aphakic" and bifocals are needed. If an intraocular lens (IOL) has been implanted, it is inside the eye and provides nearpoint correction; contact lenses or glasses can provide any additional distance correction needed.

Sunglasses or tinted lenses are simple optical enhancements for individuals who are light sensitive. Albinism and achromatopsia are two examples of eye conditions that have photophobia as a symptom, but anyone for whom daytime glare is a problem might find tinted lenses helpful.

In most cases, glasses or contact lenses can correct refractive errors sufficiently to provide normal or near-normal vision. (Glasses cannot correct retinal problems, optic nerve defects, or optic tract malfunction; they also cannot improve visual impairment caused by brain dysfunction.) When it is not possible to provide a full correction (it may be impossible to make lenses powerful enough–they would be too thick and heavy to wear–or distortion-free), the individual may not have normal vision even with glasses. Depending on the amount of vision available, it may be possible to prescribe special devices to be used in addition to glasses, and a Low Vision Evaluation is usually recommended.

The Low Vision Specialist will check acuities at far and near, and usually also checks peripheral fields. The best possible spectacle correction is also determined before considering additional optical devices. The Low Vision Specialist will discuss with the individual what tasks need to be accomplished (reading, filing, shopping, driving, doing needlepoint, drawing, etc.). Based on each person's individual needs (and there may be more than one), a number of optical devices are tried out, in varying powers. They may include magnifiers, telescopes, or prism lenses. Whichever devices seem to help the individual perform his/her desired tasks are then prescribed, and ordered. "Loaner" devices are sometimes given until the person's own device(s) becomes available. A brief training session in how to use the device(s) is usually provided in the clinical setting, but the person must usually practice using the device(s) independently, in practical applications. When instruction is not given in the clinical setting, the individual must learn to use the device(s) on his/her own, and motivation becomes a big factor in successful use. In the case of a school student, the special teacher of visually impaired students may provide instruction in the use of the device(s); sometimes the Orientation and Mobility Instructor assumes this responsibility. If proper instruction is not available, the student may never learn to use his/her device(s) efficiently, and its value in vision enhancement is lost. All too many expensive and carefully prescribed optical devices end up on a shelf or in the individual's pocket because no instruction in their use was given, or the instruction was inadequate. Coordinated efforts between the Low Vision Specialist and the school personnel could greatly alleviate this problem.

Types of optical devices can be grouped by magnifiers, telescopes, prism lenses, and electronic devices. Each type has different applications, and an individual may use more than one type for different tasks.

Magnifiers enlarge an image so that it utilizes more of the retinal surface, and provides more information to be transmitted to the brain. Magnifiers may be attached to the glasses (usually for close work, such as needlework or fly-tying), may be hand-held (the most familiar kind), or may be stationary (bar magnifiers, stand magnifiers, mirror magnifiers). Some models of hand-held or stand magnifiers have their own illumination systems that light the page or object being viewed; usually, an electrical outlet is required for these models. All magnifiers come in different "powers" (ability to enlarge). Generally, the smaller the lens, the higher the power, but also the more restricted the viewing area.

Telescopes are intended to bring distant objects closer. They are not only used for travel purposes but may also be used to see the blackboard from the back of a classroom, or to see printed music on a music stand at arm's distance away. Telescopes are usually used with one eye and are called monoculars. They can be clipped onto a pair of glasses, attached permanently, or hand-held. The higher the power, the more restricted the viewing area (or "field"). One kind of distance device mounted permanently on glasses is a "full field" telescope system; it uses two telescopes, one for each eye, and thereby restricts the viewer to only what can be seen through the telescopes. the viewer has no nearpoint or peripheral vision while using the telescopes, and should not walk around while wearing them. They are only useful for specific purposes (e.g., watching TV). Another kind of telescope is one mounted behind the eyeglass lens (that is, immediately in front of the eye); these devices are used like a bifocal, by moving the eye down to look through the telescope and then up to see through the glasses.

"Bioptics" are small telescopes which are permanently mounted into a pair of glasses; there may be either one or two telescopes, mounted just above or just below the straight-ahead line of vision. The individual must usually move his/her head up or down to use the telescope. They are sometimes used for driving by people with low vision, and some states permit driver's licenses under these conditions.

Prism lenses bring the peripheral environment into the user's functional fields. Usually, the prism lenses are mounted directly onto the viewer's glasses, either on both lateral edges, or above/below the central lens area. Because the image is distorted, the viewer must learn to use the information through practice.

Another optical device used by persons with fields restrictions is a "reverse telescope." Instead of enlarging distant objects, it makes them smaller, but it includes more of the distant environment in the field of view. Good central acuity is essential. This device is not recommended for mobility purposes but for orientation to a new environment.

There are a number of electronic systems for vision enhancement. The most commonly known device is the closed circuit television (CCTV), which is actually a small video camera that projects an enlarged image on a video monitor. The user can control the enlargement size, contrast, and polarity (black letters on a white background, or white letters on a black background). The system is not portable, however, unless a student pushes an audiovisual cart from room to room. Rapidly advancing technology will probably miniaturize this system in the future.

Computer systems often have software programs to enlarge print on the display monitor. Larger monitors and screen magnifiers can also be used. The rapid increase in microchip technology is already beginning to spur the development of new systems for vision enhancement. One of these is a device worn on the head like glasses, and contains both video cameras and a small screen in front of the wearer's eyes; it is claimed that the size of images produced are similar to sitting 4′ away from a 60 TV″ screen. The device can be connected to a VCR, computer, or compact video disk to allow the viewer to see movies or the computer screen. These newest systems are cost prohibitive for schools, at present, but they reflect what may be in the future for optical devices.

NONOPTICAL VISION ENHANCEMENT

Nonoptical ways of enhancing visual functioning include procedures, and devices/materials. Among the procedures are lighting, seating and/or positioning, adapting materials, and giving extra time. Many visually impaired persons find that extra light is helpful if it is diffused and indirect (to minimize glare), but light directed on the task should come from over the shoulder opposite to the dominant hand (i.e., over the left shoulder for a right-handed person). Glare is a serious problem for individuals with cataracts or corneal opacities, and can be a discomfort for others; shiny surfaces on pages, desks, and blackboards can reflect light that is visually uncomfortable; nonglare paper for reading and written tasks, a desk-sized piece of light-colored matte surface paper to cover a shiny desk surface, and window shades to control direct light on blackboards are all possible remedies for glare problems. Some eye defects include light sensitivity as a symptom (e.g., albinism, achromatopsia); for these individuals, protection against glare, and strict lighting control are essential. A cap with a visor and/or tinted lenses can shield against glare, and lighting should be average or less for visual comfort.

Classroom seating can enhance visual performance if it places the student where the lighting level matches his/her visual needs. Multiply disabled students may have special positioning requirements, but these should consider whether medication affects ocular pupil size; if the pupils are dilated most of the time, facing a light source will be uncomfortable; positioning should be facing away from the light source.

Adapting materials includes increasing contrast, adding color, adjusting spacing (especially between math problems), increasing size (enlarging), and simplifying (outlining, eliminating extraneous detail, reducing "clutter"). The procedures selected should match the visual needs of the student, since what may help one child may not help another. When central vision is reduced, enlargement or magnification will utilize more of the retinal area; however, when peripheral vision has been lost, enlargement is counterproductive.

Giving extra time for the completion of a task may be helpful for students who must exert extra energy in seeing. "Trying to see" requires energy and often results in fatigue, so allowing extra time can help.

Nonoptical vision enhancement devices or materials include reading stands (to position reading material so that the student is not constantly bent over to see it), felt-tip pens (both black and colors), nonglare paper (dark-lined), typoscopes (a card with a rectangular hole to expose a few words or a line at a time), "underliners" (a piece of construction paper held under the line to be read, to keep from losing the place when moving from one line to the next), trays to contain manipulatives within view, and large print. Notice that "large print" should is the last item; this is intentional. Any student who "needs" large print should explore other means of enlargement first (magnifiers or magnification systems). The student's ability to read anything he/she *chooses* to read should be the first consideration. Supplying large print limits the student to only what is provided.

THE FUTURE OF VISUAL ENHANCEMENT

The inability to see is a major disability. It interferes with nearly all functions of daily living and restricts a great many leisure or pleasure activities. It is not surprising, then, that bioresearchers are studying ways of providing some kind of artificial vision for those who cannot see. The most promising research seems to be in developing retinal or cortical implants. Currently, there are attempts to implant electronic "chips" in the retina, but success has been limited because the present level of technology does not allow the chips to be made small enough. In theory, the chip is intended to act as a photoreceptor (to receive light, transform it to electrical impulses, and transmit the impulses to the optic nerve), but the chip cannot yet approximate the function of retinal receptors. When one considers that there are 137 million photoreceptor cells in the retina, packed into an area smaller than most postage stamps, the enormity of the problem becomes evident. Almost seven million cones take up a space about 1.5 mm in diameter (the fovea centralis), and 130 million rods are located in the remainder of the retina. To put it in another context, the cones number about the same as the population of greater New York City, and the rods would be like the whole population of the United States standing on a postage stamp (Gregory, 1966, p. 63). Current technology has just not yet figured out how to miniaturize sufficiently. The retinal chips now available process such gross bits of light energy that the chip is not able to relay much really recognizable information to the brain. All is not lost, however, for bioresearchers are studying nanotechnology possibilities. If a chip could be made small enough to receive enough bits of discrete information (light energy), it may yet be possible to create an artificial retina.

Cortical implants have some of the same problems as retinal chips. Brain cells are so numerous and tiny that a small burst of energy sent to the cortical implant literally blasts the corresponding cells. It might be compared to a giant's foot stepping on a gnat. Consider the size of brain cells: if one person was the size of a single brain cell, the entire population of the earth could be held in one pair of cupped hands and it still wouldn't be enough cells for one human brain! Obviously, more research in nanotechnology will be needed before cortical implants will be able to target individual brain cells.

Children often ask why they can't get an eye transplant to help them see better; the answer is that the optic nerve would have to be severed to remove the eye, and surgeons have not yet figured out how to reconnect optic nerves. (There are too many tiny nerve bundles to reconnect.) Perhaps if nanotechnology can refine surgical techniques, it may become possible in the future to join tiny nerve connections, and ocular transplants could become a reality. Until then, however, ophthalmologists will be limited to what surgical procedures are possible.

SUMMARY

This chapter has described the ways in which impairments can be improved in function, using optical and nonoptical means. Most visually impaired students will have some amount of useful vision, and individualized adjustments in materials, the environment, or enhanced visual functioning can make the learning process both easier and more efficient.

REFERENCES AND RECOMMENDED READING

Barraga, N. & Erin, J. (2001). *Visual impairments and learning* (4th Ed.). Austin, TX: ProEd.

Bernas-Pierce, J. (Ed.). (1998). *Pediatric Visual Diagnosis Fact Sheets.* San Francisco: Blind Babies Foundation.

Bishop, V. (1986). *Selected anomalies and diseases of the eye.* Unpublished manuscript; available on the Texas School for the Blind website.

Bishop, V. (1988). Making choices in functional vision evaluations: Noodles, needles, and haystacks. *Journal of Visual Impairment and Blindness, 82,* 94–99.

Cassin, B. & Solomon, S. (1990). *Dictionary of eye terminology.* Gainesville, FL: Triad Publishing Company.

Catalano, R. & Nelson, L. (1994). *Pediatric ophthalmology.* Norwalk, CT: Appleton and Lange.

Cogan, D. (1966). *Neurology of the visual system.* Springfield, IL: Charles C Thomas.

Corn, A. (1980). Optical aids in the classroom. *Education of the Visually Handicapped, 12,* 114–119.

Corn, A. (1983). Visual function: A theoretical model for individuals with low vision. *Journal of Visual Impairment and Blindness, 77,* 373–377.

Corn, A. (1986). Low vision and visual efficiency. In Scholl, G. (Ed.), *Foundations of education for blind and visually handicapped children and youth.* New York: American Foundation for the Blind.

Corn, A. & Koenig, A. (1996). *Foundations of low vision: Clinical and functional perspectives.* New York: American Foundation for the Blind.

DeMatteo, B. (1986). *Terminal shock.* Toronto: New Canada Publications.

Fraunfelder, F. (1989). *Drug-induced ocular side effects and drug interactions* (3rd Ed.). Philadelphia: Lea & Febiger.

Gregory, R. (1981). *Eye and brain.* New York: McGraw-Hill Book Company.

Isenberg, S. (1989). *The eye in infancy.* Chicago: Year Book Medical Publishers, Inc.

Jose, R. (1983). *Understanding low vision.* New York: American Foundation for the Blind.

Levack, N. (1994). *Low vision* (2nd Ed.). Austin, TX: Texas School for the Blind and Visually Impaired.

Newell, F. (1992). *Ophthalmology principles and concepts* (7th Ed.). St. Louis: Mosby/Year Book.

Ornstein, R. & Thompson, R. (1985). *The amazing brain.* London: Hogarth Press.

Restak, R. (1984). *The brain.* New York: Bantam Books.

Smith, A. & O'Donnell, L. (1992). *Beyond arm's reach: Enhancing distance vision.* Philadelphia: Pennsylvania College of Optometry Press.

Stein, H., Slatt, B., & Stein, R. (1992). *Ophthalmic terminology.* St. Louis: Mosby/Year Book.

Vaughan, D. & Asbury, T. (1980). *General ophthalmology* (9th Ed.). East Norwalk, CT: Appleton & Lange.

Ward, M. (2000). The visual system. In Holbrook, C. & Koenig, A. (Eds.). *Foundations of education,* Volume 1. New York: AFB Press.

Wright, K. & Spiegal, P. (Eds.). (2003). *Pediatric ophthalmology and strabismus.* New York: Springer.

Zimmerman, G. (1996). Optics and optical devices. In Corn, A. & Koenig, A. (Eds.), *Foundations of low vision: Clinical and functional perspectives.* New York: AFB Press.

Part Two

LEARNING

Chapter Six

LEARNING THEORY

INTRODUCTION

In order to discuss "learning," it is necessary to examine the various groupings of development theory, and then to see how learning theory relates to those groupings. There are a number of ways to group theories of human development, and at least four ways are found in most educational theory texts. The first might be by emphasis: "Psychoanalytical" theorists base their philosophy on human interactions; "Cognitivists" believe intellectual development to be the most important facet of human growth; "Behaviorists" place their emphasis on human behavior and its shaping; and "Humanists" are people/feelings oriented.

A second way of viewing human development is through a hierarchy of needs gratification. This hierarchy is typified by Maslow's description of steps, from physiological (hunger, thirst, elimination), to safety-security (order, routine, lack of danger), to love and belongingness (friends, spouses), and finally to esteem (self-respect, self-esteem); an even higher level, seldom reached in reality by many people, is what Maslow called "self-actualization" (the realization of full potential). The infant's needs are at the lowest level, the toddler and preschool child cross the next two levels, and the school-age child usually can achieve the fourth level. Some adults, however, never achieve the third and fourth levels, and, in some cultures or societies, few people rise above the first level. The highest level is reached by few people, although it is always a goal for which to aim.

Educators who have taken courses in "Child Development" will recognize the guidelines in the third general group of theories. These "keys" to development include the idea that human beings develop from general to specific, gross to fine, head to foot (cephalocaudal) and near to far (proximodistal). These "keys" seem to match the direction of physical development (gross motor before fine motor, torso before extremities, head control before arm control before leg control) but they seem to overlook the element of cognition in the developmental process.

Another way of looking at developmental theory is through the "nature vs nurture" approach. "Naturists" describe human development from a physical and maturational viewpoint, with an intact infant as the focal starting point. "Nurturists" see the environment and external factors as more important in shaping development; and "Nature-Nurture" fence-sitters think both the child and the environment *interact* in contributing to the development of the child. The last group places great emphasis on cognitive growth, and attributes much of development to the expanding cognitive system (see Figure 7).

The grouping of developmental theories that may have the most direct relationship to learning theory is the "Nature-Nurture" group. If one believes that the individual has a preprogrammed rate and sequence for growth, and that maturation will take care of development, then there will be "readiness" periods that will make a child "teachable," and not before. However, if one thinks that the child is born ready to be programmed, the environment will shape development, "education" will emanate from external sources, and then learning will result from whatever the teacher does or says. If neither of these theories seems satisfactory, then perhaps a little of both will satisfy: both natural maturation *and* the environment will play a role in development, and learning will require the interaction between both the child and the environment. The reader is urged to examine his/her own educational philosophy to see which developmental theory best matches that philosophy.

It is important to recognize the heterogeneity of learners, and that one theory may be better for some learners than another (see Figure 8). There is no single "right" theory for all children. (Educational systems seem to get this wrong repeatedly as they experiment with "new" teaching approaches implemented across a school system.) The ideal might be to use whatever instructional approaches produce learning, *for each child,* but this concept seems to elude many educators, even within the special education system. The cur-

	"Nature"	"Nurture"	"Nature-Nurture"
Common Descriptor	Developmental	Environmental	Interactional
Emphasis	Physical maturation	External control	Cognition
Person Associated with Theory	Gesell	Skinner	Piaget
Other Descriptors	"Age types"	Behaviorism Conditioning Behavor modification	Stages: Sensori-motor Preoperational Concrete Operations Formal Operations

Figure 7. Selected Developmental Theories

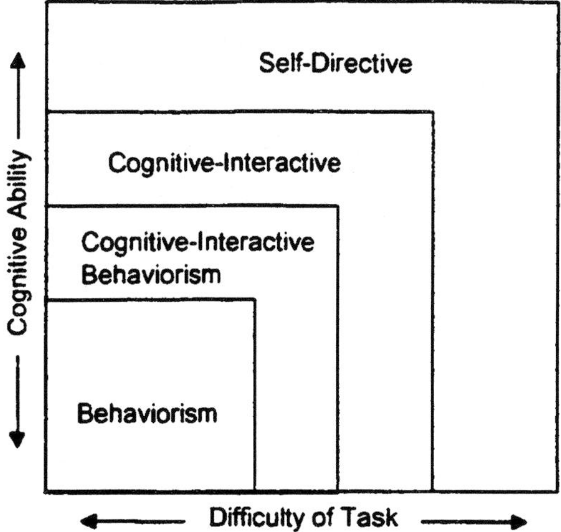

	Behaviorism	Cognitive-Interactional	Self-Directive
Instructional Goal	Skill acquisition	Development of reasoning	Independent learning
Methodology	Programmed instruction Behavior modification	Experience learning "Discovery" learning "Work Centers" Assumes stage acquisition; readiness	Child centered "Open education" Affective emphasis Assumes maturation/ readiness
Method of Assessment	Data collection Standardized tests	Observation Criterion-referenced tests	(non-graded)
Role of the Teacher	Teacher centered	Teacher is mediator	Teacher assists
Potential Problems	Lack of generalization of skills	Requires creative teacher	Lack of structure

Figure 8. The Relationships Between Learning Theories and Learning

rently popular phrase "All children can learn" is only true if instructional methodology is matched appropriately with each child's learning style, cognitive level, and unique needs.

This author's underlying philosophy of education leans heavily on the interactional (Piagetian) model for a number of reasons:

1. It is sensory based and process oriented;
2. It respects individual maturation and readiness levels;
3. The equilibration theory seems to match current brain theory;
4. It encourages independence on the part of the child;
5. It allows the teacher to be a facilitator instead of a director;

PIAGETIAN STAGES
Order is Invariant; Development is Cumulative

Stage	Age Range	Characteristics	Progression from Beginning to End of Age Range
Sensorimotor*	B - 2	Own actions dominate	Reactive to Active
Preoperational	2 - 7	Egocentric Language begins No conservation/ reversibility	Empirical to Logical
Concrete Operational	7 - 11	Acquisition of mental reversibility	Absolute to Relative
Formal Operations	11+	Mental hypothesis testing	Abstract Reasoning

*Sensorimotor Period includes:

Reflexive	B - 1 month
Primary Circular Reactions	1 - 4 months
Secondary Circular Reactions	4 - 8 months
Coordinated Secondary Schemes	8 - 12 months
Tertiary Circular Reactions	12 -18 months
New Means via Mental Combinations	18 -24 months

Figure 9.

6. It is easily adapted to learners with special needs; and
7. It has the potential to make learning a pleasant experience (even "fun!").

THE BRAIN

In order to develop a theory about learning, there must be some understanding of how the cognitive control center–the brain–works. Neuroscientists still have many questions, and do not always agree on conclusions, but the explosion of information in neuroscience reflects a growing body of knowledge. For example, there is general agreement about how the brain is constructed (all of the many parts), but not always universal agreement on what each part does. Researchers have suggested that there are specific areas of the cortex that are directly related to the processing of information collected by the senses, but scientists are not in agreement about where data is stored *after* processing, and how it is retrieved. In other words, we don't have *all* the answers yet, but we are learning. The brain continues to provide an intriguing area for research (see Figure 10 and Table 2).

A few observations of neural brain function may have implications for learning. Connections between brain cells appear to be strengthened or weakened by experience (positive or negative), and repeated stimulations cause increased neurotransmitter release (the chemical "bridge" between neurons). Repeated sensory input can also actually modify areas of the brain. At least two studies (cited in Schwartz & Begley, 2002) found that the somatosensory cortex of persons who were fluent braille readers was much larger for the "reading finger" than for the fingers of non-braille readers; the somatosensory cortex of violinists' left hands was noticeably larger than for non-violinists. The cortical region that processes sensory input had expanded to meet the increased needs (and use) of particular hands or fingers. This

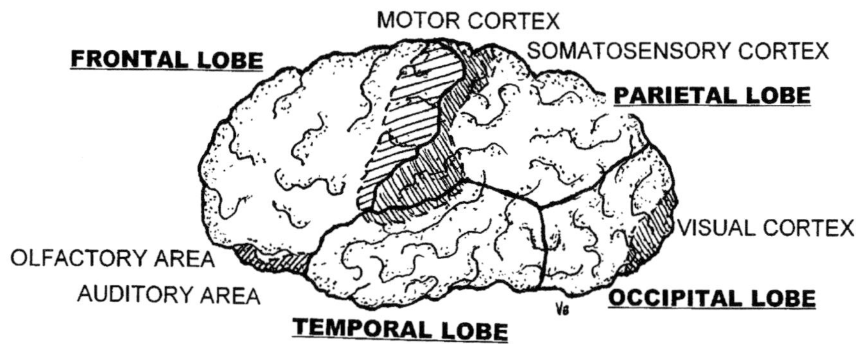

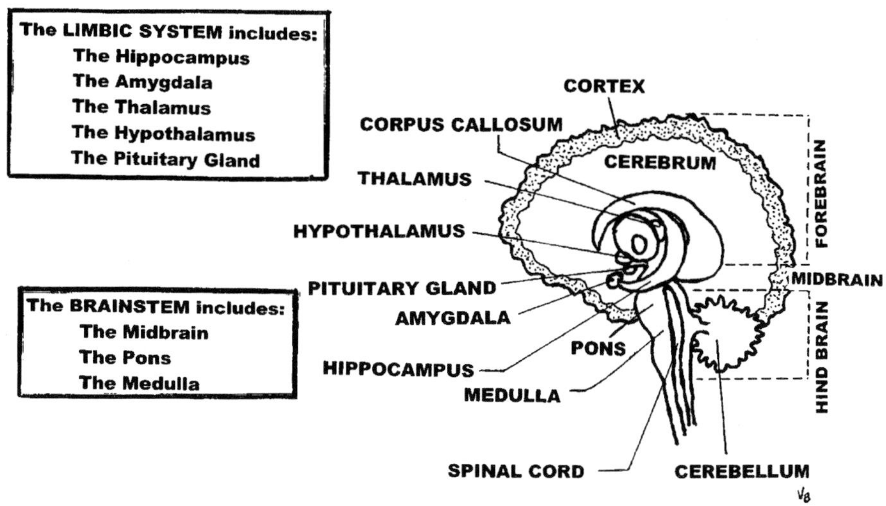

THE BRAIN

Figure 10.

TABLE 2. AREAS OF THE BRAIN AND THEIR FUNCTIONS

The Brainstem:	includes the medulla (lowest area), pons (middle area, or "bridge") and the midbrain (the highest area); this is the oldest part of the brain, and the most primitive; it is believed to control survival functions (breathing and heart rate) and determines the general level of alertness.
The Cerebellum:	"the little brain," located behind the brainstem; controls posture and balance; coordinates muscle movements; related to spatial orientation.
The Limbic System:	a group of structures between the brainstem and cortex, that regulates involuntary body functions (including pupillary reactions). The *Hippocampus* and *Amygdala* are believed to be related to memory (hippocampus monitoring spatial memory, as in maps or drawings; the amygdala related to emotional memory). *Thalamus:* initiates consciousness; relays signals. *Hypothalamus:* regulates involuntary body functions, such as hunger, thirst, sleep, body temperature, blood sugar levels, blood pressure. *Pituitary gland:* the "master gland;" controls distribution of other hormones.
The Cerebrum:	the two brain "hemispheres," each sensorily responsive to opposite sides of the body; hemispheres are connected by the *corpus callosum,* which is supported on a pillar called the *septum pellucidum* (which lies between the hemispheres) "Left Brain"–language/verbal/math; logical/analytical/rational; sequential "Right Brain"–spatial/artistic/musical; intuitive/synthetic; patterns; Gestalt
Cortex:	a 1/8th inch thick layer of nerve cells, covering the Cerebrum in folds, in order to fit within the skull; it is separated into four lobes on each side. *Frontal lobe:* responsible for planning, decision-making, reasoning. *Parietal lobe:* receives sensory input from the body. *Occipital lobe:* primary visual processing area. *Temporal lobe:* auditory processing area; responsible for perception and, perhaps, memory.

finding has applications for instructional theory: repetition ("practice") *does* work, and there is a physiological/neurological explanation. Moreover, the brain may retain its plasticity longer than was once thought, since the subjects in the above studies were all adults.

The way the brain appears to "learn" also has implications for educators. As new or novel information is sent to the brain, processing involves seeking a familiar pattern from memory. If the new information is not too dissimilar from the already recognized pattern, the brain accepts the new pattern and "accommodates" (a Piagetian term for "accepts-and-files"). Thus, the brain maintains a state of equilibrium. Educators could learn from this process, and *always* proceed from the know to the unknown in instruction.

Another lesson from brain function: when teaching a *tactual* skill (like braille, or touch typing), establish only *tactual* patterns in the sensory cortex; permitting vision to assist only slows the learning process because the sensory route into the brain becomes detoured through the visual cortex. The motor pattern needs to go directly to the tactual portion of the cortex if it is to be truly a motor (touch) skill.

ASSUMPTIONS ABOUT THE BRAIN

It should be evident that understanding how the brain works is a prerequisite to developing any learning theories, since the brain is the "control center" for learning. For the purposes of this book, certain assumptions about brain function will be made.

1. The human brain is unusual in its ability to respond to characteristics that are uniquely human (faces, voices, expressions, emotions).
2. The human brain works systematically; sensory information is encoded, stored, and translated into recognizable response patterns.
3. The human brain functions as an entity; parts of the brain may be differentiated according to function, but the data is interconnected, both between centers and between hemispheres.
4. The human brain is capable of establishing, expanding, and applying elaborate coding systems that include language, mathematical symbols, and complex connections between ideas.
5. The human brain (especially the young brain) has the ability to use/develop portions of the brain wired for one purpose (e.g., seeing) for other purposes; this capability is called "plasticity."
6. The beginning of communication between brain hemispheres coincides with the myelinization of the corpus callosum; coincidentally, this is about the same time as Piagetian "reversibility" of thought and "conservation" (remembering a former state of matter or an object) are acquired cognitively;
7. "Sensitive" times for learning ("readiness" and receptivity) coincide with periods of brain growth; these times include all of the preschool years (but especially when language is acquired), when "reversibility" is finally present, and when formal (abstract) reasoning begins.

(Languis et al., 1980)

LEARNING THEORY

The first attempts at learning are the infant's acquisition of sensory knowledge about the environment. All knowledge of the world beyond the self comes by way of the senses, so this is the first level of brain intake. Without this input, the brain will not grow, and cannot establish beginning patterns of information. Gradually, the brain attaches meaning to the sensory input (mother's voice, smile, touch, which mean comfort and security). The first acts of cognition are the brain's attempts to make sense of experiences, to perceive relationships between bits of sensory data. Piaget describes this process as "equilibration"–when a current "scheme" (or pattern of responses) assimilates a new bit of information, and, by absorbing it, becomes changed a little) accommodates).

Learning, then, is a change in behavior because of experience. *Doing* something provides experience that aids in understanding. The Montessori method of learning is basically the provision of experiences to build understanding–"discovery learning" at its best. Process-oriented teaching creates environments to be explored, provides challenges to be met, and problems to be solved.

In learning relationships, structure and natural "order" are "discovered." The ability to generalize learning depends on the perception of similar structure. This requires a level of cognition not present in some severely delayed learners, and may explain why a conditioning instructional approach works better with these children.

Learning that is only the acquisition of unrelated information will not generalize. It needs to be related enough to be applied to other situations. If it can be applied, the third step should be to evaluate how well it worked. Scientific method is a higher form of this kind of learning–the proposal of a hypothesis, the application of known information, and the measurement of efficacy. The "spiral curriculum" also operates on a similar premise–that later learning is based on (and may be an expansion of) prior learning.

In summary, then: learning is the gradual acquisition of sensory data, which is sorted and categorized by the brain (perception). As patterns of responses are formed in the brain, neuronal connections are strengthened. When new data is received, the response patterns are altered or new patterns are created and stored. When enough patterns have been acquired that applications are possible, thought processes are able to manipulate them to form conclusions or to create new ideas. The human organism has progressed from a receiver, to a doer, to a thinker.

THE ROLE OF VISION IN DEVELOPMENT AND LEARNING

The human being is born totally helpless; it cannot move itself from place to place, cannot obtain or prepare food or feed itself, cannot clothe itself, cannot communicate very well with others, and cannot even dispose of its own body wastes. All it can do is sleep and indicate discomfort. It will take at least 15–18 years for that human being to acquire all the skills it needs, to be able to function independently. The acquisition of independence (and the ability to perpetuate its species) is a systematic set of developmental steps and learning experiences, and vision plays a major role in nearly every aspect of that system. An analysis of those accomplishments and experiences can help put "education" (and teaching) into a useful perspective.

The first year of life is primarily devoted to getting the infant into an upright position, preparing it to move. Each step of motor development is either motivated by vision or monitored by vision. Head and neck control is acquired because the baby wants to *look* at something of interest; reach is initiated and practiced because the infant wishes to examine, explore, or acquire something it *sees.* Sitting independently allows the head and torso to twist and turn, and frees the hands for more precise manipulation of whatever the child has acquired. Standing, and subsequent walking, are motivated by "what's out there to get to." *Vision* had been the motivator, the lure, the monitor, and the reason for each successive step in motor development.

Although the first year focuses primarily on motor skills, and the coordination of arms, legs, body, and head, it is vision that "pulls it all together." This is not to say that other systems are not functioning; indeed, they are, but at a different level. The foundations for language, communication, and cognition are being laid as the infant *looks* around, assigns meaning to particular objects or people, compares sizes, shapes, colors, distances, and gets a sense of "how things work," and what they are called. The infant brain is very busy that first year, collecting information, categorizing it, and filing it away for future reference. The baby is largely a passive observer/learner until it can move itself into the world around it, and vision has allowed exploration of the immediate environment without moving into it directly. The one year old has built a considerable storehouse of information in its brain, enabling it to begin layering new information *based on the old.* This is a basic principle of learning (and teaching): there must be something in the brain's database to relate to, or learning will not take place. (It is not coincidental that a good teacher establishes a "current level of functioning" before beginning instruction.)

The second year of life is when the toddler "moves out" and begins to explore the world for him/herself. Vision helps to maintain physical balance and provides the continuing lure to "go see." Toddlers *see* something they want, and go after it. They *watch* what happens when they initiate some action. They *observe* how other humans behave. Vision is their primary information gathering sense, with hearing and touch acting as reinforcers. The combined experiences of seeing, listening, and touching expand the brain's database to include names of things, how they work, how they compare, and how they change or stay the same. Vision enables the toddler to connect activities and objects. The child *watches* as Mama removes food from the refrigerator, prepares it at the sink or stove, and places it on a plate ready to eat. The toddler *observes* the water going into the bathtub, *sees* the tub toys bobbing among the bubbles, and *watches* the water disappear down the drain. The toddler *sees* the sky get dark at bedtime, *observes* the clouds and raindrops, and *watches* human beings perform their daily routines of work, play, moving around, laughing, crying, hugging, and talking. All of these experiences are added to the brain's database for future reference.

At around age 2, the toddler has pretty well refined the ability to get around and "into things," and has discovered his individuality–that he/she is a being separate from others, and capable of decision-making; the toddler can do or not do, according to his/her own preference. The toddler even takes this newly acquired control to another level, and begins to "do for him/herself." The toddler observes and imitates–feeding, dressing, toileting, playing. The era of "self-help" has begun, and its success is based largely on the ability to *watch* how others do things. Even play depends on the ability to imitate and replicate what has been *observed.* Vision continues to play a primary role in development and learning.

The preschool years, 3–5, are a time of expanding and refining. The young child coordinates his body better (running, climbing, jumping, hopping, skipping, riding a tricycle) and expands his/her repertoire of basic concepts and social behaviors. The preschooler continues to *observe* and imitate, but also experiments, *watches* what happens, and compares. Many (if not most) basic concepts (size, shape, color, length, height, distance, spatial location) rely on vision for understanding, and the many properties of matter become an important foundation for future learning. When objects or phenomena that are out of reach (clouds, stars, mountains, extinct animals, tornados, electricity) must be explained, there will need to be a database of concepts to draw upon ("It's like . . ."). Visual experience, and visual memory, will provide that foundation of information.

When a child enters school, he/she brings along all of the experiences (or lack thereof) in his/her own personal database. Learning success in school will depend heavily on the quantity and quality of that database. Hopefully, each teacher during a child's school years will make an attempt to access each child's individual storehouse of experiences, and build instruction on that base. Most of the child's school instruction will rely heavily on vision (blackboards, textbooks, computer screens, pictures and drawings, maps, charts, graphs, signs, demonstrations, etc.); even the acquisition of social skills will depend on the child's ability to observe peer behaviors, dress codes, and disciplinary limits. The simple process of organizing assignments, notebooks, and schedules assumes visual reference. We live, for the most part, in a visual world, and a great many instructional techniques are visually based. The entire educational system assumes that the learner can see, has had visual experiences, can make visual comparisons, has visual memory, and can use vision to expand knowledge. This assumption is invalid for learners who are visually impaired, and it is the responsibility of the teacher of students who are visually impaired (TVI) to "fill in the gaps" at all levels. The remainder of this book will try to help the TVI (and anyone who knows–or wishes they knew–a visually impaired person) understand how to modify instruction so that visually impaired learners are not at a disadvantage.

HOW DOES A VISUAL IMPAIRMENT AFFECT LEARNING?

Characteristics of the visual impairment itself may determine the degree of impact on early development and learning. Total blindness forces other sensory channels to provide initial sensory input data to the brain, but this information does not have the same motivational power as vision does. In congenitally blind infants, sometimes the other senses are able to take over the area of the brain reserved for vision, thus somewhat strengthening the quality of information collected. (This ability of the young brain to reprogram itself is called "plasticity.") It should be noted that this does not happen spontaneously or automatically; intervention must take place to provide the experiences that encourage brain use.

When an infant has *some* vision, early stimulation with black and white pictures/patterns (not light alone) can help to maximize the development of available vision, but the amount of available vision can affect both learning and early development. The more vision an infant has, the more likely it will be that normal (or near-normal) development is possible. This is not to say that totally blind infants are incapable of reaching "normal" developmental milestones; they are. It just takes more practice and appropriate intervention.

If the visual impairment is present at birth (congenital), it is more likely to affect development and learning than if it is acquired later (adventitious). Even a few years of vision can provide spatial orientational data to the brain; it has been observed that children with retinoblastoma, who have had their eyes surgically removed (usually within the first two years of life), seem to have uncanny perceptions of the space around them. The brief period of vision before surgery may be the reason.

When a visual impairment is related to, or caused by, a disease or brain hemorrhage, other factors may also cause difficulties in early development and learning (e.g., brain damage which affects cognitive ability, orthopedic defects which affect mobility). When the visual impairment is one of several disabilities, the problems become more severe and complex. (Multiple disabilities are discussed in Chapter Ten.)

Since early development is the beginning of the learning process, any impairment that affects development will also have impact on learning. (Visual impairment and early development will be discussed in greater detail in Chapter Seven.) A visual impairment interferes with beginning social attachments ("bonding") when eye contact is not made with the caregiver. Intervention can help the caregiver accept this lack of eye contact, and can encourage continued tactual/auditory contact (cuddling, holding, and talking). Absent or diminished visual stimulation can interfere with the observation of the environment that initiates brain programming, and can obstruct the reaching out to people or objects that initiates interaction with the environment. A visual impairment may prohibit or discourage the voluntary movement that begins cognitive data collection. Unless caregivers are reminded to stimulate and encourage body movement in the young child with a visual impairment, the resulting overprotection can prevent necessary sensory stimulation. Early exploration of space is essential to the internalization of "what is out there" and where it is.

Movement is critical, not only for the maturation of the motor system, but also for the opportunity to interact with the environment. Cognitive growth depends on sensory input derived from repeated contact with and exploration of objects, people, and space. Concept development and the child's construction of reality depends on interaction with the environment. Meaningful language acquisition relies on first-hand contact with a variety of things and actions. The more experience a visually impaired child has with his/her environment, the more data will be stored in the brain for future reference and recall.

Many skills that are learned incidently by sighted children (e.g., self-feeding, teeth brushing, bathing, dressing) may be delayed in visually impaired children because they do not have the visual abilities necessary for watching and imitating. Even play (which is an imitated and remembered ability) may be affected if a child has not seen what adults or peers *do* with objects.

Self-image and self-concept are often difficult to establish in a visually impaired child since self-identity separates the "me" from the "not me"–a visual concept. Social skills that make children acceptable to each other (and to adults) are not always present in children with visual impairments; they must be taught intentionally. Since success in mainstreaming depends a great deal on social acceptance, this area of learning is important in the early years.

Visual impairments are known to interfere with age appropriate acquisition of classification, conservation, and spatial imagery (all cognitive skills based on experience). Without intervention (and specific instruction), this delay in cognitive development can also delay the acquisition of reasoning skills and problem-solving capabilities. Many visually impaired children have difficulty getting past the concrete stage of learning into the abstract arena unless extra emphasis is placed on early cognitive opportunities.

It may appear that blindness or visual impairment is a devastating blow to an otherwise intact child, but intervention can minimize the delays caused by absent or reduced vision. Intact visually impaired children, *can* acquire the same milestone skills that sighted children achieve, but they may take longer to get there. Early identification of the type and degree of visual impairments, and immediate provision of special intervention by a teacher of visually impaired students can minimize delays and, in some cases, prevent them. It takes prompt action as early as possible in the child's life to give a visually impaired child an equal chance to learn at a normal rate and acquire age appropriate skills at appropriate times. If a solid foundation of services is provided early enough, delays can be minimal. These services include early Orientation and Mobility instruction, a wide range of hands-on experiences with objects and environments, and a structured program of self-help and social skills training. The early years of learning are critical for all children, but they are crucial for visually impaired children who may need extra time and experience to become able to compete adequately with their sighted peers in school.

REFERENCES AND RECOMMENDED READING

Atkinson, J. (2000). *The developing visual brain.* New York: Oxford University Press.

Barraga, N. & Erin, J. (2001). *Visual impairments and learning.* Austin, TX: Pro-Ed.

Bower, T. (1977). *The perceptual world of the child.* Cambridge, MA: Harvard University Press.

Cook, C., Sulik, K. & Wright, K. (2003). Embryology. In Wright, K. & Spiegel, P. (Eds.), *Pediatric ophthalmology and strabismus* (2nd Ed.). New York: Springer.

Forman, G. & Kushner, D. (1977). *The child's construction of knowledge: Piaget for teaching children.* Monterey, CA: Wadsworth.

Languis, M., Sanders, T., & Tipps, S. (1980). *Brain and learning.* Washington, DC: National Association for the Education of Young Children.

Ornstein, R. & Thompson, R. (1985). *The amazing brain.* London: Hogwarth Press.

Restak, R. (1984). *The brain.* New York: Bantam Books.

Schwartz, J. & Begley, S. (2002). *The mind land the brain: Neuroplasticity and the power of mental force.* New York: Harper Collins.

Chapter Seven

HOW DOES A VISUAL IMPAIRMENT AFFECT EARLY DEVELOPMENT?

INTRODUCTION

"Development is the organism's striving to implement hierarchical organizational goals . . . lack of vision interferes with all other systems, which are biologically geared to realize themselves in feedback with vision" (Als, Tronick, and Brazelton, 1976). This statement presents in a nutshell the problems encountered with a blind child. Early development is the child's attempts to organize himself and the world around him/her. Vision is the primary feedback sense that enables the child to get body systems operational and refined, and helps in the accumulation of information to make sense of the environment. When vision is reduced or absent, nearly all aspects of early development can be affected: motor, cognitive, language, self-help, and social.

Surprisingly, there has been very little research on how vision loss (specifically, blindness) affects early development. Much of what little research there is appears to be flawed.

Gesell (1949) studied vision itself in great detail, and formulated much of what is known about early development and vision. He also studied a single blind child and documented the developmental deviation ("lags") exhibited by that child. By inference, these conclusions were to be extrapolated to all blind children, but the individuality of each blind child (his/her family, environment, genetics, etc.) was overlooked in the implications. Gesell did, however, advance two ideas that have applications to this discussion. The first is that "blindness profoundly alters the structure of mental life, but does not disorganize it in an otherwise normally endowed individual. The greater the original endowment, the greater the constructive driveness to achieve integration and satisfaction" (Gesell, p. 265). Teachers who have worked with a wide range of ability levels in blind children will tend to agree that a higher level of intelligence helps the blind child cope with the special situations that must be solved in order to learn. The other statement Gesell contributed to an understanding of blindness and early development is "Vision . . . defers to maturation. The patterns of visual behavior reflect the maturity status of the entire action system" (p. 268). The child who is developmentally delayed, therefore, is likely to have a visual system more related to his/her *developmental age* than chronological age. (There will be more about this in Chapter Ten.)

In the Norris, Spaulding, Brodie study (1957), of 66 blind children, 85 percent were born prematurely and developed RLF; two thirds of the group were female. Later follow-up identified at least seven children with brain damage, and seven with enough vision to be considered sighted; one child had died. Despite the obvious sampling problem, the major conclusion from the original study (and which the follow-up study confirmed) appears to be valid: that blindness itself does not present developmental problems, but *the lack of opportunity to learn* (because of the blindness) does affect development.

The most often-quoted research study (Selma Fraiberg, 1963–1973) involved only ten blind children, three of which had RLF, three others had optic nerve hypoplasia, and four had a variety of diagnoses. Both RLF and optic nerve hypoplasia have their own unique related characteristics, so this sample may not have been either large enough or representative of the heterogeneous population of blind children. In addition, Ms. Fraiberg focused on the ego development of the children, and only secondarily studied posture, locomotion, hand use, and language. Her research was well documented through films and notes, however, and contributed much towards a beginning understanding of how blind babies develop. The observed motor delays are of particular interest, since the earliest system organized is motoric and is the basis for all other areas of development.

PROJECT PRISM

A more recent study (Project report dated 1998) on early development and visual impairment was Project PRISM, a longitudinal data collection done by Dr. Kay Ferrell. She developed a consistent protocol (data collection system) and enlisted the help of seven agencies across the United States who provided early intervention for 202 visually impaired infants and toddlers, aged birth to five. These children had moderate low vision to total blindness, and included both those who were only visually impaired and those who had additional disabilities. Over a five-year period, Dr. Ferrell collected data on the acquisition and sequences for 19 developmental milestones (selected by an advisory board as milestones most likely to be affected by a visual impairment). She analyzed developmental patterns based on the quantity of available vision (moderate low vision, severe low vision, light perception, and total blindness), etiology, and presence or absence of additional disabilities.

Her 230-page project report has many tables, charts, and statistical analyses, but the primary finding was that 12 milestones were acquired later than typically developing children, and five milestones were acquired within the normal range of acquisition. (There were two milestones that produced insufficient data for reliable conclusions.) This information would not be terribly surprising, but when the *sequences* of acquisition were analyzed, some unique patterns were discovered. Six milestones were acquired in a different sequence than for sighted children, and there were differences in sequences when the degree of visual impairment was analyzed. (About one-third of the children were totally blind.) Some of the differences were unexpected; for example, children with severe low vision had more difficulty learning to play interactive games than the subjects who were blind or had only light perception.

When varying etiologies were compared to the acquisition ages for milestone skills, children with Retinopathy of Prematurity were more significantly delayed than those with Cortical Visual Impairment or albinism. (About a fifth of the group had a visual diagnosis of ROP and another fifth were those with CVI; optic nerve hypoplasia was the next largest group by etiology.)

When the participants were subdivided into those without additional disabilities and those who had multiple disabilities, there were 81 intact children (who were only visually impaired), 45 with mild additional disabilities, and 76 whose additional disabilities were labeled "severe." The comparison of skill acquisition between the intact group and the larger group with multiple disabilities (60% of the subjects) showed that (not surprisingly), the age of acquisition for 12 of the 19 milestones was significantly later for the children with multiple disabilities.

Although the PRISM data has not yet produced "norms" for young visually impaired children, there is rich analytical data to be explored. It is hoped that Dr. Ferrell will make her findings public and available, so that teachers who provide intervention will find rationale for their early contacts with infants and toddlers who are visually impaired.

CURRENT PRACTICE

Since there are currently no "norms" for early development of young children who are visually impaired, a deviation model of intervention may be the only available structure for measuring the timing and appropriateness of intervention. That is, blind children may continue to be compared to sight-

TABLE 3. PROJECT PRISM DATA
Ferrell, K. (1998). Final Report

MILESTONE	*Typical Attainment (in mos.)*		*All PRISM Children*	*Visually Impaired Only*	*VI-MI*
	Median	*Range*			
Reaches for and touches object	5.4	0–5	8.3	8.1	10.6
Transfers object hand to hand	5.5	6–11	9.3	8.3	10.1
Searches for removed object	6.0	6–11	15.0*	13.4*	18.2*
Sits alone 5 seconds without support	6.6	6–11	10.9	9.2	11.9
Feeds self bite-sized food	7.4	6–11	12.6*	11.1*	18.8*
Produces 1 or more consonant-vowel sounds	7.9	6–11	10.9	9.5	11.8
Moves 3′ or more by crawling	9.0	6–11	12.8*	11.4*	18.3*
Plays interactive game	9.7	6–11	11.4	9.3	13.1
Walks without support 10′	13.0	12–17	19.8	19.0	26.6*
Points to at least 1 body part on request	17.5	12–24	19.5	18.8	20.2
Removes simple garment without help	20.5	24–35	22.7	19.2	24.8
Generally follows daily routine directions	20.5	36–47	24.3	19.3	25.0
Uses 2-word utterances to express meaningful relationships	20.6	24–35	28.2*	24.9	36.1
Uses pronouns I, you, me	24.0	24–35	25.8	24.8	36.1
Controls bowel movements regularly	30.0	24–35	36.5*	24.9	38.6*
Repeats 2-digit sequence	30.0	24–35	33.4	25.0	37.0*
Walks down stairs alternating feet	30.0	36–47	33.4	30.2	36.2
Copies circle	33.0	36–47	31.8*	37.2	30.0*
Relates past experiences	40.0	36–47	37.3	36.9	37.7
			n = 202	n = 81	n = 121

* = out of sequence

ed children when deciding age-appropriateness for skill acquisition. This chapter will describe the probable deviations, based on sighted norms, although it should be recognized that early intervention *can* erase or minimize many of the delays. It must also be recognized that quality and quantity of vision makes a difference; the more useful vision a young child has, the more likely it is that early intervention can eliminate or reduce delays (given the intactness of other body systems). Total blindness is not the norm; most visually impaired babies and toddlers have some degree of vision, from object perception to very useful near vision. The word "blind" will be used in this chapter to mean a severe vision loss, and the delays described are more likely to occur more often among the most severely visually impaired children.

MOTOR DEVELOPMENT

The eyes can be said to be the "explorers" of the young child's world. They motivate motion, whether caused by a face, a person, or an interesting object. The blind child has the *physical* ability to activate and strengthen muscles, but he/she often lacks the motivation to move because there seems to be no reason to do so. The first delay is in head control, a critical postural achievement. The blind baby may "fuss" when placed on his/her tummy, and "Mommy" obliges by turning him/her over; the supine (on the back) position does not encourage the baby to hold his/her head up. Babies need to spend short, supervised periods on their tummies (prone position) even though they don't like it. Talking to the baby while on its stomach, and stroking his/her back, can make it a more pleasant experience; it also encourages the arching of the body that helps to lift the head. This neck strength and head control is a vital first step in upright posture, which is the initial phase of developing independence.

The second common area of delay in motor development seems to be the ability to reach. Vision not only serves to motivate reach but also refines the coordinated movements needed to achieve it. Without vision, there is nothing to reach *for,* and no opportunity to practice the movements needed. Other "lures" must be used to encourage a baby to reach; a favorite sound producing toy or cuddly blanket can be used if it is not too far beyond the child's arm distance (i.e., close enough to make accidental contact). Success in attaining the object reinforces the action. Only when the baby is sure the object can be obtained is it safe to move it to *extended* arm's reach distance, thus encouraging a full reach with effort. Objects that are beyond arm's reach do not exist for a blind baby unless they produce continuous sound. (Note: The ability to reach towards sound is not usually acquired by a sighted child until late in the first year, since the auditory processing center is located deep within the brain. Therefore, sound, even in the most "normal" blind child, may not become a useful "lure" until late in the first year). Objects that have pleasing textures or have meaning (e.g., a favorite blanket, furry animal toys, bottle, breast) may be better immediate "lures" in the first half of the first year.

When upright posture is achieved (sitting without support), the baby's hands are free to explore/manipulate objects. Many blind babies continue to support themselves with their hands, since balance uses visual input to verify position in space. Until a blind baby can achieve independent sitting, however, his/her hands are not free to develop the fine motor coordination needed for object manipulation and exploration. One delay compounds another. Supported sitting (as in a high chair, with rolled towels on either side of the child's trunk) can encourage free hands to explore objects placed on the tray in front.

Without vision, the progress from total body contact with the environment (laying on the floor) to sitting (*less* body contact with the environment) to standing (only the soles of the feet in contact with the floor) is a scary process. Blind babies are not usually *interested* in standing, although they are physically able to do so; there is little *reason* to stand, and less information about the environment is available through the soles of the feet. It is probably better to put off shoe wearing (and even socks or booties, unless for warmth) for some periods of each day, just to allow the blind baby to gain exploratory information with his/her feet. Once shoes are a daily habit, all contact with the floor is minimal; a whole new set of references must be learned.

One way of encouraging standing (as well as movement) might be to place a reasonably taut strap across the middle of the playpen, in such a way that the baby can hold either the top rail of the playpen or the strap (or both) for upright support and to maintain balance. As confidence is gained in the upright position, the baby may begin to sway or swing while holding on; with a little verbal encouragement, he/she may even begin to "cruise" around the sides, or take a step from side-rail to strap. The skill of walking alone may take longer to develop, and may require both encouragement and practice. (Note: The blind baby should never be left alone in a playpen with the strap across the center; standing play should be supervised and/or observed by an adults close-by.)

Hand use (and its global title "fine motor development") depends on opportunity and practice. As soon as the baby's hands are no longer needed for support (weight bearing), they are free to explore independently from the rest of the body. Opportunities must be provided to hold, shake, bang, pat and rub with the hands, poke, or probe with the fingers. Repeated opportunities offer the practice prerequisite to acquiring finger skill. This is critical for the blind child, who will do much of his learning (and most of his reading) tactually. Independent finger use is essential for pincer grasp (which is basic for "finger-feeding") and will become important later in writing braille or using a keyboard to type or compute. Manipulative skills will provide a foundation for developing basic concepts and learning simple math, and will serve the child well all of his life.

COGNITIVE DEVELOPMENT

The preschool years are critical for the development of intelligence, in both sighted and blind children alike. As early as 1964, Benjamin Bloom declared that a (nonhandicapped) four-year-old child probably has 50 percent of the intelligence he will have at age 17. Ten years later, a Health, Education and Welfare (HEW) study added that by age 8, that child will have 80 percent of his adult capacity. A recent *Wall Street Journal* article cited a report by the Carnegie Corporation of New York, which described several findings:

1. Brain development before age one is more rapid and extensive than we thought, and is more vulnerable to lasting environmental influence; early stress is a negative factor.
2. Environment affects how many brain cells are developed and how they are connected.

Wall Street Journal, Tuesday April 12, 1994, p. B1

It is well known that vision plays a large role in the development of intelligence; both developmental scales and standardized intelligence tests are highly visual-experience oriented. Blind children's intelligence may develop in a different way, by different routes, but it *does* develop. There are some possible early delays, however, that require structured intervention, and "hands-on" experiences may be the key. "People permanence" may develop before object permanence, because people are more reliable and real in the blind baby's early months; objects take longer because there isn't the same reliability; they appear and disappear as if by magic. Cause-and-effect relationships are harder to understand when the cause or its effect cannot be seen; cause/effect toys can provide extra experience in this area. Physical change is observed directly when a sighted toddler sees his mother get eggs out of the refrigerator, break them into a skillet, and make an omelet; unless the blind child is intentionally included in that process, *his/her* eggs appear magically on a plate. One-to-one correspondence must be experienced physically by the blind child ("one for you; one for me"), whereas the sighted child *sees* everyone getting a knife, fork, and spoon at every meal. The properties of matter are *observed* by sighted children, but they must each be taught specifically to blind children. It is impossible to compare and categorize until properties of matter or actions (basic concepts) are learned.

Visual memory is the basis of play (pretending), self-help, and social skills (gestures, manners, acceptable behaviors). Blind children must be specifically taught each action or behavior physically, since they will not have visual memory. All of the perceptual abilities learned spontaneously by sighted children must be systematically taught to blind children, including discrimination (same/different), closure (missing parts), spatial orientation/position in space (both for self and objects), and figure-ground (selecting main properties or ideas from a distracting background, whether auditory or tactual). The entire goal of early intervention for blind preschoolers is to provide the opportunities it takes to learn and develop intelligence by constructing alternate neural pathways in the brain.

LANGUAGE DEVELOPMENT

At the preverbal stage of language ("babbling"), blind children are at no disadvantage since most of this "language" is auditory exploration or auditory imitation. It is when the labeling begins (attaching words to objects, people, and actions) that delays occur because the blind child doesn't see the relationships. Many blind children learn to use words without having clear understandings of their meanings ("verbalism") because language takes on social significance; to be socially accepted, people talk. It is not unusual to discover a totally erroneous concept in a blind child because the word meanings underlying it were unclear. Other areas of language difficulty are in pronoun use (distinguishing the "me" from the "note me"), in describers (adjectives and adverbs, which are often visual concepts), and in the applied uses of language (asking questions, initiating/continuing/ending conversations, creative writing).

A kind of language that is observed in some blind children is "echolalia"–the repetition of sounds/words purely for sound's sake; this kind of language serves no purpose, but is sometimes mistaken for verbal ability until the repetitious nature is noted. True echolalia is probably a social device (attention or acceptance seeking), however, a few blind children (and children with other disabilities as well) learn to use language to mediate actions. That is, they appear to be repeating what the teacher has said, but are really "talking to themselves through" the execution of a task. This application of language is useful, although probably should progress to a subvocal level; echolalia serves no purpose, is not a result of blindness itself, and, if possible, should not be allowed to persist.

SELF-HELP SKILLS

Preschool sighted children learn to feed, dress, and care for themselves largely through imitation ("doing what the big people do"). Blind children do not have the spontaneous models to watch and imitate, and must be specifically taught the motor behaviors necessary for self-feeding, dressing, grooming, and toileting. Hand-over-hand instruction, with the instructor behind the child, is probably easiest for feeding, dressing, and grooming. Toilet training, which is even difficult for some sighted children, is also a problem for blind children, who do not understand why body excretions must be in a specific place and then disappear; to the child, these excretions belong to *them,* and they do not *see* adults disposing of them. A lot of discussion, repeated toilet flushings, and even feeling the water (clean) as it swirls around the toilet bowl, can facilitate the toilet training experience. The mother of a toddler with low vision related that the task of teaching her son to urinate standing up was frustrating (and messy) until she hit upon the idea to tell him to "aim until you hear the splash." It worked for that child.

There is no one "best" way to teach self-help skills. The TVI may have developed other "tricks" to teach such skills as shoe tying, the use of fasteners, or using eating utensils. Whatever "works" is the "right" way to teach it. The more independence a visually impaired child has when he/she enters school, the more likely he/she will be accepted by both peers and classroom teacher.

SELF-CONCEPT

The sighted child looks in a mirror and sees the image of himself/herself looking back. The blind child has no mirror in which to see a reflection and know what he/she looks like. The child's self-image is largely based on how he/she is treated by others, and by how much control he/she can exercise over self or environment. Many blind children are dependent and passive because no one has allowed or encouraged choices, decision-making, and independent action. Blind children need to learn, as early as possible, that they can interact with other people and their environment, and can exercise some control over themselves and the environment. They also need to learn (as do all children) that there are consequences related to decisions, that responsibilities are to be assumed, and there are limits to behaviors that are socially acceptable. They also need to be accepted as an individual, worthwhile and valued. There is no room for pity or overprotection in the life of a young blind child if he/she is to develop a positive self-image.

SOCIAL SKILLS

Social skills are often learned through visual observation and limitation. Blind children have no way of observing how others behave and interact with each other, or what behaviors are socially acceptable. The gestures and body language sighted people use without thinking about it must be taught, one by one, to blind children. Smiling, shaking hands, waving "bye-bye," using head nods or shoulder shrugs to indicate "yes," "no," or "I don't know," covering one's mouth when yawning or sneezing, not picking one's nose in public, taking turns and waiting patiently–these are all social skills that must be taught, and the beginning is in the preschool years. Good manners and a sense of humor have their roots in preschool experiences, and will go a long way towards social acceptance in later years.

PRESCHOOL INTERVENTION

Part C of the 1997 amendments to IDFA mandates early intervention services for children B–3 who have developmental delays (or are at risk for developmental delays) *and their families.* Because the family is a crucial factor in the early development of a child, the needs of the family are included in both assessment and planning. The Individual Family Service Plan (IFSP) must include:

- An objective statement of the child's present level of development–physically, cognitively, socially, emotionally, adaptively, and in the area of communication;
- A statement of the family's present resources, priorities, and concerns;
- A statement of the family's outcomes, how they are expected to be achieved, the timelines, and the criteria for achievement;
- A description of specific intervention services needed, including who will provide them and how often;
- When services will begin, and how long they will last;
- Who will coordinate services and see that they occur; and
- How the toddler will transition to services available when he/she reaches his/her third birthday.

Source: 20 U.S.C. 1436, 636(d) (June 4, 1997)

In the case of a child with a visual impairment, the disability must be identified (through vision screening or a medical report submitted at the time of referral), documented (eye specialist's examination and report), and the impact of the visual impairment on development determined (an appropriate developmental scale administered, a functional vision evaluation and learning media assessment done). (See Part Three for further discussion of assessment.) The process should take place as quickly as possible, so that intervention can be timely.

The TVI is usually called in to do the functional vision evaluation and learning media assessment, and, thus, becomes a member of the ECI (early childhood intervention) team. Intervention can be provided directly during home visits by the TVI, or as a part of a global plan by the entire team (e.g., transdisciplinary efforts). Whenever possible, intervention goals related to the visual impairment should be embedded in the child's natural routines (feeding, bathing, playtime). Few TVIs have the time for daily visits to families with infants or toddlers who are visually impaired; therefore, the best use of the TVI's time may be to teach *families* how to be aware of "vision goals" within the context of daily life. The TVI can then monitor progress, demonstrate new ideas, suggest appropriate toys or materials, or provide special equipment. Family-focused services are a hallmark of early intervention, and TVIs can release expertise to empower families or caregivers.

It is important for the TVI to understand the sequence of early development, so intervention is timely. You do not wait for a delay before intervening; you try to *prevent* (or minimize) the delay by beginning intervention in advance of the expected acquisition of a particular milestone skill. For example, rather than waiting for midline hand use to occur naturally, suggest holding the infant's own hands around the bottle, or play "Patty Cake," or help the baby discover his/her own hands by bringing them together at midline. Rather than waiting for a child to sit independently on his/her own (with hands free), when there seems to be some torso control (upright posture attempted, even though there may be imperfect balance), prop the infant in a high chair with rolled towels on both sides to help maintain upright position; provide toys to manipulate, on the high chair tray. This encourages hand use from an upright position, even though independent sitting may not quite be achieved. Anticipate major milestones, and start "practicing" ahead of time. Most young visually impaired children will need extra practice anyway, so beginning a bit in advance may help to minimize any delay in acquisition.

There are a number of sources of ideas for intervention for the B–3-year-old (Anthony, 1993; Bishop, 2000; Brody and Webber, 1994; Ferrell, 1984; Ferrel, 1985; Harrell and Akeson, 1987; Hug et al., Kekelis and Chernus Mansfield; Meyers and Lansky; Moore, 1985; Pogrund et al., Recchia; Schmitt and Armenta-Schmitt, 1999; Simmons and O'Maida, 1992; Trief, 1992). (These are listed at the end of the chapter.) Some are written directly for parents (all of the publications from the Blind Children's Center), while others are for professionals. There are also a number of videos (listed at the end of the chapter) that are "parent friendly" and can be loaned for viewing. Every TVI who works with young visually impaired children should keep a ready supply of materials to share with families, including hand-out fact sheets, books and pamphlets, lists of vision-related resources (clinics, schools, libraries, etc.), and videos.

It may also be the TVI's responsibility to assist in transition planning for young visually impaired children who are about two and a half years old. In some states, where B–3 services and three to five programming are under the aegis of different state agencies, the transition may need to be carefully orchestrated. There may be radical changes in services offered, personnel, and focus. The TVI may be the only link between the two programs and should make every effort to effect as smooth a transition as possible. Keeping families informed, and maintaining their level of team participation during the transition planning can go a long way towards smoothing out any "bumps in the road."

In other states, where both B–3 and three to five services are part of the state's education agency responsibilities, this transition only means rewriting the plan to reflect the change in emphasis from family-focused services to child-centered programming; the IFSP becomes an IEP (Individual Education Plan), and the legal mandate shifts from Part C of IDEA to Part B. Services may continue to be offered at the child's home, but may also change to community-based, center-based, or school-based programs (since Part B offers "a continuum" of educational choices). Service personnel are provided by the local school district and are usually on a school-year plan (instead of year-round). The emphasis on programming is still highly individualized but shifts focus to developing independence, concept development, and social/personal skills. The years three to five reflect the child's growing ability to act as an individual (get around on his/her own, care for personal needs, and prepare to compete with normally sighted peers in the educational setting).

The following broad goals offer a selection of instructional areas, whether provided at home or in a class. Goals are intentionally broad (but inclusive), and specific objectives should be designed to meet the child's individual needs–personal, academic, and visual.

Goal #1: To develop basic concepts through alternative senses.

1. Identify properties by finding the one object in a group of two that is:

big/little	soft/hard	wet/dry
smooth/rough	hot/cold	long/short
wide/narrow	fat/thin	round/square

2. Identify location by placing an object:

in/out	over/under
on top/underneath	in front/in back

3. Identify weight by finding the one object in a group of two that is:

   light/heavy

4. Identify sound tones as:

	high/low	loud/soft	fast/slow
5. Identify by taste:	sweet/sour	hot/cold
6. Identify:	one/more than one	few/many

7. Determine like or different by selecting from a group of three, either two the same, or one that is different.

Goal #2: To compare by properties (i.e., "classify").

1. Sort groups of objects by properties:

   Size: big/little, long/short
   Shape: circle, square, triangle
   Texture: soft/hard, smooth/rough
   Temperature: hot/cold
   Weight: light/heavy
   Taste: sweet/sour
   Smell: "good" odors/"bad" odors

2. Sort groups of objects by use:

   Foods, toys, clothing, tools, fruits, shoes

3. Sort objects by double properties:

   Shape and color, shape and size, shape and texture, size and color, size and texture.

Goal #3: To acquire one-to-one correspondence:

1. Match one peg to one hole.
2. Match nut to bolt by size.
3. Distribute objects to containers, one per container.
4. Distribute objects to people, one per person.
5. Count people, one by one, touching each as counted.
6. Count objects, one by one, touching each as counted.
7. Count objects, one by one, by pointing to each as counted.

Goal #4: To refine motor skills.

1. Demonstrate gross motor skills of: jumping, hopping, running, climbing
2. Demonstrate fine motor skills by using implements efficiently: writing/coloring implement

   scissors paste/glue
   eating implements
3. Demonstrate independent finger movement by:

   wiggling each finger separately
   using each finger independently to point
   using each finger independently to poke

Goal #5: To improve language skills.

1. Use gestures appropriately:

   shaking head "yes" shaking head "no"
   pointing with index finger shaking hands
   using facial expressions to indicate emotion (e.g., smiling, frowning)
2. Expand vocabulary by understanding the meaning of:

   things (nouns) actions (verbs)
   pronouns (he, him; she, her; it; we, us; they, them; me; I)
   simple describers (adjectives/adverbs)
   Note: "understand" means to demonstrate through appropriate use and/or explanation.
3. Demonstrate listening skills by:

   following one-step directions
   following two-step directions
   retelling events/simple stories in proper sequence
4. Use proper grammar/syntax:

   noun/verb sentences
   use of pronouns as subjects
   descriptors
   agreement of pronoun form (with verb; as subject)
5. Initiate a conversation by asking a question.
6. Listen to a question and give a relevant response.
7. Use "polite words" appropriately.

Goal #6: To acquire age-appropriate social skills.

1. Demonstrate the use of appropriate gestures.
2. Play with peers cooperatively.
3. Take turns.

Goal #7: To acquire age-appropriate mobility skills.

1. Move independently in familiar environments.
2. Demonstrate trailing technique (if appropriate for level of functional vision).
3. Demonstrate the use of a sighted guide (if appropriate for level of functional vision).
4. Demonstrate appropriate use of a T-bar cane (if appropriate for level of functional vision).

Goal #8: to decrease inappropriate/self-stimulative behaviors.

1. Hold head up when sitting or standing/walking.
2. Use echo-locator skills only when not disturbing others.
3. Decrease/ eliminate: thumb-sucking eye-poking
   (if applicable) rocking "finger-flicking"

Goal #9: To adhere to age-appropriate behavior expectations.

1. Follow the rules of the classroom.
2. Take turns.
3. Stay in line when required.
4. Recognize that behaviors have consequences.
5. Use "good manners" in social situations.

Goal #10: To increase the level of independence in self-help skills.

1. Eating:
   a. Use a spoon/fork for self-feeding.
   b. Use a napkin appropriately.
   c. Drink from a cup and/or use a straw as appropriate.
   d. Clean up after own spills.
2. Dressing:
   a. Remove all of own clothing independently.
   b. Put on specific items of clothing independently:
      pull-on shirt or sweater coat or jacket
      pull-on pants hat/mittens (if applicable)
      socks shoes (may need help tying)
   c. Manipulate fasteners:
      buttons snaps/hooks/eyes
      zippers (may need help with jacket or coat zipper)
3. Grooming:
   a. Wipe own face with a napkin.
   b. Wash/dry hands.
   c. Brush teeth.
   d. Comb hair (may need help with final touches).

4. Toileting
   a. Indicate the need to use the bathroom.
   b. Handle own clothing in the bathroom (off/on).
   c. Wipe self after a bowel movement.
   d. For a boy, use a urinal.
   e. Wash/dry hands after bathroom use.

Goal #11: to acquire prebraille skills if indicated.

1. Acquire concepts: start/stop; begin/end; go/stop; first/last; side; corner; center/middle; dot, line, page; book; follow/trace; find; that words can be written down and read.
2. Acquire skills:
   a. Following a raised line with one or more fingers.
   b. Following the line from left to right.
   c. Finding the next line.
   d. Turning pages in a book, one at a time.
   e. Locating the position of the page number (for a right-hand page: upper right; for a left-hand page: upper left.

REFERENCES AND RECOMMENDED READING

Als, H., Tronick, E., & Brazelton, T. (1976). Affective reciprocity and development of autonomy: The study of a blind infant. *The Journal of the American Academy of Child Psychiatry, 19,* 22–40.

Anthony, T. et al. (1993). *First steps: A handbook for teaching young children who are visually impaired.* Los Angeles: Blind Children's Center.

Bernas-Pierce, J. (Ed.). (1998). *Pediatric Visual Diagnosis Fact Sheets.* San Francisco: Blind Babies Foundation.

Bishop, V. (1991). *Preschool children with visual impairments.* (Unpublished Manual, available from author.)

Bishop, V. (1998). *Infants and toddlers with visual impairment.* (Unpublished Manual, available from author.)

Bishop, V. (2000). Early childhood. In Holbrook, C. & Koenig, A. (Eds.). *Foundations of education* (2nd Ed.), Volume 2. New York: American Foundation for the Blind.

Bishop, V., Shafer, S., & Shier, S. (1984). *Individualized programming for blind and visually impaired infants and young children.* (Unpublished Manual, available from author.)

Blakely, K., Lang, M., & Hart, R. (1991). *Getting in touch with play.* New York: The Lighthouse, Inc.

Blakely, K., Lang, M., & Sosna, B. (1995). *Toys and play: A guide to fun and development for children with impaired vision.* New York: The Lighthouse, Inc.

Bloom, B. (1954). *Stability and change in human characteristics.* New York: John Wiley and Sons.

Brody, J. & Webber, L. (1994). *Let's eat: Feeding a child with visual impairment.* Los Angeles: Blind Children's Center.

Carnegie Report cited by Sharpe, R. (1994). To boost IQs, aid is needed in first three years. *Wall Street Journal,* April 12, 1994.

Chen, D., Friedman, C., & Calvello, G. (1990). *Parents and visually impaired infants.* Louisville, KY: American Printing House for the Blind.

Chen, D. & McCann, M. (1993). *Selecting a program: A guide for parents of infants and preschoolers with visual impairments.* Los Angeles: Blind Children's Center.

*Chernus-Mansfield, N., Hayashi, D., Horn, M., & Kekelis, L. (N.D.). *Heart to heart: Parents of blind and partially sighted children talk about their feelings.* Los Angeles: Blind Children's Center.

Dodson-Burk, B. & Hill, E. (1989). *An orientation and mobility primer for families and young children.* New York: American Foundation for the Blind.

Ferrell, K. (1984). *Parenting preschoolers: Suggestions for raising young blind and visually impaired children.* New York: American Foundation for the Blind.

Ferrell, K. (1985). *Reach out and teach.* New York: American Foundation for the Blind.

Ferrell, K. (1998). *Project PRISM: A longitudinal study of developmental patterns of children who are visually impaired.* Final Report, CFDA 84.0203C, Grant H023C10188. Greeley, CO: University of Northern Colorado.

Ferrell, K. (2000). Growth and development of young children. In Holbrook, C. & Koenig, A. (Eds.), *Foundations of education* (2nd ed.), Volume 1. New York: American Foundation for the Blind.

Fraiberg, S. (1977). *Insights from the blind.* New York: Basic Books, Inc.

Gesell, A., Ilg, F., & Bullis, G. (1949). *Vision: Its development in infant and child.* New York: Harper & Brothers.

Harrell, L. & Akeson, N. (1987). *Preschool vision stimulation: It's more than a flashlight!* New York: American Foundation for the Blind.

H.E.W. study cited by Roos, P. (1974). Trends and issues in special education for the mentally retarded. In Kirk, S. & Lord, F. (Eds.), *Exceptional children: Educational resources and perspectives.* Boston: Houghton Mifflin.

*Hug, D., Chernas-Mansfield, N., & Hayashi, D. (N.D.). *Move with me: A parent's guide to movement development for visually impaired babies.* Los Angeles: Blind Children's Center.

Kastein, S., Spaulding, I., & Scharf, b. (1980). *Raising the young blind child.* New York: Human Sciences Press.

*Kekelis, L. & Chernus-Mansfield, N. (N.D.). *Talk to me: A language guide for parents of blind children* and *Talk to me II: Common concerns.* Los Angeles: Blind Children's Center.

Lueck, A., Chen, D., & Kekelis, L. (1997). *Developmental guidelines for infants with visual impairment.* Louisville, KY: American Printing House for the Blind.

Meyers, L. & Lansky, P. (N.D.). *Dancing cheek to cheek: Nurturing beginning social, play, and language interactions.* Los Angeles: Blind Children's Center.

Moore, S. (1985). *Beginnings: A practical guide for parents and teachers of visually impaired babies.* Louisville, KY: American Printing House for the Blind.

Norris, M., Spaulding, P., & Brodie, F. (1957). *Blindness in children.* Chicago:

University of Chicago Press.

Off to a Good Start Fact Sheets. (1999). San Francisco: Blind Babies Foundation.

Pogrund, R. & Fazzi, D. (Eds.). (2002). *Early focus: Working with young blind and visually impaired children and their families* (2nd Ed.). New York: American Foundation for the Blind.

Pogrund, R. Healy, G., Jones, K., Levack, N., Martin-Curry, S., Martinez, C., Marz, J., Roberson-Smith, B., & Vrba, A. (1993). *Teaching age-appropriate purposeful skills: An orientation and mobility curriculum for students with visual impairment (TAPS).* Austin, TX: Texas School for the Blind and Visually Impaired.

Recchia, S. (N.D.). *Learning to play: Common concerns for the visually impaired preschool child.* Los Angeles: Blind Children's Center.

Schmitt, P. & Armenta-Schmitt, F. (1999). *Fathers: A common ground.* Los Angeles: Blind Children's Center.

Simmons, S. & O'Mara Maida, S. (1992). *Reaching, crawling, walking: Let's get moving (Orientation and mobility for preschool children).* Los Angeles: Blind Children's Center.

Trief, E. (1992). *Working with visually impaired young students: A curriculum guide for birth–3-year-olds.* Springfield, IL: Charles C Thomas.

Warren, D. (1984). *Blindness and early childhood development* (2nd ed.). New York: American Foundation for the Blind.

VIDEOS

From Blind Babies Foundation (San Francisco, CA):

Pesavento, M. (N.D.). *Getting there: A look at the early mobility skills of four young blind children.*

From Blind Children's Center (Los Angeles: CA):

Heart to heart
Let's eat

From Visually Impaired Preschool Services (VIPS), Louisville, KY:

Seeing things in a new way: What happens when you have a blind baby
Learning about the world: Concept development
Becoming a "Can Do" kid: Self-help skills
Making friends: Social skills and play
Going places: Orientation and mobility
Through their eyes: An introduction to low vision

---

*Also available in Spanish.

Moving through the world: Gross motor skills and play
Hands on experience: Tactual learning and skills
Successfully adapting the preschool environment
Power at your fingertips: An introduction to learning braille
Full of hope

Chapter Eight

HOW DOES A VISUAL IMPAIRMENT AFFECT EDUCATION IN GENERAL?

INTRODUCTION

Visually impaired children have been educated in public school since the early 1900s, three fourths of a century before it was federally mandated. Schools and families have always known that it was desirable to attend a local school whenever possible, but they have also known that public schools have not always offered the best educational programs for their children who were visually impaired. Residential schools sometimes offered better educational opportunity, and should continue to be an option for placement. However, the fact remains that as many as 90 percent of visually impaired students are attending public school, where they receive their education in regular classrooms with their sighted peers. In the best situations, a certified teacher of visually impaired students (TVI) is available to support the classroom teacher, and to provide special instruction in disability-related curricular areas (see Chapter Nine). Chapter Eight will focus on subjects taught by the regular classroom teacher, and the impact a visual impairment can have on those subjects. Special emphasis will be placed on why a visual impairment has the impact it does, and what modifications or adaptations can be made to compensate for the visual impairment's effects.

It should be emphasized that when visually impaired students are "mainstreamed" (included in regular classes with their sighted peers), it is still the responsibility of regular classroom teachers to provide instruction in academic areas, and in such classes as physical education, art, music, home economics, and industrial arts. The TVI is *not* a tutor in these subjects, but can suggest ways to make classroom instruction more effective for the visually impaired student. An understanding of how visual impairments affect learning in academic areas (and the other subjects mentioned above) can provide a basis for understanding what modifications are needed when and for what purposes. This chapter will discuss each classroom subject area separately and suggest ideas for adapting teaching strategies, materials, and learning environments.

PRESCHOOL

At the preschool level, the TVI may be both interventionist/teacher and consultant, depending on the age of the child. During infancy and the toddler years (birth to three), the TVI usually helps parents or primary caregivers with strategies to minimize or eliminate developmental delays in the child. This intervention is commonly provided in the child's home, and anticipates periods of potential delay (e.g., suggests ways of *preparing* the child for the next level of development, rather than waiting for delays to occur before intervening). For this reason, a TVI should always be a part of the early childhood intervention team when a visual impairment has been identified or is suspected. Waiting until school age to call the TVI can be detrimental to development; valuable years of experiential learning can be lost, and never made up. The early years are critical for visually impaired children, and the TVI needs to be involved as early as possible.

During the preschool years of 3–5, center-based programs for visually impaired children can combine the skills of a TVI with the knowledge of the child's parents or primary caregivers. It is important to choose a preschool program carefully for visually impaired children; early childhood special education classes may not be the best choice for an intact visually impaired child, who needs positive role models and appropriate peer interaction to stimulate optimum development. If there is a "regular" nursery school, prekindergarten, or kindergarten available, it might be a better choice than a "special education" class, depending on the visually impaired child's abilities and the personality of the classroom teacher. The TVI should always be available for ideas, suggestions, and support. Programming emphasis should be on concept development through experience learning, social and self-help skills, meaningful language development, and independence. (See Chapter Seven for more information on early childhood programming for visually impaired preschoolers.)

Special attention should be given to "readiness," especially in the area of language arts. If a child seems likely to be a print reader (i.e., seems to have enough useful vision to see pictures, words, etc.), emphasis should be on the development of visual efficiency. If the child is blind, or seems to be a tactual/auditory learner, attention should be given to the development of tactual perception and listening skills. The TVI will probably evaluate the child's best sensory channels through a Learning Media Assessment (LMA); the data accumulated in this procedure can help in determining whether print or braille will be likely as later reading media. Some children may remain multisensory learners, and the decision for a primary reading medium may be difficult. Moreover, a few visually impaired children could end up using one medium for some tasks and another for other tasks; such children might use both print *and* braille, depending on the task. If all sensory channels are afforded opportunity for development in the early years, the choice for learning/literacy media later is made much easier.

Good listening skills can be important for the visually impaired student in later years, and the foundation is laid in the preschool years. If recorded materials will be used later, the skills acquired at the preschool level will be critical. (Students don't automatically know how to gain information through listening when recorded materials are provided; they must have developed good listening skills from their earliest year. If they haven't, the TVI must structure a program to *teach* listening skills before recorded materials can be useful for knowledge acquisition.) Encouraging careful listening to stories (for details, sequence, descriptions, names, etc.) can establish an awareness that will make listening to recorded materials more effective. (For a suggested sequence of teaching listening skills, see Appendix A.)

The curriculum at the preschool level is usually experiential, multisensory, and concrete, and the visually impaired child can profit from as much of this as can be offered. Every effort should be made to build concepts through direct experience and interaction with the environment. (See Chapter Nine for more information on "basic concepts.") The preschool years are critical times for a visually impaired child and can make the difference between success or struggle during later educational experiences.

Most intact visually impaired preschoolers need the same kinds of nursery school or kindergarten experiences as sighted children, with emphasis on the concrete (sensory) aspects. They also may need more *of* these experiences. It is good practice for the TVI to visit possible placements to see if they might be a "good match" for a particular child. Preschool programs for children with disabilities (PPCD) are not always the best choice, especially for a child whose only disability is a visual impairment. Many of these "special classes" contain children with a variety of disabilities and a wide range of severity; the intact child with a visual impairment may need more normal role models with whom to interact and from whom to learn. The TVI can suggest the best match of program and child (and sometimes the best teacher).

Once a selection is made, the TVI (and probably the O&M instructor) will prepare the child for the new placement. This is an important step for a child with a visual impairment, who may not be able to scan the new environment and orient to it. Usually, an orientation visit is arranged, with parent, child,

TVI, and O&M instructor (and, hopefully, the new teacher) present. This is usually done at a time when there are no other students present, to allow the visually impaired child opportunity to explore independently. This transitional visit is crucial for a number of reasons, especially for children whose only disability is visual impairment:

1. The *parent* sees that the new placement is appropriate and not dangerous.
2. The *teacher* is available to make initial contact with both the child and parent, and to answer any questions.
3. The *TVI* has the opportunity to suggest any necessary modifications and reassure both the child and parent that there will be continuity of personnel and services. The TVI will "be there" to help as needed.
4. The O&M instructor is present to structure the orientation process as needed, and to establish new routes of travel (which will be practiced after the transition is made.)
5. The *child* has the chance to explore the new surroundings at his/her own pace, and according to individual interests. The child can ask questions, find where he/she will sit, where his/her cane or jacket will go, and where to wash hands or listen to a story. This transitional visit is intended to remove the fear of change, for both parent and child.

For children with multiple disabilities, the success of the orientation visit may depend on the personnel and their attitudes. Parents are often as fearful of change as their children, and the chance to "get-to-know-you" and "welcome" can go a long way towards a smooth transition from home-based program to school.

General teacher guidelines for classroom teachers who may have visually impaired child in their preschool class include:

1. Lack of vision, in itself, does not inhibit learning, but lack of opportunity to function *does.*
2. The less interaction (socially as well as with objects) there is, the less cognitive growth there will be.
3. The child must act upon, not *be* acted upon.
4. If you can't take the child to the world, bring the world to the child (insofar as possible).
5. Motoric experience/development teaches spatial orientation and spatial imagery.
6. "Motor" the visually impaired child through actions, to teach him/her the imitation of movement.

7. Critical to the visually impaired child is the inability to observe the results of actions ("what happens when . . ."); concrete, hands-on experience (and creativity on the part of the teacher) can help to bridge this gap.
8. Use play as a teaching technique, but you may have to teach the child how to play. Use *real* things when possible so the child can use all of his/her other senses to supplement missing vision (e.g., plastic fruit does not *smell* like real fruit).
9. Representations of things (pictures, models) should not be used until concrete experience with those "things" has occurred.
10. Language is the manipulation of symbolic representations; until language is meaningful (based on experience), language cannot be used to mediate learning.
11. Concrete reasoning must precede abstract thought, but be sure the visually impaired student is not "stuck" at the concrete stage forever.
12. When internalization of things/objects (mental imagery) occurs, the child is ready to begin to manipulate ideas mentally (i.e., "think" and not before.

Some suggestions for early childhood teachers who have a visually impaired child in their class include:

1. Avoid using gestures alone (or facial expressions) for managing class behaviors unless you pair each with a verbal statement.
2. Make learning experiences as "hands on" (concrete, interactive, multisensory) as possible.
3. Encourage the development of listening skills whenever possible (e.g., following directions, relating story sequences, listening for details).
4. When speaking directly to a visually impaired child, use the child's name; touch his/her arm or shoulder lightly as you do so, to be sure the child knows you are addressing him/her.
5. If a visually impaired child has some useful vision, it's okay to ask him/her what an object or picture looks like to him/her.
6. Whenever possible, avoid isolating a visually impaired child as punishment (as in "time out"); it may feel the same as abandonment unless he/she can still hear your voice.
7. Watch for situations for which the child has had no prior experience (e.g., foods in different forms–corn-on-the-cob, cooked corn, popcorn, dried corn; matter in altered form–water, steam, ice, dew, condensation; sources of things–milk comes from cows; occupations–what jobs people perform; "what happens when . . .").

Ideas for Activities for the Preschool Visually Impaired Child

Most of the activities suggested below will appear to be very much like standard nursery school/kindergarten activities. Visually impaired children need many of the same kinds of tasks and experiences, but just may need more *of* them, and more emphasis on the concrete (sensory) aspects of them.

Motor Activities

Gross Motor: marching, running, jumping, hopping, climbing, rolling, stretching, twisting
circle games (where children hold hands, follow directions, do directed movements, e.g., "The Hokey Pokey") and action songs

Fine Motor: finger plays (e.g., "Where is Thumbkin," "Two Little Blackbirds," "Eensy Weensy Spider")
pounding (play dough, clay, bread dough); kneading
pouring (dry rice, beans, sand, water)
block play (Duplo®, Lego®, "bristle" blocks, cubes)
finger painting and "pudding painting"
"school" skills: coloring, cutting, pasting, tracing stencils (both with fingers and a writing tool)

Sensory Activities

Using Vision: (whenever applicable) Easter Egg Hunt, Treasure Hunt (using large or brightly colored objects)
talking about what things *look* like (shape, size, color, weight, texture)
looking for things in the environment that resemble circles, squares, triangles, rectangles

Using Hearing: listening games (e.g., "Simon Says")
listening for details in stories read to him/her
music: singing songs (especially songs with actions), using rhythm band instruments
listening for sounds in the environment (e.g., birds, traffic, airplanes, voice, motors)
following directions (beginning with simple one-step directions and progressing to more difficult two-step directions)

Using Touch: sorting by texture (blocks, cloth samples, etc.)
talking about what things feel like (e.g., smooth, rough, soft, hard, furry, "picky," bumpy, etc.)
"Feely Meely" box (guess what is in the box, purely through touch)
tracing raised lines (avoid raised-line pictures at this point; they usually contain too much detail; following a line with the index

finger is sufficient)
sorting shapes blindfolded (all the children in the class, not just the visually impaired child)

Using Smell: talking about how things smell ("good" or "bad")
pointing out particular and specific smells when on walks or trips (e.g., the bakery, a paper mill)
"Sniff cans" (used film cans filled with things that have unique smells, e.g., chocolate, vinegar, mint, licorice, orange peel, vanilla)

Using Taste: pointing out special tastes (e.g., sweet things, sour things, salty things)
playing a "tasting game" ("Guess what this is?" by taste; limit foods to familiar ones, so that identification is relatively easy)

Cooking Activities

(This is one of the best ways to demonstrate physical changes.)

Make: popcorn, Jello®, fudge, applesauce, meatloaf, hamburgers, hard-boiled eggs, cookies, s'mores, Rice Krispies® squares.
Bake: a cake, gingerbread, potatoes, slice'n'bake cookies, a pie.
Show the different forms of: eggs (fresh, soft and hard boiled, scrambled, "sunny-side-up"), fruit (apples vs applesauce, oranges fresh vs orange sections; watermelon from uncut to sliced to chunks); meat (fresh, raw hamburger vs hamburgers or meatloaf), etc.
Use "stirring" as a fine motor activity.
Use "decorating" cookies as one-to-one correspondence practice.
Use setting table as one-to-one correspondence practice, as well as self-help training.

Science Activities

(This is especially good for demonstrating physical change and conservation of matter.)

Plant seeds and watch them grow. (daily observations)
Check the weather every day; talk about forms of precipitation.
Boil water; evaporate water in a dish on the window sill.
Freeze water into ice; melt ice into water.
Have live animals in the room; feed and care for them. (Be sure the visually impaired child has a chance to touch the animal.)
Talk about temperature: relate it to weather, personal comfort, needs of plants and animals.

Dissolve solids into liquids (e.g., sugar, salt); stirring with fingers allows contact with the process, and tasting during the process provides "proof" that there has been change; the dissolved solution tastes different than plain water.

Play

Dress up in oversized clothing.
Use a toy telephone for conversation.
Make a small rowboat to get into and out of.
Use the sand table and water table for "messing" and pouring.
Do "housekeeping" activities with real (but child-sized) implements (broom, iron/ironing board, dishes, etc.).
Make a "mailbox" and "send letters." ("Letters" should be identifiable; pictures or printed names or raised dots can be used.) "Deliver" the "letters" to the right person.
Act out stories, devising original dialogue when necessary.

Field Trips

(Trips should be practical, and as "hands-on" as possible.)

Grocery store	Bakery	Firehouse	Airport
Post Office	Farm (where the animals can be touched)		

Nature walks with interaction with the environment (putting arms around a tree trunk, wading in a stream, collecting leaves or shells or stones, smelling pine trees, comparing the shapes of leaves, feeling the different flower shapes, etc.)

Note: Field trips/nature walks should have advance preparation (previous discussion) and follow-up activities.

Getting Ready for School

Preschool experiences should prepare the child to enter school. In preparing the visually impaired child for first grade, emphasis may have to be placed on skills sighted children learn spontaneously. Following is a list of areas the visually impaired child may need extra preparation/experience to learn.

Names/uses of things:	body parts	common objects
	foods	books
	coins	shapes
	actions (run, jump, hop, sit, stand, go, come, skip)	

Sequence:	Making up stories; retelling stories. Counting objects. Yesterday/today/tomorrow. First/then/next/last.
How things work:	buttons, zippers, knobs, latches, hooks, etc. opening/unwrapping (milk carton, cereal box, etc.) tools (hammer, saw, scissors, paste, crayons, etc.)
Dexterity development:	pincer grasp; poking with one finger; two-handed cooperation (using two hands to explore); use of simple tools, stringing beads; building with blocks; doing puzzles
Materials	(what things are made of)
Likenesses/Differences:	Complete/incomplete (tail-less animal, roofless house or car, shoeless person) Ordinary/unusual (upside-down car; boat used as a restaurant) Seasons; night/day; weather
Play Skills:	pouring, dumping, sorting, matching, stacking assembling/dissembling, house-keeping/pretending
Social Skills:	turn-taking, waiting, eating manners, cooperating, listening, following directions
Memory Skills:	concentration via games ("Peek-a-boo" to fingerplays); repeating back (items for shopping, characters in a story, nursery rhymes, songs, games), following sequential directions (one-step, two-step)
Self-Help:	playing dressing, eating, toileting, etc.

HELP THE CHILD TO BE A MAKER AND A DOER, NOT JUST AN OBSERVER.

PRIMARY GRADES

During the first three years of structured education (grades 1–3), the greatest emphasis is on language arts (reading, writing, spelling). The print size is often large enough for some visually impaired children to see, and few modifications may be needed. For those who have difficulty seeing primary-size print, some enlargement may be necessary. It is always better to explore alternatives to "large type" first, since they afford greater independence in selecting reading material. If an optical device (magnification tool or system) can enlarge reading material sufficiently, it is preferable to providing "large type books." When special textbooks are provided, the student is limited to reading only what is given to him/her, instead of being able to select whatever appeals to his/her interests. The TVI should be available on a regular (at least weekly) basis to provide instruction in the use of optical devices when appropriate, but will not teach reading.

When a student is blind, or appears to lean heavily on the tactual/auditory senses for learning, braille instruction may be indicated. It is important for the classroom teacher to understand that literary braille is not just an alphabetical code (i.e., it is more than the substitution of tactual dot configurations for alphabetical letters); it is a set of 189 dot configurations, some of which stand for single letters, some of which represent entire words, some of which stand for letter combinations, and some of which represent punctuation marks. In addition, there are numerous rules for when to use certain of the configurations. The teaching of braille reading is a complex process which is the responsibility of the TVI. It is different enough from print reading that the TVI may need to remove the child from the regular classroom for braille instruction, at least until the code is largely mastered. Such instruction will include the use of a braillewriter for writing; slate and stylus use ("handwritten braille") is more difficult than the use of a braillewriter, and is not usually introduced until sometime in third grade.

Because braille symbols are introduced in order of tactual difficulty (not necessarily in ABC order), braille reading material may contain different vocabulary words than the regular print readers. If contractions (two or more letters combined, with a specific dot configuration) are introduced, it further complicates the available vocabulary examples. Beginning spelling may be difficult, since the braille user has been thinking in terms of dot configurations instead of letters; he/she must learn both the letter spelling of a word as well as its braille (possibly contracted) form. For this reason, the TVI may suggest that spelling words are spelled orally, or are written twice when contractions are involved (once in letter-by-letter braille, and once in contracted form).

It should be apparent that literary braille cannot be taught effectively on a "once a week" basis. It must be practiced daily (just as print reading is learned), and instruction should be on a daily (minimum of hourly sessions) basis. Therefore, the TVI should schedule daily visits until the braille code is mastered.

A phonetic approach to word attack skills may be helpful for some students. The "window of opportunity" (best, most receptive time for instruction) for phonics is during the primary grades. The classroom teacher should be the one to introduce this approach, but the TVI can reinforce it spontaneously when appropriate.

Handwriting may present some problems for visually impaired learners.

Decisions about whether to use special dark-lined paper or black pens, how wide apart the lines should be, or how much legibility to expect will vary from student to student. The TVI should offer advice on these matters, based on a knowledge of the individual student's visual condition and available *functional* vision. For some students with useful vision, very few adaptations may be needed. Reasonable legibility may be a better goal than proper slant or exact letter formation; very few visually impaired students have neat handwriting. This can be a side effect of their visual status. Most visually impaired students will acquire minimal handwriting skills, and will use a typewriter or computer keyboard for written assignments. The use of a CCTV (optical device for magnification) may help the student read his/her own handwriting.

When a student has low vision, the TVI may need to reinforce classroom instruction in handwriting with special practice sessions apart from the class. Emphasis should be on legibility. (Instructional ideas can be found in Chapter Nine.)

The blind child will use a braillewriter to do written work, and will probably begin to use a slate and stylus sometime during third grade. Handwriting will not be a required part of his/her special curriculum until later (anytime from late middle school to high school); a few blind children will learn to print (block letters) well enough to take short-answer tests with the class, but most will probably learn only to write their own name in cursive style, using a signature guide for horizontal alignment.

Special technology use (especially computers and self-contained equipment like braille note-takers) may begin on a limited basis during the primary grades. A closed-circuit TV (CCTV) is a common optical device that can be introduced during the primary years, and some kinds of voice-producing computer software can be used by some students. Most technology, however, becomes more useful during the upper elementary or middle school years. The TVI can offer the best recommendations for an individual visually impaired child.

Math instruction in the primary grades should be as concrete as possible. Pre-requisite concepts should be present before teaching abstract processes. Among these concepts are:

many-few	more-less	large-small
big-little	tall-short	long-short
far-near	top-bottom	under-over
upper-lower	part-whole	right-left
same-different	heavy-light	around
equal	long	wide
high	middle	half

Since math is basically the processes of counting, measuring, comparing, combining, separating, and estimating, extra concrete experience in these areas can help strengthen the basic concepts needed for addition, subtraction, multiplication, and division. Manipulatives are necessities for teaching math to visually impaired students, particularly during the primary years.

"Word problems" are sometimes difficult for primary students; the ability to solve such problems involves reasoning, mental imagery, and some degree of reversibility in thinking (the ability to remember how things were before a change occurred). This capability is acquired by most sighted learners sometime between ages 7 and 11, so there may be both sighted and visually impaired primary-grade learners who "just don't get it" when word problems are presented. The classroom teacher may want to consider whether cognitive maturation has occurred if word problems are troublesome. Moreover, the visually impaired child may not have acquired sufficient experience to have good mental imagery. Keeping word problems as concrete as possible (i.e., using manipulatives) can alleviate some of the difficulties in imagery.

The use of an abacus in math is not usually taught until the basic addition and subtraction facts are mastered. A common misconception is that the abacus is a kind of calculator, but a better comparison might be that it is a substitute for paper and pencil. The student must be able to do mental arithmetic with some degree of ease and understanding before the abacus can become a useful tool.

Similarly, talking calculators should be postponed until the student understands the mathematical processes; when used by a visually impaired student, it should only be when the other (sighted) students in the class are using *their* calculators.

There is no substitute for repetition ("drill") when learning number facts or "tables," and the visually impaired student is no exception. Games and "flashcards" to help master the "facts" can be prepared in large formats or in braille. The TVI will introduce braille mathematical symbols (Nemeth Code) during braille instruction, but the classroom teacher will teach math processes and concepts.

Practical and applied math skills (telling time, using money, measuring, etc.) can be taught through the use of concrete materials and experiences. Use *real* money when teaching money skills (cardboard or plastic money does not feel like real money, and the visually impaired student may learn to recognize coins by touch). The TVI may be able to provide some special equipment (large-numeral, raised line, or braille clocks; adapted measuring tools or containers; modified scales; braille or large print number lines, etc.), and can make suggestions about how to modify classroom materials.

Science and Social Studies are usually taught in a concrete manner in the primary grades, so these subjects may not present many problems in the classroom. If the classroom teacher is alert to gaps in experience or lack of meaningful vocabulary, these deficits can usually be remediated by providing hands-on experiences. In fact, it is in the primary grades that many weak concepts in science or social studies areas can be most easily strengthened. Sand-table play, papier maché constructions, scientific "experiments" (using scientific method), neighborhood field trips to social/cultural/ethnic centers, and a variety of other "hands-on" field trips, visitors, or demonstrations can benefit *all* children (but are essential for visually impaired children). The conceptual foundations laid in science and social studies in the primary grades can go a long way towards easing learning experiences in these subjects in later grades. (See also the discussion later in this chapter on science and social studies for elementary and middle school.)

If the classroom teacher has never had a visually impaired student in his/her class, the TVI can be a source of information about how to handle such things as fire drills, playground activities, cafeteria procedures, field trips, or testing. Each visually impaired child has different needs, and the TVI can provide suggestions for that individual child. Some students may need extra light, while others may find light uncomfortable; some pupils may need to be seated at the front of the room for ease of seeing the blackboard, while others (particularly those who might use an optical device like a telescope, or "monocular") may be able to sit in any portion of the room; some students will wear glasses (but still may not see well) and others may have visual conditions that are not correctable with glasses. Each visually impaired child will have different visual needs, and the classroom teacher should not hesitate to ask questions; the TVI is there to help.

Some general guidelines can be listed for working with most visually impaired students. They follow, in the form of "Do's" and "Don'ts."

DO	DON'T
. . . feel comfortable using vision words, such as "look," "see," and "watch." . . . use the student's name when calling on him/her. . . . read out loud what you are writing on the board. . . . encourage independence; the visually impaired student needs to learn to do as much as possible for him/herself. . . . include the visually impaired student	. . . be afraid to touch the visually impaired student, but tell him/her you are about to touch him/her; respect the student's personal preferences about touching. . . . overprotect; let the student try as many things as possible for him/herself. . . . worry about your initial feelings of awkwardness; remember that you are teaching a *child*–who happens to have a disability.

DO	DON'T
in as many class activities as possible. . . . give explicit directions; avoid the words "here" and "there" since they may not give enough information. . . . fill in experiential gaps when you discover them. . . . allow extra time when needed, for tactual exploration, when appropriate, slower visual/braille reading, etc. . . . provide extra storage space for special equipment/materials. . . . encourage the use of aids/devices (*not* aides).	. . . be afraid to require a student's best work. . . . be afraid to require good behavior; administer the same discipline, if needed, as you would for a sighted child; rules *do* count. . . . hesitate to ask the student what something looks like to him/her, it may help you understand the quality of the student's vision. . . . feel you must tolerate unacceptable behavior in the visually impaired student any more than you would in a normally sighted student.

Above all, don't hesitate to ask the specialists (TVI and/or Orientation & Mobility Instructor) *any* question that you may have; the only foolish question is the one that is unasked. The specialists are there to help you make school as enjoyable and profitable for the visually impaired student as it can be.

ELEMENTARY GRADES AND MIDDLE SCHOOL

Since much of the learning in the primary years is concrete and interactive, the visually impaired student can participate in most of the activities. In fact, the more "hands on" learning there is, the easier it is for the visually impaired child to build the necessary concepts that form the foundations for later learning. It is when the instructional program begins to shift from an interactive process to an abstract level (using language to mediate learning via textbooks) that visually impaired learners must rely on whatever concepts and/or prior experiences are stored in their memories. This transition usually begins in the late primary grades and continues into the upper elementary grades.

It is also during this time that teachers must be most alert to deficits in conceptual foundations and gaps in experiences. The visually impaired student is not aware of these missing bits of information, and will often *say* he/she understands a new concept when he/she really does not. Both classroom teacher and TVIs must be constantly alert for any conceptual deficits, and should make every effort to fill in the gaps with concrete experiences. A questioning strategy is often helpful in uncovering deficits, using open-ended questions whenever possible (i.e., "Tell me about . . ." or "What do you think about . . ." or "Show me . . ."). Such questions as "Have you ever seen/been . . ." can be answered with a "yes" or "no" and the student's understanding cannot be determined accurately. Unless missing information has been filled in, new knowledge will have an uncertain conceptual foundation.

Language arts begins to shift from the acquisition of a skill to the refining of its use (sentence structure, parts of speech, grammar). Reading as a learning tool should be at grade level, whether in print, optically enlarged print or braille. The ability to use language in applications (creative writing, oral and written communication, and reading) becomes a prerequisite for learning in the upper elementary grades and upwards. If a visually impaired student cannot read at grade level, time spent on remediation can pay dividends later. Although even the best braille reading, or reading with optical devices, will not likely be as fast as "regular" reading (without optical devices), comprehension can still be equal to classmates, and should be the most important measure of reading efficiency. (The TVI should be able to evaluate the student's reading medium/literacy level by analyzing such factors as accuracy, speed, comprehension, and fatigue.)

Sometime during third or fourth grade, most visually impaired students will learn to type, both as a communication tool and as a keyboarding skill for technology use. The TVI will provide this instruction (see Chapter Nine).

Also during upper elementary school, other types of technology will probably be introduced. For a visually impaired student, this could include the use of sophisticated electronic braille equipment, translating software, synthetic speech connected to electronic reading devices, modified computer applications, and optical enlarging systems (as well as the familiar "Talking Books"/Talking Book players and tape recorders). (For a more complete description of this special equipment, see Chapter Nine.)

Math: In math, the basic processes (addition, subtraction, multiplication, and division) should be mastered before the abacus or a talking calculator are introduced. The TVI can obtain special materials to assist classroom teachers in such areas as fractions, decimals, and introductory geometry. Whenever possible, introduce a new concept concretely (e.g., part-whole puzzles to teach fractions; manipulatives to teach place value; specially marked rulers, scales, containers, protractors, etc. to teach measurement; raised-line drawing kits or wire forms to teach geometric concepts). Once a concept has been mastered, abstract problems can then be worked.

For students with useful vision, care must be taken to assure their seeing of process signs (plus, minus, multiplication, or division signs, dollar signs, cents signs, decimal points, fractions, and ratio colons). The use of graph paper can help in keeping columns of numbers in straight vertical alignment. Reducing the number of problems on a page, and possibly enlarging them, can minimize visual clutter or crowding. When grading math homework, check to see if errors are symbol-related, concept based, or the result of incorrect copying. (See also the chapter on Diagnostic Teaching.)

Although it is the responsibility of the classroom teacher to teach math, the TVI can suggest special materials, modified techniques, and hints for tactual approaches in math instruction. Learning the use of special equipment (such as the abacus, talking calculator, or Nemeth Code in braille) is the instructional responsibility of the TVI.

Social Studies: This is often considered a "safe" subject for visually impaired students since much of it involves reading. Therefore, in terms of adaptations, it appears that only the reading medium of the students requires special considerations. This is *not* the case, however. Social studies involves much visual experience and visual learning; the visually impaired student is at a disadvantage, both in foundational experience and in learning techniques. Much of social studies is based on conclusions drawn from observation–of people and of the environment. Vision is the only sense capable of integrating a variety of information and of establishing the "wholeness" of objects, environments, and events. Since social studies is a subject concerned with just such factors, impaired vision results in both subtle and not-so-subtle deficits in the study of people and their environments.

The problems in social studies for visually impaired students may be grouped into four general categories: experience/observation limitations, discussion skills deficits, reading-media related problems, and visual displays issues. Each category has its own disability related factors.

The first group of problems is related to the visually impaired student's difficulty in observing people and events. Information that sighted students absorb spontaneously may be missed by visually impaired pupils, and this deficit can cause large experiential/informational gaps. The visually impaired child is at a disadvantage in drawing conclusions or building concepts fundamental to social studies. Therefore, it is critical for educators to approach the teaching of this subject with the goals of finding out where the experiential gaps are and of filling them in. Visually impaired students often learn at an early age to give the verbal answers *expected* of them, so it is important for the teacher to probe beneath this verbal surface to determine whether there is real understanding. Students with low vision may give the impression of "seeing" more than they actually do, and may need sensory supplementation as much as the blind child. A pre-probe/post-probe (asking questions before and after any structured learning experience) can help identify where the gaps in concepts are, and if they still exist after supposed learning has taken place. In as many instructional situations as possible, try to provide a multisensory, "hands-on" approach. Constructing models, acting-out historical events, visiting historical sites, using creative materials to build landform examples (sand table, clay, outdoor environments), are all examples of making social studies concrete and sensory.

A second area of difficulty is in discussion skills capabilities. Since most social studies curricula utilize discussion as a teaching technique, it is important to determine whether the visually impaired student is able to interact verbally in a group. Beyond basic verbal ability (i.e., appropriate syntax and adequate vocabulary) is the ability to ask questions and to process answers. Questions that elicit "yes/no" or one-word answers generally do not provide much information. Students need to be able to ask questions that require thoughtful processing of responses (e.g., "What is . . ." or "How does . . . affect . . . ?"). It cannot be assumed that verbal skills are adequate because visual ability is limited; specific instruction may be necessary in order to assure adequacy in conversational techniques and questioning skills.

In teaching social studies processes (e.g., voting; the judicial process; economic systems), an effective technique can be role playing. "Pretending" can provide a learning technique that becomes an effective bridge between verbal discussion and actual experience.

Closely associated with discussion capabilities is the area of reading and reading media. The basic skill of reading should be at grade level if textbooks are to be a part of the social studies curriculum. There is a temptation to provide social studies texts in recorded form, and this is not inappropriate if the student is able to learn auditorily. However, if good listening skills have not been learned, the provision of recorded texts may be unproductive. The TVI should evaluate listening skills before providing recorded texts, and should attempt to remediate any deficits before expecting auditory learning to take place. If braille texts are being used, it must be recognized that reading speed will be slower, and assignments should take this into consideration. Even students who use adapted print texts (i.e., either use optical devices to enlarge the print, or read large type) may need additional time to complete reading assignments. In any event, reading should be only one strategy in teaching social studies; textbooks should never wholly replace experience learning, and should ideally only provide a reference for facts to supplement discussion.

One of the most critical areas of social studies for visually impaired students is the use of pictures, models, maps, globes, charts, graphs, and tables; these are all visual representations, and can provide very little useful information for the visually impaired learner unless modified. Visually impaired students must first have good orientational and directional concepts, must be able to perceive and integrate tactual information, and must be able to draw conclusions based on an imaginary whole which has been constructed from accurately perceived parts. The sighted person has an immediate visual image upon which to base conclusions; the visually impaired person must first *build* the image, piece by piece, before conclusions may be drawn. Sighted persons are able to perceive a model as a *reminder* of an object already seen, while visually impaired persons must build their entire concept upon information accumulated in sequential pieces from the same model. Therefore, models must be accurate, relay sufficient information (without becoming confusing because of too *much* information), and be able to be compared easily to familiar phenomena/objects. Map skills require directional concepts; topographical models require tactual/perceptual ability; graphs, tables, and charts require mental organizational ability; pictures for students with low vision must be sufficiently clear and concise, and have adequate contrast in color and/or lines. Globes present special problems, since they are usually, of necessity, too small to permit much detail; they also represent a difficult concept–that the world is round. The relationship between maps and globes is a difficult concept for sighted students; it is one which may need special attention for visually impaired students.

The use of three-dimensional resource materials (particularly for geographical concepts) is strongly recommended in teaching social studies, but consideration should also be given to the prerequisite skills and concepts needed to understand the three-dimensional materials. Impaired vision does not automatically result in increased ability to use the other senses for learning. The challenge in teaching visually impaired students lies in the ability to recognize each child's individual needs, deficits, and strengths. Because of the subtle involvement of vision in learning social studies concepts, this academic area may represent one of the greatest challenges of teaching visually impaired students.

Tables, Charts:

1. Spacing is important; leave space between groups of information, but keep data in proper columns.
2. Don't forget to title the chart or table.
3. Be sure the student has the necessary prerequisite concepts (e.g., column, row, frequency, percent, across, down, right, left, etc.).

Graphs:

1. If bar type, separate bars with space.
2. Use diagonal lines to fill in the bars (not horizontal or vertical lines, which can be confused with the bar shape).
3. If using textured material to indicate bars, keep it "soft" (too much texture can confuse the information to be gained from the graph).

4. If a line graph, use lines that are clearly different but easy to follow (e.g., ... and ___ ___ ___ ___ ___).

Maps:

How to Make Maps from "Scratch"

1. Points to remember:
   a. Students cannot perceive as much information by touch as they can by sight; therefore, maps must be kept as simple as possible.
   b. Outlining shapes will not be as effective as providing a solid texture for the entire shape.
   c. Making or adapting maps could be valuable learning experiences for sighted peers of a visually impaired student.
2. Ideas for materials to use:

For map bases	*For lines*	*For points*
heavy cardboard	macrame twine	hole-punched circles
corkboard	plastic-coated wire	nail heads (as on blue jeans)
Cellotex (ceiling tiles)	lines of dried glue	glue dots
Styrofoam	yarn	small beads

For semi-smooth areas (secondary or background information)

felt	polyester double-knit fabric
Naugahyde	heavy-weave linen

For tactually "bright" areas (significant information)

sandpaper	dotted-Swiss fabric (small dots, not too far apart)
needlepoint canvas	ribbed fabrics

(Adapted from: MAVIS Sourcebook 4 by Laurel Singleton; *Social Studies for the Visually Impaired Child.*)

3. Hints on making maps:
   a. Keep it as simple as possible. Fingers cannot pick up as much information as eyes can.
   b. Use "soft" colors/textures/symbols for large areas (i.e., no plaids, patterns, weave simulations, dots or anything that can be confused with information-carrying symbols).
   c. If filling in a large area, use diagonal lines, not vertical or horizontal lines.
   d. In choosing the types of lines to use on a map, consider the following:

Adequate space between dots or dashes
(. . . . . rather than ....)
(___ ___ ___ ___ rather than _ _ _ _ _ _ _ _ _)
"Soft" curves or angles
( rather than )
( rather than )

e. Tactual maps should always be horizontal (e.g., on the desk or table), not on the wall; "north" is not "up."
f. Raised-line drawing kits (which use plastic sheets as a base) or aluminum sheeting are good bases; a sewing tracing wheel can make useful lines, but the map-maker must think in reverse (the imprint will be on the reverse side of the map material).
g. If the TVI has access to a thermoform machine, raised maps or figures can be made on a plastic material called "braillon."
h. Don't leave out the "key" since it establishes the "code."

4. How to use maps:
   a. Prepare the student for map use by teaching topographical map concepts with a sand table or water table.
   b. Be sure the student understands the basic landforms vocabulary (e.g., continent, island, peninsula, ocean/sea/lake, bay/inlet, river, mountain/hill, waterfall, cliff, mesa, canyon, etc.).
   c. "Scale" is a concept that must be taught.
   d. Introduce the "key" first, since it contains the "code" to understanding the map.
   e. Use a "point-of-reference" technique in reading a map (i.e., use a magnet, push-pin, sticker, or finger to hold a place with one hand while the other hand is exploring nearby areas.
   f. Use compass directions for verbal references (e.g., "Chicago is at the southern end of Lake Michigan.").
   g. Use a "whole" concept that assumes details exist within a specific area or context; explore the entire map first before locating details.
   h. Keep a horizontal orientation for tactual maps (i.e., flat on a desk or table).

Science: As with all academic areas, basic concepts must be secure before proceeding with abstract learning. In the area of science, however, much of the "abstract learning" can continue to be concrete. Science that is well-taught involves the use of scientific method (hypothesizing, experimenting, observing, and drawing conclusions). For visually impaired students, "discovery learning" can incorporate scientific method, since the *process* is a large part of science. If basic concepts are secure (weight, area/volume, temperature, etc.), observation that involves a multisensory approach can make science an exciting subject for visually impaired learners.

Special materials can be created specifically by the instructor for teaching a particular concept, already-available instructional modules and equipment can be used, or existing approaches can be modified for the visually impaired learner. The use of real objects (seeds, small live animals such as fish, crayfish, snails, snakes, etc.) is preferable to models, but accurate replicas can also be used (animal pelts, life size but preserved real animals, lifesize take-apart models). Adapted equipment can be obtained from several sources (the American Printing House for the Blind, Science for the Blind, SAVI/SELPH), and entire instructional modules (complete with modified equipment and instructions) can be purchased from both American Printing House for the Blind and SAVI/SELPH. The TVI can be an excellent source of ideas and suggestions for including the visually impaired learner in regular class science activities.

When units are visual by necessity (e.g., using a microscope or telescope), the visually impaired student should not be a passive participant (e.g., the "notetaker"); models or raised-line drawings can be substituted for what is seen through the microscope; three-dimensional models of the solar system can be used to illustrate relative sizes and positions of planets. A replica of an erupting volcano can be constructed by the class, using safe chemicals to simulate the overflowing lava. Physical change can be demonstrated in simple ways (making applesauce from apples, popcorn from corn kernels, dissolving sugar or salt in water, etc.) or in more complex ways (freezing or evaporating water to show change from liquid to solid or gas). The possibilities are almost endless for making science a wholly hands-on experience, and the creative science teacher can feel comfortable in including the visually impaired student in nearly every activity.

Tips for Teaching Science to a Visually Impaired Learner

1. Keep it real; use as many real objects or animals as possible.
2. Be sure materials are sturdy enough for tactual exploration (large seeds, green leaves rather than dry or brittle leaves, a goldfish rather than a minnow, a box turtle rather than the small turtles found in pet stores, earthworms, beetles, etc.). When it is difficult to examine a live animal (such as a bird), stuffed models can be substituted, especially to show wingspan, claws, fangs, etc.
3. Use "discovery learning" whenever possible. By asking preliminary questions ("What do you think will happen if we . . . ?"), allowing hands-on participation, and reminding the student to draw a conclusion ("What happened? Why?"), learning is active and participatory.
4. Encourage an organized approach to recording data. Use divided containers (e.g., egg cartons or muffin tins) for sorting, and labels in appropriate

reading media (large print or braille). Create columnar formats for written data.

5. Use a "buddy system" when necessary, but encourage the visually impaired student to be actively involved in the experiment.

6. Encourage questions. Visually impaired students may not have the capacity to observe side effects or unexpected results of a particular experiment, and can't ask about what they don't see. Create a learning climate where no question is considered "stupid."

7. Help the visually impaired student to make generalizations, especially about the environment (balance of nature, food chain, pollution, natural selection, etc.). Visually impaired learners may have difficulty applying scientific concepts to a world they cannot observe.

Art: Visual impairment should not be a reason for excluding a student from art class. There are many art media that visually impaired students can utilize successfully, and many modifications that make other media more accessible. Most three-dimensional media (metal, wire, clay, collages, foil, papier maché, wood, ceramics) can be utilized with little or no modification, so long as the end product is not compared with those of the sighted children in the class. For the visually impaired student, the *process* of art may be more important than the product; the pleasure may be in the "doing." Moreover, participation can be a "vehicle" for the expression of feelings, and representation of how the visually blind student perceives his/her world. The art teacher needs to recognize that creativity is not limited to sighted people, and that is quite all right to try activities in unusual ways without knowing in advance whether they'll work or not. The TVI might suggest alternatives to certain projects, but the art teacher should still reserve the right to "try anything."

It may be important to evaluate prerequisite concepts (up-down, wet-dry, right-left, top-bottom, hard-soft, shapes, sizes, colors, etc.) and tool skills (use of scissors, glue, paste, stapler, paper punch, brushes) prior to the introduction of an art media. The TVI may be able to reinforce any weak concepts or tool skills, but practice should occur in the art class. Allow "mess" and extra time; the expression of emotion or the creative urge may take more time than a class period.

Some media can be adapted for use by a visually impaired student. Drawing can be done with a bold marker for students with low vision, or with a raised-line drawing kit or screen board for blind students; either plastic sheets or lightweight aluminum can be used for raised-line drawings. Painting may require no more modification than a larger sheet of paper for a student with low vision; for the blind child, various textures can be added to the paint (grades of sand or other "gritty" material) to produce different textures to correspond with different colors.

Photography is an underutilized media for some visually impaired students. Those with low vision may enjoy creating pictures with this medium, and may surprise everyone with what they can see by using special lenses or filters (e.g., a telephoto lens or wide angle lens). Because the range of visual function is so great among individuals with low vision, photography should not be ruled out as a possible art medium.

If an art class visits a museum, the art teacher should be aware that many museums have special exhibits for blind and visually impaired visitors. Even if they don't, an advance inquiry may alert the museum to the need, and they may be willing to allow special "touch privileges" for the one or two visually impaired students in the class. (This suggestion also applies to *all* museums and many other field trip destinations.)

Music: Visually impaired students can usually participate in most aspects of music classes with very few modifications. This is not to imply that visually impaired students will all have talent or interest in this subject, for reduction in vision does not automatically result in an increase in auditory abilities. Real talent occurs about as often as in normally sighted individuals, and good listening skills must often be intentionally taught. Music can enhance or reinforce these listening skills, however, and many visually impaired students enjoy music classes. They can participate in all of the auditory aspects of these classes with no modifications. The only changes may be in the medium of the printed music or lyrics. There is a separate braille music code which can be used for modifying vocal sheet music or instrumental music, and lyrics for choral music can be transcribed into literary braille. The blind musician usually memorizes the braille music, since his/her hands are needed to play the instrument; some students with low vision will use this technique as well. (The TVI normally obtains or transcribes any needed braille music).

Home Economics: Many classroom teachers of home economics are not aware that visually impaired students are capable of participating in their class. In fact, this class can provide needed opportunities for visually impaired students to learn daily living skills such as clothing care, the use of appliances, and how to survive in the kitchen. Parents have too often barred their visually impaired child from the kitchen, believing it is dangerous for them, but guided instruction in basic kitchen skills is a necessary experience in developing independence. The home economics teacher may have to adapt or modify many approaches (with the help of the TVI) but it *can* be done. Using elbow-length oven mitts, adapted dials, outlined switches or outlets, specially designed "gadgets" (e.g., an audible liquid-level indicator), large type cookbooks or recipe cards, a whistling teapot, and modified/labeled measuring tools or containers can make survival in the kitchen a reality. Even sewing can be learned on a limited basis with sewing machine magnifiers and finger guards and needle threaders; much will depend on the amount of functional vision available to the student.

The use of microwave ovens, washer and dryers, vacuum cleaners, and other common household appliances can be learned with a minimum of modification; the TVI can suggest alternatives, obtain special materials, and help "brainstorm" solutions to problems when a skill is desirable and needs to be learned. The TVI may even ask to use the home economics facilities for teaching other "survival skills" and home care techniques (making beds, cleaning/dusting, sorting laundry, ironing). Usually this separate teaching supplements the regular home economics curriculum (does not take its place). The TVI may even wish to use the home economics curriculum as a resource for individual instruction; the visually impaired student and TVI could do the grocery shopping for the home economics teacher for a specific unit, meal, or project. The TVI can be a real support to the home economics teacher, and the home economics teacher can provide opportunities for the TVI to extend instruction to the student in daily living skills. If viewed in this cooperative context, both teachers can use each other's special expertise to benefit the visually impaired student.

Tips for Home Economics when a visually impaired student is part of the class:

1. Wooden-handled utensils conduct less heat than metal ones.
2. Splatter screens help to prevent hot oils or grease from causing painful burns.
3. Hand mixers may be harder to manipulate or control than a stand model.
4. A meat-carving board with a meat holder may facilitate carving and slicing of the meat.
5. Fitted sheets facilitate bed making.
6. When using spray cleaners (as for dusting), spray the cloth rather than the object to be cleaned.
7. Use a pattern approach to dusting or vacuuming. (i.e., Image a "grid" and use horizontal or vertical strokes to cover the area.)

Industrial Arts: The "shop" teacher may feel apprehensive about having a visually impaired student in his class because safety is a big factor in industrial arts programs. The visually impaired student is viewed as a risk around power tools and other machinery or engines. Much depends on the creativity and willingness of the teacher, however, and there are very few visually impaired students who cannot learn *something* in this class.

Some areas of industrial arts are more amenable to modifications or adapted instruction, and are more likely to provide success for the visually impaired student. Woodshop (with closely supervised use of power tools), metalshop with supervision, some aspects of auto and/or small appliance repair, the use of hand tools for simple home repairs, "business" simulations, and general home maintenance (including changing fuses and lightbulbs) are examples of such instructional areas.

There are many special measurement tools that can be used in an industrial arts class. Large print or braille rulers, protractors, calipers, micrometers, and audible levels are a few examples of such tools. In addition, many precision engineering tools have been modified for blind engineers (audible calculators, audible liquid-level indicators, audible calipers, audible light sensors). Protective guards are available for power saws (table saw and band saw). Rehabilitation centers may be good sources of information about shields, guards, and special equipment.

Tips for Including Visually Impaired Students in Industrial Arts:

1. Encourage organization and neatness in storing equipment and materials.
2. Design beginning projects that allow the visually impaired student to use hand tools to produce a product.
3. Develop a safe *approach* technique when using power tools, and see that the student practices it.
4. Help the student recognize which machines make which sounds and where they are located.
5. When teaching the student to use a power tool, first help him explore the operational parts and controls (with the equipment off and unplugged); establish safe patterns of hand movements to control and operate the equipment (best done while the machine is *on,* and the student has adequate supervision).
6. Alert the student to the fact that a machine that is on and operating usually vibrates; this clue can help a student know to avoid exploring that machine until it is off and quiet.
7. Learn to utilize alternative sensory clues for safe equipment operation (e.g., listening for auditory changes as a task is in progress; using touch to identify heat, belt tension, or vibration; smelling warning signs as an engine overheats, or using odors to identify substances/materials). (Note: These tips were adapted from McConnell, J. (1984). Integration of visually handicapped students in industrial education classes: An overview. The reader is strongly urged to read this article, written by an industrial arts teacher.)

Physical Education: In the past, visually impaired students were often excluded from physical education, either by choice or because the gym teacher was uncertain about what the student could do. Because visual impairments restrict the ability to observe the activities of others, visually impaired students may have been unaware that they could move around actively and safely, or they may have learned the passivity and inaction that usually accompanies overprotection. In a few cases, eye specialists have recommended "limited activity" or "no contact sports" when retinal detachment was a risk. However, the high prevalence of barring visually impaired students from gym "for safety reasons" was usually because of misunderstanding; physical education is no more "dangerous" for most visually impaired students than for sighted students, given informed instructional methodology and standard safety precautions applicable to *all* students.

Visually impaired students consume a considerable amount of energy in seeing and moving, and require extra stamina to maintain postural control or to practice good mobility skills. A good program in physical education, from kindergarten or first grade on, can build motor skills, increase body awareness and position in space, and enhance mobility skills (especially laterality, directionality, balance, posture, and gait). There are enough good reasons to include visually impaired students in the physical education program that federal mandates for inclusion (or the provision of an adapted program) are almost superfluous. Despite this positive philosophy, there are still visually impaired students "sitting on the sidelines" during gym, even though it is illegal (unless for reasons given by an ophthalmologist, in writing).

Inclusion in physical education requires few modifications at any age or grade level, and the benefits are many. Some activities or sports require no modification (tug or war, parachute play, canoeing, tandem bicycling, swimming, walking, jogging on a track, yoga, mime, and using physical fitness equipment). Other activities or sports require only minimal modifications (bowling, water skiing, dancing, wrestling, tumbling and some gymnastics, large-ball play, running in tandem, hiking). Visually impaired people (including some blind people!) have even learned to snow ski (both downhill and cross country), sail, fish, play golf, and enjoy archery. There are few limits to what a physically fit and active visually impaired individual can do, given the opportunity and some instruction.

The use of special equipment (e.g., audible balls, an audible goal locator) or modified methods of instruction (use of precise verbal instruction and manual manipulation of the learner's body) can make it possible for visually impaired students to participate in many physical education activities. Wrestling coaches have discovered that some blind wrestlers are even able to outperform their sighted opponents. The creative physical education instructor can find many ways of including visually impaired students in class activities at all levels.

Even ball games can include visually impaired students. For those who have useful vision, using a larger or more brightly colored ball can work well (e.g., using a beachball to play volleyball). Using an audible goal locator, attached to the basketball backboard, can enable a blind player to shoot baskets. The visually impaired student can act as server in volleyball, and a softball can be batted from a tee. Brightly colored balls can be used for kickball or basketball, or, if the student can see the black and white soccer ball, no modification is needed at all.

A number of physical activities have special value for visually impaired students. Use of a balance beam, or heel-to-toe walking can increase balance and improve posture. Jumping rope, doing "jumping jacks," and deep knee bends can improve body control. Moving towards a designated sound (a bouncing ball, audible locator, clapping) can help to build directionality. Games teach cooperation and sportsmanship; success in any phase of the activities can build self-confidence and generate positive attitudes toward physical activity.

The most long-lasting effect of participation in a good physical education program may be the establishment of good habits, both health-wise and of a recreational nature. Sports learned in school may become leisure/recreation activities when the visually impaired student graduates or leaves the the school system. Moreover, such activities establish a basis for continued inclusion with sighted peers in society.

General Suggestions for Classroom Teachers During the Upper Elementary and Middle School Years:

1. Allow preferential seating or "roaming privileges" for best use of available vision.
2. Allow enough time for the student's best work–and *expect it.* Don't "give" grades; expect the student to earn them.
3. Monitor lighting conditions; especially watch for glare. (Do not stand with your back to windows when lecturing, as this forces the visually impaired student to look into the light source.)
4. Encourage the visually impaired student to take responsibility for his/her own time management and assignment completion; encourage neatness and organization.
5. Provide clear, dark copies of notes if a visually impaired student is a visual learner.
6. Verbalize whatever you write on the board.
7. Remind blind students in particular to face the speaker (orienting both face and body in that direction). Some students with low vision may also need to be similarly reminded. Reminders should be as unobtrusive as possible, so as not to embarrass the student in front of his peers.

Factors to Consider When Making Adapted Materials

1. What is the purpose of the lesson? (The materials should end up serving that purpose.)
2. What is the material supposed to teach? (Extraneous details can be eliminated so long as they do not delete any information intended to be learned.)
3. What is the best learning channel(s) of the child? (Knowing that the child is a visual or auditory or tactual learner, or any combination thereof, can help in deciding what sense to use most in modifying the materials.)
4. Can the lesson's purpose be enhanced by the material in its adapted form? (Sometimes, the purpose is lost in the process of modification; in this case, look for alternative materials, rather than trying to modify.)
5. Will the learner gain the same information from the adapted material as the sighted students do from the original material? (This may be a difficult decision; the TVI can often help in interpreting what the visually impaired student can absorb through the media proposed.)
6. Are the prerequisite concepts for acquisition of knowledge/concepts present in the learner? (The TVI can help to determine this.)
7. Have you eliminated extraneous detail, but still retained the concept(s) intended to be learned?
8. Can you measure learning as a result of the materials?
9. Are the materials sturdy, reusable, minimal in cost?
10. Are the materials non-toxic?
11. Do the materials have a single purpose? One-time use? Or can they be used in other contexts? (It takes *time* to modify materials; if they can be used over again, or for other applications, the time is more efficiently spent.)
12. Are the materials multisensory?

Examples of Modifications/Adaptations in Materials:

Darkening — Enlarging — Minimizing glare
Adding color — Adding texture — Eliminating detail
Reducing clutter — Simplifying — Spacing
Reducing extraneous detail (visual, tactual, auditory)
Shifting from two-dimensional to three-dimensional)
Shifting from pictures to models or (preferably) the "real thing"
Giving extra time — Using different paper (non-glare, darker lined, graph, wide-lined)
Changing the media (written to oral, written to taped, verbal to graphic)

Factors to Consider When Adapting Environments

1. What is the problem? (light? glare? body position? low contrast? inappropriate location in the classroom?)
2. What are several solutions? (Pick the one that fits the student's individual needs and the situation.)
3. Which is the best for *this* child? (Each student will have unique visual needs; the TVI can help interpret these.)
4. Can it be easily arranged spontaneously by the child as needed? (It is always desirable for the visually impaired student to assume as much responsibility for his/her unique needs as possible, given the maturity and ability.)
5. Do others (peers, teachers) understand why any change in the environment is necessary? (Usually, the TVI will explain to teachers, and expect teachers to explain to the other students in the class.)
6. Is the change socially acceptable? (Seating the student in the front of the room may be difficult socially; similarly, the student may be embarrassed to move up the board to see, if his/her peers are watching and critical. Clear explanations are necessary if the need is to meet with understanding and acceptance.)
7. What will it cost? (Most environmental modifications do not cost anything (e.g., adjusting seating or lighting), but if an extra electrical outlet is needed, to support the visually impaired student's electrical equipment, there may be necessary cost involved. Most schools do not mind such an expense since it is usually minimal.)
8. Who will take responsibility for making the adaptation? (Preferably the student, but if the modification is extensive or involved, some adult may need to take the initiative and follow through.)
9. Are there any "side effects?" (Glare may come with additional lighting; special seating may cause unexpected social problems. Each "problem" must be individually solved.)
10. Does the *student* want the modification, and will the student use/do it when the TVI is not around? (If the change is not accepted as useful by the visually impaired student, it may not be practiced consistently. For this reason, it is always desirable to include the student in the decision making process when possible.)

Examples of Adaptations/Modifications in the Environment:

Seating (location; size of chair, desk, table).
Lighting (natural or artificial).
Glare reduction (window shade controls; illumination control).
Organization (storage space, shelves, closets, lockers).

Use of color or contrast to outline steps, outlets, switches.
Giving extra time when assignments are extensive or in testing.
Space (establishing specific areas for specific tasks; keeping classroom arrangements reasonably consistent.)

SECONDARY SCHOOL AND BEYOND

High school subjects are so diverse it is hard to make general statements about modifications. Many of the same suggestions for prior years will still apply to instructional methods (concrete and "hands on" whenever possible). Classroom modifications will remain highly individualized and dependent on the unique visual needs of each visually impaired student. Textbooks will be in the student's primary reading medium (braille or print) but may be supplemented by auditory (taped) editions. (The visually impaired student who is college-bound will need to know that there will be no braille or large print texts in college; he/she will depend on recorded textbooks and/or human readers). The use of sophisticated technology (both computer related and self-contained) will help the student access information as well as submit assignments in print (even though the student may be a braille user). Special braille codes (music, scientific notation, foreign languages) may be taught by the TVI if the student encounters the need. Students with low vision should be using their optical devices with increasing ease and proficiency, and should be making choices about when to use them (and when alternative information access would be more efficient.) Problem-solving/decision-making skills should be practiced and refined. Abstract reasoning ability will depend on the quality of the student's past experiences and his/her memory capability. The TVI should be gradually expecting the student to do more and more for himself/herself, and the Orientation & Mobility Instructor will probably be introducing more complicated travel experiences. The visually impaired student should be able to sit in on his/her own IEP meetings and advocate for his/her own needs. Every objective should reflect the core goal of independence insofar as is possible, and opportunities to practice this independence should be available. (There will be no TVI after graduation.)

During the high school years, the transition to adulthood has begun. Although the educational program has begun to be specialized and have alternatives (i.e., higher education oriented or vocational planning), social adjustment may take a primary position among the transitional changes. Academics are still the responsibility of the classroom teacher, and the TVI may become less visible as more independence is expected of the student. The visually impaired learner is expected to take more responsibility for his/her own needs (including the necessary modifications or special materials because of the visual impairment). The TVI should be weaning the student away from regular support, and encouraging the student to make decisions or solve problems independently. By the time the visually impaired student is 15 or 16, other support agencies should have become members of the transition planning team, and some long range planning should be the directing force behind course selections, behavior motivations, and part-time employment possibilities. Such questions arise as "What do I want to do after I graduate?" "How will I earn a living?" "Where will I live?" and "How will I arrange transportation, both for routine needs like food or clothing shopping, and for the purpose of getting to a place of employment?" The TVI should become a facilitator (providing lists of resources and teaching the student the realities of job searches, credit cards, and bank accounts).

The high school years are also times to prepare visually impaired students for entry into the adult world of work, community, and family. The TVI may spend time emphasizing such things as personal appearance, hygiene, and job readiness skills so that the best possible impression is made by the visually impaired young adult. Refining social skills and social adjustment may be part of the TVI's role, and classroom teachers should support these efforts by providing practice situations to reinforce the special instruction.

Coping skills are another possible area of need. Although problem-solving techniques should have been taught and (hopefully) practiced for most of the educational years, they may need to be specifically encouraged during the high school years. A sense of self-advocacy and self-sufficiency is the goal. Classroom teachers can help by encouraging and allowing the visually impaired student to solve his/her own problems, and by providing equal access to opportunities whenever possible for the growth and the realization of potential. Visually impaired students can only become productive visually impaired adults if they are valued as unique individuals who have the ability to make positive contributions to society.

SUMMARY

In the current educational trend towards "full inclusion" (despite the federal mandate for a full continuum of placement options to meet individual needs), the reality is that most visually impaired students are in inclusive settings (including many students with disabilities in addition to visual impairment). In regular class placements, the TVI provides support to the regular class teacher(s), may suggest environmental modifications, and provide adapted materials or special equipment, but does not tutor or teach any subject material covered by the regular teacher(s). The role of the TVI is to interpret the child's visual status and needs, to evaluate what special (vision related) skills are needed, and to provide instruction in those special skill areas (see Chapter Nine). Chapter Eight has provided explanations about how visual impairments impact general education, and how to modify the learning environment or materials in ways that help the visually impaired learner to compete with sighted peers.

REFERENCES AND RECOMMENDED READING

Buell, C. (1966). *Physical education for blind children.* Springfield, IL: Charles C Thomas.

Gallagher, P. (1986). *Educational games for visually impaired and sighted children.* Denver: Love.

Jan, J., Freeman, R., & Scott, R. (1977). *Visual impairment in children and adolescents.* New York: Grune & Stratton.

McConnell, J. (1984). Integration of visually handicapped students in industrial education classes: An overview. *Journal of Visual Impairment and Blindness, 78,* 319–323.

Rhyne, J. (1981). *Curriculum for teaching the visually impaired.* Springfield, IL: Charles C Thomas.

Science activities for the visually impaired (SAVI) and Science enrichment for learners with physical handicaps (SELPH). Berkeley, CA: Center for Multisensory Learning.

Scott, E. (1982). *Your visually impaired student: A guide for teachers.* Baltimore: University Park Press.

Singleton, L. (1979). *Social studies for the visually impaired child.* (MAVIS Sourcebook 4). Boulder, CO: Social Science Education Consortium.

Warren, D. (1994). *Blindness and children.* Cambridge, MA: Cambridge University Press.

Also see Volume 2 of: Koenig, A. & Holbrook, C. (2000). *Foundations of education* (2nd ed.). New York: American Foundation for the Blind.
for chapters on: Literacy (Koenig, A. & Holbrook, C.); Social Studies and Science (Ross, D. & Robinson, M.); Mathematics (Kapperman, G., Heinze, T., & Sticken, J.); Arts Education (McNear, D.); Physical Education and Health (Farrenkopf, C. & McGregor, D.).

Chapter Nine

THE EXPANDED CORE CURRICULUM: THE SPECIAL SKILLS NEEDED BY A VISUALLY IMPAIRED STUDENT

INTRODUCTION

The term *core curriculum* commonly refers to a group of courses that form the basis (core) of a particular educational plan. An academic core curriculum would include English, Maths, Sciences, Social Studies, and Languages–all subjects geared towards preparing students to enter college.

In the field of visual impairment, there is an *expanded core curriculum*–a group of instructional areas that are unique to students who are visually impaired, and which teach compensatory skills that are necessary because of the limitations a visual impairment places on a learner. These instructional areas–the expanded core curriculum–have a threefold purpose:

- To eliminate or minimize any possible developmental delays caused by the visual impairment;
- To provide a variety of supplementary and compensatory skills that will enable the visually impaired student to compete on a par with his/her sighted peers; and
- To help the visually impaired student to realize his/her full potential.

Every qualified/certified TVI has been prepared to provide special instruction in expanded core curriculum areas, although not every visually impaired student will need to learn all of the skills in this curriculum. Type and severity of visual impairment, whether it is congenital or acquired, cognitive level, past experiences, level of sensory awareness, presence or absence of other disabilities–all of these factors are considered by the TVI when evaluating individual needs for special skills instruction for each visually impaired student. The Individual Education Plan (IEP) should reflect which of these skills are needed by each visually impaired student, and that those skills will be taught by the TVI.

The expanded core curriculum includes:

1. Sensory skills (awareness, discrimination, perception)
   a. Vision (when there is any useful vision), including vision stimulation and visual efficiency
   b. Hearing (including Listening Skills)
   c. Touch
   d. Smell and taste
2. Motor development (especially for infants and young children)
3. Concept development
4. Communication skills
   a. Early language skills
   b. Braille, when indicated (readiness, reading, writing, math, foreign languages, music, scientific notation)
   c. Handwriting
   d. Typing/Keyboarding
   e. Technology (computer use, electronic braille equipment, note-takers, etc.)
   f. Tactual/visual graphics
   g. Organizational and study skills (including library skills)
5. Social skills (non-verbal communication, manners, etiquette, personal interactions)
6. Self-help/Daily living skills
   a. Food related (eating, food preparation, food purchasing, food storage)
   b. Clothing related (dressing, clothing purchases, clothing care)
   c. Grooming and hygiene
   d. Home maintenance/Home care (housecleaning, simple repairs)
   e. Time management
   f. Money management (shopping, banking, budgets, credit, taxes, consumerism)
7. Human sexuality
8. Using low vision devices
9. Leisure and recreation skills; management of leisure time
10. Career awareness/vocational choices/job readiness
11. Self-advocacy and Accessing Information (beyond the educational environment); Problem-solving and Decision-making
12. Orientation and Mobility (taught by a specialist with a separate certification)

Different visually impaired students will have different needs, and the age/grade at which specific special skills are introduced may vary according to need or capability of the individual student. Some skills will be taught on an ongoing basis (e.g., braille, listening skills, social skills, orientation and mobility) while others may only require a specific time period (e.g., typing/keyboarding, using low vision devices, basic concept development). Some skills are taught in hierarchical order (e.g., from self-feeding to food preparation, from dressing to clothing selection and care, from simple bathing to shaving or applying make-up), while others expand capabilities (e.g., from how to play to how to manage leisure time, or from career awareness to actual job readiness). The decisions about when it is appropriate to begin instruction in a particular skill area, or how long to continue that instruction (based on an estimated level of probable proficiency expected) should be based on the TVI's recommendation, since appropriate special evaluations and professional judgments may be needed.

This chapter will describe the general content of the expanded core curriculum, and why the additional skills are important.

SENSORY SKILLS

When the primary sense is absent or impaired, the other senses do not automatically become more adept. Additional dependence on the other senses may tend to increase their perceptual awareness, but a structured program of instruction makes them more useful in gathering information for the brain. It is essential that sensory channels become as efficient as possible, since they must provide information that will substitute for vision. Even the most acute hearing and touch are incomplete substitutes for vision, but they may be all the senses available to the learner; their capabilities must be as well-developed as possible.

Vision: When a child still has some useful vision, it should be utilized; it cannot be "conserved" by not using it, as was once thought; it must be practiced to reach maximum efficiency. Programs of instruction in "visual stimulation" and "visual efficiency" can be designed by the TVI. These programs are adapted to the age and ability of the child, and usually begin at an awareness level. Light, color, shape, shadows, reflections, and movement are some of the stimuli commonly used. If there is sufficient vision, some level of visual discrimination (for shapes, outlines, and details) may be achieved. Depending on the age and cognitive level of the learner, it may even be possible to teach applications (e.g., using visual clues to identify people, objects, and perhaps even large letters). The Orientation and Mobility instructor will be especially interested in the development of visual efficiency, since it may provide environmental information that will be useful for movement and mobility purposes. If the learner can use optical devices, they are incorporated into the program of visual efficiency development, since the additional information provided with an optical device can enhance visual functioning. Maximum use of available vision is always the goal of any vision development program.

Hearing: The auditory sense is probably the next best information-gathering sense available to a visually impaired learner, although it is a poor substitute for vision. It does not provide the rich variety of information that vision does, and is not as precise. It is a distance sense (i.e., is sensitive to stimuli beyond arm's reach) but is largely sequential in nature. Whereas vision can take in a variety of information at one glance, hearing must usually concentrate on sounds that are sequential and continuous in order to gain useful information. Efficient use of hearing requires the learner's concentrated attention, and a minimum of auditory distractions. The learner must be aware of a sound, pay attention to it, and decipher its meaning.

Localizing of sound is usually the first level of auditory training. Because of the location of a child's ears on opposite sides of his/her head, it is possible to learn to determine the direction of a sound source (the two ears receive just slightly different information, and the brain can use this difference in determining direction). It is more difficult to determine auditory height of the sound source, but direction alone can give useful information.

Identifying the sound source takes more time, experience, and reasoning ability. Much practice with a wide range of sound-producing objects, is required before the learner can begin to categorize sounds. Human voices have unique characteristics and may be the easiest sounds to learn first. Familiar objects (toys) or environmental noises (animals, the telephone, wind, traffic, horns) are usually next to be identified. It should be apparent that a specially planned and sequenced program of exposure to sounds will help in establishing references for auditory discrimination.

The progression of skills in a program to teach listening skills should move from simple sound identification to tonal and volume discrimination, to the reproduction of sound, to discriminating between similar or different sounds. A program in phonics can enhance the use of sound in speech and in word attack skills in reading. Then, auditory applications are introduced (extending the auditory attention span, following directions, using words in applications, recognizing auditory sequence). Finally, more sophisticated applications of language are introduced to sharpen the cognitive auditory link (discriminating fact from fiction, listening for details, listening for specific information, and using listening for evaluative purposes). An outline of the sequence in developing listening skills follows.

Listening Skills for Visually Impaired Students:

Level I: Discrimination and Perception

A. Preschool, kindergarten, early primary grades
   1. Awareness of sound
   2. Attention to sound
   3. Localization of sound
   4. Discrimination of sound (loud/soft, high/low, fast/slow)
   5. Recognizing, identifying, and imitating sounds in the environment (animals, things, voices, musical instruments, etc.)
   6. Matching sounds (rhyming; beginning speech)

B. Kindergarten and early primary applications
   a. Following directions
   b. Selective listening (auditory figure-ground)

Level II: Phonics/Grammar

A. Word matching (likenesses and differences) (by sound) (rhyming; endings; initial, medial, final consonants; vowel sounds; word "families")
B. Word meanings (things, action words, describers)
C. Word use (sentences; following more complicated directions)

Level III: Abstract Comprehension (auditory)

A. Details (who, what, when, where, why)
B. Main ideas (in sentences, paragraphs, stories, books)
C. Summarizing
D. Taking notes during a listening experience

Level IV: Applications (auditory)

A. Separating fact from opinion
B. Auditory studying (accumulating information through listening)
C. Miscellaneous applications
   1. Using sound clues in mobility
   2. Giving directions
   3. Using auditory clues (words, tones) to discern feelings, personalities, attitudes)
   4. Other auditory study skills (previewing, scanning, locating information on a tape)

Note: Some suggested games or activities for teaching listening skills are listed in the Appendix under "Listening Skills."

Touch: The sense of touch is limited by the length of the learner's arms. It is also dependent on the child's tactual awareness, motivation to explore tactually, and cognitive ability to make sense out of what has been touched. Unless an object or substance is touchable, the visually impaired learner cannot acquire tactual information from it. Therefore, although the sense of touch is a valuable support sense, it should not be relied upon solely to provide information; it should be a reinforcing sense to verify auditory and/or visual information.

The most basic level of tactual training is awareness. A child must be intrigued by differences in textures, and must *want* to explore them with fingers, hands, feet, and sometimes with the entire body. Providing a wide variety of textures to explore is critical to motivating tactual learning. Note that the visual appearance of the object to the teacher should not be the deciding factor in selecting textures; some common but visually unattractive objects (like plastic kitchen scrubbers or carpet squares) may be tactually attractive to a blind child, similarly, objects that may be visually attractive may be tactually boring. Many blind children find smooth plastic uninteresting. If in doubt, let the visually impaired child have a chance to explore the substance tactually; interest will usually be obvious in the way the child holds, rubs, probes, and manipulates the object.

A few visually impaired children will be "tactually defensive" (i.e., may seem to reject tactual contact). The TVI will probably try first to determine possible causes. (e.g., Some visually impaired children have had extensive medical treatment early in life and have experienced discomfort from unexpected tactual contact; such negative experiences may have made them tactually apprehensive. Other possibilities include over-stimulation or unusual tactual sensitivity.) If no apparent cause can be determined, the TVI will probably develop a program of gradual and pleasant introduction to tactual stimuli. The less vision the child possesses, the more difficult the program may be, and the more gradual the introduction of tactual stimuli. It is also true, however, that the less vision present, the more important the development of tactual perception becomes. A blind child will need to acquire a high level of tactual ability in order to learn braille, and the program of tactual stimulation can be a critical instructional area for that child.

Smell and Taste: These senses are interrelated, and can be stimulated either separately or together. The TVI will probably structure a program to introduce a variety of odors and tastes, especially to a young visually impaired child. Although these senses may be minor in their ability to provide useful information, they can be used effectively to discriminate substances for safety purposes (particularly in the kitchen, but also sometimes in the bathroom). The sense of smell can also provide mobility clues for individuals with low vision or who are blind.

MOTOR SKILLS

The instructional program in the area of motor development is concentrated primarily in the preschool years, when motor development is a major skills area. Appropriate intervention, done early enough, and on a continual/sequential basis, can minimize motor delays. Even a totally blind child can develop nearly age appropriate motor capabilities, especially in the gross motor areas (walking, running, jumping, climbing). Fine motor skills may take additional time and practice to acquire proficiency, but the TVI can include some objectives in this area on the IEP if needed. (Examples of fine motor skills include grasping, manipulating objects in the hands, using fingers independently to probe or poke, finger feeding, manipulating clothing fasteners, holding a writing implement, using scissors, tracing/tracking with fingers, etc.)

The Orientation and Mobility instructor can also work on motor development through instruction in body image, posture, gait, and body movement. School-age visually impaired students can refine motor skills during physical education activities and on the playground, with suggestions from the TVI or O&M instructor for emphasis or modifications. (See also Chapter Seven for suggestions in motor development during the preschool years.)

CONCEPT DEVELOPMENT

This instructional area is primarily a preschool concern but may need reinforcement during later school years. The kind of activities commonly offered in nursery school and kindergarten are structured specifically to build basic concepts, but the visually impaired child may need extra emphasis on the auditory and tactual aspects of these experiences. When basic concepts are not mastered at the preschool level, the visually impaired child must have additional experience and instruction during the primary years. The TVI may need to review and/or reinforce basic concepts before the child can have success in his/her academics. A list of selected basic concepts might include:

Size: big, little, large, small, fat, thin, wide, narrow, long, short, tall

Shape: round, circle, square, box, rectangle, triangle, pyramid, cone, oval, star, cross, X

Location: right, left, up, down, top, bottom, middle, back, front, beside, center, between, inside, outside, behind, in front of, in back of, next to, above, below, skip (as in "skip one")

Distance: far, near, close, away (as in "go away"), nearest, farthest, away from

Height: tall, short, high, low
Weight: heavy, light
Color: names of colors (red, blue, yellow, green, orange, purple, black, brown, white)
names of shades (pink, gray, aqua/turquoise, lime, maroon, tan, beige, charcoal, auburn, blonde, brunette)
Texture: rough, smooth, hard, soft, scratchy, bumpy, crisp
Temperature: hot, cold, warm, cool, tepid, freezing, boiling
Moisture: wet, dry, damp, moist, sweaty
Smell: sweet, comparisons (like chocolate, like perfume, like oranges, etc.)
Taste: sweet, sour, salty
Sound/Pitch: high, low, loud, soft
Quantity: few, many, more, less, a lot, half, some, whole, several, pair, zero/none, equal
Comparison Terms: like, different, same, almost, as many, matches, alike, most, least, enough, not enough, too many
Time: today, yesterday, tomorrow, week, month, year, present, past, future, minute, second, hour, night, day, seasons
Mobility Concepts: corner, intersections ("T," "X"), angles (right angle, 45° angle, parallel, perpendicular, adjacent to/next to, right hand/left hand, block (as a city block), building, driveway, sidewalk, curb, stairs, steps, railing, elevator, escalator, moving walkway, compass directions (north, south, east, west), room, floor, ceiling, doorway, window
Ordinals: first, second, third, fourth, fifth, etc., last

COMMUNICATION SKILLS

Chapter Seven has discussed the impact of a visual impairment on early language development, but language is only one aspect of communication. Nonverbal communication (gestures and body language) is primarily visual and must be taught; this area of communication is usually included with social skills instruction.

Reading readiness, whether in visual or tactual media (i.e., print or braille), may not occur as early as in sighted children, and the TVI may pay special attention to the particular and preparatory skills needed to make a visually impaired child ready for a structured reading program. For a child with useful vision, basic concepts will need to be well developed, and visual efficiency instruction may be needed. For blind children, a separate set of readiness factors may be involved; these include basic concepts in auditory and/or tactual form, postural independence (the ability to sit alone, in an upright position, without using the hands for support), hand/finger dexterity (independent finger use, range of hand movement, tactual sensitivity), an awareness of braille as a reading media, and a sense of "bookness" (knowing that language can be written down in sequential form to create sentences and stories on pages in order).

Structured reading instruction will depend on the medium selected. For visually impaired children who will be print readers, instruction can occur in the regular classroom with sighted peers; modifications or adaptations may be needed (and will be suggested by the TVI) but actual reading instruction will be provided by the regular classroom teacher. For students who will learn braille, the TVI will provide the instruction (usually on a "pull-out" basis, since the process differs from print reading instruction, and may be noisy when a braillewriter is used). A few students may receive instruction in both print reading and braille when the literacy medium choice does not indicate a clear preference, or when a dual media decision is possible; in such cases, the classroom teacher may be providing print reading instruction while the TVI will provide instruction in braille.

After the basic literary code has been mastered (both in reading and writing, using the braillewriter), other braille codes can be introduced as needed. Sometimes the math code (Nemeth) is introduced simultaneously with the literary code, or shortly after the greater part of the literary code has been presented. Foreign languages, music, and/or scientific braille codes are only introduced as needed (usually well after the literary code has been mastered).

Sometime during about the third grade, the slate and stylus is introduced as an alternative means of writing braille. This tool is useful for note-taking, or when a portable literacy device is needed.

Handwriting: Sighted children observe others using pencils, pens, or other writing tools to make meaningful marks on paper; they imitate this behavior, first by scribbling, making individual marks, and then by forming those marks into letters. They "write" before they know what writing really is. Visually impaired children may not observe others using writing implements and don't imitate because they haven't observed. They may not be motivated to "write" because they are not aware that people write. Part of readiness for writing consists of establishing a familiarity with writing as a communication technique. Visually impaired children must be shown, either visually or tactually, that abstract configurations (letters or raised dots) have meaning, that they can be combined to form words, sentences, and stories, and that people can record them in some kind of re-usable form. It is the ability to record their abstract configurations that constitutes "writing."

The teaching of handwriting takes very different forms and directions for visually impaired children, depending on the amount and quality of available vision. For those with a great deal of useful vision (the children that will probably be print readers), handwriting instruction may require no more than a modified approach and adapted materials (paper with dark lines, a soft lead pencil or black felt-tip marker). Block printing becomes a collection of figures formed from horizontal, vertical, diagonal, and curved lines. The easiest letters use only vertical and horizontal lines (E, F, H, I, L, T) and the next group adds diagonals (A, K, M, N, V, W, X, Y, Z). When curves are added to straight lines, another set of figures can be formed (B, D, J, P, R, U). The letters formed from *all* curves are added (C, G, O, Q) and the final, most difficult letter (S) completes the alphabet. When lower case letters are introduced, a similar approach can be followed. Those with similar configurations are presented in groups (a, c, e, o; m, n, h, r; l, t, f; v, x, w, y; b, d, p, q, g; i, j) and the similarities between some lower case and upper case letters are pointed out (Cc, Kk, Oo, Pp, Ss, Uu, Vv, Ww, Xx, Zz). Differences in height or line position can be emphasized by showing that some are "turtle letters"– stay within the half-space (a, c, e, i, m, n, o, r, s, u, v, w, x, z), some have tall necks like a giraffe (b, d, f, h, k, l, t), and others have tails like a monkey (g, j, p, y). A dark ruled line can be drawn to indicate both side margins of the paper so the child knows where to begin writing and does not write off the edge of the paper.

When letters are put together to form words, some visually impaired students have difficulty spacing between words. Suggest that the child place the index finger of the non-writing hand at the end of the word and begin the next word on the other side of the finger. Emphasis should be on legibility, rather than "penmanship" form. Handwriting is not usually very neat for most visually impaired students, but it should be legible.

For students with low vision, writing may be larger and darker than normal and may require wider spacing between dark lines. If a low vision device is used (e.g., a hand-held or stand magnifier or CCTV), the TVI will probably coordinate handwriting practice with instruction and practice using the magnification device.

The blind child will probably not learn handwriting until much later, and the proficiency level will vary from a simple signature to the use of block letters. A few exceptional blind students may acquire sufficient handwriting (printing) skill to give written responses to short-answer questions on tests, but the legibility may be marginal. All blind children should learn to sign their own name, using a signature guide (special tool to align their writing in an appropriate position), and some may become proficient enough to write checks independently (using a special check guide). The TVI will assume responsibility for teaching either script writing or printing to blind children when the skill is appropriate.

The blind child who is motivated to "write" (beyond a signature) may be able to use the format of the braille cell to learn the configurations of block letters. Since the dots are numbered (from top to bottom, left column first), most configurations can be taught by numbers (e.g., C would be 4-1-2-3-6; L would be 1-2-3-6; E would be 4-1-2-5-2-3-6; etc.). The process of learning block letter configurations in this manner is slow, but motivation can make up for time if a blind student wants very much to communicate with peers. Again, introduce similar letters by similar configurations. Raised line models may help in building the perception of shape.

The braille cell can also be used to teach a simple script; it will appear "squarish" but will be legible. (See Appendix C for the alphabet in block letters, using the braille cell as a reference.)

When the visually impaired child who has learned manuscript printing is ready to learn cursive writing (and some visually impaired children never make this transition successfully, but should be given the opportunity to try), the TVI will probably be involved in the instructional process. Correct letter formation is important, and instruction should be closely supervised. It is easier for a visually impaired child to learn the connecting technique if all letters are taught as *beginning on the line* (as *a* not *a*). Use familiar, easy words as practice exercises as soon as possible (possibly even spelling words, if all letters in the words have been introduced). This teaches the connective technique at the same time the letters are introduced. Special attention should be given to letters connecting with b, o, v, and w. The connective ending of these letters affects the beginning of the next letter. Combination errors occur commonly when m, n, and x follow o or w, but attention should be given to *any* letter following b, o, v, or w.

Introduce similar letters individually or in groups, depending on how quickly the child masters them. A suggested order or grouping that introduces several vowels early (facilitating the practice with words) may be as follows: c, a, d, g, o, q; i, u, w, t; j, p; b, h, k; f; m, n; v, x, y, z; r; s. If difficulty is experienced in any group or on an individual letter, do not progress to the next letter or group until the difficult ones are mastered.

Postpone capital letters until lower case letters are mastered. (The reverse is true of manuscript printing–the child usually begins with block capitals and progresses to lower case.) Capitals may be introduced in a different order than the lower case. Begin with those that resemble their matching lower case "brother" (A, C, M, N, O, P, Y, Z). Progress to those that resemble the block printing capital (B, D, E, H, K, L, R, S, U, W, X). Finally add the more difficult capitals (F, T, G, I, J, Q, V). Point out those capitals that may connect to the following lower case letter (A, C, E, I, J, K, L, M, N, Q, R, U, Y, Z) and those that must end independently of the following lower case letter (B, D, F, G, H, O, P, S, T, V, W, X). Listing of names, places, days of the week, and months of the year will give adequate practice with capital formations. A technique that might also be used is to list children's first names that begin with each letter of the alphabet.

A copy of suggested form of the cursive alphabet (lower case and capitals) is Figure 11. Where formation differs from the handwriting program's suggested use in the school, adapt it for the child.

To summarize important points about handwriting instruction:

1. The visually impaired child must have certain prerequisite *skills:*
   a. The ability to grasp and hold a writing tool;
   b. A concept of directionality (including the ability to change direction when making a curved line);

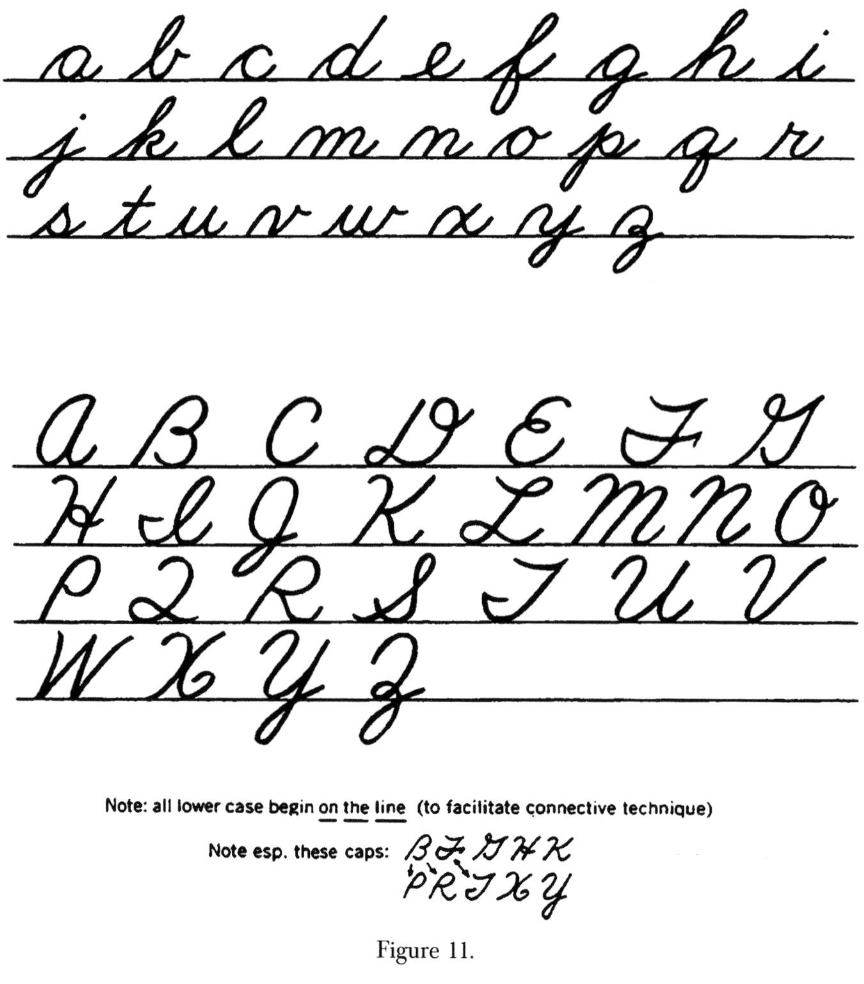

a b c d e f g h i
j k l m n o p q r
s t u v w x y z

A B C D E F G
H I J K L M N O
P Q R S T U V
W X Y Z

Note: all lower case begin on the line (to facilitate connective technique)

Note esp. these caps: B F G H K
P R T X Y

Figure 11.

c. The ability to remember shapes and/or shape combinations; and
d. The motivation (or incentive) to write.

2. The visually impaired child must have certain prerequisite *concepts:*
   a. For block printing: top, bottom, right, left, up, down, upper, lower, middle, halfway, center, corner, side, horizontal, vertical, diagonal/slanting, round curve, circle, right curve, left curve;
   b. For cursive writing (in addition to the above): point, dot, cross, loop, hook, mountain, valley, right loop, left loop, upper loop, lower loop.
3. Practice materials might include:
   a. Fingerpaints, blackboard and chalk, paper and crayons, screenboard and crayons
   b. Clay and pointed dowels, aluminum sheets and a ballpoint pen, raised-line drawing kit
   c. Dark-lined paper of various widths, raised-line paper, graph paper
   d. Markers, felt-tip pens, crayons
   e. Writing guide, signature guide, check guide
4. Reminders:
   a. The amount of available vision will determine which approach to use, and how much legibility to expect.
   b. Teach *applications* of handwriting (e.g., note taking, labeling, check writing, signatures).

Typing/Keyboarding: The visually impaired child will, at some time during the educative process, add the skill of typing/keyboarding to his/her personal skills. Since handwriting is often poor, typing/keyboarding offers a means of preparing assignments in neat, organized form, and is a means of written communication for personal purposes.

In the current technological environment, word processing (the use of a computer instead of a typewriter) may be an equal or better skill than typing, but the initial learning of basic keyboard letter positions serves both typewriter use and computer applications. The fact that computers are being introduced as early as kindergarten (effective or not) has generated some discussion about how to begin keyboard instruction. Should a child be allowed to "hunt and peck" to maintain interest in the process of access, or should correct keyboard position be taught at the start? A number of factors may need to be considered when deciding which route to take:

1. What is the extent of the visual impairment? Can the child see the keyboard or screen clearly enough to make visual use of the display data, and will he/she use that vision also to locate keys? Or, will a voice synthesizer be required to interpret the screen output? The intent of both typing and computer use is to simplify the communication process; if there is just enough

vision to hunt for keyboard keys, the amount of vision may be a *handicap* for efficient keyboard use, and a totally nonvisual approach to computer use (touch typing and voice output) may be indicated.

2. Is there sufficient hand size and manual coordination dexterity to use a keyboard with both hands? Most children in kindergarten or first grade do not have big enough hands, wide enough finger reach, or adequate coordination to learn to type or use a two-handed approach to a computer keyboard. Neither typing nor keyboarding will be appropriate until these problems are resolved.

3. Personality and motivation may be factors in using either a typewriter or computer keyboard. Few young children are able to (or should be expected to) sit still long enough to learn proper hand position. Learning to type or use a keyboard requires concentration, attention, and repeated practice–none of which are common among young children.

4. Is the "pay off" big enough? Unless there is fun, learning that is pleasurable, or an increase in function, typing/keyboarding instruction may be a waste of time until the rewards are worth the effort. For most children (including those who are visually impaired), that point is usually not reached until around third grade.

5. Will print be useful reading media for this child? If he/she cannot read what has been typed/printed, errors cannot be self-corrected, and the end product may be as bad as the child's own handwriting. If the child is (or will be) a braille reader, self-correction may depend on a screen reader or a "spell-check" program. Blind children will probably learn to type or use a computer keyboard (given sufficient cognitive ability) out of necessity–to create documents in print for sighted teachers or employers. In the current job market, a computer user has a decided advantage (an employability "edge"); therefore, the skill of typing/keyboarding must be taught at some point in school.

The decision for visually impaired students is not *whether* to begin typing instruction and/or keyboarding, but *when,* and is highly individual; the TVI can provide expertise in assisting with that decision. If the child has been "playing" with a computer keyboard for several years, there may be some bad search and locate habits to break. It is vital that hand position be taught, however, if any speed or efficiency is to be expected. Tactual motor patterns ("reach" patterns) must be established in the brain without visual interference. (Each time a student *looks* to find a key or to establish hand position, the motor pattern is interrupted and the delay interferes with the development of speed; the best typists rarely, if ever, look at the keys.) Supervised typing/keyboarding instruction is essential, and supervised practice is highly desirable, so that correct "reach patterns" are established in the brain. Slow,

TABLE 4. PRINT ENLARGING SYSTEMS: VIDEO

Name	*Advantage*	*Disadvantage*
Closed Circuit Television (CCTV); uses a small TV camera to enlarge to a TV monitor; models include: Optelec, Vantage, Clear View, Big Picture	Enlarges anything (including handwriting and relatively flat objects like coins); has the ability to increase or decrease contrast, provide black print on white background or white print on black background, or color; can be placed in a classroom or library.	Electrical outlet needed; print may be too big; large, bulky, not easily transported, difficult for users with fine motor coordination problems, only a portion of a page can be viewed at a time (a problem for charts, tables, graphs, pictures, etc.)
Flipper Clarity Classmate	Small microscope type device which has the same features as larger desktop CCTVs. This device is very portable and can be used for distance or near viewing.	Requires a TV monitor or with an adaptor a computer monitor in each viewing situation.
Flipper Port Jordy	Allows near and distance viewing on sunglass type monitor.	Can disorient user. Can make the student socially uncomfortable
Pocket Viewer Traveller	Allows truly portable viewing on books, paper, handwriting tasks.	No distance viewing. Expensive.

repeated, rhythmic strokes are preferable to "fast" typing; speed will come naturally as the motor patterns become firmly established in the brain. (A sequence of adapted lessons to teach typing can be found in Appendix B.)

TECHNOLOGY

The literal explosion in technology within the past twenty years has revolutionized the area of communication for everyone. It has been a mixed blessing in the field of visual impairment; it has opened opportunities for communication while at the same time required both additional funding for extremely expensive special equipment and teachers who are prepared to teach the applications.

At one time, visually impaired students had only a typewriter, tape recorder, Talking Book Machine (special-speed record player), and/or a braillewriter as special equipment. Although these devices helped to make integrated school placements simpler, they didn't solve all problems. The

TABLE 5. PRINT ENLARGING SYSTEMS: COMPUTER SOFTWARE

Equipment	*Software*	*Comments*
Macintosh	inLARGE (Mac OS 7–9), not available for OS X Closeview (included free with Mac OS	Only enlarges, enlarges from 2X to 16X; works with all applications.
Windows Compatible: Windows 95, 98, ME, 2000, XP	ZoomText Xtra Level 1	Magnifies up to 16X, three font styles, usable with any other applications.
	Level 2	Screen enlargement same as Level 1, also includes voice output reading functions. Reads menus, dialog boxes, typing.
	Bigshot	Made by the same company as ZoomText, but allows magnification from 1.5 to 2X only. No speech output.
	Magic	Software application which includes screen magnification and speech.

special teacher still had to translate braille homework into print, so that the regular classroom teacher could read it, and many textbooks were unavailable in recorded form or in braille. Despite these difficulties, hundreds of visually impaired students succeeded in school because creative TVIs and cooperative classroom teachers worked together to make the educational process effective.

Today, available technology has the potential to increase visually impaired students' control over educational materials and can allow direct contact with classroom activities. There are systems and software to enlarge print spontaneously, software to enable computers to "talk," self-contained electronic equipment to allow blind students to take notes or to read print, and software that will translate braille to print. The visually impaired student in the regular classroom is only limited by the availability of technology and a TVI to instruct how to use it.

The following charts describe some selected technology currently available. By the time this book is in print, there will probably be even more. Hopefully, software designers will also have solved such current problems as how blind computer users can recognize increasingly visual screen formats–e.g., "icons," or graphical user interface (GUI). This screen accessibility has

TABLE 6. SOFTWARE TO MAKE COMPUTERS "TALK": SCREEN READERS

Equipment	*Software*	*Comments*
Macintosh OS 7–9	OutSPOKEN	This screenreader is not supported on OS X. Best results are achieved when color is turned off. Screen readers read not only what the user types, but menus and dialog boxes and other user controls.
Windows	JAWS	Available for all versions of Windows up to XP. Also called JFW: JAWS for Windows. Voice output for all applications and menus, dialog boxes, and other user controls.
	Window-Eyes	Can be used with any version of Windows up to Win XP. Voice output for all applications and menus, dialog boxes, and other user controls.
Self-voicing applications	Math Flash	Arithmetic drill and practice program. Includes voice output and large fonts. Teacher can control the difficulty level and the operations used (i.e., two digit subtraction).
	Learn Keys	When user types letters or control keys on the keyboard, Learn Keys speaks the letter or function.
	Talking Typer	Drill and practice touch typing instruction with voice output. Saves data to report speed, errors, letters used.
	Termite	
	Torpedo	

TABLE 7. SOFTWARE TRANSLATORS:
(SOFTWARE THAT CHANGES PRINT TO BRAILLE)

Equipment	*Software*	*Comments*
Macintosh OS 7–9	Duxbury	Translates print to Braille and Braille to print. Contracted (Grade 2) or uncontracted (Grade 1) Braille may be selected, as well as different levels of contracted Braille (Braille Fundamentals curriculum clusters) are included.
Windows Win 95 to XP	Duxbury Megadots Developed for DOS, but can be used in Windows	Translates print to Braille and Braille to print. Contracted (Grade 2) or uncontracted (Grade 1) Braille may be selected, as well as different levels of contracted Braille (Braille Fundamentals curriculum clusters) are included.

the potential for expanding job opportunities for visually impaired people, and for reducing the high unemployment rate among them. Although employment is largely an adult problem, and beyond the scope of this book, the preparation process must begin during the school years; the efficient use of technology is part of that preparation.

TACTUAL/VISUAL GRAPHICS

Chapter Eight contains discussion of modifications for tables, charts, graphs, maps, and other representational data presentations. The TVI will be able to make suggestions for classroom applications, particularly in math, science, and social studies, but will assume the responsibility for teaching the visually impaired student how to utilize these modified graphics most efficiently. Many basic concepts are necessary for effective use of graphic material, and the TVI should evaluate each student's level of understanding; remediation will be part of the IEP when basic concepts are determined to be lacking or poorly developed. Such remediation can be as basic as concrete explorations of forms, tactual completion of three-dimensional puzzles, or practice in tracing lines with the fingers. Whole-hand exploration provides more information than finger tracing, but raised-line drawings may require

TABLE 8. SELF-CONTAINED TECHNOLOGY: NOTETAKERS

Braille keyboard: Braille 'n' Speak 640 APH Braille Scholar Braille Lite (refreshable Braille display) Braille Lite Millenium (refreshable Braille display) *QWERTY keyboards:* Type 'n' Speak Type Lite (refreshable Braille display)	DOS-based portable note taking device. Includes word processor, scientific calculator, phone book, apointment calendar. Input is in Braille, output may be print or Braille (requires external printer or embosser), synthesized speech, can transfer files to and from a Windows computer, requires external disk drive. Options include spell checker, games, checkbook program. Useful for students from about third grade and above.
Braille keyboard: BrailleNote BT (refreshable Braille display) VoiceNote BT *QWERTY keyboard:* VoiceNote QT BrailleNote QT (refreshable Braille display)	Windows CE based portable note taking device. Include word processor, email, daily planner, book reader, address list, web browser, and scientific calculator. Files can be easily transferred between the note taker and Windows computers. Includes built-in slot for compact flash memory card. Ethernet port for connection to high speed Internet. Optional global positioning system.
Braille keyboard: PAC Mate BNS *QWERTY keyboard:* PAC Mate TNS	Windows Pocket PC based device. Uses JAWS screen reading software to access the Windowns Pocket PC operation system. Includes word processor, calculator, web browser, email. Uses off-the-shelf Windows Pocket PC software if they are compatible with JAWS. Uses USB port to sync with computer to transfer files. Includes built-in slot for compact flash memory card. Ethernet port for connection to high speed Internet. Refreshable Braille display optional.
Mountbatten Braille Writer Mountbatten Pro	Electronic Braille writer. Is capable of producing Braille without an external embosser. Files may be transferred to and from the Mountbatten to a computer. Text may be input with a computer keyboard. Can be connected to a printer for print copies.

TABLE 9. MISCELLANEOUS TECHNOLOGY

Franklin Language Master	A small speech enabled dictionary and thesaurus; has a small QWERTY keyboard, headphones, and a large type display.
Orion Talking Scientific Calculator	Based on the popular TI-34 calculator from Texas Instruments with speech output. Allows general ed math teacher to assist the blind student.
Tiger Braille Graphics Embosser	Windows based embosser which can produce tactile graphic displays of any graphic produced in Windows. Can also produce Braille. The best choice for producing maps, graphs, and other math, science, and social studies graphics.
Accessible Graphing Calculator	Works in Windows as a fully functional graphing scientific calculator. Has multisensory feedback which allows the visually impaired student to use it. Interfaces well with the Tiger for output of tactile graphs.
Book Port A previous version of this device was called the Road Runner	Portable device designed to read electronic books to blind students. Two by four inches in size, has a built-in text to speech synthesizer for reading electronic text and web pages. Also plays digital audio files such as MP3 and DAISY digital talking books. Transfers files from computer to device via USB port or compact flash. Contains built-in microphone for recording.

(The technology charts were reviewed and updated by Sharon Nichols, Outreach Technology Consultant at the Texas School for the Blind and Visually Impaired. Sharon's help is gratefully acknowledged and greatly appreciated.

the understanding of single-line representations. A visual picture does not always translate easily to a tactual outline that provides the same information; therefore, the visually impaired student may need practice in tactual interpretation. This ability will be crucial to understanding the "codes" used in "keys" for maps and graphs, and may need to be taught specifically by the TVI.

ORGANIZATIONAL AND STUDY SKILLS

This is an area that is usually *assumed* (rarely specifically taught) for sighted learners, but for visually impaired students, there are many related skills that must be specifically taught. "Organization" is largely a visual concept, so alternative methods must be devised to make it a tactual or auditory capability. It is the foundation for good study skills, and is usually introduced as early as possible.

The organization of time and information is the first level, and includes keeping a desk neat (everything in a specific place), loading a backpack efficiently (many visually impaired students use backpacks to carry bulky materials from class to class), keeping shelves or locker reasonably neat, labeling shelves or drawers, using pocket pages and dividers in a notebook, and keeping an assignment book current. Another organizational tool is learning to manage time by prioritizing and planning, based on the due dates and extent of time needed to complete assignments. Visually impaired students may miss reminders on the blackboard, and need to be constantly aware of impending assignment due dates. Having a visual impairment is no excuse for handing in assignments late, and it should not be tolerated by classroom teachers unless there are extenuating circumstances. The visually impaired student should have notified the teacher in advance if such is the case (e.g., the unavailability of a print reference on tape or in braille, although the student should have attempted to *get* it read on tape by an aide, librarian, or volunteer). Information management (a filing system, or some orderly means of keeping notes in consecutive order) and time management are two basic skills that, if well-learned in school, will serve the visually impaired student well in life.

Specific study skills that might be taught by the TVI include:

1. Listening for information;
2. Note-taking alternatives;
3. Methods of obtaining information written on the blackboard;
4. Use of skimming/scanning techniques in reading;
5. Use of acronyms or mnemonics to facilitate memorizing;
6. Using indices and/or tables-of-contents effectively;
7. Use of tools (stapler, scissors, glue/paste, paper clips, paper punch, etc.);
8. Special test-taking techniques (using special answer sheets, multiple-choice-questions attack methods, oral testing, alternatives to matching on tests, etc.);
9. Library skills (accessing printed materials, using dictionaries and encyclopedias, understanding the card catalogue system, using note-cards in braille or print, making outlines);

10. Procedures for getting equipment repaired when the TVI is not available to help;
11. Procedures for ordering special texts or adapted editions of texts;
12. Locating and using human readers effectively;
13. Using the telephone to access information;
14. Using a computer to access information;
15. Making the best of audio-visual formats (transparencies, filmstrips, videos, films, etc.); and
16. Using tactual graphics effectively.

SOCIAL SKILLS

This is one of the most important special skill areas of the core curriculum for visually impaired students since social skills are critical to positive life adjustments for visually impaired persons. Even the earliest social interaction between a visually impaired infant and its mother (e.g., making eye contact, smiling, "bonding") may be adversely affected by the child's impaired visual abilities. Preferential smiling may be more the result of hand contact with a familiar caregiver's face, hands, or body, since visually impaired infants are more likely to use smiling as a *response* (rather than an initiating behavior). The first consistent initiating social behavior involves reaching toward a familiar voice (which occurs at about the same time as "reach-to-sound" and people permanence, about 10–12 months of age). A delay in the ability to initiate social interaction may already have begun before a visually impaired child is a year old.

As the visually impaired child begins to structure his/her world of things and people, other delays in social skills may appear. The identification of "me" and "not-me" or "mine" and "yours" may depend on the child's ability to discriminate between self and others, and the visual sense contributes a considerable amount of information in this process. The more useful vision a child has, the easier this transition to "self" vs others will be. Moreover, it will be easier to recognize authority figures, anticipate problems, and develop personal values related to self and others.

As gestures become an important part of social interactions (e.g., head-nodding to indicate "yes" or "no," hand-shaking as a greeting, facial expression to show emotion), a visual impairment can interfere with the spontaneous learning of these behaviors. Structured observation, evaluation, and instruction in gestural communication may be essential parts of an educational program for visually impaired children. Even basic courtesies (such as waiting patiently in line, acknowledging the presence of a respected elder, or requesting information from a stranger) involve the ability to see, and impaired vision impacts upon the development of these skills.

In public situations (i.e., in the presence of other people, whether sighted or visually impaired), the lack of vision may affect social confidence and social interaction. The degree of visual efficiency may have a direct relationship to the extent of social behaviors that are productive and effective. Blind persons may have difficulty in initiating conversation if they are unaware of who is nearby and their exact location. As a result, many visually impaired persons choose to remain socially passive, rather than risk embarrassment. If social skills, particularly those involved in interpersonal relationships, were evaluated and taught in educational settings, the integration process might be less painful and more productive. Research has shown that social skills may be one of the most important areas to evaluate in determining readiness for mainstreaming in school and society. Therefore, a careful observation of the quality and quantity of a child's social skills should precede a carefully structured program of instruction in this critical area of daily living.

Some examples of social skills that might be included in a structured program of instruction in this area include:

1. Nonverbal communication (gestures: waving, head nodding/shaking to indicate "yes" or "no," pointing, shoulder shrugging, shaking hands, hugging/kissing appropriately, covering the mouth when yawning;
2. Recognition of and appropriate expressions of emotion;
3. Conversation (initiating, maintaining, ending; facing the speaker; voice modulation);
4. Good manners (Please/Thank You/Excuse Me; greeting someone; use of a napkin; sitting appropriately–with legs crossed or closed, for a female; covering mouth when sneezing or coughing; extinguishment of negative behaviors such as nose picking, scratching, twitching, rocking, swaying; public behaviors such as eating at a restaurant vs eating at a fast-foods establishment;
5. Social dancing;
6. Taking turns;
7. Introducing two people (the protocols);
8. Participation in group games;
9. Dating/sexual behaviors that are appropriate;
10. Telephone use/telephone manners;
11. Using a vending machine;
12. Using leisure time appropriately;
13. Asking friends or acquaintances to use "sighted guide" technique, correctly and appropriately;
14. Informing others about own visual impairment.

There are also some guidelines for instruction, in the form of a list of "Do's" and "Don'ts."

DO:

1. Encourage independence.
2. Encourage the development of leisure skills, both personal and in groups.
3. Learn survival skills (handling money, traveling, etc.).
4. Practice reciprocal conversation.
5. Learn acceptable manners.
6. Learn to manage emotions; a sense of humor helps.
7. Learn the difference between assertiveness and aggression.
8. Learn the basics of good grooming.
9. Develop a knowledge of the world of work.
10. Develop helping skills; the visually impaired person needs to be able to offer a sighted helper something in return.
11. Learn coping strategies ("What do I do if . . . ?").
12. Learn to show appreciation and reciprocal behaviors.
13. Learn the vernacular.
14. Conform to groups mores until comfortable with the group. (Individualism is good, but not until it is appropriate.)
15. During the learning period, keep anxiety at a minimum by making social situations relatively brief.

DON'T:

1. Teach skills in isolation; they must be transferrable.
2. Expect to be like someone else; each person is unique.
3. Overschedule activities; hurrying creates confusion.
4. Monopolize conversations; listening is part of the game.
5. Expect special privileges; "belonging" means fitting in.
6. Expect others to solve your problems; learn to problem-solve independently.
7. Confuse aggressive and assertive; one feels angry, while the other is calm.
8. Expect perfection; "Rome wasn't built in a day!"
9. Accept withdrawal; social means interaction.
10. Try to joke too early; humor is a useful tool, but can be embarrassing if used inappropriately.

Remember that the visually impaired child has only others to teach appropriate social skills; silence does not teach these skills.

Social skills instruction at school may be ineffective if there is no "carry-over" at home. Part of the role of the TVI may be to talk with the visually impaired student's family, and to make suggestions for their involvement in the social skills instructional program. Some tips for parents might include:

1. Teach acceptable manners, in a variety of situations.
2. Teach practical skills.
3. Encourage problem-solving.
4. Encourage independence.
5. Encourage the development of interests, talents, and capabilities.
6. Discuss social situations, before and after . . .
7. Provide structured activities that practice social skills.
8. Encourage group participation activities (clubs, social groups, teams, Boy/Girl Scouts).
9. Help the child to dress as his/her peers do.
10. Explain visual cues/body language.
11. Don't accept inappropriate behavior–EVER!
12. Give family responsibilities, and expect performance.

(The list of "Do's" and "Don'ts" and the list of parent tips were adapted from a presentation by Olivia Schoenberger, the Vision Consultant from the Region 19 Education Service Center in El Paso, Texas.)

SELF-HELP/DAILY LIVING SKILLS

Sighted children have learned to feed themselves, dress themselves, wash their hands, and brush their teeth largely by watching other people perform these tasks. Visually impaired children are often unable to observe even the most simple of these activities, and may even be unaware that they can do them. A whole set of independence skills must be taught specifically to visually impaired students, and this part of the core curriculum spans the educational years from preschool through high school. From the first attempt to pull off a bootie or hold a bottle until clothing colors are matched appropriately, make-up is applied neatly, a napkin is used in socially accepted ways, each self-help skill must be taught to each visually impaired child. The TVI should include an evaluation of proficiency in life skills as part of the comprehensive assessment and will probably include objectives related to independent self-care in the IEP. Instruction can take place at school when an appropriately related site is available (e.g., home economics suite that includes a kitchen, bedroom, and living areas) or at the child's home when it can be arranged. Real-life settings are preferable to "pretending" (e.g., teach shopping skills at a mall or grocery store; teach clothing care by actually using a washer or dryer; make real telephone calls on a real telephone). There are checklists and special curricula available that list skills in sequential order, and the TVI should have these available when providing life skills instruction.

Examples of life skills include:

1. *Clothing-related skills:* removing clothing; putting on clothing (including special items, such as pantyhose, bra); tying shoe laces; manipulating fasteners (snaps, zippers, buttons, hooks, buckles); selecting/buying clothing; organizing clothing; caring for clothing (laundry, dry cleaning, etc.); clothing repairs; elements of style (matching colors/styles, dressing appropriately for the occasion, peer styles).
2. *Food-related skills:* using utensils (spoon, fork, knife) and tableware (cup, bowl, plate); using a straw; table manners (using a napkin; using a "pusher"); pouring; drinking from a fountain; eating specialty foods (appropriate use of the fingers with corn-on-the-cob, watermelon, fried chicken; use of utensils with spaghetti).
3. *Hygiene and Grooming skills:* toileting (use of a urinal for boys; concept of privacy; for young children, indicating the need to use the bathroom); washing hands, hair; brushing teeth; brushing or combing hair; bathing/showering; blowing and wiping nose; use of deodorant/mouthwash; shaving; applying/removing make-up; feminine hygiene.
4. *Home Management skills:* food shopping/storage/preparation; measuring both liquids and solids; disposing of garbage; dusting/making a bed; folding towels; watering house plants; changing lightbulbs; changing fuses/using a circuit breaker; opening/closing doors (both room and cabinet); manipulating locks; using trash containers; organizing storage.
5. *Practical Safety skills:* dealing with strangers; dialing 911; answering the door; using a telephone; knowing one's name, address, phone number, and social security number; what to do in case of fire, tornado, flood.
6. *Practical School-related skills:* managing a lock on a locker; using public toilets; going through the cafeteria line; managing medications when necessary; what to do if the school bus is missed at the end of the school day; using vending machines and public telephones.
7. *Personal/Financial Management skills:* self advocacy; time management; consumerism; money (coin identification, identifying/storing bills, making change); banking; checking accounts; bills; budgets; credit; taxes; insurance.

HUMAN SEXUALITY

Human sexuality is a controversial topic when related to educational curriculum offerings. The ethical and moral considerations must be balanced with the realities of ignorance. Some students may have no other reliable source of information than their school, and some parents may prefer to let the school provide this instruction. Family preferences should always be respected; guidelines (a course outline and/or sample materials) should be provided to parents in advance of actual instruction, and permission obtained to provide the instruction (preferably in writing).

The fact remains that much of the information students accumulate about sexuality has a visual base, and visually impaired students are at a disadvantage in learning about male-female bodies and body changes, roles, and relationships. It may be extremely important for these visually impaired students to have a specific, carefully planned and structured sex education course in school. Such a course should be sequenced and concrete, utilizing anatomically accurate models (even at the earliest levels). Care must be taken to balance the physiological aspects of sexuality with the interpersonal (moral and sociological) implications, so that visually impaired students have sufficient and correct information upon which to develop their own standards of conduct. In a world where the consequences of sexual ignorance can be literally fatal, it is of extreme importance that visually impaired students be able to make informed decisions for their own lives.

The TVI can choose to provide special materials to the designated classroom teacher who provides instruction in human sexuality, or can use the classroom curriculum to teach the visually impaired student apart from sighted peers. Separate instruction may be preferred, since the visually impaired student will be using anatomically correct reproductive models for tactual exploration, and may feel more comfortable doing this with only the TVI present. Parents should be fully informed that instruction will be separate, and should have given written permission. (They also should have had the opportunity to review the materials to be used, and to see the models.) Occasionally, parents may elect to teach their own child what they want him/her to know, and their wishes should be respected; special materials can be loaned to parents to help them describe reproduction and its related processes. The decision about who will teach the visually impaired student about human sexuality is an individual one, and the parents should be involved in that decision.

USING LOW VISION DEVICES

When a specially prescribed optical device has been recommended by a Low Vision Specialist, instruction in its use by that Specialist is often minimal. It is usually the responsibility of the TVI (or Orientation and Mobility Instructor) to teach the visually impaired student how to use the device(s) efficiently. Since there are few structured curricula available for this purpose, the TVI may have to design a practical instructional sequence that is based on the particular device and its use with that individual student. If it is a magnifier, practice should be in a variety of settings, for multiple applications (e.g., reading books, magazines, newspapers, medicine bottles, personal correspondence, recipes, shopping lists, can/box/jar labels, price tags, etc.). If the low vision device is a telescope ("monocular"), practice must include focusing, spotting, tracking, copying from a distance, reading street signs, bus numbers, fast foods menus, etc. Too many good (and often expensive) low vision devices wind up on shelves or in pockets because the individual never learned to use them properly. The TVI should make every attempt to see that this does not occur by providing enough instruction and practice opportunities until the visually impaired student feels comfortable using his/her special device.

LEISURE/RECREATION SKILLS

Educators may not realize that play is largely visual imitation; without sufficient vision to be able to observe others playing or performing tasks, it is hard to accumulate the memories of such activities in such a way as to be able to imitate them. For visually impaired students, play is a concept that must often be taught.

There is very little research about how visually impaired children play, but several conclusions have emerged in the recent literature: the lack of vision *does* produce delays in both the quality and kind of play activities performed by visually impaired young children; the more severe the visual impairment is, the more severe the delays in the play behaviors may be. The ability to *pretend* (i.e., use a representational model or imitate a behavior) is directly related to previous experience with real objects and previous motor experience with behaviors being imitated. These conclusions should be kept in mind when evaluating or teaching play behaviors (and often they *must* be taught).

Some additional considerations should be mentioned. Delays in motor development may be related to the degree of visual loss, particularly if no early intervention program was available. Hands must have been played with before manipulative ability can emerge; a child must be able to sit steadily before his/her hands are free to explore and practice movement; kicking and throwing require a stable and balanced upright posture, as well as spatial orientation based on exploration. Sighted norms cannot be relied upon to provide a framework for play activity if visual impairment has delayed the motor development needed to allow the child to use his body to play activities. Because the population of visually impaired children is diverse in terms of usable vision (ranging from totally blind to considerable useful vision), it can be concluded that the less vision the child has, the less likely he/she will be to have the age-appropriate motor behaviors required for play activities. This is not to say that totally blind children cannot play (or cannot be *taught* to play); it simply means that (1) attention may need to be directed to the prerequisite motor skills needed for a particular activity, and (2) many varied experiences, with *real* objects and events, will have to be provided before the blind child can substitute models (i.e., toys) or representational behaviors (i.e., "pretending") for real objects and events.

Generally, play behaviors for blind children and those with low vision may be atypical in the early years. They may get stalled at the sensorimotor level (continue to mouthe, finger, rub, wave, and bang toys beyond the appropriate ages for the type of play). They may also have less on-task (sustained) play behaviors. Vision provides ideas for creative play approaches, allows the child to imitate play behaviors, and helps to sustain interest in ways that sound and touch cannot equal. Nevertheless, manipulative toys should have lots of auditory and tactual appeal for visually impaired children, and they may need to be demonstrated (physically, show the child what to do with the toy). The visual *appearance* of a toy for a blind child is not nearly as important as how it feels, sounds, smells, tastes, and what it can *do* (or what can be done *with* it).

Toys for solitary play should be interesting to the child. Whether visually appealing (bright or colorful), sound producing, or tactually unique (have a variety of textures, places to poke a finger into, etc.) will depend on the degree of visual impairment. The child with useful vision should have that sense stimulated, while a totally blind child will respond to other characteristics of a toy. (The adult who chooses a toy for a visually impaired child should try experiencing the toy without using vision, in order to evaluate the appeal for touch and hearing.)

If a visually impaired child is tactually defensive, play activities utilizing hot or cold materials, or materials that "blur" tactual sensation (fingerpaint, mud pies, paste, play dough, clay, pudding-painting) should be introduced very gradually; they may have to be discarded if the child cannot accustom to the sensation. "Gooey" materials may actually be a barrier to the development of tactual sensitivity for some visually impaired children. Each child should be evaluated separately if tactual sensitivity is a problem.

Reaching-to-sound is a skill that may not be present until late in the first year. There is a difference in presenting a sound-producing toy to a child (allowing *him/her* to produce the sound) and expecting the child to *reach* for the toy when the sound is produced by the adult. The first approach allows the child to interact with the toy, and to find out what it is or can do; the second approach requires auditory localization skill and auditory processing, and is not as interesting to the child unless he/she already knows what object is making that sound. Children with useful vision are able to combine both auditory and visual clues in monitoring reach, but blind children must depend on a single sense far less accurate than vision.

Purposeful toy play may depend on a number of factors. If the child has sufficient vision to see the cause and effect of a particular toy, or can evaluate the physical attributes (e.g., roundness), the play behaviors may be more cognitively oriented. The meaningful manipulation of moveable parts may depend on whether the child can see what results his motor actions produce on the toy. If manipulation is for its own purpose, only motor patterns are being learned; if manipulation produces observable (able to be experienced) results, learning is taking place, and control can be experienced. The taking apart and putting together of a toy may require careful instruction; the child must experience the "wholeness" before he/she can have an idea how the parts fit together to form that whole. The memory of the "wholeness" provides the goal for assembly, and may even assist in the manipulative process of taking the toy apart. If the child has difficulty in the dismantling or assembling of a toy, it may be that a cognitive skill (sequencing) may not yet be present. Observation of how a child plays with a toy can give insights into past experience and cognitive level.

Block building requires a great deal of manual dexterity and spatial orientation. The simple act of stacking blocks requires many prerequisite skills, and the act of knocking down the "tower" assumes visual ability to appreciate the effect. The blind child can learn to stack blocks and build structures, but there may not be the appreciation for the finished product that the sighted child has. Moreover, knocking down the stack is simply a noise; the child lacks the visual effect of the blocks scattering, and may not realize the possible danger to others if the blocks "go flying." These implications must be taught.

The concept of a "collection" may have to be taught, depending on the amount of vision present. A collection of objects is primarily a visual experience, and the pride or motivation involved may be a very different experience for a visually impaired child. The ultimate purpose may be to share with sighted persons, but the visually impaired collector may have to understand (be taught) the unusual value sighted people place on an accumulation of similar objects.

Solitary play has some associated concerns. If it occurs as a part of the developmental process, and is kept in perspective in the adult years, it serves a necessary purpose. However, if the visually impaired child never moves out of this stage of play, the normal social interactions of growing up and becoming a balanced individual never have a chance to occur. The educator may need to observe what emphasis the visually impaired child places on solitary play activities, and may need to intervene in order to engage the child in other types of play behaviors.

Parallel/associative play begins to involve other persons. The visually impaired child may need to be *made aware* of peers who are playing nearby or who are engaging in similar activities. The child may also need to be taught how to move into the next stage (cooperative play) by initiating social contact. Simply asking to be included ("Can I play, too?") can be a real problem for a child who cannot see how many people are present or what they are doing.

Interactive play can be difficult for visually impaired children. Helping the child to position and move his/her body through the activity or responses ("motoring" him/her through) is a useful technique for teaching this play behavior.

Both cooperative and competitive play may require considerable adaptations. Rules that cannot be observed and formats (e.g., boards, field markings, lanes) that are difficult to explain may need to be discussed, put on tape or in braille, or drawn in raised-line format. Very few games are actually impossible for a visually impaired person to play if some creative thought is given to adaptations or adjustments.

If play can be viewed as a means to learning, it may also be a facilitator of cognitive growth. Piaget believed that play was an indicator of cognitive development, and, for visually impaired children, it may be vital to their cognitive growth. The manipulation of toys, interaction with the environment, and the experiencing of events may lay the groundwork for recognizing object permanence, cause and effect, and physical properties of matter. Properly organized play activities can serve a greater purpose than pleasure for its own sake.

Expanding the topic of play to include leisure and recreational skills also expands the applicable range into adulthood. It is assumed that a broad range of experiences (a "taste" of activities in a number of areas) will be provided at the preschool and possibly through the elementary school levels. During the secondary years, students may begin to exhibit more distinctive preferences and interests. Leisure activities may then be channeled into only a few areas of interest. If a younger student expresses strong interest in (or a talent for) a particular area, this narrowing down of focus may occur earlier.

Programming decisions should be individualized, according to student abilities and interests.

Physical activities (e.g., sports) should consider the motor capabilities of the child, and may need to examine the prerequisite motor skills for a particular activity. Orientation in space and level of independent mobility may also affect the capabilities in these activities. The degree of visual impairment will determine the need for adapted techniques.

Involvement with plants, animals, and nature in general, can represent the child's ability to focus on life beyond him/herself. The extent of visual impairment *may* affect the level of awareness of the interdependency of man and nature. Camping activities are closely related to self-help skills, but require reasonably good orientation and mobility skills. Most activities usually can be adapted to meet individual visual abilities.

The creative arts may provide expressive outlets for emotion and/or creative abilities. Music and dance utilize body movement, listening skills, and emotional sensitivity. These activities may also relate to the spatial orientation and mobility of the individual. It should be noted that decreased visual ability does not result in unusual musical ability, only a more *practiced* auditory skill. Any unusual musical talent should be evaluated as objectively as possible, and nurtured, if present. Although the stereotype of the blind musician still exists, real talent probably occurs with similar frequency as in the sighted population. Both musical and artistic talent should be given every chance to be developed when they occur.

If a visually impaired student exhibits interest in or talent for artistic expression, such ability should be encouraged. Prerequisite abilities may include manual dexterity (fine motor skills), practiced manipulative skill, and the desire to be creative. Early arts and crafts experiences can help to refine hand or finger skill, as well as satisfy the urge to "make something." Photography may be a possible creative outlet for students with low vision, and the familiarity with optical devices may facilitate an introduction to the use of lenses for optical reproduction.

The use of communication media (watching television or listening to the radio/records/ tapes/CDs) may be thought of as a passive leisure activity, but active involvement could convert it into a variety of participatory activities. Creative writing, storytelling, and participation in dramatic productions could convert interest in verbal media from passive to active levels. Playing musical instruments or dancing can make an interest in music a more active pasttime.

The TVI should observe each child for signs of special interests or talents. If such are recognized, they should be developed. For children who do not seem to have any special interests, the TVI may want to introduce a variety of possibilities (attendance at sports events, concerts, museums, exhibits, plays; introducing games such as chess or cards; encouraging participation in peer groups such as Scouts; suggesting that parents provide similar opportunities at home). Managing leisure time in pleasurable, satisfying ways, is as much a skill as learning to read or write. Sighted students are visually stimulated to "do things" but visually impaired pupils may need a little encouragement. Too many visually impaired adults never had opportunities to try new things while they were in school, and end up leading sedentary, passive lives as adults. The TVI has a responsibility not to let this happen if at all possible, and can accomplish this by including at least one goal in the IEP that relates to a leisure time ("fun") activity.

Visually impaired students may need to learn that leisure time can be both constructive and pleasurable. Participating in a sport such as bowling, swimming, hiking or cycling can improve fitness levels as well as provide opportunities for social contacts. Learning to play checkers, cards, or chess can provide mental challenges as well as social pleasure. Intentional management of leisure time can prevent idleness and passivity, while also teaching self-discipline. Recreational pasttimes are rarely acquired "out of the blue" in adulthood; their introduction should be in childhood or youth, and this initial beginning is often part of the special instructional areas for which the TVI is responsible.

CAREER AWARENESS/JOB READINESS

Career awareness beings in infancy when a baby smiles, babbles, or reaches for an attractive toy; social interaction, the ability to communicate, and proactive behaviors are all necessary prerequisites for success in a chosen career. For the visually impaired infant, delays in acquiring skills can also mean delays in becoming ready to enter the world of employment. For this reason, early intervention and the development of job readiness skills are essential components of career/vocational development for visually impaired students.

During the preschool years, a number of preliminary job readiness skills should be taught. Among these are the ability to listen and communicate, independence in self-care, initiative, and a cooperative attitude. An awareness of "work" begins by knowing that "work" and "play" are different, that adults perform tasks to earn money, and that work is part of living. The young child may even begin to pretend to "work" (be a fireman, cowboy, nurse, or teacher), and should perceive these roles in positive ways. For visually impaired children who may not incidentally observe the roles adults assume as "work," intentional opportunities to gain this information should be provided (visits to places of work, mentioning the ways people work and where, and noting the contributions made by various professions or vocations in daily life (e.g., the policeman who "keeps us safe," the farmer who "grows our food," or the postman who "brings our mail").

During most of the school years, the exposure to careers increases, and many job readiness skills are (hopefully) taught or encouraged. Communication skills increase, social interaction improves, and independence develops. Opportunities arise for dealing with authority, the performance/reward process becomes more evident, and personal values/self-confidence/self-concept develops. Hobbies and special interests begin to channel abilities into possible career directions. Chores at home or in school, or part-time/summer jobs introduce children and youth to the arena of responsibility. Visually impaired students must have the same opportunities to develop healthy attitudes towards employment, and need to develop the same job readiness skills. The TVI may be responsible for encouraging good work habits, exposing the student to positive role models, and reminding classroom teachers that grades should be earned, not awarded. The TVI may have to assume the role of vocational counselor in cases where a guidance counselor feels unprepared or unsure of how to guide choices for a visually impaired student. In the best scenario, the TVI acts as an advisor to the guidance counselor and classroom teachers, but allows them to perform their functions as they would with other students.

The TVI may help in locating opportunities for work (part-time jobs, summer employment) and may help in preparing the visually impaired student to meet the job expectations. Too often, visually impaired students have not been encouraged to have part-time jobs because of low expectations, but this deprivation can have devastating long-term effects on the visually impaired student. He/she may have no idea what it takes to get and keep a job, and the personal qualities required for positive job performance. Such simple needs as transportation to and from the work site can become monumental deterrents for the visually impaired student who cannot drive and must use public transportation, and unspoken societal attitudes can erode self-confidence. Sometimes, the TVI and the Orientation and Mobility Instructor can collaborate in getting the visually impaired student ready for a job (assessing the job readiness skills of communication, reliability, promptness, and sociability; learning to use public transportation efficiently). Successful performance in part-time or summer employment can provide invaluable experience in real-world work environments and can lay the groundwork for future career planning.

SELF-ADVOCACY AND INFORMATION ACCESS

The best advocate for a visually impaired person is that person. No one else understands his/her problems, needs, and goals as well as the individual who lives that life. The challenge for everyone who comes in contact with a visually impaired student is to look past the disability and see the person. The responsibilities of the TVI are to encourage independence in the visually impaired student, to enable that student to advocate for him/herself, and to develop a sense of self-respect. The expanded curriculum should have a central purpose, from early childhood on, of building independence, self-esteem, and self-advocacy. Such qualities as a sense of humor, curiosity, and the ability to problem-solve or make decisions should be encouraged at all ages and levels of experience. The TVI will plan activities throughout the visually impaired child's educational year that encourages these qualities.

Problem-solving and decision-making are skills all independent people possess to some degree, and visually impaired students need to have opportunities to develop those skills. From the time a child can choose foods he/she likes, clothing to wear, or which toy to play with, the decision-making process is being practiced. Time management and assignment completion are further extensions of the decision-making process, and should be taught as "survival skills." Spontaneous problem solving is a related skill the TVI may have to teach; role playing or hypothesis testing can be ways of teaching this skill. The visually impaired student will encounter many situations when the TVI is not available, and the problem will need to be resolved before the TVI's next visit (equipment malfunctions, schedule changes, a missed bus, unexpected assignments). The student should have a structured approach to solving unexpected problems, and a "checklist" approach may help. The following is one possibility:

1. Identify/Describe the problem.
2. List possible solutions.
3. Project possible consequences or outcomes for each solution.
4. Select and implement one solution.
5. Evaluate the outcome.

As the student practices this process, it should become part of the student's automatic approach to unexpected situations; it should also place the locus of control where it belongs–in the hands of the student. The unwritten goal of all TVIs should be to "work themselves out of a job" (i.e., make each visually impaired student so self-sufficient that they don't "need" the TVI anymore). Independent problem solving skills place the student a step closer to that goal.

Access to information beyond the educational environment is difficult for many visually impaired persons. Techniques for doing this should be taught in school by the TVI. Such methods include the efficient use of a telephone to gather information (calling libraries, stores, agencies), keeping a current file of resources (medical rehabilitation, readers, drivers, shoppers), and maintaining personal records (financial, medical, etc.). Whenever possible, the visually impaired student should be exposed to such things as pay telephones, ATMs, drive-through fast food services, FAX machines, and vending machines. The TVI should be present, to teach the realities of using public technology. As computers become more common, the visually impaired student will need to understand how to use them to access information through E-mail, Internet, and other "tracks" in the information highway. The visually impaired student also needs to know when to ask for help and when to perform a task independently. If instruction in information access occurs during the educational years, the transition to independent adulthood should be smoother and more satisfying.

ORIENTATION AND MOBILITY

It is critical that every visually impaired student have the opportunity to learn to move safely through space and to travel independently. This skill is taught by a separately certified person (the "O&M" instructor) who will evaluate each visually impaired student's need for such instruction. Such an evaluation can occur as early as preschool, and is sometimes ongoing to determine the optimum time to begin structured mobility instruction. Each child's needs are different, often based on the amount and quality of available vision.

Although actual travel skills are taught by the O&M Instructor, the TVI can prepare the young child for this special instruction by teaching basic concepts, body image, visual efficiency, and sighted guide technique (the *proper* way of "leading" a visually impaired person who needs help in getting from one place to another). The O&M Instructor will evaluate the level of basic concepts, body image, and visual efficiency before designing an individualized program of instruction in mobility. The need for and use of a long cane is an individual decision (not all visually impaired people use canes), as is the use of a dog (used only by adults) or electronic travel aids (sonic guide, laser cane, Mowat Sensor) (used primarily by adults). The O&M Instructor is specially trained to assist in decisions about which devices will be best, at what age.

It may be an oversimplified statement to say that all visually impaired students should have O&M instruction, but most visually impaired students *will* profit from having at least an O&M evaluation; the decision about whether to teach special mobility techniques will be based on the individual student's level of travel competency and need to move about safely and independently. Even visually impaired students in wheelchairs may be able to learn skills that will enable them to be more mobile.

O&M instruction includes travel in both familiar and unfamiliar environments. The O&M Instructor can help orient the student to new settings (different schools; community), and may transport the student off campus for some instructional sessions. Special situations (halls, stairs, doorways, curb cuts, restrooms, restaurants, banks, hotels, swimming pools, parks, etc.) or techniques (trailing, "squaring off," protective technique, sighted guide), and dealing with unusual encounters (ice/snow, guy wires, gratings, escalators, revolving doors, elevators, trains, planes, etc.) are all part of O&M instruction. The goal is to increase independence by making travel both possible and safe.

INDEPENDENCE IS THE "NAME OF THE GAME"

Both classroom teachers and TVIs can fall into the dependency trap. In their zeal to "help" the visually impaired student, they can inadvertently send messages of learned dependency to the student, in the way they handle instructional situations. Decide which way *you* would handle the following situations, and think about which approach is most realistic in terms of developing independence.

Situation	*This response*	or	*This response*
Every time the five-year-old visually impaired student learns a new braille alphabet letter,	the TVI claps and cheers		the TVI calmly tells the student he/she did a good job, and affixes a scratch-and-sniff sticker to the paper as a reward.
When the TVI plays games with the visually impaired preschooler,	the student always wins.		about half the time the student wins, and half the time the TVI wins.
When a high school student needs more time to complete an assignment,	the TVI talks to the classroom teacher to clear it.		the student talks to the classroom teacher and arranges to come in after school to complete the assignment.

Situation	*This response*	or *This response*
When ordering books in braille or tape for the college-bound visually impaired high school student,	the TVI takes care of ordering the books, and hands them out when received.	the TVI may give ordering instructions, but the student obtains a book list and fills out necessary forms.

(Thanks to Cindy Wenrich, Montgomery County Public Schools, Christiansburg, VA for the above situations and solutions.) Realistic situations, experiences, and expectations need to be part of an independence-building educational experience for all visually impaired students in mainstreamed settings.

REFERENCES AND RECOMMENDED READING

Cleveland, J., Levack, N., Sewell, D., & Toy, R. (2002). *Braille FUNdamentals: A braille curriculum for students with visual impairments from primary to high school levels.* Austin, TX: Texas School for the Blind and Visually Impaired.

Corn, A. (1989). Employing critical thinking strategies within a curriculum of critical things to think about for blind and visually impaired students. *Journal of Vocational Rehabilitation, 3,* 17–36.

Corn, A. & Bishop, V. (1984). Acquisition of practical knowledge by blind and visually impaired students in grades 9–12. *Journal of Visual Impairment and Blindness, 78,* 552–556.

Fullwood, D. (1988). *A start to independence for your visually impaired child.* Melbourne, Australia: Royal Victorian Institute for the Blind.

Hatlen, P. (1990). Meeting the unique needs of pupils with visual impairment. *RE:view, 22,* (2), 79–82.

Labossiere, S. & Rhodes, K. (1991). *Braille requisite skills inventory (BRSI).* Houston, TX: Region IV Education Service Center.

Levack, N. (1997). *Annotated bibliography of curricular materials.* Austin, TX: Texas School for the Blind and Visually Impaired.

Livingston, R. (1997). *Use of the Cranmer abacus* (2nd ed.). Austin, TX: Texas School for the Blind and Visually Impaired.

Loumiet, R. & Levack, N. (1993). *Independent living: A curriculum with adaptations for students with visual impairment* (2nd ed.). Austin, TX: Texas School for the Blind and Visually Impaired.

Miller, C. & Levack, N. (Eds.). (1997). *A paraprofessional's handbook for working with students who are visually impaired.* Austin, TX: Texas School for the Blind and Visually Impaired.

O'Sail, B., Levack, N., Donovan, L., & Sewell, D. (2001). *Elementary concepts for students with visual impairment.* Austin, TX: Texas School for the Blind and Visually Impaired.

Olson, M. (1981). *Guidelines and games for teaching efficient braille reading.* New York: American Foundation for the Blind.
Perwein, V. & Levack, N. (1996). *From IEP to teaching strategies . . . How do we get there?* Austin, TX: Texas School for the Blind and Visually Impaired.
Pogrund, R., Healty, G., Jones, K., Levack, N., Martin-Curry, S., Martinez, C., Marz, J., Roberson-Smith, B., & Vrba, A. (1995). *Teaching age-appropriate purposeful skills: An orientation and mobility curriculum (TAPS)* (2nd ed.). Austin, TX: Texas School for the Blind and Visually Impaired.
Rhyne, J. (1981). *Curriculum for teaching the visually impaired.* Springfield, IL: Charles C Thomas.
Sacks, S. (Ed.). (1992). *The development of social skills by blind and visually impaired students.* New York: American Foundation for the Blind.
Smith, A. & O'Donnell, L. (1992). *Beyond arm's reach: Enhancing distance vision.* Philadelphia, PA: Pennsylvania College of Optometry Press.

See also:
Koenig, A. & Holbrook, C. (Eds.). (2000). *Foundations of education,* Volume 2. New York: American Foundation for the Blind (AFB Press).
Visual Efficiency (Corn, A., DePriest, L., & Erin, J.)
Assistive Technology (Kapperman, G. & Sticken, J.)
Independent Living Skills (Kelley, P. & Smith, P.)
Social Skills (Sacks, S. & Silberman, R.)
Recreation and Leisure Skills (McGregor, D. & Farrenkopf, C.)
Career Education (Wolffe, K.)
Orientation and Mobility (Griffen-Shirley, N., Trusty, S., & Rickard, R.)

Chapter Ten

WHAT ABOUT MULTIPLE DISABILITIES?

INTRODUCTION

Chapters Six through Nine have focused primarily on intact visually impaired learners (i.e., those with no other disabilities besides the visual impairment). Chapter Ten will discuss students with multiple disabilities who are also visually impaired (i.e., two or more disabilities, one of which is a visual impairment). These multiply disabled students have been attending public school programs of some kind since federal legislation (P.L. 94-142, The Education for All Handicapped Children Act of 1975) was enacted to make it both possible and mandated. Every disabled child in the United States is entitled by law (both federal and state) to a "free appropriate public education" (FAPE) in the "least restrictive environment" (LRE). In most cases, this is the local public school. The educational system has had to accommodate the needs of *all* of its students, not just those who were physically, emotionally, and mentally intact. The efforts to provide appropriate educational programs for disabled students has resulted in what is commonly referred to as "special education" (although current trends are in the direction of "inclusion"–the *combined* efforts of special educators and regular educators).

Probably at least 60 percent of all visually impaired students have one or more additional disabilities. Among these other disabilities are hearing impairment, speech and language disorders, mental retardation, learning disability, cerebral palsy, and emotional disturbance. A brief description of each of these disabilities can help in understanding the interaction between different impairments.

HEARING IMPAIRMENT

The second most important sensory channel in learning is hearing (second only to vision). The terms used in describing hearing loss depend on an understanding of how hearing works. Sound waves enter the outer ear and cause the eardrum (tympanic membrane) to vibrate; this vibration is transferred to the middle ear, where tiny bones ("hammer," or malleus; "anvil," or incus; and "stirrup,: or stapes) also vibrate. Any problems in the outer or middle ear (e.g., canal blockage, ruptured ear drums, or damaged bones) result in a "conductive" hearing loss.

The vibration of the bones in the middle ear produces waves in the liquid within the outer and inner chambers of the cochlea (a structure with circular chambers, located in the inner ear), which, in turn, cause tiny hairs within the liquid of the middle chamber of the cochlea to ripple. This movement transforms mechanical vibration to electrical energy; the tiny hairs become the auditory nerve, which transmits the electrical impulses to the brain. Any malfunction in the cochlea or auditory nerve causes a "sensorineural" hearing loss.

Hearing loss is defined by both type ("conductive," "sensorineural," or "mixed") and severity. The measurement unit is decibels (dB), and measures the intensity or loudness of sound. Normal hearing is the ability to hear sounds of 20 dB or less (see Figure 12).

Deaf-blindness is a special (and extremely low prevalence) multiple disability; it is defined as a hearing impairment and a visual impairment, the combination of which requires programming different from that available for either hearing impaired or visually impaired students. Note that the severities of neither impairment are defined; it is the *combined* sensory loss that qualifies for special services. There may be useful vision and useful hearing, but there is insufficient vision for a communication method like lip reading, and inadequate hearing for most efficient auditory learning. Very few "deaf-blind" students are totally deaf or totally blind, but the combined losses require instruction in unique communication systems.

For students who are dually sensorily impaired, a specialized educational approach is often needed. This may take place in a regular school, but is also often accomplished effectively in a residential setting (most commonly at a school for blind students). Special teachers there are experienced in both sensory areas and have specialized training in communications methods. Since most deaf-blind student also have cognitive delays, these teachers are also capable of using unique approaches to instruction that focus on functional "life skills" as well as communication. (The reader who is particularly interested in deaf-blindness is encouraged to seek further information on special instructional techniques from other more specific texts.)

Descriptor	Range of Loss (unable to hear)	Functional Characteristics
Mild	between 25 and 45 dB	Speech not a problem; distance sounds difficult to hear
Moderate	between 45 and 70 dB	Normal voices hard to hear; speech articulation may be affected
Severe	between 70 and 90 dB	Unable to participate in normal conversation; may hear an occasional word; hearing aid may be helpful
Profound	greater than 90 dB	Hearing not useful; hearing aid may be helpful, but normal speech usually not possible

Note: Most children have bilateral hearing losses, when a hearing loss is present.

LEVELS OF HEARING LOSS

	Types	
Level of Hearing Loss	Conductive	Sensorineural
Mild to moderate	Middle ear infections Associated with cleft palate	Noise pollution
Severe		Genetic factors (most are autosomal recessive) Diseases (rubella, meningitis, toxoplasmosis, cytomegalovirus, herpes virus) Anoxia at birth

Note: In about half of the cases of hearing loss, the exact cause is unknown. (Batshaw & Perret, 1981)

CAUSES OF HEARING LOSS

Figure 12.

SPEECH AND LANGUAGE DISORDERS

In a young child, beginning speech is the experimenting with and practicing of sound production ("babbling"). As the brain begins to mature and becomes capable of processing auditory stimuli, language emerges (by about age 3). Two types of language capabilities develop: receptive language (the ability to *understand* heard language) and expressive language (the ability to *produce* meaningful language, or speech). Language disorders are classified as "receptive" or "expressive;" if both types of disorders exist together, it is called a communications disorder.

Speech problems commonly involve expressive language and include articulation disorders (the inability to generate speech sounds correctly), rhythm disorders (e.g., stuttering), and voice production problems) pitch or voice quality). Many children with cerebral palsy have expressive speech problems because of poor motor control. Augmentative communication ("language boards" and other adaptive devices) can be used to supplement expressive language problems. "Speech therapy" is a planned program to remediate articulation, rhythm, or voice problems.

Children with brain damage (e.g., due to hydrocephalus) may articulate sounds correctly but their receptive language is affected (they may not understand, or "process," what they hear). Language therapy is usually recommended in cases of receptive language disorders.

Speech and language disorders probably occur in conjunction with a visual impairment in similar proportion as they occur in the rest of the population; however, the causative factors may determine the incidence more accurately. When speech or language disorders occur along with a visual impairment, and no other disability can be identified, the speech therapist and the TVI should share expertise to coordinate their separate services.

If the speech or language problem is the result of a hearing impairment, and there is also a visual impairment, they may be neurologically related. Depending on the severity of the hearing and visual impairments, educational programming will probably emphasize communication skills, and may be similar to educational programming for deaf-blind students.

CEREBRAL PALSY

Cerebral palsy is not a disease, but a group of nonprogressive symptoms related to brain malfunction. It can be caused by damage, inflammation, or a defect/lesion in the immature brain (in children under 16 years of age). It is not genetic in origin, and is uncurable. Underlying prenatal causes can include anoxia, maternal infection (rubella, toxoplasmosis, herpes simplex), maternal metabolic disease (diabetes, hyperthyroidism, severe asthma, heart condition), or Rh factor. Natal causes can include anoxia/asphyxia (oxygen deprivation), birth trauma, analgesics that affect respiration, and prematurity. Postnatal causes can include trauma, fever, hemorrhage, anoxia, hydrocephalus, brain tumors, or cysts. In many cases of cerebral palsy, there is no identifiable cause. It can occur in any race, nationality, or economic strata.

Cerebral palsy results in weak muscles, a lack of muscle coordination, and postural defects. If the brain area affected is the motor cortex or cerebrum, spasticity (tightening of muscles, or "hypertonia") occurs. When the midbrain is affected, "athetosis" occurs; this is characterized by involuntary and uncontrolled movements (usually slow and twisting), facial grimacing, drooling, and speech problems related to poor facial muscle control. If the cerebellum is affected, there is poor balance and coordination, and ataxia (shaky, clumsy, unsteady gait) in some cases. In mixed athetosis-spasticity, the lower extremities (legs) are usually spastic, and the upper extremities are athetoid.

Athetoid cerebral palsy usually appears around 18 months, and fine motor movements become difficult. When a young child is hypotonic ("floppy;" has low muscle tone), the condition usually progresses to either spastic or athetoid forms of cerebral palsy.

In mild cases of cerebral palsy, little or no treatment is indicated. When the condition is moderate, braces or other orthotic devices can be useful. In severe cases, the individual may never achieve the ability for self-care, ambulation, or speech. Some kinds of cerebral palsy also involve seizures (less than half). Individuals who must use wheelchairs may develop scoliosis (improper spine curvature) from excessive pressure on the spine, or from continual leaning to one side without adequate support.

The presence of cerebral palsy does not necessarily mean mental retardation. Among those who have hemiplegia (both extremities on the same side affected) are many who have normal intelligence. The presence or absence of mental retardation depends on the site of the brain damage.

Cerebral palsy has visual involvement in as many as half of all occurrences; most common of the visual effects is strabimus (a muscle-control function); depending on the site of brain involvement, cortical visual impairment may also be present. Cerebral palsy can involve both visual and hearing impairments, as well as cognitive delays.

Educational programming usually considers the physical impairment as a primary disability, and the extent of mobility impairment may suggest the kinds of modifications needed (e.g., extra time allowed to get from class to class). Supplementary consultation and/or services may also be given by physical therapists, occupational therapists, TVIs, speech therapists, and hearing consultants.

MENTAL RETARDATION

Cognitive function is brain-centered; therefore, cognitive impairments occur in the brain. Causes include disease, malformation of the brain, anoxia, hemorrhages, and genetic factors. Cognitive disabilities are measured by developmental scales in young children, and by intelligence tests in older children and adults. Generally, mental retardation is indicated when IQ scores fall two or more standard deviations below normal (70 or below), when the condition is present either prenatally or during the developmental years, and there is documented impairment in adaptive ability (the ability to solve problems and make decisions). Mild retardation includes IQs between 55 and 70; moderate levels fall between 40 and 55; severe retardation includes IQs between 25 and 40; and profound levels are below 25. Severely mentally retarded adults generally have a functional level equal to a 3–4½-year-old, whereas profoundly retarded adults usually function at around the 2-year level or below.

When the brain is not intact, for any reason, it affects how well sensory data is understood and applied, and how easily learning is generalized. Mental retardation, because it is brain-based, can involve vision or visual processing. This is a critical factor when planning vision services for a severely retarded child. The best vision stimulation program may not produce the desired results if the potential for visual processing does not exist or is severely impaired. The best plan for developing visual efficiency may fail if sensory input has little meaning. The relationship between eye and brain is a critical one when considering appropriate vision services for visually impaired/mentally retarded students.

Young children with cortical visual impairment are a special group. Although many of them may also be mentally retarded, those who have only the visual cortex involved may respond to visual stimulation. Moreover, the young brain's "plasticity" (potential for reprogramming) is often a "wild card" in predicting outcomes from instructional programs. The TVI should always be consulted when cortical visual impairment is suspected, and can suggest structured ways of approaching visual programming.

Hints for Programming for Children with Cortical Visual Impairment (CVI)

1. Visual input must be controlled to avoid overstimulation. (Keep stimuli simple and present in isolation.)
2. Verbal cueing seems to help (i.e., *tell* the child what he/she is seeing).
3. Tactual cueing (i.e., tracing with a finger) may help.
4. Figure-ground difficulties are common, so keep images or objects relatively isolated and with nondistracting background. Present one object at a time, on a plain background.
5. One-to-one instruction is best, with consistent personnel and methodology. Use the same words to mean the same thing (i.e., "potty" *always* means toilet, not "have to go?" or "wet?" etc.).
6. Use common objects for play (pots and pans, spoons, cups, boxes, lids, etc.; avoid "models" or miniatures; use the "real thing."
7. Colors, especially yellow and red, seem to be effective.
8. Keep images simple, consistent, constant, and predictable.
9. Use markers or underliners to draw attention.

10. Watch for fatigue. These children use up a lot of energy in concentrating.
11. Program so that "special" activities (e.g., PT, OT, speech therapy) are separate. Too many people, too close together (or all at once) may be confusing and overstimulating.
12. Be patient. CVI is a *processing* problem, and thinking takes time.

LEARNING DISABILITY

Definitions of learning disability vary from state to state, but some aspects of the definitions have common agreement. A major characteristic of learning disability is that it is *not* caused by mental retardation, emotional disturbances, social maladjustment, or physical defects (such as vision or hearing impairments). It is generally considered to be related to brain function.

Learning disability is most often observed as a language-related disability, and involves some degree of disorder in reading, speaking, writing, spelling, or listening; it also sometimes affects the use of math symbols and calculations. Dyslexia is a severe form of learning disability. When there are persistent letter reversals past the age of about 7, or when there is a continuing inability to distinguish right from left, some degree of learning disability might be suspected.

A visual impairment can coexist with a learning disability, but in order for the child to be identified as "LD," it must be shown that the visual impairment is not the *cause* of the learning disability. This is a confusing concept unless the connection between eye and brain is considered. The optical system is *usually* intact in learning disabled students; it is the perceptual system that has the problem. TVIs do not work with learning disabled students unless there is *also* an optical system defect. Little is known about students with both optical and perceptual defects (i.e., visually impaired/learning disabled), but most TVIs have had at least one student that had this unusual (and often not clearly identified) dual disability. In such cases, the TVI addresses the visual impairment and its related factors, and may ask the special teacher of learning disabled students for assistance in understanding the perceptual aspects of the dual disability.

EMOTIONAL DISTURBANCE

Although descriptions vary for this disability, there seems to be general agreement that it must be present over a long period of time, to a marked degree, and, in school-age children, have a negative effect on educational performance. Symptoms may include an inability to learn, an inability to build interpersonal relationships, inappropriate behavior, unhappiness, and/or depression. Emotional disturbances probably occur along with a visual impairment in similar proportions as they occur in the rest of the population.

If an emotional disturbance is severe enough to interfere with behavior and school performance, it is probably considered a primary disability. Programming will address the emotional needs of the child first; all other disabilities will likely require consultant skills from specialists in those disability areas (including the TVI for any visual impairment).

Autism is a unique behavioral disorder that is generally grouped with emotional disturbances. IDEA describes autism as a significant developmental disability that:

- is usually evident before age three;
- affects communication and social interaction;
- may be associated with repetitive or stereotypical movements;
- may cause resistance to changes in the environment or in routines; and
- may produce unusual responses to sensory experiences.

Some visually impaired children appear to exhibit autistic-*like* behaviors. These behaviors include:

- failure to respond when addressed by name;
- failure to interact with others; and
- a refusal to be close to or touch others.

Although there is no research that links autism to visual impairment, several studies suggest that there is a higher-than-expected occurrence of autistic-*like* behaviors among children with Retinopathy or Prematurity (Keeler, 1958; Lowenfeld, 1963; Chase, 1974). No specific treatment is known, although a highly structured approach to this group of children seems to minimize the behaviors. A few professionals in the field of visual impairment are studying these children, to try to determine the most effective programming. For more information, contact:

Dr. Lorraine Rocissano
c/o Maryland School for the Blind
3501 Taylor Avenue
Baltimore, MD
21736-4499
1-800-400-4915

Dr. Terese Pawletko
P.O. Box 383
Portsmouth, NH
03802-0383
(603) 396-1645
teresepawl@yahoo.com

Ms. Marilyn Gense
Willamette Education Service District
2611 Pringle Road, SE
Salem, OR 97302
(503) 385-4718

MULTIPLE DISABILITIES

Certain visual conditions associated with prematurity (RLF/ROP) have been suspected of a higher-than-normal occurrence with other possibly prematurity-related disabilities (cerebral palsy or brain damage). Prenatal deformities can cross several sensory channels and can include brain malformations. Prenatal maternal infections can cause multiple disabilities (rubella, toxoplasmosis, herpes virus) as can birth trauma involving anoxia. Any brain (central nervous system) damage can affect all neurologically-based capabilities (vision, hearing, motor control, cognition). The possible combinations and severities of multiple disabilities are endless and increasing. As medical science advances, more babies of lower birth weights are being saved, and increasing numbers of these infants have multiple disabilities more diverse and complex than ever before. The challenge for educators is monumental.

Perhaps the simplest way of understanding the impact of dual or multiple impairments is to recall the example of the submarine in Chapter One. The submarine has a control center (the captain) to make decisions based on visual input through the periscope (vision) and sound data through sonar (hearing). The comparison can be extended to include steering mechanisms (motor control), and radio (communication capabilities). Even the most capable captain will have difficulty operating the submarine if both sonar (hearing) and periscope (vision) are malfunctioning or inoperable, and will need to have some kind of alternate communication system. If the captain behaves in erratic fashion, firing torpedoes for no apparent reason (emotional disturbance), the submarine will be a useless tool and could become dangerous. If the steering mechanism is faulty (poor motor control), the captain will have difficulty keeping the submarine on course, and any available sonar data (hearing) or periscope information (vision) will help in orienting the submarine; if steering mechanisms *and* one or both information gathering systems are defective, the captain will have great difficulty in achieving his goals; he may get there, but will require every bit of his intelligence and skills. If, however, the captain responds slowly and has difficulty using information in a logical manner (mental retardation), he will have trouble making best use of sonar data (hearing), periscope information (vision), and radio equipment (the ability to communicate). It becomes obvious that the more malfunctions there are, the less effective the operations become. Even when there are minor malfunctions in one or more systems, the command center must be in optimal condition in order to make compensatory maneuvers efficiently and effectively.

The comparison to multiple disabilities in human beings is inescapable: it takes an intact brain to make best use of vision and hearing, and to compensate for other malfunctions. The more severe each disability is, the more difficult it is for the person to compensate, and the more modifications or considerations are needed. The interactive/multiplicative nature of multiple disabilities requires attention to both individual disabilities and their interactions. Collaborative assessments and cooperative programming are essential elements of education for children with multiple disabilities.

For most severe combinations of disabilities, goals in education seek to provide the opportunities for and encouragement to interact with the environment. Curricular goals are dedicated to the prevention, whenever possible, of passivity and inactivity. Functional skills are emphasized in instruction, and cross-exceptionality goals are implemented by teachers who are supported by specialists. For every disability area, there should be an advisor or consultant, and they should operate as a support team to the family or classroom teacher. (See Chapter Thirteen for further discussion of "Teams.")

THE ROLE OF THE TVI WITH VISUALLY IMPAIRED STUDENTS WHO HAVE MULTIPLE DISABILITIES

One of the most often-asked questions about special programming for students with multiple disabilities is "What do I *do*?" Although there are differing viewpoints, the most effective suggestion may be simply to coordinate efforts. When there are multiple disabilities, there should be multiple consultants, but, ideally, few actual service deliverers/intervenors. Goals/objectives should be embedded into routines that are normal for each individual child, and performed as a daily function of normal life. Such routines include feeding, bathing, diapering, and playing. The few service providers can provide familiarity, consistency, and repetition in activities, and caregivers or classroom teachers are the most logical and familiar persons to provide this structure.

When providing services to children with multiple disabilities, TVIs are often expected to perform some unknown intervention that instantly activates the visual system, and suddenly makes it a useful learning channel. However, there are more factors involved than just "turning on a switch." The role of the brain cannot be underestimated in the visual process, and the capacity, type/location, or extent of injury, and integrative ability may determine whether visual function *can,* in fact, be stimulated or improved. The eyes can only "see" to the extent that the brain can "understand."

In designing appropriate services for visually impaired students who also have multiple disabilities, it is helpful to follow a specific evaluation model.* Each person who serves on the multidisciplinary/interdisciplinary/transdisciplinary team (see Chapter Thirteen) should follow much the same sequence in assessing the child. These steps include:

1. A careful review of all records, particularly medical reports;
2. At least one observation (minimum of an hour) of the child in a "normal" setting, performing familiar tasks or routines, and interacting with familiar persons;
3. Informal interviews with as many people in the child's life as possible;
4. The identification, whenever possible, of the general functional level of the child:
    a. At a biobehavioral level (primarily only sleeping or at some level of wakefulness);
    b. Able to interact and communicate through movement;
    c. Able to cooperate intentionally during the functional tasks (feeding; bathing; dressing);
    d. Able to relate familiar objects to functions;
    e. Able to understand that pictures or symbols can stand for objects;
    f. Able to use words to represent objects; language mediates actions;
    g. Able to perform functional tasks with some assistance; or
    h. Able to perform functional tasks independently.
5. Selection/performance of specific assessments (The Functional Vision Evaluation and Learning Media Assessments are the vision-related procedures.);
6. Determination of abilities and challenges, based on assessment results;
7. Development of goals/objectives, based on abilities and challenges;
8. Coordination of consultants to combine goals/objectives in cross-exceptionality behaviors (routines);
9. Designing some means of collecting data to show change (progress; learning; generalization when possible); and
10. Determination of when to modify goals/objectives (using ongoing data collection or reassessment).

Vision-specific goals (e.g., fixation, scanning or shifting gaze, tracking, using vision to monitor reach) can usually be embedded easily into daily rou-

* The evaluation sequence and functional levels have been derived and modified from a model proposed by Dr. Dixie Mercer.tines. For example:

tines. For example:

- Visual attention (fixation): "Student will *look* at the bottle just before receiving it."
- Scanning/shifting gaze: "Student will *visually scan* to locate finger foods on high chair tray."
- Tracking: "Student will *watch* tub toys move in the tub during bath time."
- Using vision to monitor reach: "Student will *visually locate* and reach for finger foods on the high chair tray."

The role of the TVI then becomes one of a consultant who assists in interpreting visual terms/reports, performs vision specific assessments (Functional Vision Evaluation and Learning Media Assessment), determines what visual skills are present and which an be improved, suggests ways of practicing visual skills during daily routines, and monitors any change or improvement in those skills over time. the consultant role is not necessarily any less time-consuming than providing direct services, but the emphasis is different. The consultant can still visit on a regular basis but will be more likely to monitor progress than to provide hands-on activities. In this way, the expertise of the TVI can be most efficiently utilized, especially when numbers of eligible students with multiple disabilities, and geographic scattering, are considered.

The efforts to provide adequate, individualized instruction that meets all of the needs of each disability can be a real challenge, but when multiple disabilities exist there is no alternative if each child is to have equal opportunity to reach his/her maximum potential.

REFERENCES AND RECOMMENDED READING

Barraga, N. & Erin, J. (2001). *Visual impairment and learning* (4th Ed.). Austin, TX: ProEd.

Batshaw, M. & Perret, Y. (1981). *Children with handicaps: A medical primer.* Baltimore, MD: Paul H. Brookes.

Blaha, R. (2001). *Calendars for students with multiple impairments including deafblindness.* Austin, TX: Texas School for the Blind and Visually Impaired.

Chase, J. (1974). A retrospective study of retrolental fibroplasia. *The New Outlook for the Blind, 68,* 61–71.

Chen, D. & Dote-Kwan, J. (Eds.). (1995). *Starting points: Instructional practice for young children whose multiple disabilities include visual impairment.* Los Angeles: Blind Children's Center.

Cushman, C., Heydt, K., Edwards, S., Clark, M., & Allon, M. (1992). *Perkins activity and resource guide: A handbook for teachers and parents of students with visual and mul-*

tiple disabilities. Watertown, MA: Howe Press of Perkins Schools for the Blind.

Erin, J. (1989). *Dimensions: Visually impaired persons with multiple disabilities.* New York: American Foundation for the Blind.

Erin, J. (2000). Students with visual impairment and additional disabilities. In Koenig, A. & Holbrook, C. (Eds.), *Foundations of Education,* Volume 2. New York: American Foundation for the Blind.

Fullwood, D., Harvey, L., & White, G. (1988). *Living and learning: A guide for parents and educators of young visually impaired children who have additional disabilities.* Melbourne, Australia: Royal Victorian Institute for the Blind.

Hagood, L. (1997). *Communication: A guide for teaching students with visual and multiple impairments.* Austin, TX: Texas School for the Blind and Visually Impaired.

Haring, N. & Romer, L. (1995). *Welcoming students who are deafblind into typical classrooms.* Baltimore: Paul H. Brookes.

Hauser, S., Levack, N., & Newton, L. (Eds.). (n.d.). *Functional academics: A curriculum for students with visual impairments.* Austin, TX: Texas School for the Blind and Visually Impaired.

Heubner, K., Prickett, J., Welch, T., & Joffee, E. (Eds.). *Hand in hand: Essentials of communication and orientation and mobility for your students who are deafblind.* New York: American Foundation for the Blind.

Keeler, W. (1958). Autistic patterns and defective communication in blind children with retrolental fibroplasia. In Hoch, P. & Zubin, J. (Eds.), *Psychopathology of communication.* New York: Grune.

Korsten, J., Dunn, D., Foss, T., & Francke, M. (1993). *Every move counts.* San Antonio, TX: Therapy Skill Builders.

Levack, N., Hauser, S., Newton, L., & Stephenson, P. (Eds.). (1996/1997). *Basic skills for community living: A curriculum for students with visual impairment and multiple disabilities.* Austin, TX: Texas School for the Blind and Visually Impaired.

Lowenfeld, B. (1963). The impact of retrolental fibroplasia. *The New Outlook for the Blind, 57,* 402–405.

McInnes, J. & Treffry, J. (1982). *Deafblind infants and children: A developmental guide.* Buffalo, NY: University of Toronto Press.

Rogow, S. (1988). *Helping the visually impaired child with developmental problems.* New York: Teachers College Press.

Sacks, S. & Silberman, R. (Eds.). (1988). *Educating students who have visual impairments with other disabilities.* Baltimore: Paul H. Brookes.

Schleichkorn, J. (1983). *Coping with cerebral palsy.* Austin, TX: ProEd.

Silberman, R. (2000). Children and youth with visual impairments and other exceptionalities. In Holbrook, C. & Koenig, A. (Eds.), *Foundation of education,* Volume 1. New York: American Foundation for the Blind.

Smith, M. & Levack, N. (1996). *Teaching students with visual and multiple impairments: A resource guide.* Austin, TX: Texas School for the Blind and Visually Impaired.

Texas School for the Blind and Visually Impaired. (1996). *Activity routines.* Austin, TX: Author.

VIDEOS

From: Blind Children's Center: *Let's Eat!* (n.d.). Los Angeles: Blind Children's Center.

From: Texas School for the Blind land Visually Impaired:

Axelrod, C., Condon, R., Durkel, J., & Wiley, D. (1993). *Ain't misbehavin': Strategies for improving the lives of students who are deafblind and present challenging behaviors.* (Also available open-captioned.)

Beothel, M. & Rudin, D. (1987). *Power of the heart: A parent involvement story.* (Also available open-captioned and in Spanish.)

Rudin, D. & Wade, A. (1987). *A lifetime of patience.*

TSBVI. (1998). *Routines: All dressed up and somewhere to go.*

Chapter Eleven

GIFTED CHILDREN WHO ARE VISUALLY IMPAIRED: A SPECIAL CASE

INTRODUCTION

Giftedness is not considered "handicap" or "disability" by the federal government; it never appeared among the descriptors in Public Law 94-142) (The Education for All Handicapped Act of 1975) or in any of the ensuing amendments (1983; 1997). Therefore, children who are gifted are not eligible for special education services unless they also have some additional disability. "Special education" is only available to children with "deficits" (physical/sensory, intellectual, emotional), or, in the case of very young children, "delays." This is a small percentage of the B-21 population, and a deficit-model of programming exists (i.e., "fix the problem").

Most textbooks on disabilities list giftedness among multiple disabilities, probably by default, since there appears to be no other place to put it. There is usually only a brief paragraph or two, and the reader is directed to other references for further information. If one views this optimistically, however, it may be a good thing: giftedness is recognized as a "difference." *This* book chooses to devote an entire chapter to giftedness, reflecting the importance of the topic to the author.

Giftedness is a unique characteristic that can co-exist with a number of other characteristics (or disabilities), but because the number of children who are gifted is so small, little research has been done on how to provide optimal learning opportunities. Every attempt has been made here, to offer known or accepted facts, but they are few. The chapter will discuss giftedness as a single exceptionality, then explore the combined characteristics of visual impairment and giftedness (children who are "twice exceptional"), and close with recommendations or suggestions for early nurturing of visually impaired children who may also be gifted.

WHAT IS GIFTEDNESS?

At one time, early in the twentieth century, giftedness was described as "high intelligence" (IQs above 130). Psychologists measured what was termed "general ability," but they were actually measuring how a person applied what had been learned. This definition satisfied most people, but it didn't account for the occasional flashes of original brilliance marking people like Thomas Edison or Albert Einstein (neither of whom did very well in school). Despite the occasional "geniuses," the link between intelligence and giftedness remained until the middle of the twentieth century, when Sputnik appeared in space. Suddenly, there was increased interest in the brightest students who could lead the way in developing the technology and techniques needed in the race into space, and researchers reexamined the concept of giftedness.

By the early 1970s, a government-sponsored study (Marland, 1972) had examined the status of gifted students in the public schools, and found it wanting; only four percent of gifted students nationally had special programs available to them. The Marland study proposed a definition of giftedness that may still be used as a model for some school programs for gifted students. That definition was:

> Gifted and talented children are those identified by professionally qualified persons who, by virtue of outstanding abilities, are capable of high performance. These are children who require the differentiated educational programs and services beyond those normally provided by the regular school program in order to realize their contribution to self and society.
>
> Children capable of high performance include those with demonstrated achievement and/or potential in any of the following areas:
>
> 1. General intellectual ability
> 2. Specific academic aptitude
> 3. Creative or productive thinking
> 4. Leadership ability
> 5. Visual and performing arts
> 6. Psychomotor ability
>
> (Marland, 1972, p. 2)

It is interesting to note that several dimensions of giftedness were added to the original concept: the *capability* (or *potential*) for high performance, the need for special educational *programs,* and the broadening of achievement areas beyond academics, to include visual and performing arts, psychomotor ability, leadership, and creativity. "Giftedness" was now defined beyond intellectual ability, and could now be called "gifted and talented."

In 1974, an Office of the Gifted and Talented was established within the United States Department of Education, and in 1975, the landmark Education for All Handicapped Children Act was passed (P.L. 94-142). Giftedness was *not* among the descriptors that established eligibility for special education, however, and continues to be a separate issue. In 1978, Joseph Renzulli suggested another dimension of giftedness: high levels of task commitment, and the definition of giftedness continued to grow.

The Jacob K. Javits Gifted and Talented Students Education Act* was passed in 1988 (P.L. 103-382), and an even more comprehensive definition of giftedness emerged:

> . . . students, children, or youth, who give evidence of high performance capability in areas such as intellectual, creative, artistic, or leadership capability, or in specific academic fields, and who require services or activities not ordinarily provided by the school, in order to fully develop such capabilities.
>
> (20 U.S.C., Part B; P.L. 103-382, Title XIV, p. 388)

More recently, psychologists and cognitive researchers have broadened the definition of giftedness even further. Gardner (1993) has suggested that there are *multiple* intelligences: linguistic, logical/mathematical, visual/spatial, musical/rhyming, bodily/kinesthetic, interpersonal, intrapersonal, and naturalist. Goleman (1995) added yet one more kind of intelligence: emotional intelligence (presumed to be based on new theories about how the brain works). Perhaps as neuroscientists map the brain more accurately, the relationships between the many types of intelligences will be clarified, and the parameters of giftedness will be better defined. But for now, some combination of the Marland definition of giftedness, and the one given in the Javits Act will have to do.

HOW DO YOU BECOME GIFTED?

Most researchers agree that there is a strong genetic factor that determines intelligence, but exactly *how* important it is, and whether it can be modified is still not clear. The generally accepted conclusion is that genes account for about half of the differences in intelligence from one person to another (Begley, 2003). Recent research has identified at least five genes that appear to occur more frequently in persons with high IQs, but the mechanism of

*The Jacob K. Javits Act (reauthorized several time) offered financial support to a research center on giftedness, to model programs, and to personnel preparation. It did not guarantee student rights as P.L. 94-142 had done.

how these genes affect performance is still unknown. The tentative conclusion so far seems to be that intelligence is the result of a great number of genetic interactions, both within the individual and with the environment. (Aha! The old "nature vs. nurture" debate resurfaces!) Even a slight intellectual advantage at birth may lead to a leap in intelligence if opportunities for cognitive growth are provided. The trick is to choose/provide the kinds of learning experiences that will stimulate the genes that influence intelligence (Begley, 2003). If we want to make the most of the "raw materials" provided by the genes, we have to create the kind of learning environment that will "grow" the abilities–and early! By age four, a child with no disabilities will have acquired as much as 50 percent of the intelligence he/she will have at age 17 (Bloom, 1964), and by age eight, the same child will have 80 percent of his/her adult capacity (Roos, 1974). The experiences a child has *before* he/she begins school may make the difference between "bright" and "gifted."

WHAT MAKES GIFTED CHILDREN SO DIFFERENT?

Giftedness and high achievement are not necessarily the same. High achievers may be highly motivated, and able to sustain effort on a task, but they may not be gifted. Gifted students may or may not be high achievers, depending on their interest in the ask or sphere of knowledge. Moreover, gifted children may be bored with age-appropriate activities or learning tasks, and express their disinterest by doing nothing (or by daydreaming). Gifted learners need challenges, novel ways to investigate, opportunities to express creative abilities, and answers to questions no one else even thought to ask (sometimes, including the teacher). Gifted children approach life and learning from a different perspective, bring different skills to the learning experience, and acquire knowledge through different processes. They are a different kind of person, and a different kind of learner.

Gifted individuals are not just smarter or brighter; they are *different.* They think, grow, and behave differently, and they approach life from a different direction. They are unique individuals–mentally, emotionally, socially, and physically. These differences have implications for school programs, home environments, learning opportunities, and life experiences. Accelerated learning and enrichment experiences are not enough. These children need to know "it's *okay* to be different" and that there are opportunities to grow and learn in multiple directions. While other children may be learning at the recall or comprehension levels, gifted children need opportunities to apply information, put it together in creative ways, and evaluate its value (Bloom, 1956). Gifted children need nurturing, encouragement, and the sense that learning opportunities are unlimited.

There are currently a large number of books and many websites about giftedness. Most are designed to be resources for parents of gifted children, who are searching for ideas, techniques, and tips on living with/nurturing their gifted children. There are also many lists of characteristics of gifted children of all ages. Gifted children may show many of these characteristics, and parents usually recognize them quite early. The following are selected descriptors for two groups of gifted children: the very young and those of school age.*

Young gifted children are extremely alert and visually attentive during the first six months of life; (1) have a fascination for patterns; (2) have a highly sensitive sensory system (may exhibit distinct preferences for particular sounds/music, textures, tastes, or smells); (3) have high levels of energy, may need less sleep than other children; (4) are able to entertain themselves for large blocks of time; (5) may use toys/objects in unusual or creative ways; (6) have an insatiable curiosity; (7) may have early language development; and (8) may exhibit a high appetite for books and pictures.

School-age gifted children may exhibit uneven development (one system may be more highly developed, or more delayed, than the others); (1) may have super-sensitive senses (loud noises may be frightening; certain textures may be preferred; may have "picky" food preferences); (2) have abundant imaginations (imaginary companions are not uncommon); (3) are capable of intense feelings; (4) show a creative nature; like to "make things;" (5) may be perfectionists and have high expectations for themselves; (6) usually have exceptional memories; (7) show an unusual ability to concentrate on topics of interest, and do *not* want to be disturbed when concentrating; (8) may be characterized as "strong-willed" but actually have a high level of inner drive or motivation; (9) want to know "how" and "why"–incessantly; (10) do things "differently;" (11) build strong emotional attachments; (12) may exhibit discrepancies between the ability to think and the ability to produce (the mind is ahead of the hands); (13) have a strong sense of humor; and (14) are exhausting to live with because of their high energy level.

Notice that these characteristics are observable, and most parents can identify them easily. It is not necessary to wait until an IQ test can be administered (at the upper preschool period, at the earliest) to suspect that a child may be gifted.

* (Selected from: Rivero, 2002; Walker, 1991; Smutney et al., 1989; Galbraith, 2000; Rogers & Silverman, 1988; Smutney, 1997.)

WHAT ARE/SHOULD BE THE INSTRUCTIONAL IMPLICATIONS FOR GIFTED LEARNERS?

If we can recognize the characteristics of a gifted child early, we may also be able to offer special opportunities to encourage the development of the potential for giftedness. Following are some suggestions for nurturing possible giftedness, with greatest emphasis on the preschool years (when the "window of opportunity" to encourage intellectual growth is greatest).

At the Preschool Level:

Birth–3: Building and refining motor skills
Activating and enhancing the sensory system
Building language, both receptive and expressive
Providing opportunities to experiment/play with a variety of materials (liquids, prisms, sponges, paper, wood, metal, foods, etc.)

Ages 3–5: "Discovery-learning" opportunities that explore properties (sizes, shapes, colors, textures, etc.) and observe cause-effect relationships
Providing a variety of picture books
Encouraging "story telling" (from experience, and from the memory of books or stories read *to* the child)

During the School Years:

Encouragement of creative thinking and the creative process (divergent as well as convergent thinking); "thinking outside the box"
Exploring topics in different ways (using the higher levels of Bloom's Taxonomy)
Developing research skills and self-directed study skills during independent studies
Encouragement of individual interests and talents
Development of a positive self-image (including feeling comfortable with "differentness")

GIFTEDNESS AND VISUAL IMPAIRMENT

Giftedness occurs in only two percent to five percent of the school population (Johnsen, 1986; Johnsen & Corn, 1989), whereas visual impairment is present in about .1 percent of children B–17 years of age (Nelson & Dimitrova, 1993). Since both giftedness and visual impairment are low incidence exceptionalities, the group of children who are both visually impaired *and* gifted is extremely small. There is very little in the literature about this unusual combination of exceptionalities, but most TVIs who have been teaching for any length of time can recall one or two students who could be called "gifted visually impaired." The recollections are usually pleasant, and the students are remembered fondly, although teaching them probably required more attention to the giftedness than the visual impairment. They are students who would very likely have succeeded academically with or without help; this author speculates that they used their giftedness to compensate for their visual impairment. How much more could have been done if the giftedness had been recognized and nurtured!

Although the group of twice-exceptional gifted-visually impaired children is small, there is an unusual cluster within this small group. At least three studies (Thurrell & Josephson, 1966; Williams, 1968; Witkin et al., 1971) have observed higher intelligence in totally blind children who have had bilateral retinoblastoma.* (Chase (1970) has suggested that *particular* cognitive functions (global articulation, specifically tactual discrimination) were more highly developed and accounted for the higher scores. TVIs who have had students whose eyes were enucleated because of retinoblastoma, often report that these children seem "very bright" when compared to sighted peers, and have exceptional spatial perception (despite having no eyes). One theory for this unusual capability is that the children had some degree of early vision (prior to the enucleation) and the brain "remembers" the spatial aspects of what was seen.

The most interesting aspect of the relationship between retinoblastoma and higher intelligence is the genetic factor. If there are genes that determine any portion of intelligences (as is currently believed), it may be that the genetic nature of retinoblastoma is linked in some way to the intelligence-determiner genes. Further neuroresearch is needed to support or disprove this theory.

HOW CAN WE IDENTIFY GIFTEDNESS IN VISUALLY IMPAIRED CHILDREN?

---

*Retinoblastoma is a tumor (cancer) of the eye(s) and is genetically linked. It is caused by the absence of or damage to both suppressor genes on chromosome 13 (Angier, 1987). The absence of or damage to the suppressor genes is initially a spontaneous mutation (i.e., does not occur in other family members) but becomes hereditary thereafter. Treatment often involves the removal of one or both eyes, within the first few years of life. There is a probability of recurring cancer in the hereditary types of retinoblastoma, and the lifespan may be shortened. (Isenberg, 1989; Catalano & Nelson, 1994)

A major problem in identifying giftedness in children who are visually impaired is the assessment process itself. There are, at present, no universally accepted procedures, especially for children under 6. Developmental scales are usually based on sighted norms, and measure expected "normal" development (not necessarily a characteristic of gifted children). Moreover, giftedness may still be in its formative period during the early years. Very few early childhood texts have addressed the unusual characteristics of giftedness, leaving TVIs who work with young children with visual impairment without guidelines for recognizing possible giftedness. This author has taken a position about the identification process, and suggests that characteristics of giftedness have some universality; that is, gifted indicators would probably be present despite the presence of single sensory disabilities. (This premise assumes that there are no other disabilities.) In this belief, two checklists have been developed, based on general characteristics of giftedness The checklists are intended to be screening instruments only, and can be used by a TVI who suspects that a young visually impaired child might be gifted. (The author would welcome feedback from any TVI who uses the checklists, regardless of the results.) (See "Possible Indicators of Giftedness" for Infants and Toddlers, and for Preschoolers at the end of this chapter.)

Another screening checklist, developed by a TVI who had an endorsement in gifted education, also taps characteristics of giftedness (Johnson, 1987). The TVI who developed this scale was a teacher in a self-contained class for visually impaired students, in a regular school, and had a blind pupil who appeared to be very bright. The checklist was designed specifically to identify characteristics of giftedness in visually impaired students, and is offered as a possible screening tool for school-age students who are visually impaired and may be gifted.

TVIs work closely with their students (commonly on a one-to-one basis), and are in an ideal position to notice characteristics that might suggest giftedness. It is the TVI who would probably use a screening tool to initiate the evaluation process. Once the TVI can provide data to support "gut feeling," referral to an assessment team would be a logical next step. This team would collect information and conduct testing, in order to establish the likelihood of giftedness. Intelligence testing is usually only one part of the data collection process, and may present challenges for the examiner (see Chapter Fourteen). Other types of data collection could include interviews, questionnaires, anecdotal records, achievement test scores, grade transcripts, student interviews, creativity inventories (Hackney, 1986) and portfolios of the student's unusual and/or creative work. Whatever battery of procedures or sequence of data collection is established by the team, it should be as visually neutral as possible (i.e., as little dependent on visual ability or visual experience as possible, or at least not disadvantageous to the visually impaired student). This may a difficult criteria to observe, but it helps to focus on the giftedness and not the visual impairment. There is a need for the development of such a disability-neutral process, and perhaps if TVIs begin to ask for it when they suspect giftedness in their students, the need will become more widely recognized.

How Can We Best Serve Visually Impaired Students Who Are Also Gifted?

There may be two layers to the provision of services to visually impaired students who may also be gifted. The first layer might be called "growing the potential" and applies to preschool children (B–5) identified as visually impaired. The second layer could be titled "realizing the potential," and would apply to school-age children who are visually impaired.

"Growing the potential" means paying attention to characteristics of the child that may be early indicators of giftedness, and providing the stimulating opportunities and experiences that will allow those characteristics to develop whatever potential there is for giftedness. These children could be called "at promise" (as opposed to the negative "at risk") (Kay, 2000, p. 293). The preschool years would be devoted to fulfilling that promise (of potential giftedness).

For infants and toddlers who may also be gifted (or have the potential to become gifted), it is important to intervene at the right time–before delays appear. Remediating deficits is harder than facilitating development. Many otherwise intact but visually impaired infants and toddlers can achieve developmental milestones "on time" (or within a normal range) if given early intervention. Those children who may be gifted are even more apt to achieve milestones normally since there is usually a higher level of motivation, or inner drive. Some general guidelines can provide direction for intervention planning:

1. Stimulate/develop the senses as early as possible; provide high contrast (black and white) patterns to look at, for children with usable vision. Use music to calm and soothe the high energy bursts (Mozart is highly recommended). Use soft textures for blankets, bedding, and clothing. As the child goes from infancy to toddlerhood, provide a variety of textures and patterns, so that the child begins to compare and choose (show preferences). Provide toys that can be explored tactually (not just listened to or watched), and that have a variety of textures and tactual details.
2. Provide *interactive* experiences and toys. The child should have to *do* something to make a toy work, or should have to respond to continue an experience. For the child who cannot observe visually, he/she must *participate*–

initiate an activity, continue the activity, and terminate the activity. This can be as simple as kicking to activate a mobile, or as complex as using switches, buttons, or levers. The goal is participation–making something happen.

3. Try to set as few limits as possible. Encourage safe and sustained independent exploration. Gifted children have their own speed and style of learning. Provide opportunities, and then get out of their way!
4. Allow for (and accept) highly individual likes and dislikes. Most gifted children don't do things "like everyone else," and this extends to personal preferences. An early sense that "It's okay to be different" can go a long way towards developing a healthy sense of self-esteem.
5. Giving a child some kind of "advanced warning" when a change in routine is about to happen can alleviate arguments. For example, let the child know that it is 15 minutes until bedtime; it helps him/her begin to reorient his/her system to change.

For preschool children (3–5), the general suggestions for infants and toddlers also apply, but now begin to get more focused. Sensory development will depend on the degree of visual impairment; blind children will need more experience in auditory and tactual skills, while children with some useful vision may also need structured experiences to make their available vision as efficient as possible. Interactive learning goes beyond toys in the home and family members; it can extend to the natural outdoor environment, the community, and preschool programs. "Limits" begin to consider safety as the child is able to move more independently through his/her environment, and O&M instruction may begin. Opportunities to explore, investigate, identify, compare, and classify are almost endless, but are essential. The gifted child who is visually impaired must build a repertoire of cognitive memories, many of them tactual or auditory, to draw upon when structured learning begins, and language begins to mediate. (See Chapter Seven for an expanded description of ideas for experiences.)

School-aged children who are both visually impaired and gifted present a special challenge. Not all schools have gifted programs (nor are they required by law to have them), and not all gifted programs are good ones; some only provide opportunities for acceleration, advanced studies, or "enrichment." Unfortunately, some of the latter are simply "extra work" to keep the gifted students occupied. Gifted students needs more than extra work to keep them interested and involved in the learning process. (See Appendix D for *Characteristics of a Good Gifted Program.*)

If a school *has* a gifted program, the TVI should determine its structure, purpose, goals, and expertise of the faculty. (Most good gifted programs will have a mission statement, and will encourage visitation.) The TVI can then judge whether a particular visually impaired gifted student could profit from being enrolled in that gifted program (in terms of time/scheduling, curriculum, goals, and personnel/faculty). Accelerated or enrichment models may not be the best match for a visually impaired gifted student, who already has to work overtime to complete regular assignments. However, a program that focuses on creative thinking, research skills, and independent study could be an exciting learning outlet for the special learning styles of a gifted student who is visually impaired.

A good gifted program can offer more than a creative learning opportunity. It can be a nurturing environment that values individual differences, pays attention to learning styles and preferred modalities, focuses on individual potential, and encourages compensatory learning strategies (Kay, 2000). Good gifted programs often provide career exposure, mentors, and leadership opportunities (Corn, 1986). Sighted gifted learners tend to accept differences and treat other gifted learners as equals, despite any limitations (Paskewicz, 1986). A good gifted program can do much to nurture the visually impaired gifted student, who may be more like the gifted students than the age peers.

What, then, is the responsibility of the TVI with a gifted visually impaired student? Certain aspects of the expanded core curriculum will have special importance when the student is gifted, and the TVI should focus on those skills that will enable the visually impaired student to access the gifted curriculum. Among these are communication skills (including braille if indicated, typing/keyboarding, efficient use of technology and/or low vision devices when recommended, and effective use of tactual/visual graphics). Organizational and study skills (including library and internet access) are also essential abilities for the gifted visually impaired student. The TVI can help the visually impaired student become his/her own advocate, and can teach techniques to facilitate the ability to solve problems and make decisions independently. Gifted program faculty and the TVI can work jointly on the development of age appropriate social skills (a common weakness of gifted children with and without other exceptionalities). There is so much to be gained by including the gifted visually impaired student in a good gifted program that educators should welcome the opportunity.

Twenty-five years ago, Berthold Lowenfeld tried to alert educators about the inadequacies of services for visually impaired gifted and talented persons. In part, he said:

> The gifted and talented have been with us in public and residential schools for a long time and we have enjoyed them. But have we done everything possible to assist them in using their talents and gifts? We have in most instances let them fend for themselves. . . . Here is an area where the basic work remains to be done, and it will be a rewarding effort.

(Lowenfeld, 1979, p. 12)

Have we done the work 25 years later? The dearth of studies and lack of literature on gifted visually impaired children suggests that we have not. Until we do so, there will be no reward.

POSSIBLE INDICATORS OF GIFTEDNESS IN VISUALLY IMPAIRED CHILDREN

Infants and Toddlers

Behaviors should be noticed most of the time, not just occasionally. Check all those that apply.

____ Unusually alert; often appears to be listening intently; may try to turn towards an interesting stimulus.

____ High levels of energy; may need less sleep; always "on the go;" "gets into things;" always moving.

____ Fascinated with patterns, especially those with high contrast.

____ Explores toys carefully and experimentally (probes, fingers, pokes, pats, rubs, shakes, taps, etc.).

____ Experiments with sound; compares similar sounds (as in bells or rattles); plays with own verbalizations (loud/soft, high/low, or unusual–clicking, lip smacking, gurgling, "blowing bubbles").

____ May use toys in unique and unexpected ways (after the "correct" use has been demonstrated and understood). Example: instead of building structures with blocks, uses them in a row to outline areas.

____ Able to entertain self contentedly for blocks of time; may become absorbed in an independent activity.

____ May exhibit dissonance in development (one system may lag behind the rest, for no apparent reason).

____ May have distinct sensory sensitivities (marked performances or aversions to specific textures, foods, odors, sounds).

____ Noticeable empathy for others who are sick or disabled.

The more checks, the more likely that giftedness is a possibility. (Bishop, 2003)

POSSIBLE INDICATORS OF GIFTEDNESS IN VISUALLY IMPAIRED CHILDREN
Preschoolers

Behaviors should be characteristic and frequent, not just occasional. Check all those that apply.

____ Continues to use toys/objects in unusual and creative ways.

____ High level of curiosity; wants to know "how" and "why."

____ Appropriate (and possibly early) meaningful use of language.

____ Begins to understand multiple word uses (e.g., "rest" as in *to* rest or *the* rest) and "plays" on words; likes riddles.

____ Sense of humor; chuckles or laughs at incongruities.

____ Independently spends time in comparing properties (hard/soft, high/low, loud/soft, smooth/rough, etc.).

____ Seems to have a high level of inner "drive" or motivation; may resent authoritation direction.

____ Gets annoyed when interrupted during periods of intense concentration; has own timeline and speed for accomplishing tasks.

____ Interested in (and can retell) stories; if vision is sufficient, enjoys pictures and what they mean.

____ Responds to explanations better than orders.

____ May continue to exhibit dissonance in development (mind may be ahead of hand and body coordination).

____ May be a perfectionist; gets annoyed when he/she cannot get something "right."

____ May prefer the company of adults or older children to peers.

____ Often has a highly developed imaginary world, that can include imaginary companions.

____ May appear to flit from activity to activity, but has the ability to concentrate intensely when an activity is of interest.

____ Sensorily sensitive; may have distinct preferences and dislikes for specific kinds of music, particular foods, or textures.

____ May become fixated on a specific topic and essentially "live" in that world (e.g., dinosaurs, fish, insects); usually acquires a high level of knowledge about that topic.

____ Has an exceptional memory.

____ Seems to have an unending supply of energy (parents report that these children are exhausting to live with).

The more checks, the more likely that giftedness is a possibility. (Bishop, 2003)

POSSIBLE INDICATORS OF GIFTEDNESS
IN VISUALLY IMPAIRED CHILDREN
School-Age Children

YES	NO	CHARACTERISTIC
____	____	Is curious about many things.
____	____	*Is perceptive of the environment.
____	____	Becomes impatient when an explanation is "fuzzy."
____	____	Has a good sense of humor.
____	____	Is sensitive to injustice.
____	____	Understands quickly and easily.
____	____	Has original responses.
____	____	*Has a lively imagination.
____	____	Originates many ideas from a stimulus.
____	____	Becomes excited about learning because it is fun.
____	____	Has accelerated academic achievement in relation to peers.
____	____	Scores in average or high average against sighted peers, in one or more areas.
____	____	Has advanced vocabulary for age or grade level.
____	____	Has quick mastery and recall of facts.
____	____	*Understands abstract concepts.
____	____	Wants to be independent.
____	____	Is willing and eager to try new things.

*Very difficult for blind or visually impaired students.

The more "yes" judgments there are, the more convincing the argument is in favor of giftedness.

From "Teaching the visually impaired gifted youngster" by L. Johnson (1987). In *Journal of Visual Impairment and Blindness, 81* (2), p. 51. Reprinted with permission from the American Foundation for the Blind.

REFERENCES AND RECOMMENDED READING

Angier, N. (1987). Light cast on darkling gene. *Discover, 8* (3), 85–96.

Begley, S. (2003). Good genes count, but many factors make up a high IQ. *Wall Street Journal,* June 20, 2003, B1.

Bloom, B. (1956). *Taxonomy of educational objectives: The classification of educational goals. Handbook 1. Cognitive domain.* New York: McKay.

Bloom, B. (1964). *Stability and change in human characteristics.* New York: John Wiley & Sons.

Bloom, B. (1985). *Developing talent in young people.* New York: Ballentine Books.

Chase, J. (1970). Cognitive patterns in subjects blinded by retinoblastoma. In *Proceedings of the International Council for the Education of the Visually Handicapped* (pp. 100–109). New York: UNESCO.

Clark, B. (2002). *Growing up gifted.* Columbus, OH: Charles Merrill Company.

Corn, A. (1986). Gifted students who have a visual handicap: Can we meet their educational needs? *Education of the Visually Handicapped, 18,* 71–84.

Corn, A. (1999). Intellectually gifted children with sensory impairments. In Cline, S. & Schwarts, D. (Eds.), *Populations of gifted children.* Upper Saddle River, NJ: Merrill.

Galbraith, J. (1999). *The gifted kids' survival guide for ages 10 and under.* Minneapolis, MN: Free Spirit Publishing.

Galbraith, J. (2000). *You know your child is gifted when . . . .* Minneapolis, MN: Free Spirit Publishing.

Galbraith, J. & Delisle, J. (1996). *The gifted kids' survival guide: A teen handbook.* Minneapolis, MN: Free Spirit Publishing.

Gardner, H. (1993). *Frames of mind: The theory of multiple intelligences.* New York: Bantam Books.

Gardner, H. (1993). *Multiple Intelligences: The theory of practice.* New York: Basic Books.

Goleman, D. (1995). *Emotional intelligence.* New York: Bantam Books.

Hackney, P. (1986). Education of the visually handicapped gifted: A program description. *Education of the Visually Handicapped, 18* (2), 85–95.

Johnsen, S. (1986). Who are the gifted? A dilemma in search of a solution. *Education of the Visually Handicapped, 18*(2), 54–70.

Johnsen, S. & Corn, A. (1989). The past, present, and future of education for gifted children with sensory and/or physical disabilities. *Roeper Review, 12* (1), 13–23.

Johnson, L. (1987). Teaching the visually impaired gifted youngster. *Journal of Visual Impairment and Blindness, 81* (2), 51–52.

Kay, K. (Ed.). (2000). *Uniquely gifted: Identifying and meeting the needs of the twice exceptional student.* Golsum, NH: Avocus Publishing, Inc.

Lowenfeld, B. (1979). *The challenge of the coming decade for the educational of blind children.* Unpublished presentation to the Mid-Atlantic Regional Conference of the Association for Education of the Visually Handicapped.

Marland, S. (1972). *Education and the gifted and talented.* Washington, DC: Commission of Education, 92nd Congress, 2nd Session, USCPO.

Nelson, K. & Dimitrova, E. (1993). Severe visual impairment in the United States and in each state, 1990. *Journal of Visual Impairment and Blindness, 87,* 80–85.

Paskewicz, M. (1986). Mainstreaming the gifted visually impaired child. *Journal of Visual Impairment and Blindness, 80* (9), 937–938.

Public Law 94-142. The Education for All Handicapped Children Act of 1975, 20 U.S.C. 1401 et seq.

Public Law 103-382, Title XIV. The Jacob K. Javits Gifted and Talented Students Education Act of 1988, 20 U.S.C.

Renzulli, J. (1978). What makes giftedness? Reexamining a definition. *Phi Delta Kappan, 60,* 180–184, 261.

Rimm, S. (2001). *Keys to parenting the gifted child, 2nd Ed.* New York: Barron's Education Series, Inc.

Rivero, L. (2002). *Creative home schooling for gifted children: A resource guide.* Scottsdale, AZ: Great Potential Press.

Rogers, M. & Silverman, L. (1988). Recognizing giftedness in young children. *Understanding our Gifted, 1* (2), 5, 16, 17, 20.

Roos, P. (1974). Trends and issues in special education for the mentally retarded. In Kirk, S. & Lord, F. (Eds.). *Exceptional children: Educational resources and perspectives.* Boston: Houghton Mifflin Company.

Scholl, G. (1986). Visual impairment and other exceptionalities. In Scholl, G. (Ed). *Foundations of education for blind and visually handicapped children and youth.* New York: American Foundation for the Blind.

Smutney, J. (1997). *Teaching young gifted children in the regular classroom: Identifying, nurturing, and challenging ages 4–9.* Minneapolis, MN: Free Spirit Publishing.

Smutney, J., Veenker, K., & Veenker, S. (1989). *Your gifted child.* New York: Ballentine Books.

Thurrell, R. & Josephson, T. (1966). Retinoblastoma and intelligence. *Psychosomatics, 7,* 368–370.

Walker, S. (1991). *The survival guide for parents of gifted kids.* Minneapolis, MN: Free Spirit Publishing.

Warren, D. (1984). *Blindness and early childhood development* (2nd Ed. Revised). New York: American Foundation for the Blind.

Warren, D. (1994). *Blindness and children: An individual differences approach.* New York: Cambridge University Press.

Webb, J., Meckstroth, E., & Tolan, S. (1989). *Guiding the gifted child: A practical source for parents and teachers.* Scottsdale, AZ:P Gifted Psychology Press.

Williams, M. (1968). Superior intelligence of children blinded from retinoblastoma. *Archives of Diseases of Childhood,* 43, 204–210.

Winebrenner, S. (2000). *Teaching gifted kids in the regular classroom: Strategies and technologies every teacher can use to meet academic needs of the gifted and talented.* Minneapolis, MN: Free Spirit Publishing.

Witkin, H., Oltman, P., Chase, J., & Friedman, F. (1971). Cognitive patterning in the blind. In Hellmuth, J. (Ed.). *Cognitive Studies, Volume 2.* New York: Brunner/Mazel.

Chapter Twelve

THE LEARNING ENVIRONMENT

INTRODUCTION

"Least restrictive environment," the "continuum of alternative placements," and the "most appropriate placement" are all descriptors of learning environments, and they need to be understood within the context of their intent. In Chapters Seven and Eight, learning environments were the home and the classroom, and suggestions were given about how to modify these environments. This chapter will broaden the concept of learning environments, including the legal mandates and implications. TVIs need to be able to recommend placements that will best meet individual students' needs, and to do that, TVIs should be able to advocate for the most appropriate learning environment possible for each student. An understanding of the options should help in making those recommendations.

THE CONTINUUM/ARRAY

Public Law 94-142 (The Education for All Handicapped Children Act of 1975) specifically described "a continuum of alternative placements" that included "regular classes, special classes, special schools, home instruction, instruction in hospitals and institutions" as well as resource rooms or itinerant instruction "in conjunction with regular class placement" (20 U.S.C. 1412 (5) (B).) The most recent IDEA amendments did not change that wording or intent (C.F.R. Section 300.550(b).) It is clear that federal law intended for parents and IEP teams to have choices in placement, and still does.

Many schools do not have the full set of choices available, and prefer *not* to if services can be provided in a setting they *do* have (most often, the regular classroom). However, the federal Office of Special Education Programs (OSEP) has issued a statement to remind schools that "availability of space, or administrative convenience" may *not* be determiners of placements (Heumann & Hehir, 1995). In other words, schools *will* provide what the student *needs,* not just what the schools *have.* TVIs can gather support from both law and OSEP directives when recommending what kinds of services or service delivery system a particular student needs.

The term "continuum" has often been graphically represented as a line, either vertical or horizontal. Because the line has a beginning and an end, the implication may be that one end is positive ("good") and the other end is negative ("bad"). Thus, systems at one end of an educational continuum are presumed to be better than those at the other end. In the case of special education, the service models at one end are more separate (e.g., residential schools) and those at the other end are more inclusive (e.g., regular classes, in a regular school). The implications are equated to "less restrictive" and "more restrictive," although this assumption is erroneous (and will be discussed later).

In an effort to equalize the values of placement choices, the field of visual impairment has arranged them in a circle, and called it an "array" (see Figure 13). By putting the child in the center, the choice of placement is focused on the student. Each of the placements might have a particular value at a specific time during the child's educational years, and no single placement is "better" or "worse" except in its ability to meet the child's needs. The TVI (and the IEP team) should understand the instructional capabilities of each type of placement (see Table 4).

Nearly all visually impaired students can be served satisfactorily in one of these placements, but there is no reason why two options could not be combined, if that combination met a particular student's needs best. For example, a student could be in a regular class and receive instruction from both an itinerant TVI (who would focus on a particular area) *and* a Vision Resource Room teacher (who could provide broader support on a daily basis). The child's *needs* should drive the decision for service delivery models.

Mention should be made of placement choices at the preschool level. Although most vision services will likely be provided in the child's home during the B–3 age period, parents should be able to choose support from a center-based program if the center can provide professional expertise not available elsewhere. During the 3–5-year-old period, the TVI should be in close contact with preschool programs in the area, and should know which are appropriate (or inappropriate) for particular children. (See Chapter Eight for more information about selecting preschool programs.)

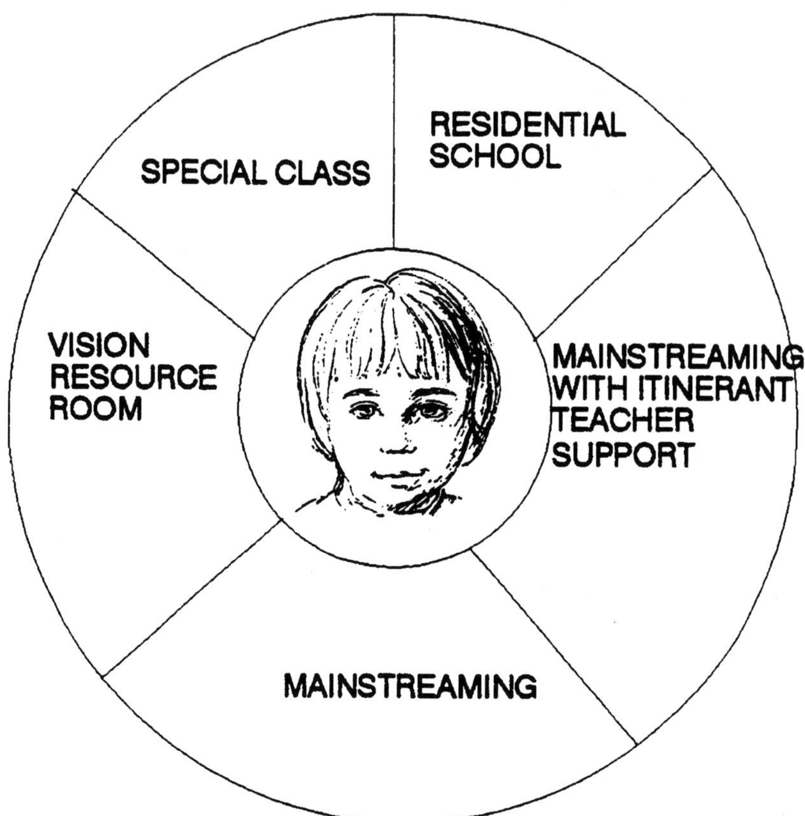

THE ARRAY OF SERVICES

Figure 13.

INCLUSION: PLACEMENT, PROCESS, OR GOAL?

P.L. 94-142 directed that handicapped children should be educated with children who are not handicapped "to the maximum extent appropriate" and that removal of handicapped children from the regular educational environment should occur "only when the nature or severity of the handicap is such that education in regular classes with the use of supplementary aids and services cannot be achieved satisfactorily" (20 U.S. C. 1412 (5) (B); 1414 (a) (1) (C) (iv).). The most recent amendments (IDEA, 1997) and their ensuing regulations (34 C.F.R. 300.1–300.756) use essentially the same language, but substitute "disabled" for "handicapped." In the discussion portion of the reg-

TABLE 4. DESCRIPTION OF PLACEMENT OPTIONS
FOR VISUALLY IMPAIRED STUDENTS

The regular class: with consultative support from the itinerant TVI	The student who only needs to be monitored, has very few special equipment/material needs or environmental modifications, and can function relatively independently.
with itinerant TVI instructional support	The student who has specific instructional needs beyond the regular classroom (i.e., any or all of the expanded core curriculum areas) but who is able to compete academically with sighted peers in the regular classroom, given adequate and appropriate materials, equipment, special compensatory study skills, and environmental modifications.
The regular class, with a *vision* resource room supplment Note: This resource room is staffed by a certified TVI and is not meant to serve children with other disabilities.	The student who may need special vision related assistance some part of every day; the Resource Room teacher is available as needed, to teach special skills or adapt materials, as well as support the regular classroom teachers.
The special "vision class" (can be located in a regular school, if there is enough visually impaired students, or can be a "day program" at a residential school, usually in an urban area, where transportation is available).	The student who is not ready for participation in regular class programs, and who needs daily, intensive study in expanded core curriculum areas.
The residential school for blind and visually impaired students.	Depending on the residential school, for students who have highly specialized needs (e.g., deafblind students, severely multiply disabled visually impaired students, or those who require intensive instruction in some vision-related area; instruction can be short-term (as in summer programs, or 6-week placements to strengthen particular skills) or long-term (a year or more).

Note: These are general descriptions only. The TVI should become familiar with the variety of possible service delivery models in his/her own geographical area.

ulations, it is reiterated that "regulations have always required that placement decisions be based on the individual needs of each child with a disability and prohibited categorical decision making." Further, placements are to be "as close as possible to the child's home," and "in the school that he or she would attend if nondisabled" (34 C.F.R. 300.552(b) and (c).). The regulations discussion portion clearly states: "The overriding rule in this section is that placement decisions for all children with disabilities, including preschool children, must be made on an individual basis."

It would appear that federal law contradicts itself by requiring regular class placement *and* requiring placements to be based on individual needs. However, one needs to step back and remember that disabled students were once *denied* public school placement *because of their disability.* The various federal laws were intended to open the public schools and grant *access* to students with disabilities.

In the field of visual impairment, there has been a philosophy of access since the early 1800s (Koestler, 1976) and blind children have attended public school since 1900 (Davis, 1976). Long before P.L. 94-142, 80 percent of the larger school systems in the United States had teachers of visually impaired children (Jones & Collins, 1966); these were especially trained teachers for students who were blind or visually impaired. We have had over 100 years to learn how to integrate visually impaired students in the public schools, and, interestingly enough, we still have residential schools because they continue to fill a need.

The "inclusion" urged by the "least restrictive environment" (LRE) requirements of federal law is not meant to dump all disabled children into regular classes. Rather, it is meant to say that students with disabilities have a *right* to that placement–if it is appropriate for them and meets their unique needs. It is the last part of that statement that the federal mandate intends most.

It seems, then, that the problem lies in determining when a designated "LRE" meets (or does *not* meet) a particular student's unique and individual needs, and therein lies a process. There must be a thorough evaluation of the child, *and,* ideally, an evaluation of the possible placement options. Research has identified at least 70 factors that lead towards successful (appropriate) inclusion for visually impaired students; only about half of the factors are pupil related. A fourth are characteristics of the school, and the rest are about evenly divided between parent/family factors and community supports (Bishop, 1986). The TVI and IEP team should look at all aspects of a particular placement before recommending it, for "simply putting an impaired child together with other children without impairments is naive and may lead to negative results" (Nixon, 1991, p. 19). We should *never* set up a student to fail if we can avoid it.

It should be remembered that a particular placement is not (and should not be) permanent. As the problem for which the placement was recommended is solved, or needs met, the placement should be re-evaluated; it may need to be changed or modified, to meet the new needs of the student. IEPs are not "carved in stone" and should reflect changing needs–and, perhaps, changing placements. The more sensitive an IEP team is to the evolving needs of the growing child, the more accurately the placement will reflect needs, and the less restrictive to learning it will be. "Appropriate integration, in which disabilities are taken into account but do not inhibit opportunities for interacting and developing relationships, does not occur by chance" (Nixon, 1991, p. 19). It is the responsibility and goal of every IEP team.

For some visually impaired children, inclusion may be a goal, not a placement. For a young visually impaired child, an extra year of nursery school, kindergarten, or a center-based vision program could provide the strong basic concepts that will enable interaction later with sighted peers in an inclusive setting in school. For a blind child of normal intelligence, there are many compensatory skills that must be acquired (e.g., braille reading and writing, the use of technology, independent mobility) before inclusion will provide successful and satisfying learning experiences; these children will need daily and intensive tool-skill instruction early in their school years, and it is difficult to provide this satisfactorily in an inclusive setting. ("Pull-out" instruction by the TVI, or a short-term special placement may be needed.) Visually impaired students with multiple disabilities (particularly deaf-blind children, and those with severe cognitive delays) may have difficulty communicating their needs and interacting appropriately; providing a one-on-one full-time personal aide does not mean the child is "included" and full inclusion may be an unattainable, unrealistic goal. In fact, inclusion for some visually impaired children (particularly those who have multiple disabilities) can be an extremely isolating experience. (Blindness alone is isolating.) Hoben (1976) studied students who were hearing impaired or visually impaired but "mainstreamed" and found a high level of social isolation among them. They were "included" but still left out. Heumann and Hehir (1995) caution that *harmful* effects of potential placements should be considered when recommending them. The TVI and IEP team have many factors to consider and should never take this responsibility lightly.

For very young visually impaired children (B–3), the "natural environment" is considered "inclusion" (or a downward extension of that concept). Federal law (Part C of IDEA, 20 U.S.C. 1431–1445) requires that B–3 services be delivered in the child's "natural environment" ("settings that are natural or normal for the child's age peers who have no disabilities" (20 U.S.C. 1435–1436).). The preceding discussion of LRE and inclusion can be applied to young visually impaired children as well. Thorough assessments, and consideration for family needs/priorities direct the Individual Family Services Plan (IFSP) and determination of any alternative instructional settings; if other than the child's "natural environment" is suggested, the IFSP must include a rationale for the alternative or supplementary recommendation (Family-Centered Practices for Infants and Young Children with Visual Impairments: A Position Paper, 2003).

WHAT IS "THE MOST APPROPRIATE PLACEMENT?"

Determining the most appropriate placement for a visually impaired child requires an ecological model of data collection. It is not enough to assess only the child; consideration should also be given to variables within the school, the family, and the community. The more indicators there are to consider, the more accurate the placement recommendation will be (Bishop, 1990).

An ecological data collection is an organized, orderly accumulation of relevant bits of information that can be used to help determine the best, most appropriate placement that will be least restrictive to learning. It is a means of evaluating factors that are *known* to contribute to successful inclusion for visually impaired students (Bishop, 1986). Although specific forms or checklists can be used to collect data, the format is not as important as the types of information. Much of it is normally collected during the process of acquiring eligibility data and "current level of functioning" information. Moreover, the good TVI generally talks to a number of people informally (teachers, parents/family, counselors, etc.) as a part of other evaluations; therefore, much of the ecological data collection process is familiar and procedurally routine. The most important feature of ecological evaluation is *making sure* that all aspects of the data collection have been addressed. (These include pupil variables, data about the school, family characteristics, and resources available in the community.)

The pupil variables will determine the direct instructional needs of the visually impaired student. The TVI usually asks:

- Is the student performing at grade/age level? If not, why not?
- Is the pupil *capable* of performing at grade/age level? If not, why not?
- Is the student's visual impairment interfering with achievement? Can anything be done to improve or enhance visual functioning?
- Given the student's available vision and ability, what are the best learning tools and instructional techniques *for this child?*
- How independent is the student?
- Are compensatory skills adequate for the student's age/grade or needs?

(Assess sensory efficiency for all senses, alternative communication methods, mastery of technology, mobility, etc.)
- Are other areas of the expanded core curriculum (ECC) age appropriate? (Evaluate social skills, self-help skills, leisure/recreation skills, study skills, ability to problem solve/make decisions, etc.)

Any area above that suggests a deficit is an area of concern (i.e., a need that requires attention or instruction). This need-profile should drive the IEP (or IFSP), which is simply a plan to help the student acquire the skills that will allow him/her to realize his/her potential.

Once the instructional needs of the student have been established, the next step is to determine:

- which areas should receive priority for instruction (sometimes there are more needs than can be addressed, and the list must be prioritized);
- how many hours of instruction each week will be needed (the answer to this question may help to decide the answers to the last two questions);
- who will provide instruction in each area of needs; and
- where instruction will take place.

(The reader will note that these are the basic components of the IEP.) When the answers to the first three questions have been decided, the answer to the last question (where?) should include an examination of the other remaining ecological variables: the school, the family, and the community. The IEP team will need to answer the following questions:

- Is there someone in the home-school who can provide the appropriate instruction? (Usually, it is a TVI or O&M instructor.)
- Can that person give sufficient time? (Beginning braille instruction, for example, requires a minimum of an hour a day.)
- Is there a place in the home-school for this instruction to take place? Is there storage space for equipment, books, and supplies, and are there enough electrical outlets for special equipment?
- Will the administrator and classroom teacher support the efforts of the TVI? (The positive attitude of the classroom teacher is the single most important variable in successful inclusion for a visually impaired child; without it, the placement may not be appropriate.)
- Does the student's family have realistic expectations for what can be accomplished? Are they willing to follow through when home practice of skills is suggested?
- Are the family members supportive of the goal of independence for their visually impaired child?

- What community resources are available? (Public transportation? Public agencies? Rehabilitation centers? Medical facilities? Libraries? Parks and playgrounds? Boy Scouts/Girl Scouts? YMCA? Volunteer groups, especially readers and/or braillists?)

The more positive answers there are to these questions, the more likely that there are enough factors in place to predict the appropriateness of the recommended placement.

The regular class is *not* an appropriate placement if:

- The administration and/or classroom teacher(s) are not supportive (are resentful, do not claim the student as "one of their own," or believe there is "some other place" for the student);
- The student does not "fit" with his/her peers (the class does not welcome him/her, the student has poor social skills, or there is little social interaction between the student and peers); or
- The student cannot participate in class activities (does not have the tool skills; is not on grade level, particularly in reading and writing; or can only participate with the assistance of a personal aide).

Regular class placement is risky if the student's family is not supportive and unwilling to follow through on school assignments (i.e., check to see that homework is done, communicate with the classroom teacher directly if problems arise, or encourage home practice of skills learned in school).

If the student's individual needs *can* be met in a regular class, with TVI/O&M support to some degree, then that placement does not restrict learning and would be appropriate. If, however, there are not enough factors in place to meet the needs of the student in his/her regular school/class, that placement would *not* be appropriate and may actually restrict learning. It is the match between student needs and available support that determines the appropriateness of the placement, and this premise must *always* drive any placement decision.

THE TVI: ROLES AND RESPONSIBILITIES

The teacher of students who are visually impaired (TVI) is a specially trained professional who has had a number of courses beyond general teaching methods. Although university teacher preparation programs vary in their requirements, there is a general content that includes:

- a history of and philosophical foundation for educating students who

are visually impaired;
- structure and function of the visual system;
- academic methods for the visually impaired learner;
- methods for teaching students who are visually impaired and have additional disabilities;
- braille;
- introductory Orientation and Mobility.

Some universities also offer courses in early childhood, in assessment, and in advanced braille/technology. This coursework is both broad and specific, preparing TVIs to perform a wide variety of functions with and for visually impaired learners. In fact, a widely accepted position paper (published by the Division of Visual Impairment, Council for Exceptional Children) states that "every infant, child, and youth with a visual impairment is entitled to the services of a TVI, regardless of the severity of the disability or the presence of additional disabilities" (Spungin & Ferrell, n.d.). In addition, Goal 3 of the National Agenda directs universities to prepare enough TVIs to meet the needs for such personnel across the nation (Corn et al., 1995). Despite national and local efforts, there remains a shortage of properly trained and certified TVIs, and IEP teams may have difficulty finding a TVI to perform the required assessments and provide the necessary services for visually impaired students. (The federal law says that an expert in the area of the child's suspected disability *must* participate in the assessment and IEP team planning process.)

The TVI may be employed in any of the array (continuum) roles: at a residential school, in a special class of visually impaired students, in a VI resource room, or as an itinerant teacher serving multiple locations where there are students with visual impairments. Although the roles and responsibilities of the TVI may vary with the employment model, they include some basic responsibilities. A brief review of these functions follows.

1. *Assessment* of visually impaired children of all ages (infants and toddlers, preschoolers, school-aged students), including the Functional Vision Evaluation, the Learning Media Assessment, and disability-related testing; interpreting vision-related portions of medical records, including the eye report; assisting in team assessments, particularly with visually impaired infants and toddlers, or with students who have multiple disabilities; using assessment results to:
   a. establish the "current level of functioning" for developing IFSP/IEP goals and objectives;
   b. help identify appropriate instructional methods, materials, and necessary environmental modifications;

   c. help direct decisions for placement;
   d. suggest appropriate learning and literacy media; and
   e. establish the need for specific technology needed by the visually impaired student.
2. *Consultation* with parents, classroom teachers, administrators, diagnosticians/psychologists, and other professionals, to interpret the unique and special needs of each individual visually impaired child.
3. *Participation* in IFSP and IEP planning meetings, to assure the appropriateness of services and placements.
4. *Assuring* that modifications in materials, methods, and the environment are implemented, including:
   a. obtaining and providing textbooks and other teaching materials in appropriate media (e.g., braille, enlarged print, or in recorded form);
   b. recommending environmental modifications that meet the student's individual needs;
   c. obtaining and setting up appropriate technology devices;
   d. suggesting any modifications needed in testing or assignments; and
   e. interpreting the child's individual visual needs to classroom teachers and all others who may have contact with the visually impaired student.
5. *Providing direct instruction* in expanded core curriculum areas, as needed by each individual visually impaired child, including:
   a. communication skills, including braille reading and writing, braille math, braille music, and other braille codes;
   b. listening skills;
   c. sensory development, including visual efficiency development and tactual discrimination skills;
   d. the efficient use of low vision devices;
   e. handwriting for blind students or those who have low vision;
   f. typing and keyboarding skills;
   g. the use of unique technology (computer access, screen readers, braille note takers, braille translators, computer screen print enhancement, etc.);
   h. organizational and study skills;
   i. motor development (particularly with infants and toddlers who are visually impaired);
   j. concept development (especially at basic levels);
   k. problem-solving/decision-making skills;
   l. daily living skills/self-help skills;
   m. human sexuality;
   n. leisure and recreation skills (including play);
   o. social skills;

p. vocational/career awareness and job readiness; and
q. introductory orientation and mobility.*

6. *Community interaction* (exploring the community for recreational opportunities for visually impaired students; reaching out to community organizations for material and social support for visually impaired students; identifying vocational opportunities for visually impaired students).
7. *Professional development* (attending professional conferences, workshops, and inservices to expand professional skills; participating in professional organizations to develop networks of professional support). (See also the Position Paper: *The Role and Function of the Teacher of Students with Visual Handicaps,* by Spungin and Ferrell.)

It should be apparent that the TVI is a unique special educator, equipped with highly developed special expertise. Generic special education teachers do not have these skills, nor do regular teachers and administrators. If appropriate placements and programs are to be designed to meet the individual needs of visually impaired learners, there must be a TVI available to provide special assessments, interpretations, and suggestions. Although TVIs are scarce, every effort should be made to find or train one. To do less invalidates the intent of federal law.

REFERENCES AND RECOMMENDED READING

Bishop, V. (1986). Identifying the components of success in mainstreaming. *Journal of Visual Impairment and Blindness, 80,* 939–946.

Bishop, V. (1990). Educational Placement Decision-Making: An ecological model. *Journal of Visual Impairment and Blindness, 84,* 350–353.

Corn, A., Hatten, P., Heubner, K., Ryan, F., & Siller, M. (1995). *The national agenda for the education of children and youth who are visually impaired, including those with multiple disabilities.* New York: AFP Press.

Davis, F. (1976). *Education of the blind: Using the past to challenge the future.* Address presented at the 53rd Biennial Conference of the Association of Education of the Visually Handicapped, July 1976, Louisville, Kentucky.

Family-Centered Practices for Infants and Young Children with Visual Impairments: A Position Paper. (2003). Division of Visual Impairment, Council for Exceptional Children.

Heumann, J. & Hehir, T. (1995). OSEP policy guidance on educating blind and visually impaired students. In Koenig, A. & Holbrook, A. (Eds.), *Foundations of educa-*

* The COMS will have the responsibility for structured Orientation and Mobility instruction, but the TVI can teach sighted guide techniques, general motor skills, sensory awareness, and directionality; these are essential skill areas for getting the student ready for structured travel instruction.

tion, Volume 2. New York, AFB Press.

Hoben, M. (1976). *Reducing isolation in the mainstream: Final report.* Minneapolis: Hennepin Technical Centers.

Jones, J. & Collins, A. (1966). *Educational programs for visually handicapped children.* Washington, DC: U.S. Government Printing Office.

Koestler, F. (1976). *The unseen minority.* New York: American Foundation for the Blind.

Nixon, H. (1991). *Mainstreaming and the American dream.* New York: American Foundation for the Blind.

Public Law 94-142 (The Education for All Handicapped Children Act of 1975). 20 U.S.C. 1400 et seq.

Public Law 105-17 (The Individuals with Disabilities Education Act amendments of 1997). 20 U.S.C. 1400 et seq. C.F.R. Section 300.550(b). Final Regulations, Federal Register, March 12, 1999.

Spungin, S. & Ferrell, K. (n.d.). *Role and function of the teacher of students with visual handicaps.* Position Paper of the Division for the Visually Impaired, a division of the Council for Exceptional Children, Reston, VA.

Part Three

TESTING AND TRANSITIONS

INTRODUCTION

Assessment is a critical part of an appropriate instructional program for visually impaired students. Not only is it a philosophically sound component of the educational process, it is also a legal mandate in special education. The assessment process establishes eligibility for special services, and provides data that directs the individual education plan. Federal law is specific about test characteristics (e.g., non-discriminatory, in the child's native language, administered by knowledgeable personnel, and are valid) and scope (assessment in all areas of suspected disability) (P.L. 105-17, IDEA Amendments of 1997). In the case of disabled infants or toddlers (B–3), assessment areas include levels of development in cognition, communication, social/emotional areas, physical abilities, and adaptive skills *and* the family's resources, priorities, and concerns (Part C of IDEA). Assessment is the foundation of program planning, for children with disabilities of all kinds, and of all ages, and an entire section of this book will be devoted to the assessment process.

Testing should begin as soon as possible after a referral is logged in. Schools have designed both a procedure (a "paper trail") and a designated team to follow the procedure. Chapter Thirteen of this section will discuss referral follow-up and teams. Chapter Fourteen will discuss assessment terminology, who performs which tests, and the role of the psychologist/diagnostician. A number of test instruments are critiqued, and guidelines for test modifications are given; suggestions are given for reporting test results. Chapters Fifteen, Sixteen, and Seventeen are devoted to assessment procedures the TVI is responsible for implementing, from the Functional Vision Evaluation and Learning Media Assessment, to O&M screening, technology evaluations, and assessments in areas of the expanded core curriculum (ECC). Chapter Eighteen pulls the assessment results together into a goal-based intervention plan (the IFSP or IEP). Diagnostic teaching (systematic ongoing assessment) for students with visual impairments is discussed in Chapter Nineteen, and the final chapter outlines all of the transitions in the life of a visually impaired student and his/her family.

This section is an extended commentary on assessment for students with visual disabilities, and should help TVIs become more knowledgeable and confident in assessing these children. Since TVIs are often (and *should* be) liaison personnel with other members of assessment teams, particularly psychologists/diagnosticians, it is important to have access to as much information about assessment as possible. These final chapters are a contribution to that end.

Chapter Thirteen

REFERRAL AND TEAMS

Federal law specifies a "multidisciplinary" assessment prior to the meeting during which the individual educational plan (IEP) is generated, but the term "multidisciplinary" was used in a generic sense in the law. The intent was to accumulate as much information as possible, from a wide range of "specialists" (medical *and* educational), in order to make informed decisions about the best way to educate each individual exceptional child. The parents (or primary caregivers) were to be active members of the decision-making team, but legislation rarely creates reality, and the "dream-team" was no exception.

As regulations were written for the federal law, the terms used in the statute were studied and questioned, and definitions emerged that still left room for a variety of interpretations. The "multidisciplinary team" was one of the terms that was left somewhat vague. Required members were defined loosely.

The most recent amendments to the original law use the term "IEP team" without using the term "multidisciplinary," although team members are expected to have "particular knowledge or expertise to bring to the team" (Discussion notes from Section 300.344.). Required members of the team include:

1. "The parents of the child;
2. At least one regular education teacher of the child;
3. At least one special education teacher of the child, or if appropriate, at least one special education provider of the child;
4. A representative of the public agency who is:
   a. qualified to provide or supervise the provision of specially designed instruction to meet the unique needs of children with disabilities;
   b. knowledgeable about the general curriculum; and
   c. knowledgeable about the availability of resources of the public agency.

5. An individual who can interpret the instructional implications of the assessment results;
6. At the discretion of the parent or the agency, other individuals who have knowledge of or special expertise about the child, including related service personnel as appropriate; and
7. If appropriate, the child." (34 C.F.R. 300.344)

The accompanying discussion to the recent regulations states that there is no limitation on the number of individuals who can attend IEP meetings. The TVI should always be a member of the IEP team when the child is visually impaired, and some states require it.

The persons who conduct the assessments are usually members of the IEP team as well; in actual practice, they are commonly the person(s) who have expertise in areas of suspected disabilities and the psychologist/diagnostician, but could include anyone the parents or school designate (including someone who is familiar with applicable laws, the child's needs, or has conducted an independent evaluation of the child).

The intentionally vague descriptions left teams and their members largely up to the states to specify; they could *add* as many members as they chose, but could not have fewer. As a result, the exact functioning of the team left room for interpretation, so long as their reports following the assessment were timely and provided useful information for program planning.

At least three team models emerged in theory from the broad guidelines set by law, and a number of combinations of these can be found in practice. Each model will be discussed in its purest form, before comments are made about the actual applications.

MULTIDISCIPLINARY TEAMS

Strictly interpreted, the multidisciplinary team is made up of a number of specialists, and the number may vary according to the range and/or severity of the child's disabilities. Among the specialists might be a psychologist, a neurologist, a pediatrician, an ophthalmologist or optometrist, an audiologist, a speech and language specialist, an orientation and mobility specialist, a TVI, an occupational therapist, or a physical therapist. Although the parents are considered to be members of the team as well, they usually act in a supportive role during both the assessment and programming phases of the educational process. Each specialist performs an independent assessment of the child and presents an independent report at the IEP planning meeting. Services, if indicated, are also also independently provided as well. The parents provide information and follow recommendations made by the team,

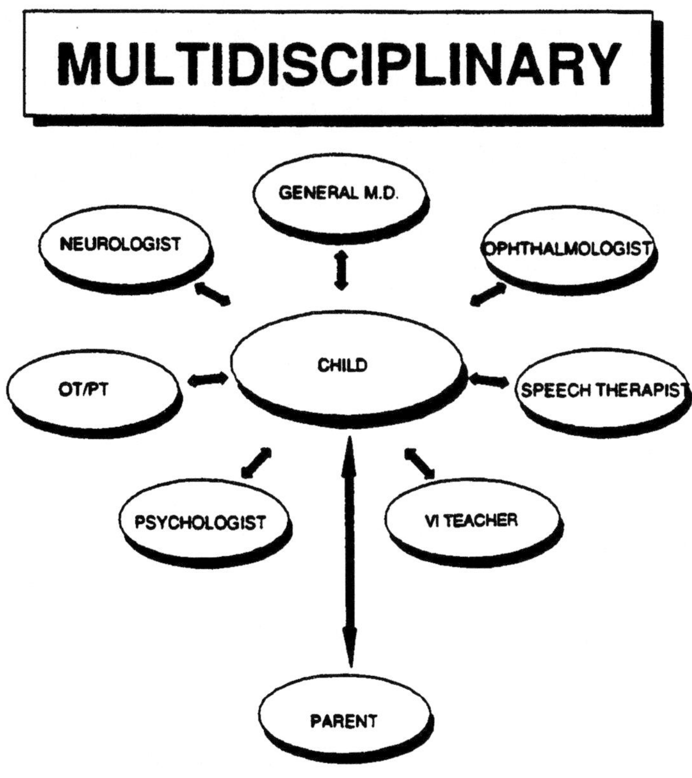

Figure 14.

but are rarely actively involved in either assessment or programming. In fact, many parents may believe that their role is to remain passive and accept the recommendations of the specialists because they "know best." The only time the entire team meets face-to-face is during the initial evaluation meeting and during the three-year re-evaluations. Annual reviews of the IEP are usually done with the minimum number of required team members (with written reports available from absent members). (See Figure 14.)

INTERDISCIPLINARY TEAMS

This team is made up of the same range of specialists, but the major difference from the multidisciplinary team is improved communication. The specialists talk to each other prior to performing assessments and may even work in two's or three's to do their testing. There is consultation before, during, and after the assessment process. The parents are either present during or consulted before and after testing. During the IEP planning, findings may

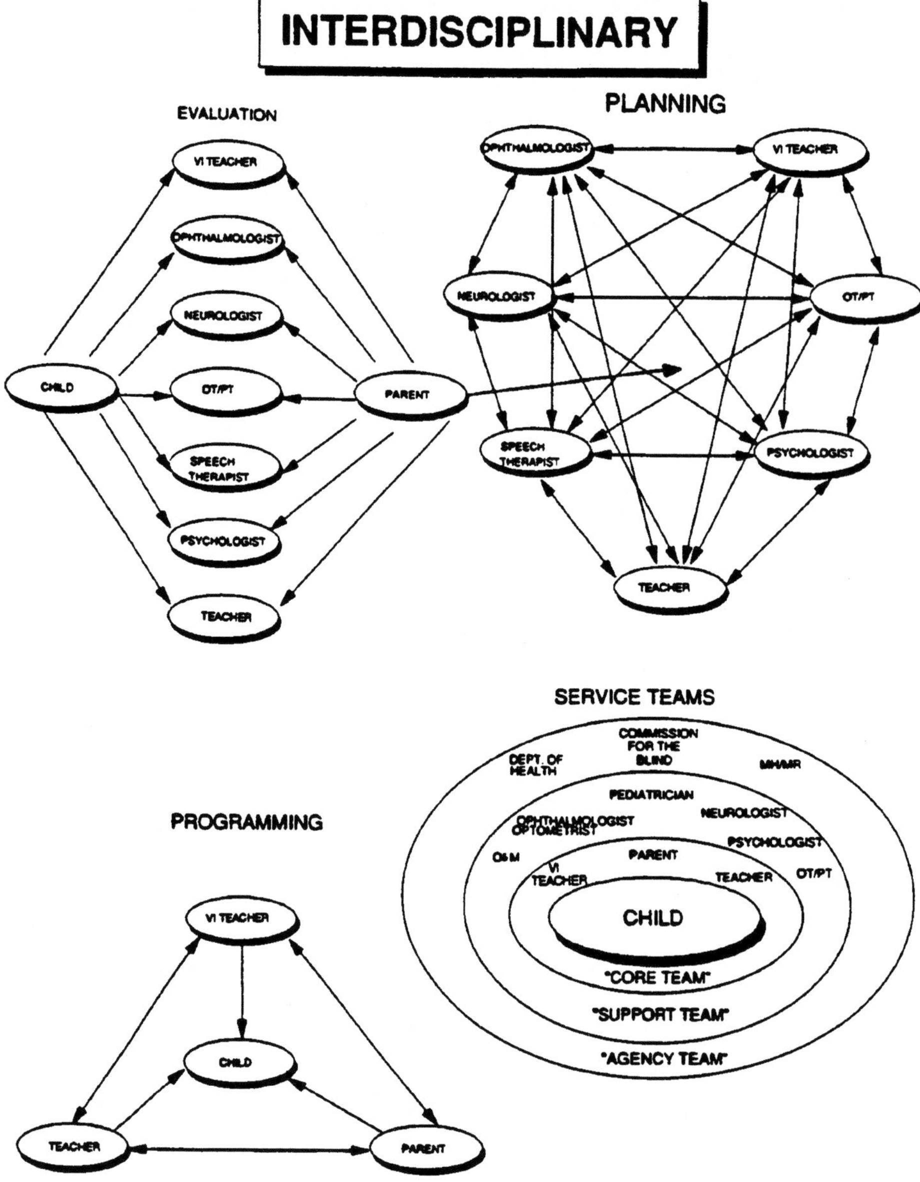

Figure 15.

be presented jointly or independently, and discussion is open. Parents are considered contributing members of the team and are included in all discussions. Goals and objectives are agreed upon jointly by all team members (including the parents) and they may even overlap. For example, vision-related goals may be infused into daily activities in the classroom. Each specialist will probably continue to deliver independent services throughout the school year, but there is ongoing sharing of progress noted among the team members. Everyone learns a little bit about everyone else's area of expertise, and the child receives an integrated program. Parents usually like this kind of team because they (the parents) are encouraged to take an active role in their child's educational program (see Figure 15).

TRANSDISCIPLINARY TEAMS

The major difference from the other two team models is the transfer of expertise. In both assessment and programming, one or two of the team members (usually the classroom teacher, or parent in the case of a very young child, and sometimes a designated medical "leader") assume the major responsibilities in both testing and service provision. Medical assessments may be performed independently but the information obtained is channeled through the medical leader (often a pediatrician). Educational services are provided solely by the classroom teacher or parent, under the supervision of the specialists; that is, each specialist teaches the teacher or parents how to do what is needed; there is role and expertise release. Parents are usually actively involved in the entire process (see Figure 16).

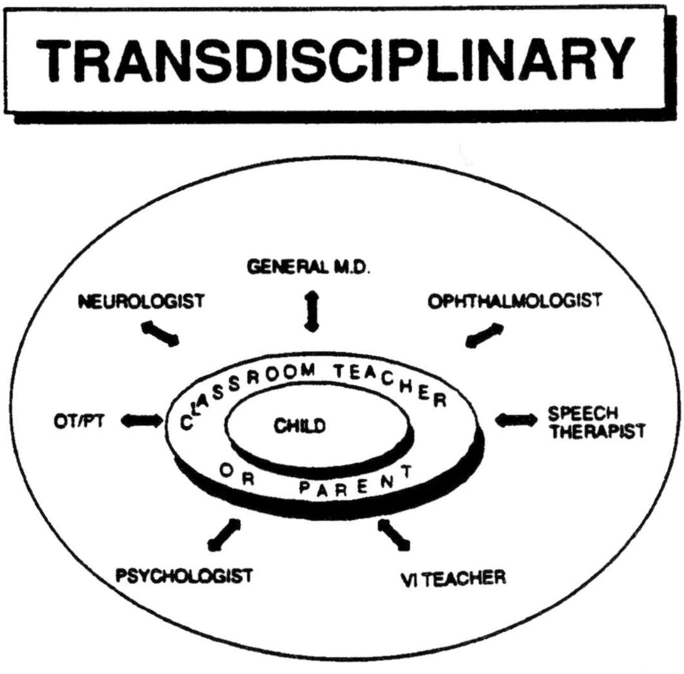

Figure 16.

A COMPARISON OF THE MODELS

Each of the models has advantages and disadvantages, and most teams, in reality, use a little of all three models. The multidisciplinary model provides strong, in-depth expertise in both assessment and programming, but there is little sharing of knowledge; parents are often more observers than participants. The interdisciplinary model still retains some separation of expertise, but there is more communication and interaction between/among the team members; parents are more involved at all levels. The transdisciplinary model looks good on paper, but rarely works smoothly in practice. Specialists don't give up their expertise easily, and the primary service provider(s) may feel overwhelmed by the quantity of information they are expected to absorb and implement. The smoothness of operation may depend on the personalities of the team members and their willingness to release traditional roles.

In actual practice, the strong expertise of the specialists is usually a requirement (especially for multidisabled students), but open communication may not occur until the sharing of reports at the IEP planning meeting. Goals and objectives may be jointly agreed upon, and sometimes infused

COMPARISON OF THE THREE MODELS

	MULTIDISCIPLINARY	INTERDISCIPLINARY	TRANSDISCIPLINARY
EVALUATION	- Each team member does a separate evaluation & prepares a report.	- Each team member does a separate evaluation - Some informal discussion with other team members before evaluation - Separate reports	- Team members do a joint evaluation. Preliminary discussion among team members essential.
PLANNING	- Each team member presents own report & plans for own services.	- Although separate reports are presented, much discussion occurs across disciplines - Services are inter-related.	- Team members develop a joint service plan, implemented by a primary service provider.
PROGRAMMING	- Each team member delivers own services & charts progress in own area of expertise.	- Team members deliver own services but utilize suggestions from other team members. - Chart child's progress in own area of expertise.	- Primary service provider delivers services & charts progress of child.
ROLE OF PARENT	- Largely a contributor - Occasionally an implementer.	- A contributor & an implementer	- May be the primary service provider & often a strong component of the team.
ROLE OF THE VI TEACHER	- A member of the team & a direct service provider.	- A member of the team but may share role with others.	- Contributing member of the team, but rarely a direct service provider.
ADVANTAGES	- Child receives in-depth evaluation and programming in a number of disciplines.	- Team members learn from each other. - Programming usually better coordinated - Parent is more likely to be included at the programming level.	- Team is a unified force and shares both responsibility and expertise. - Parent is fully involved.
DISADVANTAGES	- Segmented evaluation and programming. - Parent often on the "side-lines".	- Still some separation of disciplines.	- Success depends on team personalities & level of committment and on ability/receptivity of primary service provider.

Figure 17.

into coexisting services, but the specialists still retain their own roles and service provision. The role of parents still seems to vary from school district to school district, and may depend on the philosophy of the administrator. Even twenty-five years after P.L. 94-142 was legislated, there are still situations where parents are encouraged (and sometimes even told) to accept whatever services are offered without comment or question. Their role as a participating team member may be seen more as a threat to authority than as a vital contribution. It is hoped that these situations are few and rapidly disappearing, for parents should play a very important role in the education of their children, particularly if those children have disabilities. Parents are vital team members, and their participation in the assessment, planning, and programming processes is critical to the success of the system.

THE DECISION-MAKING PROCESS

The IEP is the result of decisions made at the planning meeting where assessment information is presented, discussed, and interpreted. Goals and objectives should <u>not</u> exist on paper at the beginning of the meeting; they should be ideas in the minds of the team members, subject to review and discussion during the meeting. Otherwise, the IEP will not represent a team decision.

Eligibility for services is generally based on the recommendations of the appropriate specialist(s), who should be able to support that eligibility with documented assessment results. In the case of visual impairment, the eye report is only one document of support; the Functional Vision Evaluation should have accumulated much more information about how vision is actually used. Numbers (acuities) are only one piece of data and often do not reflect actual visual functioning. Few states today still use a numerical definition of eligibility for services from the TVI or O&M specialist, since it has now been recognized that the quality of vision is more important than the quantity. Therefore, for a visually impaired student, the TVI will present the documentation for eligibility.

Other specialists should also document whatever criteria are required for eligibility for other services. The cognitive assessment should present data to support mental retardation or giftedness; the speech and language specialist should document any need for speech or language therapy; the audiological report should identify any hearing loss that will qualify the child as hearing impaired. The occupational and/or physical therapist should describe any physical abnormality that might require therapy. Whatever other disabilities are suspected should have been investigated and eligibility for special services either supported or ruled out. By the end of all the reports from team members, it should be clear what sorts of "labels" are appropriate (by law, a label must be attached before services can be provided). In the case of multiple disabilities, it may be difficult to establish the "primary" disability, but, for administrative purposes, this must be done. In most cases, a visual impairment is considered a primary disability because of its critical role in learning. If mental retardation is identified, however, it may be used as the primary label for placement purposes; in these cases, visual impairment should be the second label. In most states, funding is tied to labels, and the number of available special teachers may depend on the "head counts" of students. It is important, not only for appropriate service provision but to keep administrators aware of the need for special teachers, to see that visual impairment is among the top two or three labels assigned to a multiply disabled student.

The decision of placement should rest on the *individual needs of the student,* not the availability of services. It should not be interpreted on a restrictivity continuum. Least restrictive environment (LRE) has been interpreted to mean "mainstreaming" or "inclusion," and if appropriate services can be provided in the student's home school, this is ideal. Federal law still mandates a "continuum of services" that includes itinerant teacher support, a resource room (for visually impaired students, this is *not* a generic resource room or an "LD" resource room, but one staffed by a certified TVI), a special class, and a residential school. These alternative programs are not on a continuum of good to bad, or even "least restrictive environment" to "most restrictive environment." A residential school might be able to provide a learning environment more conducive to learning for the visually impaired student than the local school can provide (i.e., *less* restrictive for the visually impaired student). Therefore, it might be more appropriate to call the placement choices for visually impaired students an "array" of service options. Each has advantages that might best fulfill the needs of *that* particular visually impaired student at *that* time; review of placement should be annual, and should be changed when the needs for which the student was placed there have been met. This is an important concept for placement decision-making for visually impaired students, and should be clear to all team members and parents (see Figure 13).

Recommended program modifications (the "goals and objectives" of the IEP) should be based on the assessment results. For every goal and its objectives, there should be a "current level of functioning" established through prior testing. Recommended goals should never be generic or based on instinct (no matter how good); <u>they should be the outgrowth of assessment</u>. The purpose of testing should be to identify what the student knows/can do (strengths) or doesn't know/can't do (needs). With a realistic profile of potential in mind, learning should mean progress in the acquisition of skills needed. Therefore, goals and objectives should reflect the incremental steps of skill acquisition that can be realistically achieved in a given time period (usually a school year). This is what an IEP should be (see Chapter Eighteen).

Chapter Fourteen

COMPREHENSIVE ASSESSMENTS

Teaching visually impaired students requires ongoing assessment of their skills, knowledge -base, and ability to access information. Much of this on-going assessment can be done through diagnostic teaching (see Chapter Nineteen), but sometimes it is necessary to do other kinds of evaluations. This chapter will focus on several aspects of individual assessments: purposes of testing, sequence of testing, who should test what, how test modifications affect test results, and how to report test results. A few of the many intelligence tests will be described, including which are useful and which are not recommended. Some unique assessment procedures will be described. A number of terms commonly used in discussing assessment will be reviewed to refresh the reader's memory.

There are a number of ways to group tests, including formal/informal, standardized/nonstandardized, group/individual, verbal/performance, norm-referenced/criterion-referenced, and skill or knowledge based/outcome based. The criteria for groupings depends on the particular characteristics of the procedures. Briefly, the major differences are shown in Figure 18.

TERMS RELATED TO TESTING

The terms used most commonly to describe test structure and/or results (usually applied to formal, standardized, and norm-referenced tests) include validity, reliability, standardization, percentile, stanine, grade level equivalent, and normal distribution (mean, mode, median). An understanding of these terms is essential to reading test manuals or making sense out of the computer print-outs of scores. Each will be discussed briefly.

Validity asks whether the test actually measures what it *says* it measures. Content validity means that there are enough items to evaluate the skills, knowledge, or behavior, sampling across a broad range of possibilities. That

Formal	Informal
Timed	Generally untimed
Strict instructions	Less strict instructions
Quantitative (numerical) score standardized	Qualitative (no numbers) results Non- standardized
Formal; normed	Informal; no norms
Implications depend on the amount of deviation from the norm	Implications are individualized

Verbal	Performance
Verbal answers given	Demonstration of tasks
Non-verbal child will not do well	Blind/visually impaired child may have difficulty since most tasks require a visual orientation
Blind/visually impaired child may give "correct" answers but may not understand the meanings implied	Tactual/auditory analogs may not test the same concepts

Note: Some tests of intelligence have aspects of both types; may contain both verbal <u>and</u> performance items.

Norm-referenced	Criterion-referenced
Individual scores are compared to norms (other students of similar age/grade)	Skill mastery is individualized (not compared to other students)
Examples: Achievement tests Intelligence tests Developmental scales Adaptive scales	Examples: Check lists Observational data collection Anecdotal data collection Occupational data collection (e.g., work samples) Ecological data collection

Skill/Knowledge-based	Outcome-based
Assesses a particular skill or knowledge (e.g., spelling, reading speed, math calculations) with little attention to how the skill/knowledge will be used in the long term	Determines whether a broadly-stated, long-term goal has been reached (e.g., efficient mobility within a community, caring for personal needs, communicating effectively via speaking and/or writing); the goal determines the acquisition process and sequence

Figure 18.

is, there are enough items to give an accurate measure of the skill, knowledge, or behavior being measured. Criterion validity is how well this test compares with other already-known-to-be-valid measures. Construct validity means that the skill/knowledge or behavior being measured is based on sound and proven theory.

This concept of validity has implications when part or all of a test is modified (put in an alternate sensory form, or the timing/instructions are altered). Changing a standardized test *in any way* can affect its validity.

Reliability asks how *well* the test measures; would it give essentially the same results if given to the same group twice? Generally, the more items on the test, the more likely it is to be reliable.

Again, modifying a standardized test disrupts its reliability, unless the *exact* same changes are used the second time, with the same group. Also, when a visually impaired student's vision fluctuates for any reason, the performance may not be the same in a retest situation, and the test results may appear to be unreliable. It may not be the fault of the test, but a function of the visual status.

Standardization means that a large, well-defined group has been the "norm" group; the group usually contains a representative sample (e.g., equal numbers of males and females, percentages of ethnic groups or socioeconomic levels that approximate the general population). Most norming groups do not include visually impaired persons in enough numbers to be representative, and there are few tests that have separate "norms" for the visually impaired population. Also, since there are a variety of factors in visual impairments that can affect performance (e.g., age of onset, severity of the visual impairment, diagnosis, past experiences, presence of other disabilities), it may be next-to-impossible even to *develop* norms for the visually impaired population. If norms for visually impaired people do exist, they may lack meaning because of the heterogeneity of the group.

Percentiles, stanine scores, and *grade level equivalents* are all ways of comparing an individual score to the "norm." The percentile is based on 100, and tells what percentage of the population is *below* the individual score. (Thus, a 95th percentile is high performance and 45th percentile is below average.) Stanine scores are mathematical equivalents, using a mean of 5; they range from one (lowest) to 9 (highest). The advantage to using stanine scores is that they are single digits which can be stored easily in computer databases, and on punchcards, without taking up too much room or memory. Grade level equivalents compare an individual score to an easily recognized grade level in school.

Measures of central tendency are ways of looking at an entire group's set of scores; the individual score is only one of the group. The *Mean* is the mathematical average of all scores. That is, all scores are added up, and the total divided by the number of scores. It is the measure most often used in reporting statistics because it has been mathematically derived and can be studied mathematically. The *Mode* is that score which occurs the most frequently; it requires only a simple counting up of how many scores fall at each level. Because it is not mathematically obtained, it has little statistical value. The *Median* is the middle score; half of the scores are higher and half are lower. It is not a mathematical statistic that is useful except in describing the group.

In an *exactly* normal distribution, the Mean, Mode, and Median would be theoretically the same, but few distributions of scores are exactly normal; most show different locations on the curve for Mean, Mode, and Median. Bimodal distributions have two modes (two "humps" in the curve). In distributions that have the highest point of the curve to the right or left of center, the high point will be the Mode; the Median and the Mean will be somewhere on the side of the longer slope.

PURPOSE OF TESTING

Assessment should never be an arbitrary procedure; it should always have a purpose. The goal is usually to collect some kind of information for categorization (labeling or grouping), placement, or programming. Sometimes, testing is used to determine the need for special instructional techniques, materials, or adaptations. In all cases, the purpose of testing should determine the type of test selected, its sequence in the assessment process, and who should administer it. For example, if initial information about visual functioning is desired, such an evaluation would include both formal and informal measures, should precede all other assessments, and can only be administered by a TVI or O&M Instructor. If a measure of cognitive functioning is needed, a standardized intelligence test would probably be administered; this would occur *after* the Functional Vision Evaluation (and after a conference with the TVI or O&M Instructor, whichever one administered the Functional Vision Evaluation). Cognitive testing is usually limited to a specially trained diagnostician or psychologist (depending on the state's designated examiner title). If content mastery is to be evaluated, the test would probably be criterion-referenced, administered by a teacher, at whatever point the student was believed to have learned a designated quantity of information or skills. Sometimes, different types of tests can be used to assess the same skill, but for different reasons (e.g., to test a math concept, a standardized test will tell how a student's performance compares with a grade level or norm, but a criterion-referenced test will measure the student's own performance over time. To determine the level of early development, an observational checklist can uncover strengths or weaknesses, but a developmental scale can document delays as compared to the "norm"). It should be evident that the type of test chosen should yield results that fulfill the original purpose for the assessment.

SEQUENCE OF TESTING

There is a unique sequence for the initial assessment (and every three-year reevaluation) of visually impaired students. The eye report should be available first, and then the TVI (or O&M Instructor) will conduct a Functional Vision Evaluation; the results of this assessment should establish eligibility as a visually impaired student. A Learning Media Assessment can be added to the Functional Vision Evaluation (see Chapter Fifteen). Once the visual status, learning channels, and reading media have been established with some degree of certainty, all other initial assessments may take place (psychological testing adaptive scales, social maturity measures, etc.). If achievement evaluation or special skills assessments (O&M, daily living skills, braille, social skills, etc.) are indicated, these tests usually follow the second group (see Figure 19).

It is critical to establish the quality of useful vision, the best learning channel(s), and, when appropriate, the most efficient reading medium *before* other tests are administered because this information could influence both the choice of tests and how they are administered. It may also affect the interpretation of the results. The teacher of visually impaired students should be able to translate Functional Vision Evaluation and Learning Media Assessment information into recommendations (best media, best seating/positioning, best lighting, use of optical devices, fatigue factor, characteristics of specific eye conditions, etc.).

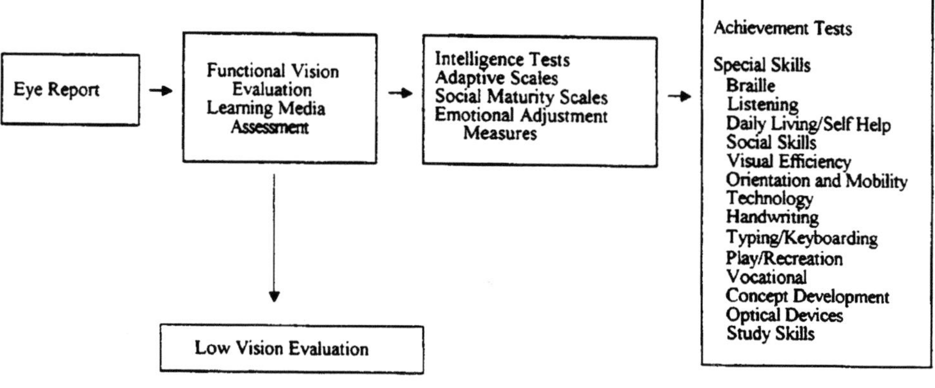

Figure 19.

WHO TESTS WHAT?

Generally, the TVI is responsible for evaluating visual functioning, learning media, and all disability-related skills except mobility; the O&M Instructor may sometimes do the Functional Vision Evaluation, but always does the O&M evaluation. (A Low Vision Specialist, usually a specially trained optometrist or ophthalmologist, does the Low Vision Evaluation in a clinical setting.) A diagnostician or psychologist usually conducts the psychological testing, completes the adaptive scale, or evaluates social/emotional status. Classroom teachers commonly assess achievement, while special teachers evaluate skills related to or unique to particular disabilities (e.g., the speech therapist will assess speech and language; the physical therapist will check physical abilities).

Assessments that a TVI might conduct include:

1. Functional Vision Evaluation
2. Learning Media Assessment
3. Disability-specific skills in:
   a. Braille reading and writing, including both braillewriter and slate/stylus;
   b. Typing/Keyboarding
   c. Handwriting (for blind students or those with low vision);
   d. Special-tool efficiency (abacus, tape player, calculator, braille translators, braille note-takers, unique computer software use, CCTV, low vision devices);
   e. Social interactions and behaviors;
   f. Daily living/Self-help skills;
   g. Play and Recreational skills;
   h. Concept development;
   i. Early development for young visually impaired children;
   j. Visual efficiency;
   k. Organizational and study skills; and
   l. Listening skills.

These evaluations can be done on an annual basis or as needed. If IEP goals include any of these special instructional areas, at least annual assessment is indicated.

MODIFIED ASSESSMENTS

A few visually impaired students are able to be tested without any modifications in test materials or procedures, but most visually impaired students will require some kind of adaptations. These changes can range from extended timing to the use of optical devices to enlarge materials, to changes in media (from print to braille or audio tape, or from visual to tactual procedures). The decision to modify should rest jointly with the TVI and the examiner, and should depend wholly on the individual visual needs of the student. Modifications may differ from student to student, and test to test. Some general guidelines may help in deciding when or how much to adapt a test.

A test should probably be modified when:

1. The medium of the test is different from the student's primary reading medium or chief learning sense;
2. The test is strictly timed (most visually impaired students are slower readers because of their visual disability);
3. "Bubble sheet" answer forms are used (the constant back-and-forth looking is extremely difficult and fatiguing for a visually impaired student); or
4. When graphics (tables, charts, diagrams) or small symbols (as in math or science) are used in the test.

Options to consider when modifying a test include:

1. Changing the reading medium (print to enlarged* type, braille or audio tape);
2. Changing of pictures or diagrams to enlarged* versions or raised line equivalents, or by increasing contrast (outlining with a dark pen) or decreasing unnecessary detail;
3. Changing of charts or tables to braille or enlarged* type;
4. Extending the timing, especially when visual fatigue might result; an often-quoted guideline is "time and a half" for enlarged* print readers, and double time for braille readers;
5. Using taped instructions to minimize reading time;
6. Using special answer sheets (either tactual or enlarged*);
7. Preparing parts of the test ahead of time (e.g., the list of choices in matching tasks);
8. Omitting items (only when absolutely necessary; this is only an option if the child is blind and the test item is visual, e.g., tracking an object, reaching, or is based on visual experience, e.g., colors);
9. Reading the test *to* the student, and allowing him/her to record answers

*Note that the word "enlarged" has been used when "large print" is indicated, to suggest that optical devices may also be used to make print and/or test items larger or more visible.

in the preferred medium (including dictating to a tape recorder); or
10. Providing an amanuensis (a sighted person to write down whatever answers the visually impaired student gives).

Other modifications that may affect the testing situation (but not the test itself) include:

1. The provision of additional lighting (or reducing the lighting) if needed;
2. Spotlighting the task with a flashlight;
3. Reducing glare by using a dull surface under any manipulative task items;
4. Increasing contrast by using a lighter or darker background under manipulative task items;
5. Using a reading stand to position printed reading materials closer to the eyes;
6. Adapting seating (the right size/height of chair; feet supported if they don't reach the floor; proper positioning in a wheelchair if normally used);
7. Providing visual and physical rest-breaks as often as the test procedure permits;
8. Using a tray to contain test items (to keep them from falling on the floor or rolling off the table or desk);
9. Using real objects instead of toys or models whenever possible;
10. Making the testing environment as comfortable as possible temperature-wise, and as quiet as possible to minimize auditory distractions;
11. Allow the student to become familiar with the room before testing begins; and
12. For multiply disabled-visually impaired students, consult with the physical therapist and/or occupational therapist for best positioning to allow maximum use of available vision.

There are a number of cautions to observe when modifying test items or procedures. These include:

1. Obtaining permission from the test publisher; technically, permission in writing is required before making any modifications; some publishers are even willing to help (usually by providing a large print edition) if contacted.
2. If items are omitted, be able to support why; this is usually described in the report or results.
3. Be sure modified items measure the same skill. For example, putting a diagram into tactual form makes it a tactual-perceptual integration task,

very different from a visual-perceptual integration task.

4. Remain aware that modifying for a blind student may be very different from modifying for a student with low vision; braille reading is not the equivalent of visually reading enlarged print, either physically, perceptually, or cognitively.
5. Watch for errors that are braille related, not the result of faulty comprehension; the braille code used by most school-age students is not a letter-for-letter translation; some entire words are represented by a single symbol.
6. Oral administration of a test is not the same as the student reading the test for him/herself, and an oral description of a picture or diagram is not the same as a visual interpretation made by the student. The listening vocabulary is nearly always greater than the reading vocabulary.
7. It cannot be stressed too strongly that any modification of a standardized test (both procedures and test items) can affect the validity and/or reliability of the test. Adapting items may change the task/skill being tested; changing the media affects reading speed; and omitting items may leave certain skills or tasks under-represented in the test.

The reader may be feeling a sense of frustration by now, and might reasonably ask whether there are any tests just for visually impaired students, or what happens if test modifications are *not* made to allow for individual visual differences? The answer to the first question is that there are very few (if any) standardized tests, of any kind (including intelligence tests) only for visually impaired students, with norms for this low prevalence population; the population is so heterogeneous (even though few in number) that "norms" are difficult and expensive to obtain.

The answer to the second question is that test results would be invalid for the visually impaired student if no modifications were made because he/she would not have had full opportunity to be tested. If the student cannot see the test materials, appropriate answers cannot be given. If the student cannot find the correct "bubble" to fill in on the answer sheet, answers may be placed inaccurately. If certain items on the test are impossible to complete because of the visual impairment or the lack of visual experience, those items will not test fairly.

Attempts have been made to adapt some standardized tests solely for visually impaired students (e.g., the Hayes-Binet and Perkins-Binet intelligence tests, Maxfield-Buchholz Social Maturity Scale for Preschool Blind children–an early adaptation of the old Vineland Social Maturity Scale), and to modify the media (large print and/or braille editions of some achievement tests). The Hayes-Binet and Maxfield-Buchholz tests are generally considered obsolete (outdated); moreover, the Maxfield-Buchholz Scale was standardized on a population of blind children that included an unusually high percentage (60%) of subjects with the visual diagnosis of RLF/ROP–a disease with unique characteristics that may not be representative of the entire preschool blind population. The Perkins-Binet test was withdrawn from use because of technical problems related to reliability.

The Haptic Intelligence Scale for the Blind (HIS) is not recommended for several reasons. Miniature objects in the test kit may not represent the real object to a blind child; coding dots are too large for rapid finger perception; the "assembly" items (a doll and a hand) are not realistic enough to elicit recognition; and the abacus in the test kit is a *Chinese* abacus (which is not constructed like the abacus a blind student might use). A major flaw in the standardization process is that blindfolded but sighted adults were used to simulate a blind population; obviously, these persons had prior visual experience to use that would not be available to a congenitally blind person.

The Ohwaki-Kohs Tactile Block Design Intelligence Test for the Blind is another flawed test. It utilizes tactual block designs, which may or may not measure the same skill as the visual equivalent, and it was normed on blind persons in Japan. Cultural and educational differences may not transfer easily to American experiences.

The Blind Learning Aptitude Test (BLAT) is a possible supplement to verbal portions of intelligence tests (e.g., the Wechsler Scales). The BLAT uses a tactual approach to assess learning ability (not acquired information) and evaluates the blind student's tactual ability to discriminate differences, note similarities, and perceive relationships. BLAT results, although *not* a measure of intelligence, correlate well with the WISC verbal scores, and have a lower-but-still-significant correlation with the Stanford Achievement Test. The BLAT may provide important information about *how* a blind student learns, and should probably be among the test procedures used to test the abilities of blind students.

Perhaps the most promising efforts in the testing of intelligence in blind children may be the ITVIC (Intelligence Test for Visually Impaired Children) developed by Dekker and her colleagues in The Netherlands. The ITVIC has been developed within the last ten years, and appears to test various facets of intelligence (orientation, reasoning, spatial ability, and verbal ability); the subscales measuring reasoning and verbal abilities correlated highly with school achievement in the initial standardization process. The test is not yet widely known or used in the United States. The standardizing population (106 blind children without useful vision and 49 visually impaired children with some minimal vision, ages 6–15 years) was found in The Netherlands; the assumption is that children are children, wherever in the world they live, but differences in educational programming or culture may need to be examined more closely. Replication of Dekker's results in the United States could strengthen the validity and reliability of the test. (See a more extensive discussion of the ITVIC in the Warren reference.)

There appear to be some performance similarities among visually impaired students on subtests of the WISC-R, but deficits increase as the vision decreases. Items requiring auditory memory (e.g., "digit span") may be inflated, but the examiner might be concerned if this area is low. "Comprehension" scores may decrease markedly as the amount of vision decreases (that is, a blind child may perform less well than a child with low vision). "Information," "Similarities," and "Vocabulary" may depend more on actual ability. In the performance subtests (which are usually only attempted with students who have some useful vision), "Picture Arrangement" and "Picture Completion" require considerable visual perceptual ability. Students with low vision may do well on the "Block Design" subtest, but may have difficulty with "Object Assembly" because it relies on visual memory. The "Coding" subtest is nearly impossible for most visually impaired students because of the reduced ability to scan and track efficiently. Therefore, the verbal portions of the Wechsler series can yield useful information in many cases, but it should be viewed guardedly and supported by other test results.

The Diagnostician or Psychologist who is faced with the task of assessing intelligence in a young visually impaired student must use some judgment in selecting and administering a test and in reporting the results. Both the Bailey Scales and the Battelle Inventory are heavily visually oriented (as are most developmental scales at the early levels), so they should be used with caution and reported as possibly measuring inaccurately. Since there are presently no developmental norms for blind or visually impaired children, comparisons may be to sighted norms by default. The verbal portion of the WPPSI (preschool) and primary (Wechsler Scale) may yield useful information, but the performance portion may be more dependent on visual/perceptual ability than on intelligence.

Suggested tests include (with cautions indicated):

1. Verbal portions of the *Wechsler series (WPPSI, WISC-R, WAIS-R)* with guarded interpretation; if the performance sections are given, use them more for observing function than for reporting scores.
2. *Woodcock-Johnson Psych-Educational Battery:* some portions may be useful, depending on the severity of the visual impairment.
3. *Leiter:* often too performance-oriented; consider the amount of available vision.
4. *Detroit Tests of Learning Aptitude:* some subtests (e.g., auditory memory) may be useful; much depends on the quality and quantity of available vision and past visual experience.
5. *Kauffman Assessment Battery:* some portions may be useful, but interpret

cautiously.

6. *Test of the Non-Verbal Intelligence* (TONI) and *Peabody Picture Vocabulary Test* (PPVT): both utilize pictures and are useful only if the child can see the pictures clearly.

7. *Hiskey-Nebraska Test of Learning Aptitude:* visually oriented; depends on the quality and amount of available vision.

8. *Blind Learning Aptitude Test* (BLAT): not technically an intelligence test (yields a "learning age") but may provide useful information on a blind child's ability to learn.

9. *Slosson Intelligence Test:* valuable in analyzing patterns of errors; score less important than patterns; many items based on visual experience. (A more complete list appears in the Appendix of this book.)

10. *Developmental Activities Screening Inventory* (DASI and DASI-II): the Manual contains suggestions for adaptations for visually impaired children, but there are no norms for a visually impaired population.

11. Brazelton and Gesell scales are heavily visually based (since early development leans strongly on vision).

12. Achievement tests: in general, not commonly normed for visually impaired students; some are available in large print or braille from the American Printing House for the Blind, but even using the special editions, most visually impaired students will score lower–not because they have not acquired skills or knowledge but because their reading speed is slower. Both the *Brigance Basic Inventory* and the *Stanford Diagnostic Reading Test* are available in braille, as is the *Key Math* test.

13. Language development measures (*Test of Adolescent Language,* or TOAL, *Test of Written Language,* or TOWL, and *Test of Language Development,* or TOLD): many have some parts that are useful, but it is critical to remember that oral administration may invalidate the test; oral comprehension is not the same as written/silent comprehension.

14. Vocational tests and Interest Inventories: Some require special training from the company to use with visually impaired students (e.g., *McCarron-Dial* materials). It should be remembered that interest inventories may reflect a lack of exposure or experience, rather than real interests.

HOW TO REPORT TEST RESULTS

If modifications *have* been made on a particular test, a careful description of those adaptations should be included in the report. Mention should be made of alterations in timing or reading medium, the use of any low vision devices or special tools (e.g., abacus, braillewriter, CCTV), and whether corrective lenses were worn. If items were omitted, there should be an explanation of why. If test items were altered in any way, the changes should be described in detail. Some clear statement should advise that modifications may have affected the validity or reliability of the test. Despite the obvious limitations imposed by modifying either test materials or procedures, the performance of the student can still be described. Emphasis should be placed on the student's strengths and knowledge acquisition, especially when based on sighted standards. The results of an adaptive scale can add further information to other assessment results, and can suggest skills that have been acquired *in spite of* the visual impairment.

All test results should be viewed within the context of the visual impairment, and descriptions should note possible reasons for lack of skill/knowledge acquisition. Errors should be analyzed to determine whether they were the result of inadequate vision, lack of visual experience, poor understanding of sequence, or related to spatial perceptions; possible causes should be noted. Summaries should contain sufficient information to give direction for recommendations. It is acceptable practice to report the *range* of achievement instead of a score when a standardized test is used (e.g., "above average range" or "superior range").

REFERENCES AND RECOMMENDED READING

Anastasi, A. (1982). *Psychological testing* (5th Ed.). New York: MacMillan.

Bradley-Johnson, S. (1986). *Psychoeducational assessment of visually impaired and blind students.* Austin, TX: Pro-Ed.

Bulla, N. (1991). *Assessment of the visually impaired.* Austin, TX: Texas School for the Blind and Visually Impaired.

Dekker, R., Drenth, P., Zaal, J., & Koole, F. (1990). An intelligence test series for blind and low vision children. *Journal of Visual Impairment and Blindness, 84,* 71–86.

Groenveld, M. (1990). The dilemma of assessing the visually impaired child. *Developmental Medicine and Child Neurology, 32,* 1105–1113.

Groenveld, M. & Jan, M. (1992). Intelligence profiles of low vision and blind children. *Journal of Visual Impairment and Blindness, 86,* 68–71.

Heinze, T. (2000). Comprehensive assessments. In Koenig, A. & Holbrook, C. (Eds.), *Foundations of education, Volume 2.* New York: AFB Press.

Johns, J. (1991). *Basic reading inventory: Pre-primer-grade 8* (5th Ed.). Dubuque, IO: Kendall/Hunt.

Roscoe, J. (1975). *Fundamental research statistics for the behavioral sciences* (2nd Ed.). New York: Holt, Rinehart, & Winston.

Siskind, T. (1993). The instructional validity of statewide criterion-referenced tests for students who are visually impaired. *Journal of Visual Impairment and Blindness, 87,* 115–117.

Warren, D. (1994). *Blindness and children.* Cambridge, MA: Cambridge University Press.

Chapter Fifteen

ESTABLISHING ELIGIBILITY

The first step in establishing eligibility for special services is to know and understand the definitions, since special education is only available to children who meet the definitions. The federal definition for visual impairment is.

> an impairment in vision that, even with correction, adversely affects a child's educational performance. The term includes both partial sight and blindness. (20 U.S.C. 1401(3)(A) and (B); 1401(26))

Deafblindness is defined as

> concomitant hearing and visual impairments, the combination of which causes such severe communication and other developmental and educational needs that they cannot be accommodated in special education programs solely for children with deafness or children with blindness. (20 U.S.C. 1401(3)(A) and (B); 1401(26))

Notice that there are no numbers or qualifying levels; determination is left in the hands of the education professionals and the IEP team.

Every TVI should also find out what his/her state definitions are for visual impairment and deafblindness. States may be more specific but not less defined. A few states still have numerical criteria (i.e., Snellen notations) as eligibility criteria, but most states have moved to more functional definitions. This places a large responsibility for identifying children who are visually impaired or deafblind on the TVI, and the functional vision evaluation helps to collect the information that will assist in that decision. Note that it is *not* the eye specialist's report that establishes eligibility; it is the IEP team's decision, which is based on the TVI's recommendation.

When a child is suspected of having a visual impairment, the TVI is called in to determine whether there is cause to evaluate. The suspicion may be the result of school vision screening and subsequent referral to an eye doctor, or, in the case of early childhood programs, a result of *their* preliminary screening. In either case, the child should already have seen an eye doctor, who will have provided whatever optical correction is possible and will have submitted a written report documenting the findings. The TVI should have the eye specialist's written report in hand before proceeding with the functional vision evaluation.

The eye report should, at minimum, provide a visual diagnosis (etiology) and acuities at near and distance. Ideally, it should also note any ocular abnormalities (eyes not in alignment, fields defects, degenerative conditions, etc.) and establish "legal blindness" (an essential documentation for Federal Quota registration). The information from the eye report should help the TVI decide "where to start" in evaluating functional vision.

A word of caution is in order, however; if an eye report simply says "blind," that is not enough reason to bypass the functional vision evaluation. There are many degrees of "blindness," from "legal blindness" to total absence of vision. The TVI has the responsibility of establishing the degree of useful vision. (A "rule-of-thumb" might be "Never assume total blindness unless there are no eyes.")

Once the eye report has been received, there are several preliminary steps before the actual evaluation occurs. The first is a thorough "records review." This means *any* records: school (achievement scores, previous testing), medical (visual and other health-related/medical), and anecdotal. The more that is known about the child in advance, the easier it will be to target procedures.

Another source of information can be interviews, with families, teachers, counselors, or anyone who has observed the child. These interviews can be formal (via checklists or questionnaires) or informal (a phone call or chance meeting in a school hallway). The goal is to learn what other people have observed in the child's visual behavior that suggests a visual problem. These interviews can often provide hints about how a child uses vision, and this information can be useful during testing.

The last preliminary procedure before doing a functional vision evaluation is an observation of the child. This observation should be at least an hour in length, and ideally, in multiple settings (e.g., the home, classroom, playground, cafeteria, hallways). The TVI should be looking for unusual behaviors that suggest visual problems (e.g., squinting, holding things close to examine them, head tilting or head turning, leaning forward, avoiding looking, etc.). If possible, observe the child as unobtrusively as possible (perhaps from a distance) to assure "normal" visual behaviors.

The TVI should have a pretty good sense of how much (or how little) vision a child has, or is using, after collecting all of the preliminary data. The information should be in writing (as reminders later, when composing the final report). The next step is the actual functional vision evaluation itself.

FUNCTIONAL VISION EVALUATION (FVE)

TVIs should be aware that there is no single "right" way to do a functional vision evaluation. Approaches will depend on the age or developmental level of the child, and the "style" of the TVI. There are numerous checklists for structure-oriented TVIs, or the TVI can develop his/her own approach. Each TVI should have a "kit" of materials (to be discussed later), a general knowledge of child development (what is "normal," both developmentally and visually), and be willing to improvise. The procedure for conducting a functional vision evaluation is highly individualized, both on the part of the examiner, and as it concerns the child. There are, however, some general suggestions that may answer the "What do I do?" question.

First, decide which general category matches the child. Is this an infant/toddler, preschooler, school age child? Does the visual impairment appear to be the only problem, or are there likely to be multiple disabilities? Is there a probability of total blindness or really low vision, or is there likely to be useful vision? The answers to these questions will help in selecting materials, tasks, and approaches. For the purposes of deciding approaches, it may be helpful to think in terms of three or four general categories: relatively intact infants/toddlers, intact preschoolers, intact school-age children, and children with multiple (usually severe) disabilities. The last group *could* be approached like the younger two groups (under-6-year-olds), since they are usually developmentally in that age range.

For children who are developmentally or chronologically B–3 years: The TVI will have little control over the plan; these children are egocentric and are not always concerned with pleasing (cooperating). The most effective approach is usually to *play* with the child, and observe carefully. Look at the child's eyes while you are playing, and watch how the child uses available vision. Look for fixation, alignment, steadiness, and ability to track. Check pupillary response, if possible (although it is difficult with children who have dark eyes, and may be sluggish or absent if the child is receiving medication). Look for the position of a light reflection–it should be at the same position in both eyes. Observe whether the child can follow a moving target. Notice whether there is a visually-directed reach. Watch to see if the child uses vision to examine things. Observe the child's visual response to: familiar (but silent) people, unfamiliar people, black and white designs, reflective objects, bubbles, balls, balloons, ring on a string. Watch how the child plays with familiar toys, and with unfamiliar or novel toys (yours). Observe whether there is sustained visual attention, or more "fingering" than looking. Document both the child's visual behaviors (orienting, fixation, following) and the characteristics of stimuli that engage the child's attention (size/shape/color of objects and distance when the child noticed them). It may be possible to structure situations that require the child to choose (e.g., scanning or shifting gaze to select finger foods, or to decide between a toy and a bottle). Be prepared for the child to lose interest quickly, fuss, or cry, and/or totally ignore the examiner. Although it is possible to draw conclusions from a one-hour visit, be prepared for more than one session.

For children who are developmentally or chronologically 3–5: These children have a short attention span but respond to praise or rewards. Many of them may not be able to match, but "find one like mine" may be a viable procedure for some. Objects will be of more interest than pictures, but some children will find books (with simple pictures) interesting. Activities should be short (5–10 minutes) in duration and varied. At this age, cognition has become an integral part of vision; the child has the ability to understand function, and can comprehend "cause and effect." Toys that the child can operate are usually interesting. Also useful are mirrors, flashlights, utensils, food (finger foods; Cheerios, etc.), and novel toys (a spiny ball, a Slinky®, pinwheels). Again, observe both the child's eyes and how vision is used. If structured vision testing is attempted, it will be most effective at ten feet or less (beyond that, the child loses interest). Use a play approach, using both familiar and unfamiliar toys/objects. Watch how the child approaches the stimuli, how it is manipulated, and how far away it can be before the child "loses" it visually. Note the size/shape/color of stimuli and the distance. Be aware that cognitive ability plays a major role in visual function; children whose intellectual development is delayed may not use their visual skills as well as they could. Developmental age may be a better grouping factor than chronological age. (The eyes can only "see" what the brain can understand. Visual age cannot exceed cognitive age.)

School-aged Children: Most of this group can respond to both structured tests and functional tasks. Structured tests include:

- Distance charts (Snellen, Lighthouse, Feinbloom, STYCAR, HOTV, LEA, etc.)
- Nearpoint cards (Snellen, Lighthouse, HOTV, continuous text, etc.)
- Confrontational fields testing (using white styrofoam balls on wands)
- Visual efficiency testing (Diagnostic Assessment Procedure, or DAP)
- Perceptual evaluation (Motor-Free Visual Perception Test)

Examples of functional tasks (choose according to age):

Reaching accurately	Matching
Stringing beads	Copying
Doing Puzzles	Coloring within lines

Tracing
Cutting
Identifying details in pictures
Pasting
Imitating funny faces

Avoiding obstacles when walking
Walking towards a designated target
Pouring liquids
Measuring quantities of liquids or solids
Walking on a sidewalk
Using tools (ruler, hammer, screwdriver)

Reading various type sizes and fonts in:
Textbooks
Newspapers
Encyclopedias
Dials
Magazines
Dictionaries
Computer screen
Schedules

Identifying money
Applying make-up
Shaving
Using prescribed low vision devices
Selecting food in a cafeteria line
Sorting laundry
Copying from the blackboard

Be prepared to devote multiple sessions to these functional vision evaluations. There is more to evaluate, and more data to collect. The TVI should select appropriate formal tests, and age-appropriate functional tasks, and should document performance carefully. Time should also be devoted to evaluating environmental factors (lighting, seating, etc.); depending on the age of the child, some of this information can be collected through questions, trials ("Is this better, or this"), or observation.

There are a number of items that could be part of the testing "kit." The TVI will need to have a portable collection of options for testing or constructing situations where assessment can take place. The following list is made up of suggestions; the creative TVI will probably find other items that will work equally well.

THE FUNCTIONAL VISION EVALUATION KIT

A wide selection of formal tools, including distance acuity charts, nearpoint cards or charts, and at least one low vision chart. Recommended are:

- the Snellen "Tumbling E" chart for 20 feet
- the HOTV chart for 10 feet
- the Lighthouse (house/apple/umbrella) chart (10′)

- STYCAR charts for 10 feet)
- a variety of nearpoint reading cards (Snellen, Jaeger print size, Lighthouse symbols, HOTV)
- the Feinbloom chart for low vision testing
- the STYCAR toys
- LEA charts, cards

White styrofoam balls of varying sizes; at least one wand 18″ long

Lights of all kinds (in addition to sunlight and indoor light): Flashlights of several sizes, with silent switches; colored caps for at least one flashlight

Reflective surfaces: mirrors (steel or plastic); aluminum foil; mylar balloons; L'eggs® containers; silver pinwheel; shiny plastic Christmas ornaments on strings; discarded CDs that are iridescent

Black and white designs: checkerboards, bull's eyes, straight lines; zig-zap patterns; simple outline of a face

Objects/toys: angular or spiny balls in bright colors (yellow, red); balloons, bubbles, rings; cause/effect toys; blocks or toys with details for little fingers to poke into and probe.

WRITING THE FINAL REPORT

Writing the final report is a critical step in the process of evaluating functional vision. It should be comprehensive but readable, since it will be a crucial part of the IEP team's decision-making data. It should also reflect everything that was part of the assessment process, since the IEP team members were not there to observe what the TVI saw. If it is presented in organized form, in easy-to-understand language, it will serve the purpose for which it was intended (establishing the eligibility or lack of eligibility) for special education services.

There is a recommended format that can facilitate the reporting of the information compiled during testing. In summary, that format is:

- Presentation of demographic data (child's and parents' name, address, phone number; child's date of birth and age at time of evaluation; school/school placement; dates of evaluation)
- Reason for referral
- Summary of the medical records, with specific attention to the visual history (define ocular terms in parentheses)

- List of procedures used, both formal and informal (Interviews and observations should be listed under informal procedures.)
- *Objective* results of each procedure used (Avoid drawing conclusions or making personal observations.)
- Implications (this is the part of the report where the TVI can say what the results all *mean,* and how the visual impairment results in atypical functioning.)
- Statement of Eligibility (The child does, or does not meet the state's definition for visually impaired, and is entitled (or not) to special services.)
- Recommendations:
  - What other evaluations should be done? (Be careful; the school may be financially responsible for what the TVI recommends.)
  - What environmental and/or material modifications are indicated?
  - What instructional-methods changes are needed?
- Sign and date the report.

THE LEARNING MEDIA ASSESSMENT (LMA)

Some states mandate a learning media assessment as part of establishing eligibility for special education services for visually impaired students. (It is not a federal requirement.) Other states *suggest* a learning media assessment but do not require it. In actuality, the LMA is a logical extension of the functional vision evaluation and gives a great deal more depth and support to the findings. It is a procedure used by TVIs to supplement and enhance the functional vision evaluation. Some TVIs even include the results of the LMA in their final functional vision evaluation report. In the opinion of this author, the reports should be separate because they have different focuses. They are "companion" assessments and should both be considered by the IEP team when making placement/programming decisions for any visually impaired student.

The LMA is a multi-faceted, hierarchically arranged procedure that fulfills multiple needs:

- It provides a structured data collection format for determining a student's primary and secondary sensory learning channels.
- It helps to determine when a student might be ready for a structured literacy program.
- It differentiates between *functional* literacy and *academic* literacy. (Functional literacy involves survival reading and writing skills–reading street signs, menus, labels, etc.–whereas academic literacy is the conventional instructional reading and writing program that occurs in

schools.)

- It inventories and evaluates learning media found in the student's home, classroom, and other learning environments.
- It provides a structure for evaluating the efficiency of a particular reading medium (print or braille).

The kinds of information collected during the LMA are more educational/ instructional than that acquired during a functional vision evaluation (which focuses on the individual's visual function) and are crucial bits of information that will help the IEP team make recommendations for programming.

The several kinds of data collections in an LMA can be adapted for a wide range of ages and/or functional levels. The sensory channel evaluation can be used with even the youngest visually impaired children, but can also be used with older children. Emerging literacy levels can be assessed as well as established literacy media. Developmentally delayed students can be evaluated to determine the most appropriate learning media as well as functional literacy levels. Those students with an established literacy medium can be assessed to determine whether that medium is the most efficient (or whether dual media, or another type of medium might be better). The possibilities for applications of information collected during a learning media assessment are many, and warrant the use of this tool prior to placement decisions or IEP planning.

Usually included in a Literacy Media Assessment are:

1. Measures of reading rate, both oral and silent;
2. Measures of reading comprehension, both oral and silent;
3. Observation of work distance if visual medium;
4. Miscue analysis;
5. Estimate of fatigue factor; and
6. Efficiency of other literacy areas (handwriting, listening).

The Koenig & Holbrook text (1993) is a comprehensive guide for performing learning media assessments. It lays strong philosophical foundations, has clearly presented descriptions of procedures, and provides 11 checklists to use in data collection. The reader can use any preferred reading inventories to assess competencies, or can use the second and third volumes of the Assessment Kit (published by the Texas School for the Blind and Visually Impaired); these volumes contain print and braille reading inventories. The reader is referred to the Koenig & Holbrook text for reproducible materials and guidelines. (See Chapter Fourteen, Figure 18, for a diagram that places the functional vision evaluation and learning media assessment into perspective as first steps in the assessment process for visually impaired students.)

REFERENCES AND RECOMMENDED READING

Bishop, V. (1988). Making choices in functional vision evaluations: Noodles, needles, and haystacks. *Journal of Visual Impairment and Blindness, 82,* 94–99.

Koenig, A. & Holbrook, C. (1993). *Learning media assessment of students with visual impairments.* Austin, TX: Texas School for the Blind and Visually Impaired.

Koenig, A., Holbrook, C., Corn, A., DePriest, L., Erin, J., & Presley, I. (2000). Specialized assessments for students with visual impairments. In Koenig, A. & Holbrook, C. (Eds.), *Foundations of education, Volume 2.* New York: AFB Press.

Levack, N. (1991). *Low vision.* Austin, TX: Texas School for the Blind and Visually Impaired.

Sewell, D. (1997). *Assessment Kit* (a four-volume set)
Volume 1: Assessment Tools for Teacher use
Volume 2: Large Print Reading Assessments for Student Use
Volume 3: Braille Reading Assessments for Student Use
Volume 4: *Basic Reading Inventory: Pre-Primer Through Grade Twelve & Early Literacy Assessments* (7th Edition) by Jerry Johns, Kendall/Hunt.
Austin, TX: Texas School for the Blind and Visually Impaired.

Chapter Sixteen

OTHER VISION-RELATED ASSESSMENTS

At the end of the functional vision evaluation report, there is usually a section for "recommendations," and one of the things the TVI can recommend is further testing. Three of the most commonly recommended further evaluations are a Low Vision Evaluation, an Orientation and Mobility (O&M) Evaluation, and an Assistive Technology Evaluation. Although these assessments are not required to establish eligibility, they all provide useful information for program decisions. Each of these evaluations will be discussed in this chapter.

THE LOW VISION EVALUATION

The Low Vision Evaluation is a clinical assessment performed in a doctor's office or clinic, by either an ophthalmologist or optometrist who has special training in low vision. The goal is to determine if there are any ways to enhance visual functioning. An individual examination of the optical system is the first step and determines acuities at near and distance, degree of refractive error, and fields restrictions, if any. The question is usually asked "What does the patient/client want to be able to do that the visual impairment prevents or impedes?" The Low Vision Specialist then tries a number of vision enhancement devices (magnifiers, telescopes, CCTVs, bioptics) and/or adjusted illumination or environmental modifications. If a device or system is found to be effective (i.e., improves or enhances visual functioning), it is prescribed and a "loaner" device given. (Sometimes the device is actually provided as a part of the evaluation.) There is usually a brief training period in the use of the device, before the individual leaves the evaluation site, and follow-up visits are scheduled. Unfortunately, some patients never return for the follow-up visit, and the Low Vision Specialist never knows whether the device was effective or not. Sometimes, prescribed devices end up on shelves, in drawers, and in pockets if the user isn't sure how to use them. The TVI may be the one who ends up providing training for students for whom low vision devices have been prescribed, and goals/objectives become part of the student's IEP.

The terms Low Vision Evaluation, Functional Vision Evaluation, and Vision Screening are sometimes confused and the terms misused; they are very different assessments, and the TVI should be able to differentiate between them. *Vision Screening* is a preliminary identification procedure used to find individuals whose vision deviates from what is considered to be normal. Vision screening includes the group "eye tests" conducted in schools by the school nurse or a trained technician. Those who "failed" the vision screening are referred to an eye specialist for a more complete visual examination; many of these children have glasses prescribed to correct their refractive errors. For young children (B–3 or preschoolers, 3–5), vision screening involves observation and informal testing, to identify those who need follow-up eye examinations or eye care. At all levels, vision screening is a preliminary procedure for the simple purpose of identifying children who may need glasses.

The *Functional Vision Evaluation* is the procedure used to determine how a child *uses* the vision he/she has. It always *follows* the visit to the eye doctor (should not precede it). Not all children who are identified in vision screening will receive a Functional Vision Evaluation; only those who have had a thorough eye exam with an ophthalmologist or optometrist, and whose vision was not able to be corrected fully (if at all) with glasses, will be referred for a Functional Vision Evaluation.

The *Low Vision Evaluation* (described earlier) is a "next step" after either the eye doctor's exam or the Functional Vision Evaluation. Its purpose is to devise ways to improve visual function optically (i.e., with special lenses or devices).

Vision screening is usually the first level of identifying a visual impairment and leads to the eye doctor's examination. The Functional Vision Evaluation follows the receipt of the eye report. The Low Vision Evaluation can be done any time after the eye doctor's examination, but is commonly a recommendation that is an outreach of the Functional Vision Evaluation. (See Chapter Fourteen, Figure 19, for a graphic representation of this sequence.)

THE O&M EVALUATION

The TVI is generally not trained to conduct a full O&M Evaluation unless dually certified (i.e., is both a TVI and a certified orientation and mobility specialist–COMS). The TVI can do an O&M *screening,* however, as a rationale for recommending a full O&M Evaluation. There does not seem to be any universal agreement about how or when the screening is done, and there does not appear to be any generally accepted form for data collection. The TVI should probably try to document indicators in note or list form, however, to support the recommendation for further O&M evaluation. During the preliminary interviews and observations (prior to the Functional Vision Evaluation), there should be ample opportunity to observe how the child gets around, and whether any mobility problems appear to be present. During the "play" sessions of the Functional Vision Evaluation, there may be opportunities to find out whether the child understand some basic concepts and can identify body parts. The TVI should not focus specifically on the O&M screening, but should note any observable problems. Figure 20 is a possible format for recording behaviors that might suggest the need for further investigation by a COMS.

ASSISTIVE TECHNOLOGY EVALUATION

The federal government has recognized the impact of technology on society, and has acknowledged its value to students with disabilities. Public Law 105-17 (the IDEA amendments of 1997) defines an assistive technology device as:

> any item, piece of equipment, or product system, whether acquired commercially off the shelf, modified, or customized, that is used to increase, maintain, or improve the functional capabilities of a child with a disability. (20 U.S.C. 1401(1))

The law further mandates an evaluation of the child's particular need for technology, authorizes the purchase or lease of devices, and requires training or technical assistance for both the child and the professionals who provide services to the child (20 U.S.C. 1401(2)). Services include:

> selecting, designing, fitting, customizing, adapting, applying, maintaining, repairing, or replacing assistive technology devices. (20 U.S.C. 1401(2)(c))

The deciding factor about whether a particular device is needed is whether that device will enable the child to access a free appropriate public education (FAPE). In the case of visually impaired students, there are a large number of devices that would fall under that definition; among these are CCTVs, refreshable braille, computer-screen enlargement software, screen readers, talking calculators, electronic writing tools, braille note-takers, braille translators, and a variety of other electronic equipment. How a particular student would use these devices can only be determined by an individualized assis-

O&M Screening Information

Student________________ Age____ TVI________________ Date______

Totally blind?______ Has some useful vision?_____
Wears glasses?_____ Uses 1 or more low vision devices?_____

Has upright posture?_____ Walks/moves independently?_____
Sits alone?_____ Uses a walker?_____
Stands alone?_____ Uses a wheelchair?_____

"Trails" correctly?_____ Uses "sighted guide" technique correctly?_____

Body Image: identifies body parts (circle all those that apply)
head yes nose mouth ears hair
arm hands fingers legs feet toes
shoulders stomach back elbow knee wrist

Basic Concepts: can point to: up/down top/bottom above/below
in front/in back side middle

can move: forwards/backwards up steps/down steps

can follow directions: stop go come here

can identify: circle (ball) square (block) triangle

can describe or demonstrate: parallel right angle perpendicular

Has difficulties with:
_____surface changes (rugs/tile; grass/concrete)
_____lighting changes (indoors/outdoors)
_____obstacles (bumps into objects or people)
_____glare/shadows
_____steps/stairs
_____curbs/drop-offs
_____finding particular areas in school
_____crossing streets
_____getting lost

Comments or observations:_____________________________________

____

____

Figure 20.

tive technology evaluation.

There are many variables to consider when evaluating a visually impaired student's need for assistive technology. Some of them will already have been addressed during the Functional Vision Evaluation (efficient use of available vision) or in the process of the Learning Media Assessment (preferred and most efficient reading media). other variables will be further investigated when expanded core curriculum areas are assessed (auditory and tactual capabilities, keyboarding skills, use of low vision devices). The assistive technology evaluation itself should pay special attention to such variables as size/style of print most easily read; whether optical devices can enhance print reading speed or comprehension; whether information access is more efficient visually, tactually (braille), or auditorily (recorded materials or via readers); how written communication is best generated; how notes are taken; what level of keyboarding skill has been acquired; familiarity with personal computers, pointing devices and related equipment (scanners, printers, braille embossers). Some consideration should also be given to the student's long-range applications (e.g., technology use in the workplace, or at post-secondary higher learning institutions). An example of a comprehensive checklist can be found in Koenig et al. (2000).

The assistive technology evaluation can be done as a recommended assessment following the Functional Vision Evaluation, or at any time the TVI is able to schedule it. Because the quality of information collected, and the "show me" nature of many of the components of the assessment, it may take considerable time. For this reason, this assessment may be a part of the IEP team's recommended services.

It is probably true that most visually impaired students will need an assistive technology evaluation at some point in their educational years. The sooner it is done, the greater the chances are that the student will learn skills that could increase his/her participation in regular school learning activities.

DEVELOPMENTAL SCALES

Part C of the 1997 IDEA amendments (P.L. 105-17) requires that a young child (B–3) receive:

> a multidisciplinary assessment of the unique strengths and needs of the infant or toddler. (20 U.S.C. 1436)

which document "present levels of physical development, cognitive development, social or emotional development, and adaptive development, based on objective criteria" (10 U.S.C. 1436). In order to collect that information, developmental scales are commonly used, however, many of these are inappropriate measures for visually impaired infants and toddlers.

Chapter Six discussed the crucial role of vision in early development, and most developmental scales reflect that role. Moreover, the scales have been normed on a population that did not include blind or visually impaired children. Therefore, these scales do not give a true picture of early development for young visually impaired children. Project PRISM verified the disruptions in the developmental sequence when there is a severe visual impairment. Despite these anomalies, early childhood programs often use such developmental scales as the Bayley, Battelle, or Denver, which will suggest that visually impaired children are delayed. The "delays" are misleading, however, when the scales are examined for visual weighting. One researcher (Hatton, 1997) examined growth curves for over 200 visually impaired children evaluated by the Battelle Scale and found them depressed. The conclusion was that the Battelle did not fairly measure early development in young visually impaired children, and should not be used to evaluate them. The same conclusion could be drawn for other scales whose norms are based on a sighted population sample.

Alternatives to standardized scales are the *Oregon Project (OR Project)* and *Growing Up;* both of these instruments were designed specifically for young visually impaired children (B–6). The *OR Project* is contained in a large 3-ring binder, with the assessment booklet as a separate document for each child. *Growing Up* is a 3-volume, spiral-bound curriculum linked to a parent-informant procedure (card sort). Both instruments provide curriculum designs based on, and linked to, individual assessments. The student profile for the *OR Project* is less informative than that for the *Growing Up* materials because it is in terms of percentage of items completed; the *Growing Up* profile is a detailed, horizontal bar graph that shows specific skill development levels clearly. Both *OR Project* and *Growing Up* are individual-oriented, even though there are year-groupings for skills. Both curricula have specific references to the impact of visual impairment on certain skills or skill areas.

The assessment procedure for the *OR Project* involves an evaluation of skills in each of the developmental areas (motor, cognitive, language, self-help, social); results are recorded individually for each developmental area. OR Project also has separate evaluations for "Compensatory Skills" (skills that would be particularly important for blind children) and "Vision" (skills that might be more appropriate if the child has some useful vision). The "Vision" assessment is NOT a substitute for a Functional Vision Evaluation, however, and is very visually based. There is no global profile except in the "percentage of items completed" format.

In the *Growing Up* assessment/curriculum, parents provide assessment information by sorting a set of cards into three piles: "can do," "can't do," and "don't know." From this sorting, a student profile is constructed that shows all five areas on one page; gross motor and fine motor are even broken out into two separate results sections; all areas have many sub-skill sections. It is clear from viewing the profile what the child has accomplished and what is still to be learned. There is a direct link between the assessment profile and curriculum objectives.

TVIs who use the *OR Project* like its portability (contained in a single, large 3-ring binder); *Growing Up* is a spiral-bound, in three volumes. Teachers who prefer *Growing Up* usually find more detail in the continuously sequenced assessment data format. Growing Up profile forms are available for infants/toddlers, birth to 24 months, and for the entire range of years, birth to six years.

For severely disabled visually impaired children (especially deafblind children), the *Callier-Azusa Scale* provides useful information that can be used in programming. It is a developmentally-based instrument, with fine steps in sequences. Extensive observational time is required to produce a developmental profile, but strengths and weaknesses will be clearly indicated. Since this protocol was standardized primarily with deafblind children, it is most useful with this population.

MEASURES OF PARENT/FAMILY NEEDS

Public Law 105-17 requires:

> a family-directed assessment of the resources, priorities, and concerns of the family and the identification of the supports and services necessary to enhance the family's capacity to meet the developmental needs of the infant or toddler. (20 U.S.C. 1436)

The results of this assessment are reflected in the portion of the IFSP that describes (the family's resources, priorities, and concerns." It seems appropriate to describe several methods of obtaining such information, especially from parents of visually impaired infants and toddlers.

Commonly, the early childhood program is responsible for evaluating parent/family needs, and the process may vary from program to program. Sometimes, a social worker is the staff member who initiates contact with the family, and a structured interview is conducted. "Forms" are completed, and specific screening begins. Often, the interview and forms are questionnaires to establish the need for financial assistance or agency referral. Rarely are early childhood personnel trained or experienced in evaluating the needs of families who contain a visually impaired infant or toddler. Even more rare are staff with counseling experience targeted to the psychological and emotional concerns about having a child with a visual impairment.

Although TVIs are not specifically trained as counselors, they are aware of the kinds of emotional "ups and downs" associated with having a child with a visual impairment. The TVI can act as liaison with early childhood personnel, alerting them to the impact of a visual impairment on the family. The TVI can also suggest several types of evaluation procedures that can help in determining parental needs.

Notice that the law specifically states "family-directed assessment." This does not mean telling the family what they *ought* to have, or what interveners can do. It means finding out what the parents/family *themselves* see as their needs or wants, or are concerned about. Parents may not be able to verbalize what they are feeling or need, and may need guidance.

There are a great many questionnaires developed to *help* families identify and prioritize their concerns. Two of these (*Family Needs Survey,* Bailey & Simeonsson; *Family Needs Scale,* Dunst et al.) are listed among the references at the end of this chapter, and provide a checklist approach to collecting data to identify family concerns. They are not, however, vision-specific, and should be used with caution.

Another self-analysis procedure, specifically designed for parents of visually impaired children, is the *Parent Needs Inventory* (Robinson & DeRosa, 1980). This procedure is a "card sort" approach, where parents sort descriptors (brief descriptions of possible concerns) according to how much *like* or *unlike* themselves they are. The cards are placed on a sorting board with blank squares the size of the cards; the squares are arranged in pyramidal shape, with those in the largest bottom row being "mosts" and the few top cards being "leasts." Also built into the process are evaluation gradings, with cards to the left of center being "like me" and cards to the right of center denoting "unlike me." The center vertical column of cards are the neutral (or "undecided") concerns.

Several areas of concern are measured by this instrument: the grieving process, knowledge of child development, and knowledge of local resources. The emphasis is on enabling parents to take charge of their own feelings and actions. This parental needs measure appears to fulfill the legal mandate for "family-directed" assessment better than checklists or questionnaires, which are externally controlled.

Another method of finding out what influences there are in a family's life (what supports and resources are available, and how useful or helpful they are) is the ecomap. If an early childhood program has not already used this approach, it is worth exploring. Basically, an ecomap is a graphic representation of the family within a larger community of relatives, friends, and resources. The map is drawn as information is given; it begins with the child in the middle, with his/her parents and siblings; grandparents and other relatives are identified above the center box, as informal supports; formal supports (agencies, programs, financial aid) are arranged below the center box. To each side of the center box are "intermediate supports" (religious affiliations, people at work, neighbors). The boxes are connected to the center box by different kinds of lines; thick or dark means strong support; thin or light lines suggest minimal support; dotted lines infer stressful relationships. The quality of information depends on the willingness of the parents to share their feelings and concerns, and the accuracy of their perceptions. The skill of the interviewer in asking non-threatening questions can also affect the quality of information. When complete, an ecomap provides insights into what parents see as useful channels of communication, information, and help. An ecomap does not identify needs or priorities, but it helps to analyze sources of support. (See Figure 21 for an example of an ecomap.)

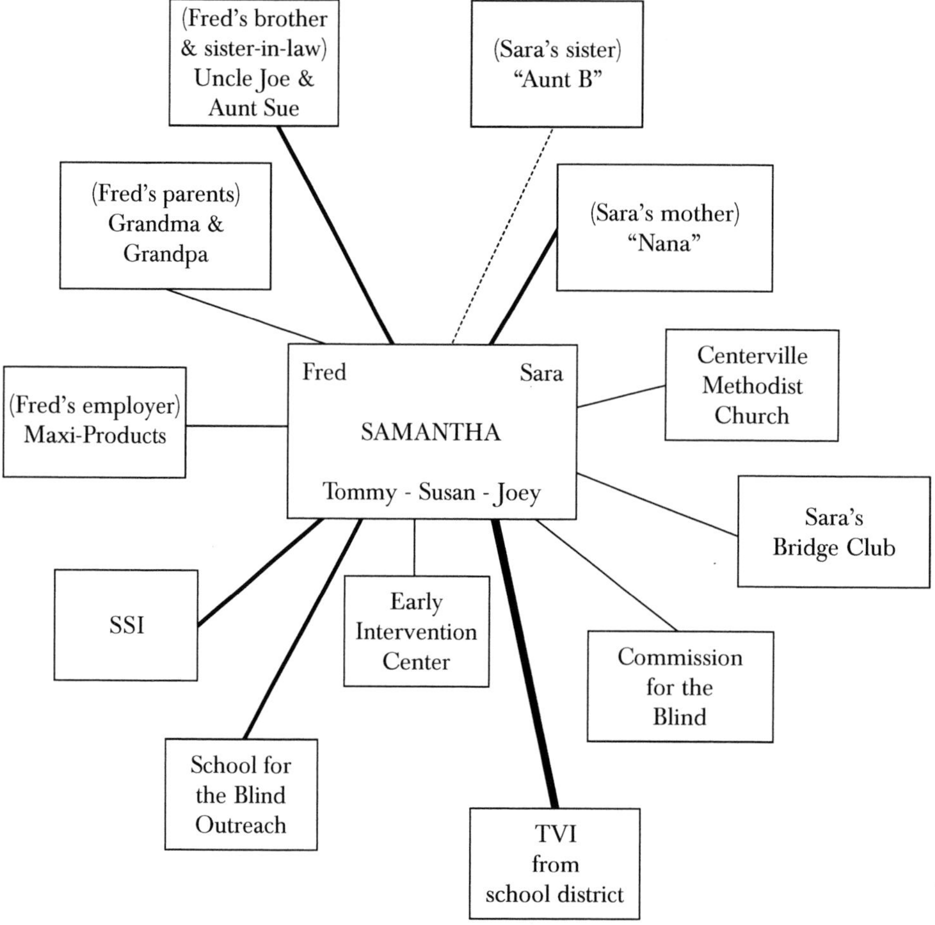

Figure 21.

REFERENCES AND RECOMMENDED READING

Bailey, D. & Simeonsson, R. (1990). *Family needs survey.* Chapel Hill, NC: University of North Carolina, Frank Porter Graham Child Development Center.

Brown, D., Simmons, V., & Methvin, J. (1991). *ORegon Project for visually impaired and blind preschool children.* Medford, OR: Jackson Education Service District.

Cratty, B. & Sams, T. (1978). Body-image screening test for blind children. In Swallow, R., Mangold, S., & Mangold, P., *Informal assessment of developmental skills for visually handicapped students.* New York: American Foundation for the Blind.

Croft, N. & Robinson, L. (1984). *Growing up: A developmental curriculum.* Ogden, UT: Parent Consultants.

Dunst, C., Cooper, C., Weeldreyer, J., Snyder, K., & Chase, J. (1988). Family needs scale. In Dunst, C., Trivette, C., & Deal, A. (Eds.), *Enabling and empowering families: Principles and guidelines for practice.* Cambridge, MA: Brookline Books.

Griffen-Shirley, N., Trusty, S., & Rickard, R. (2000). Orientation and mobility. In Koenig, A. & Holbrook, C. (Eds.), *Foundations of education, Volume 2.* New York: AFB Press.

Hatton, D., Bailey, D., Burchinal, M., & Ferrell, K. (1997). Developmental growth curves of preschool children with visual impairments. *Child Development, 68*(5), 788–806.

Jose, R. (1983). *Understanding low vision.* New York: American Foundation for the Blind.

Kapperman, G. & Sticken, J. (2000). Assistive technology. In Koenig, A. & Holbrook, C. (Eds.), *Foundations of education, Volume 2.* New York: AFB Press.

Koenig, A., Holbrook, C., Corn, A., DePriest, L., Erin, J., & Presley, I. (2000). Specialized assessments for students with visual impairments. In Koenig, A. & Holbrook, C. (Eds.), *Foundations of education, Volume 2.* New York: AFB Press.

McWilliam, R. (2001). *Understanding the family ecology.* Chapel Hill, NC: Project INTEGRATE, Frank Porter Graham Child Development Center, University of North Carolina at Chapel Hill.

Michigan School for the Blind. (n.d.). *Pre-cane mobility and orientation skills for the blind.* Lansing, MI: Author.

Moore, M. & McLaughlin, L. (1992). Assessment of the preschool child with visual impairments. In Nuttall, E., Romero, I., & Kalesnik, J. (Eds.). *Assessing and screening preschoolers.* Boston: Allyn & Bacon.

Robinson, L. & DeRosa, S. (1980). *Parent needs inventory.* Ogden, UT: Parent Consultants.

Stillman, R. (Ed.). (1978). Callier-Asuza scale. Dallas, TX: Callier Center for Communication Disorders.

Wilkinson, M. (1996). Clinical low vision services. In Corn, A. & Koenig, A. (Eds.). *Foundations for low vision: Clinical and functional perspectives.* New York: AFB Press.

Chapter Seventeen

EXPANDED CORE CURRICULUM (ECC) ASSESSMENTS

The Expanded Core Curriculum (ECC) is the heart of what TVIs are trained to teach, and what makes them "special" educators. This curriculum goes beyond the regular school program, and includes the vision-related compensatory skills that must be specifically taught to visually impaired children. It is these instructional areas that should make up the largest number of goals/objectives on the IFSP/IEP of a child with a visual impairment.

Both the IFSP and the IEP require that a *current level of functioning* be established as the starting point for any program of instruction. This functioning level should not be a wild guess, and it should not be based simply on intuition. There should be some kind of assessment results to give direction for instruction.

Should all of the ECC areas be tested for every child? The obvious answer is *no,* but how does the TVI decide which areas to test for each child? It may help to provide some general guidelines.

1. The age of the child can set some priorities. A very young visually impaired child will probably have strengths and/or needs established when the developmental scale results are examined. Further testing in ECC areas is generally not needed, and available test instruments are often inappropriate. (Motor and sensory abilities may be the areas of emphasis.) It is usually when the child begins school that ECC assessments become useful.
2. Children with multiple disabilities are another group for whom a great many of the ECC areas are inappropriate. Concentration of assessment is usually in the self-help/daily living/independent living skills area. A few of these children may learn braille, but most skill instruction will probably be in functional areas.

3. Having set aside the youngest visually impaired children, and most of those with multiple disabilities (their assessments are more focused), it leaves a much smaller group for diverse testing, in wider areas. These are the children who are likely to end up in regular classes with itinerant support and specific age/grade-related needs. They are often the ones who can succeed academically but need tool skills (unique reading media or methods, modified math tools, competencies in technology use or low vision devices, independent mobility). They are also the ones who are most likely to need instruction in study skills, social skills, leisure and recreation skills, and self-help.

Perhaps the best advice is to look at the whole child; academics, or academic skills, are only part of the child. In order to succeed in the real world (be employed, support oneself) the individual must be able to get along with people, be able to make decisions, solve problems, care for one's personal needs, and have interests beyond the workplace. Education, for the visually impaired student, means getting ready to succeed. The ECC is not an "extra" or a luxury; it is what visually impaired students *must* have if they are to find a place in society and make any kind of contribution to it.

Therefore, assess whatever skills a particular child needs: (1) to become as independent and self-sufficient as possible; (2) to reach his/her individual potential; (3) to communicate effectively with others; and (4) to be able to compete with/get along with peers. (There will be more about these long-term goals in Chapter Eighteen.)

Because visual impairment is a low incidence disability, there are not enough students to make up a norming sample, and they are widely scattered geographically. Moreover, visually impaired students are such a heterogeneous group that it further reduces the practicality of attempting standardization of instruments to measure widely distributed characteristics. Therefore, most assessment tools for visually impaired students, in disability-related areas, are either criterion-referenced or outcome-based, and usually informal. Many are simply checklists that have evolved from careful task analysis.

TEST TO EVALUATE AREAS OF THE EXPANDED CORE CURRICULUM

Unfortunately, the TVI often has to search to locate assessment instruments in some ECC areas, and there are a few sources. This chapter will attempt to list all known assessment tools in ECC instructional areas, with sources given in the reference list at the end of the chapter. ECC areas are listed in alphabetical order. References to assessment *collections* are keyed

Sewell (indicating the TSBVI Assessment Kit) or *Swallow* (to mean the book of informal assessments). All others are referenced by the author. The TVI is encouraged to acquire as many ECC assessment instruments as possible, so that they are available as needs arise (often unexpectedly). A shelf or file full of tests should be part of the TVI's home base (office), and the TVI should not hesitate to use as many assessments as it takes, to develop an accurate record of the student's *current level of functioning* in all areas.

ASSESSMENT INSTRUMENTS IN THE EXPANDED CORE CURRICULUM AREAS

ABACUS

Abacus and Fingermath Assessment (Sewell)
Abacus Checklist for the Counting Method (Sewell)

BODY IMAGE

Body-Image Screening Test for Blind Children (Swallow)

BRAILLE

Braille Reading Readiness Skills (Swallow; Sewell)
Braille Readiness (Sewell)
Braille Assessment (Sewell)
Braille Checklist (Sewell)
Diagnostic Assessment of Braille Reading Skills (Swallow)
Braille Unit Recognition Battery (Caton)
Minnesota Braille Skills Inventory
Assessment of Braille Literacy Skills (Koenig)
Braille Writing (including basic Nemeth Code) (Swallow)
Operating a Braillewriter Assessment (Sewell)

CALCULATOR

Calculator Assessment (Sewell)

CAREER

Career Portfolio (Sewell)
Student Self-Evaluation (Sewell)
Work Behavior Evaluation (Sewell)

COMMUNITY

Community Evaluation (Sewell)
Community Profile (Sewell)

CONCEPTS

Cognitive Concepts Checklist (Sewell)
Concepts Checklist for Visually Impaired Children (Sewell)
Experimental Concept Development Checklist for Visually Impaired Students (Sewell)
Orientation and Mobility Concept Assessment (Swallow)
Tactile Test of Basic Concepts (Caton)

DAILY LIVING SKILLS

Daily Loving Skills Checklist (Sewell)
Independent Living: A Curriculum (Loumiet)
(a 3-volume set; Volume I–Social Competence; Volume II–Self-Care and Maintenance of personal Environment; Volume III–Play and Leisure)

DEVELOPMENTAL SCALES

Informal Assessment of Developmental Skills (Swallow)
(37 pages; includes self-help, psychomotor, social-emotional, language, cognition)
Growing Up (Croft & Robinson)
ORegon Project (Brown et al.)

FAMILY

Family Needs Scale (Sewell)
Family Resource Scale (Sewell)
Parent Questionnaire (Sewell)
Family Profile (Sewell)
Parent Needs Inventory (Robinson & DeRosa)

HANDWRITING

(see Scriptwriting)

KEYBOARDING

Assessment of Keyboarding Skills (Sewell)

LEISURE/RECREATION/PLAY

(see Volume III of Independent Living)

LISTENING

Informal Assessment of Listening Skills (Swallow; Sewell)

MEASUREMENT

Measurement Assessment (Sewell)

MONEY

Money Assessment (Sewell)

NEMETH CODE

Elementary Nemeth Code Checklist (Sewell)
Reference Chart of the Mathematical Symbols (Sewell)

ORIENTATION & MOBILITY

Teaching Age-Appropriate Purposeful Skills (TAPS) (Pogrund et al.)
(The assessment addresses beginning concepts as well as advanced mobility skills.)

ORGANIZATIONAL/STUDY SKILLS

Organizational and Study Skills Checklist (Sewell)
(There is one for elementary and one for secondary.)

READING INVENTORIES

Volumes 2, 3, & 4 of the Assessment Kit (Sewell)
(Contains reading inventories in print, large type, and braille.)

SCRIPT READING

Assessment of Script Writing for the Blind (Swallow; Sewell)
Assessment of Script Writing for Low Vision Students (Swallow; Sewell)

SELF-HELP

(see "Daily Living Skills")

SENSORY DEVELOPMENT

(see "Visual Efficiency," "Listening," "Tactual")

SLATE AND STYLUS

Assessment of Slate Skills (Swallow)
Assessment of Slate and Stylos (Sewell)
Slate and Stylus Assessment (Sewell)

SOCIAL SKILLS

Social Skills Rating System (Gresham)
Informal Assessment Tool for Children with Visual Impairments (Sewell)
(also see Volume I of Independent Living)

TACTUAL

Tactual Graphics (Sewell)
(Part of one of the braille checklists.)
Tactual Skills Checklist (Sewell)

TECHNOLOGY

Braille 'n' Speak Checklist (Sewell)
Braille 'n' Speak/Braille Lite Checklist (Sewell)

TIME

Time Assessment (Sewell)

TYPING

Typing Skills Assessment (Swallow)
Assessing Typing Skills of Visually Handicapped Students (Swallow)
Assessing Typing & Skills of Visually Impaired Students (Sewell)

VISUAL EFFICIENCY

Program to Develop Efficiency in Visual Functioning: Diagnostic Assessment Procedure (Barraga & Morris)

VISUAL PERCEPTION

Motor-Free Visual Perception Test (Colarusso & Hammill)

VOCATIONAL/PREVOCATIONAL

Informal Evaluation of Prevocational Skills (Swallow)
Checklist for Informal Evaluation of Prevocational Skills (Sewell)
Vocational Skills Checklist: Elementary–High School (Swallow)
Vocational Skills Checklist (Sewell)

REFERENCES AND RECOMMENDED READING

Barraga, N. & Morris, J. (1980). *Program to develop efficiency in visual function: Diagnostic assessment procedure (DAP).* Louisville, KY: American Printing House for the Blind.

Brown, D., Simmons, V., & Methvin, J. (1991). *ORegon Project for visually impaired and blind preschoolers.* Medford, OR: Jackson Education Service District.

Caton, H. (1980). *Tactile test of basic concepts: A tactile analog to the Boehm test of basic concepts,* Form A. Louisville, KY: American Printing House for the Blind.

Caton, H. & Duckworth, B. (1985). *Braille unit recognition battery: Grade 2 literacy braille.* Louisville, KY: American Printing House for the Blind.

Colarusso, R. & Hammill, D. (1995). *Motor-free visual perception test.* (Revised). Los Angeles: Western Psychological Services.

Croft, N. & Robinson, L. (1984). *Growing up: A developmental curriculum.* Ogden, UT: Parent Consultants.

Godwin, A., Martin, J., Grafsgaard, K., McNear, D., Hanson, N., Rieber, C., Hooey, P., & Tillmanus, E. (1995). *Minnesota braille skills inventory.* Little Canada, MN: Minnesota Education Services.

Gresham, F. & Elliott, S. (1990). *Social skills rating system.* Circle Pines, MN: American Guidance Service.

Koenig, A. & Farrenkopf, C. (1995). *Assessment of braille literacy skills (ABLS).* Houston, TX: Region IV Education Service Center, Special Education Department.

Loumiet, R. & Levack, N. (1993). *Independent living: A curriculum with adaptations for students with visual impairments* (Volumes 1, 2, 3). Austin, TX: Texas School for the Blind and Visually Impaired.

Pogrund, R., Healy, G., Jones, K., Levack, N., Martin-Curry, S., Martinez, C., Marz, J., Roberson-Smith, B., & Vrba, A. (1993). *Teaching age-appropriate purposeful skills.* (An orientation and mobility curriculum for students with visual impairments.) Austin, TX: Texas School for the Blind and Visually Impaired.

Robinson, L. & DeRosa, S. (1980). *Parent needs inventory.* Ogden, UT: Parent Consultants.

*Sewell, D. (Ed.). (1997). *Assessment kit: Informal tools for academic students with visual impairments.* Austin, TX: Texas School for the Blind and Visually Impaired.

Swallow, R., Mangold, S., & Mangold, P. (1978). *Informal assessment of developmental skills for visually handicapped children.* New York: American Foundation for the Blind.

*This is probably the best single source of assessment instruments.

Chapter Eighteen

GOAL-BASED PLANNING

Assessment is the bridge between referral and the IFSP/IEP. It serves to establish eligibility and to determine the *current level of functioning* in all appropriate instructional areas. The establishment of eligibility is the simpler of the two purposes for assessment, and it amounts to documenting that the child's disability meets the predetermined definition of that disability. In the case of visual impairment, the Functional Vision Evaluation and the Learning Media Assessment collect a great deal of information that should make the match relatively easy. it is the second purpose of assessment that can stimulate discussion.

The TVI bears a great deal of the responsibility for establishing current level of functioning in vision-related instructional areas. When using criterion-referenced measurement tools, reporting is usually a description of what the child can or cannot do, and this information must be clearly stated, as concisely as possible.

When a child has multiple disabilities, the TVI will be only one of several specialists reporting assessment data, and all reports are trying to do the same thing: describe what the child can or cannot do in a particular disability area. The IEP team has to compile *all* of the information and come up with a composite picture of the child's functional levels. This establishment of functional levels is the first task facing the IEP team.

ESTABLISHING NEEDS

If the current level of functioning can be satisfactorily established in the opinion of the IEP team, the next step is to determine whether there is a mismatch between the current level of functioning and the *expected level of functioning* (i.e., are there delays?). The pitfalls lie in the designation of expected levels of functioning; is it *expected* according to test norms, age appropriateness, grade level achievement, innate potential, or parental expectations? this interpretation has to be agreed upon before preceding any further.

For an infant, toddler, or preschooler, expected level might be presumed to be the developmental level, according to an appropriate developmental scale. (See Chapter Fourteen for a discussion of the appropriateness of developmental scales for visually impaired infants and toddlers.)

For children with multiple disabilities, the expected level may be more difficult to establish; external variables may carry considerable weight. Does developmental age or chronological age count more? Are parental expectations realistic or useful? Can predictions for potential (possible future achievements) actually be made? On what basis can current level of functioning be compared to some other standard? There may not be good answers to these questions, and IEP teams have to make hard decisions about what to use as a comparison for the student they are evaluating.

When a student is only visually impaired, peer performance may be one possible standard. The question for the IEP team then becomes "How does *this* student's level of functioning compare to peers?" Any mismatch can provide rationale for identifying instructional needs. Basically, the IEP team must decide: What is this student *now* doing, in relation to what he/she *should* be doing? Is it an important enough difference that special instruction should be provided? This is not necessarily the best standard to use, but it is one choice in defining "needs."

If IEP teams are having trouble determining which standard to use in evaluating discrepancies between *current* level of functioning and expected/hoped for level of functioning, they may wish to use a different approach. If the team considers long-range outcomes as standards, it may help to put annual goals into a different perspective. A set of outcomes could provide an alternative framework within which to view special needs for students with visual impairments.

Instead of using age, grade, or "norms" as a standard against which to measure discrepancies, why not use an outcome? For example, an outcome for preschoolers might be "to get ready for school." Goals and objectives would then aim towards that outcome. For students with multiple disabilities, an outcome might focus on preparing those students for "life after age 21" (learning to cooperate with caregivers; getting ready to live in an assisted care/supervised living facility; acquiring leisure-time activities or skills; preparing for some type of occupational placement).

For students with higher level needs, a broader set of outcomes might include:

- Moving through space safely and confidently (physical development and mobility);

- Caring for one's own personal needs (self-help skills);
- Interacting socially, appropriately (social skills);
- Making choices based on reason and experience (cognitive development);
- Accessing information in all forms and media (language/literacy);
- Understanding and advocating for one's own needs (self-advocacy; self-concept; self-esteem).

Goals and objectives would then fit into or match one or more of the outcomes. Looking further ahead instead of focusing on a single year might help everyone on the IEP team (including parents) view the student's growth within a broader perspective.

SETTING GOALS

Once the current level of functioning is placed within the context of long-term outcomes, the focus is on the individual child and what it will take to move closer to that end. The steps become the goals and objectives linked directly to the child's individual needs. All that remains is to identify who is available to provide instruction in the needed areas, when it will begin and how long it will last, and where it will occur. These last determiners (the *who, when,* and *where*) are the variables that lead to a placement decision (i.e., Where is the best place to implement the goals).

It is no coincidence that legal requirements for both the IFSP and the IEP reflect exactly what the process produces. Comparing the legal language for both the IFSP and the IEP, these similarities are evident. (See Table 11 for details.)

It is important to determine who will implement the instructional services plan. In the case of an IFSP, a "service coordinator" is designated by the IFSP team to be responsible for the implementation of the IFSP and to coordinate the contributions of the various agencies and/or service providers. IEP teams usually have a lead member (commonly a representative of the school district) but services are usually provided by independent providers, who may or may not be direct employees of the school district. Services in instructional areas unique to visually impaired students should be planned and implemented by the TVI and COMS; other disability areas should be addressed by specialists in those disability areas.

Problems arise when there are multiple disabilities and not enough hours in the school day to deal with all of them. (This may also be a problem for a student whose sole disability is a visual impairment, but whose skills are deficient in a number of areas.) The most practical (but not the only) solution

TABLE 11. COMPARISON OF THE IFSP AND IEP

IFSP (Source: 20 U.S.C. 1436)	*IEP (Source: 20 U.S.C. 1414)*	*What it means . . .*
"unique strengths and needs of the infant or toddler" "present levels of physical development, cognitive development, communication development, social or emotional development, and adaptive development, based on objective criteria"	"present levels of educational performance" "needs that result from the child's disability" "other educational needs that result from the child's disability"	Where the student is functioning *now*. . . .
"major outcomes expected to be achieved"	"measurable annual goals, including benchmarks or short-term objectives*	Where the student *should* be functioning. . . .
"criteria, procedures, and timelines used to determine the degree to which progress toward achieving the outcomes is being made"	"how the child's progress toward the annual goals . . . will be measured"	How you'll know when goals have been met. . . .
"specific early intervention services necessary" "method of delivery services"	"special education and related services and supplementary aids and services to be provided to the child or on behalf of the child" "program modifications or supports for school personnel"	Who will provide services. . . .
"frequency, intensity" "dates for initiation of services and the anticipated duration of services"	"date for the beginning of the services and modifications" "frequency, location, and duration of those services and modifications"	When services will be provided. . . .
"natural environments in which early intervention services shall be appropriately provided, including a justification of the extent, if any, to which the services will not be provided in a natural environment"	"an explanation of the extent, if any, to which the child will not participate with non-disabled children in the regular class"	Where services will be provided. . . .

*"in the case of a child who is blind or visually impaired, provide for instruction in braille and the use of braille unless the IEP team determines, after an evaluation of the child's reading and writing skills, needs, and appropriate reading and writing media (including an evaluation of the child's future needs for instruction in braille or the use of braille), that instruction in braille or the use of braille is not appropriate for the child."

might be to establish priorities for needs and meet the most urgent ones immediately; the less urgent needs should not be ignored, but might receive less frequent attention. Another solution is to enlist parent assistance; many parents are willing to provide experiences (and even instruction in such areas as social skills, leisure and recreation skills, or study skills), or, at the very least, "back up" support in such areas. A third possibility is to arrange out-of-school instruction for some areas; feasible areas might include agency-provided instruction in daily living skills, social skills, leisure and recreation skills, or optical device training. O&M instruction might also be provided after school in some cases, although the instructor might have to be given "comp-time" or additional reimbursement for the extra hours. Learning does not need to be limited to school hours, and creative planning at the IEP meeting can result in programming that truly meets individual needs.

It is important to add that parents should feel a part of both the planning process and the program itself. An IEP is not something to "give" a parent, but a plan in which they have been involved. They should know, from the beginning of the process, that they have the right (and perhaps the responsibility) to add to, delete, or modify whatever suggested goals and objectives are presented by the other team members. If there is disagreement, there should be discussion. Final decisions should ideally be unanimous, and this is a goal every team should keep as its prime directive. The best-written IEP will be doomed to at least partial failure if all the team members don't "buy into it;" it takes the cooperation of everyone involved for a good IEP to be implemented and accomplished.

A FINAL NOTE ABOUT GOAL-BASED PLANNING

There seems to be increasing interest in outcome-based education. That is, what do we want the end product to look like, and how do we create that end product? The first step in designing outcome-based curricula is to have a clear idea about what the outcome should be. In the case of blind or visually impaired individuals, there is general agreement that the ideal should be: AS INDEPENDENT AS POSSIBLE. This means, being able to care for one's own personal needs, being able to interact socially appropriately, being able to travel independently, being able to access information in all media, being able to advocate for one's own needs, and being able to be competitively and productively employed. This is an image that may be contrary to what most sighted persons think of blind or visually impaired persons (helpless; passive; dependent), but it is also an image that is not created overnight. It begins in the early years of life, as independent behavior is encouraged and valued. The visually impaired child learns competency by succeeding, and by interacting actively with people and the environment. The task of the educator (particularly the TVI) is to provide the *opportunities* for success and interactive experiences.

Acquiring independent behaviors is a hierarchical process. That is, it requires one-step-at-a-time, sequential learning. No step can be left out, for doing so could weaken the hierarchy. Moreover, steps should be included at appropriate times (during "windows of opportunity"–the physical and chronological ages most children acquire the skills). Skills *not* acquired at appropriate times during the developmental years are *much* more difficult to teach later. for example, if head control is not achieved during the early months, upright posture will be negatively affected, and later mobility training will have to deal with a sagging head. Intervention for visually impaired children should begin at least one month before a skill would normally be acquired by sighted children, and should continue until the skill is acquired. Blind and visually impaired students may need extra practice and additional experience to acquire some skills, and it is the responsibility of the TVI to monitor the acquisition process.

It is easy to get involved in day-to-day, week-to-week programming and lose sight of the long-term outcomes. It is also sometimes easier to do things *for* visually impaired students (or to provide a full-time aide to do things for them), but it is not a favor to the child. It is far better to teach the child how to perform a task independently (and then to give time for practice) than to step in and assist too quickly. The TVI must "release" the student, and both allow and encourage independence–insofar as the student is capable. It should be a constant reminder to TVIs that they only have the school years to provide supervised learning; after high school, students are on their own.

Part of the TVI's role is also helping parents to recognize the opportunities and possibilities for their visually impaired children. If the focus is on the disability, the vision is narrow. Focusing on the future–the long-range outcome–helps to keep the annual goals in perspective. The responsibility of the educator is to prepare the student for life, and "letting go" is part of that plan.

REFERENCES AND RECOMMENDED READING

Bagnato, S. & Neisworth, J. (1981). *Linking developmental assessment and curricula.* Rockville, MD: Aspen Systems Corporation.

Hazekamp, J. & Heubner, K. (Eds.). (1989). *Program planning and evaluation for blind and visually impaired students: National guidelines for educational excellence.* New York: American Foundation for the Blind.

Larsen, S. & Poplin, M. (1980). *Methods for educating the handicapped: An individualized educational program approach.* Boston: Allyn & Bacon, Inc.

Lewis, S. & Allman, C. (2000). *Educational programming.* In Holbrook, C. & Koenig, A. (Eds.). Foundations of education, Volume 1. New York: AFB Press.

Chapter Nineteen

DIAGNOSTIC TEACHING

When children make errors in schoolwork, the mistakes are often just tallied and a grade assigned for the work. Few teachers ask *why* each error occurred. Diagnostic teaching is an instructional approach that attempts to determine the *causes* of errors, and to remediate those causative factors if possible. For visually impaired learners, this is essential, since many types of errors are vision related (misreading or miscopying, omissions, faulty concepts based on inaccurate visual observation or experience).

The teacher of visually impaired students is trained to look for the "why" of errors because of the strong influence of vision in learning. Unfortunately, few visually impaired students have the TVI available all day, during all learning experiences. Since most visually impaired students attend public school, many of them in "mainstreamed" classes, the regular classroom teacher should become aware of how to look for causes and errors as well. This chapter will describe ways of becoming more alert to why visually impaired students make mistakes and what factors may affect this process.

REASONS FOR ERRORS

Visual impairment can affect past learning as well as current performance. Early learning experiences depend to a great extent on good vision for maximum value. When a child is totally blind, other senses (which are less efficient, even when combined) provide unequal information; the result is a world structured in a different way, and concepts may not be as well established as for sighted children. Such qualities as color and space will never be adequate; attributes such as size, shape, and temperature are "known" in tactual form. The auditory information gathered by the young blind child contributes mostly to spatial orientation. Thus, concepts may have a very different construction for blind children than for sighted children.

When there is useful but impaired vision, concepts may still be inadequate. Distance, spatial orientation, and directionality are probably imprecisely perceived, and nearpoint concepts (size, shape, color, texture) may be affected by the amount of vision for near use. "Just getting closer" doesn't always work.

Experience-based concepts are probably the most common problem areas causing errors. The visually impaired student may have developed unusual perceptions of "reality," despite correct verbal responses. One of the things the classroom teacher should watch for is a mismatch between what the visually impaired child *says,* and what he/she actually understands. For example, the definition of a square ("four equal sides and four equal angles") also meets the requirements for a Tick-Tack-Toe form, where the lines overshoot the corners, but the game form will not be the correct shape for later geometry applications. Similarly, the verbal definition of a desert ("a large, hot, dry area") may lead a visually impaired child to believe that there are only sand dunes in a desert, and no people, plants, or animals. Residents of West Texas, New Mexico, or Arizona might dispute that belief! The classroom teacher must be constantly alert for these mismatches between verbal definitions and actual meanings ("verbalisms") in visually impaired students.

Other common errors in schoolwork done by visually impaired students are more directly related to the visual deficits. Examples include mis-reading letters or words, omitting letters or words, losing one's place, copying sentences or math problems incorrectly, not being able to write "on the line," and the inability to keep columns of figures in a vertical column. (Note that letter or word reversals are *not* in this group of examples because they are perceptual problems that occur in the brain, not the optical system.)

Diagnostic teaching includes the analysis of errors, processes, tasks, and concepts. The TVI can also analyze unique-tool efficiency (e.g., braille, accuracy, typing, or keyboarding ability) which may also cause errors in schoolwork. There are different approaches to analyzing different kinds of discrepancies; therefore, each will be addressed separately.

ERROR ANALYSIS

This procedure asks the teacher to look at errors, note consistency and frequency, and determine *why* they occurred. In spelling, it could be poor auditory discrimination, handwriting or braille writing errors, or inadequate visual memory. In reading, it might be poor word attack skills, inadequate vocabulary, inability to use context clues, poor comprehension skills, or simply the reading media itself (poor braille skills, slow and laborious visual reading because of low vision, inability to use low vision devices efficiently). In math, it could be mistaking or miscopying numbers or symbols, placing numbers in the wrong columns, missing decimal points or commas, the inability to see the smaller numbers in fractions, or lack of efficiency in the braille math code. If carelessness is the culprit, the errors will be more inconsistent. If vision is at fault, errors of the same type should reoccur, and can be identified; the related causes–visual, tool use, phonics, etc.–can be addressed through environmental modifications, remedial instruction, or special skill/tool enhancement.

PROCESS-ERROR ANALYSIS

If lack of understanding of a specific process (e.g., spelling rules, math procedures, science guidelines) seems to be the cause of errors, it may be able to be verified by asking the student to verbalize exactly what he/she is thinking or doing before and when the error occurs. In this way, the teacher may be able to follow the student's thought process and identify where the lack of understanding occurs. Process errors are usually conceptual rather than visual and are often amenable to re-teaching.

TASK ANALYSIS

This procedure usually works best with physical behaviors (motor skills, sequences of actions that have a final result). The teacher observes the student try to complete the task, and notes where the student's performance breaks down; the teacher can then break the task into smaller steps, and can establish the prerequisite skills for each step. This helps to determine whether a concept or a physical ability is deficient. For example, a child who cannot tie shoes may not have sufficient grasp to hold the laces, or may not understand the term "cross over." Usually, some remedial experience can solve concept problems, and practice or materials modification can alleviate physical problems. Once the troublesome factors have been addressed, the complete and original task can be re-attempted. If the visual impairment is part of the problem, then modifications, either in materials or procedures, may be needed to solve the problem.

CONCEPT ANALYSIS

This is the type of error most often overlooked by teachers, and may be the one most often caused by a visual impairment. The more severe the vision reduction, the more likely it is that concept development will be affected. The student is usually unaware of any conceptual deficits; therefore, the *teacher* must be alert to that possibility.

A questioning strategy is usually the best way to identify conceptual gaps or deficits. Avoid questions that can be answered "yes" or "no." (Examples: "Have you seen . . . ?" or "Do you understand . . . ?") Better questions might be: "What does . . . look like to you?" or "What can you tell me about . . . ?" The purpose of questioning is to find out what the student's perception *is,* not whether it is acceptable. The teacher wants to know how much the student's perception differs from reality, so that remediation procedures can be planned and implemented.

Blind and visually impaired students may have many conceptual gaps that surprise teachers when discovered, and the gaps (or imperceptions) can interfere with later learning that depends on prior concepts for accuracy. A constant monitoring process is necessary, especially when new vocabulary words are introduced. The classroom teacher, whether elementary or secondary level, should watch for unusual misunderstandings expressed by the visually impaired student; these should raise a red flag of caution, and questions should probe the student's real perceptions of the topic in question.

TOOL/SKILL ANALYSIS

If errors do not appear to be related to processes, tasks, or concepts, the TVI can inventory tool skills, evaluate reading media, or suggest materials modifications. The skills of this teacher are available to help the classroom teacher at any point during the problem solving process.

SUMMARY

When an ongoing diagnostic/prescriptive instructional model is integrated into the regular school curriculum, particularly at the elementary level, deficits can be identified and remediated before they multiply and interfere with later learning. When remediation is not possible, modifications in materials or instructional approaches can at least minimize or alleviate the deficits. By linking ongoing assessment with daily programming, teachers can sharpen their observational skills and become more effective as teachers.

REFERENCES AND RECOMMENDED READING

Bagnato, S. & Neisworth, J. (1981). *Linking developmental assessment and curricula.* Rockville, MD: Aspen Systems.

Hall, A., Scholl, G., & Swallow, R. (1986). Psychoeducational assessment. In Scholl, G. (Ed.), *Foundations of education for blind and visually handicapped children and youth.* New York: American Foundation for the Blind.

Layton, C. (2000). Ongoing assessments: Informal techniques. In Koenig, A. & Holbrook, C., *Foundations in education, Volume 2.* New York: AFB Press.

Chapter Twenty

TRANSITIONS

PLANNING FOR CHANGE

In Chapter Six, theories of development and learning were discussed. The reader will recall that a fundamental characteristic of learning and growth is change. Unless behavior is altered, or new brain patterns established, learning has not taken place. Change may be the best indicator that learning has taken place, and is, therefore desirable. The teacher looks for changes in behaviors, knowledge, skills, and in the thinking process itself.

Most teachers recognize that learning is rarely smooth and continuous, and probably occurs more in "spurts" than in neat sequences. Good teachers try to capture students' attention at "teachable moments" (readiness periods) because it is easier to teach at those times. Teachers also know that the best instructional methods can be ineffective if a student cannot relate the new knowledge to something already known. (There may be no already-established brain pattern to retrieve and compare to, so the brain literally shuts down, and learning is blocked.)

The characteristic "spurts" in learning and growth, from birth to adulthood, often occur around the same time as transition periods in education. These periods generally include the change from a home-based intervention program to a center-based program (around age 3), the step from early childhood services to primary school (around age 6), the move from elementary school to middle school or junior high school, and then on to senior high school. The next transition is from high school to a postsecondary educational setting or to the work world. For those who attend college or a vocational training program, the final transition is to the world of employment. Each period of change can present adjustment problems, even to totally intact ("normal") individuals. For the student who is visually impaired, these transition periods can be especially troublesome, both for the student and his/her family. Advance planning can ease the changes in the lives of student and family.

TRANSITIONS

From Home to Center: Early intervention for visually impaired infants and toddlers is usually home-based. The TVI visits on a regular basis to demonstrate intervention techniques, which the parents then continue between the teacher's visits. This may be a difficult time for the parents since they may still be experiencing the shock and disbelief of finding out their child has as a disability. The emotional support and regular visits from the special teacher can go a long way to help alleviate some of the disappointment felt by parents during those early years. The TVI often leaves booklets or pamphlets about development when a child is visually impaired, so the parents can begin to gain an understanding about what to expect and when. The IFSP involves the parents from the beginning, and addresses their own particular situation.

When an infant passes through the toddler stage (around age 3), the TVI may begin to talk about the closest center-based program, and will probably encourage the parents to visit once or twice. (If there is no center-based program available, the home visits may continue until the child is old enough for kindergarten.) According to current federal law, the educational system is responsible for programs for disabled preschoolers, age 3–5. (States are permitted to designate the responsible agency for disabled children from birth to 3, and this agency may often be the state department of health, who in turn, requests the services of the TVI.) Because there may be a change of responsible agency at age 3 (the older children have an IEP instead of an IFSP), the TVI is available to provide some continuity and to assist in planning the most appropriate service delivery system.

Sometimes there is a question about the most appropriate placement for 3–5-year-olds who are visually impaired. If the child is otherwise intact (i.e., the only disability appears to be the visual impairment), a nursery school or kindergarten for normally sighted youngsters is preferable to an "early childhood special education class" because the visually impaired child needs positive peer models. Most early childhood special classes contain a wide range of functioning, from severely delayed children to mildly impaired, and expectations for the visually impaired child may not be set high enough. (Of course, if the visually impaired child is also multiply disabled, such a class may be appropriate; each placement is a decision based on individual needs.) If there is a center specifically for young visually impaired children (found usually only in larger urban areas), this may be the placement choice for the visually impaired child. The TVI should be familiar with the placement options in the child's geographical area, and can recommend which will best serve that particular child's needs best.

The TVI should visit the proposed placement center in advance, both to determine the match between the child and prospective classroom teacher, and to alert the program of the possible placement. This initial contact by the TVI can do much to prepare the center for the child's arrival. The TVI will continue to provide support services to the child at the center (unless the center is specifically for visually impaired children and is staffed by a certified TVI).

From Center to School: When the time comes for enrollment in "regular school," the decision must be made whether the visually impaired child is ready for the change. Because the competition with sighted peers may intensify as structured learning begins, it is of critical importance that readiness be carefully assessed. The first five years of *any* child's life lay the foundation for development and learning the rest of that child's educational years; it is even more critical for a visually impaired child, since so much more must be experienced and learned before school begins. This is the time to repeat a year of school (usually kindergarten) if another year of opportunity will enhance the child's repertoire of experiences. This is *not* to say that all visually impaired preschoolers should have two years of kindergarten, for some are ready to enter first grade at the appropriate time. The important factor to consider is *that* particular child's readiness. An extra year of opportunity to learn about the world before learning becomes a structured academic experience can pay off later in increased maturity and social comfort with peers.

The TVI will become a crucial member of the IEP team, since the child's unique needs will already be familiar. There should be an attempt made (when possible) to "hand pick" the first grade teacher. The attitudes and emotional climate established by the classroom teacher are critical to a successful "mainstreamed" placement, and this initial contact with the educational system should be as positive as possible.

The TVI should meet with the entire first grade "team" (from bus drivers, secretaries, and cafeteria helpers, to librarians, music teachers, art teachers, and gym teachers), in advance of the first day of school. This initial contact is to "introduce" the visually impaired child through a description of his/her visual functioning and any specific special needs (e.g., a "buddy" system for fire drills). Emphasis should always be on the encouragement of as much independence on the part of the child as possible. If special aides are assigned to the visually impaired child, the TVI should supervise their role; such aides may tend to "mother" the child instead of letting him/her do as much as possible independently.

If the child is totally blind, or has been taught to use a mobility device (such as some type of cane), it is likely that the O&M Instructor will bring the child to the school for at least one visit before school begins. This serves to orient the child to a new environment, and can help make the adjustment easier for the child. The O&M Instructor will probably talk with the administrator and classroom teacher, to gain an understanding of what parts of the building will be used by this child's class, approximately when, and in what sequence (time of day, day of the week). The O&M Instructor should have a map of the building and can then plan the most direct routes of travel to teach the child.

The time it takes to prepare for the child's arrival at a new school is *necessary.* It alleviates fears and misunderstandings about students with visual impairments, and can "pave the way" for a smooth transition from the relatively sheltered preschool environment to one that is much more complex and competitive. The time *does* "pay off" in minimized problems later on.

Elementary School to Middle School: Some of the same suggestions for the preceding transition also apply to this and later transitions. Preparatory introductory visits by the TVI should prepare each new set of teachers *each and every year,* and the O&M Instructor will probably teach new travel routes prior to the beginning of the each school year. The major difference in this transition to middle school is in the increased complexity. There will probably be many more teachers to inservice (since most middle schools begin departmentalized programs) and more routes between classes to be learned. There may be more special equipment and books for which to find storage sites, and there may be an increased use of library facilities and study skills. Reading and writing will not be taught as subjects so much as tool skills, so literacy will be a requirement for the visually impaired student. The homework will probably increase in quantity, and organizational skills will become more critical. For the visually impaired student, note-taking ability will be required but may be in unique form (slate and stylus, Braille 'n' Speak, laptop computer with enlargement software). Each new challenge may require new skills that the TVI will have to devise ways to teach. These will be skill-honing years in preparation for the rapid expansion of programs in high school.

Most normally sighted students in middle school are entering new and different social phases, and visually impaired students are no different. The increased emphasis on "belonging" highlights the need for adequate social skills (which, hopefully, have been taught from preschool onwards). The acquisition of age appropriate social skills cannot be *assumed* for visually impaired students, however, since much is gained through observation and imitation. The TVI should make an effort to note the acceptable but unique dress styles or habits of the group so that such observations can be privately passed on to the visually impaired student. "Fitting in" and "belonging" can make or break feelings of success for the visually impaired student; academic prowess may not be enough.

The job of the TVI is difficult at this stage; social acceptance may be important, but special skill instruction (perhaps the introduction of more sophisticated technology) is even more important. Without the tools and the ability to use them, success in school can be seriously hampered. These middle school years will increase and refine skills introduced earlier, and should gradually result in greater independence on the part of the visually impaired student.

Upper Middle School Years of Junior High School: Most of a visually impaired student's tool skills should be fairly well established by this time. Any that are not should receive attention. Early (and possibly ongoing) assessment should occur in the skills of listening, organization, study, and time management. Creative writing should be more than an experiment by now, and technology should be "part of life." The major emphasis during these years might be placed effectively on independent reasoning skills and problem solving. Although concrete opportunities to think, reason, and make decisions should have been provided from preschool on, it is during the upper middle school or junior high school years that abstract reasoning can be introduced. Simple logic problems or puzzles are "fun" ways to introduce abstract reasoning, and practical problem solving can be spontaneous and situational. (Examples might be how to get a piece of equipment satisfactorily repaired independently, or what to do if the student needs to move closer to the blackboard and the classroom teacher has forgotten that special need.) An increasing number of the student's problems should be solved by the student's own initiative. Parents should be encouraged to allow independent problem solving when safe and reasonable. It may also be at this age (if not before) that students should learn the consequences of inaction (a paper turned in late gets a failing grade). It cannot be emphasized too strongly that "the name of the game is independence" for a visually impaired student. The TVI should be gradually withdrawing intervention support, and encouraging the student to act on his/her own behalf. Self-advocacy that is assertive without being aggressive or offensive is a skill that will serve the student well in later life, and its roots are in the gradual, supervised release of the student by the TVI. This beginning occurred earlier (when the TVI modeled advocacy intervention *for* the student), but it emerges during the junior high school years when the student begins to advocate for his/her *own* needs. (*Total* self-advocacy is a goal for the senior high school years.)

Into Senior High School: Although it has probably been evident for some time that a student is or isn't academically capable (i.e., probably college bound or not), the transition into senior high school will likely require some course or "track" selection. The counseling skills of the TVI will be called into action, and knowledge of the student's past capabilities and/or interests should help in directing him/her toward realistic post-high school goals. It should be evident that each transition looks to the next one for guidance; long-term goals determine short-term decisions. Courses selected in tenth grade may have impact on later choice of college or technical school. When in doubt, place expectations high. (The realization of full potential will never be achieved by placing expectations too low.)

The high school years (at least the summers inbetween) are ideal times for visually impaired students to obtain part-time jobs. Few actually do, but the experience would introduce them to the work world and could help connect the earning of money with the retaining of a job (a reality many visually impaired students don't face until later). The TVI may be able to help locate employment opportunities for students but should encourage the students to apply for the jobs on their own.

Goals for the senior high school years will be directed towards independence. These years should see an increase in self-advocacy on the part of the visually impaired student, and a decrease in time spent by the TVI. The goal for every visually impaired student is for him/her to be able to get along without the TVI after graduation from high school, and this does not happen a month after graduation. If the student is college-bound, the textbook ordering process must be taught, the student must learn to obtain reader service, if applicable, and to use public transportation in unfamiliar environments. The student must know how to access library materials, how to use technology efficiently, and how to manage time wisely. The student must be able to ask for modifications in materials (and must be prepared to negotiate with professors who are oblivious to those needs). In short, the visually impaired student must be prepared to deal with a real, sometimes unaccommodating world beyond high school.

High School to the Postsecondary Experience: Although the preparatory educational system ends with high school graduation, learning may be a lifelong endeavor. Public school personnel (classroom teachers and special teachers alike) may not have a direct effect on their students after graduation, but their influence will last a lifetime. The ability to deal with reality, to make independent decisions, and to care for personal needs are skills that should have been taught before high school graduation. Too many visually impaired students are academically able to go on to college but have unreal expectations of what will be done for them. They lack advocacy skills and are unable to look after their own food and clothing. Summer rehabilitation centers are full of visually impaired high school graduates who cannot make a sandwich or do a laundry. Employers will not retain disabled people who are social misfits, who arrive late to work, or who are unable to use appropriate modified technology. Part of the reason there is such high unemployment or underemployment among visually impaired adults may be that job readiness skills were not required learning during the school years. It is the responsibility of educators to educate, and if the finished product is unemployable, then an adequate education has not occurred; the schools must share in the responsibility for the failure.

Transition planning for disabled adolescents is required by federal law. In the field of visual impairment, there are case workers (sometimes called "counselors") from state offices for the blind and visually impaired who should be part of the planning team from roughly the beginning of senior high school onward. Although regulations vary from state to state, generally the counselor tries to identify the visually impaired student around age 14 or 15 and begins home visits around that time. Sometimes, the TVI will call the counselor and request his/her services, as a member of the IEP team. By the time the student is 16, there should be a written "Transition Plan" as part of the IEP. This plan includes a list of steps to effect a smooth transition from school to postsecondary life (including college, vocational training, supported employment, continuing or adult education, adult services, independent living, or community involvement). Interagency responsibilities are clearly delineated and planned, before the student leaves school. If the agency(s) does not follow through with the plan, the IEP team can be reconvened to find other ways to meet the outlined objectives. It is too soon to tell whether this "transition planning" will be effective (the law is not very old) but, if observed strictly, has the potential to provide continuing monitoring for visually impaired students past the education years.

A sometimes unrecognized advantage of "transition planning" is its applicability for multidisabled students. It is not only the visually impaired students who are college or technical school bound who can get supervision and assistance from agencies, but also the students who may need sheltered workshop employment, independent living arrangements, and rehabilitation training services. "Transition planning" is for *all* visually impaired students, and it may help some become employable.

Into the World of Work: Although educators often have little control over the availability of jobs for visually impaired students, the "work ethic" (desire to earn an independent living) can be instilled at an early age. Paper routes, babysitting, greenhouse work, and even home chores can create a sense of responsibility and satisfaction with self-earned income. If the independence so desired as a goal becomes a reality, the prospects for employability also rise.

A realistic appraisal of a student's talents, interests, and skills can happen during the school years and can influence the choice of job later on. Too many academically capable school students become academically capable college students, and then academically capable graduate students, but are unemployable because they have no saleable job skills. (What does a blind sociologist with a master's degree actually do for a living?) With the technology explosion of the past ten years, and the passage of the Americans with

Disabilities Act (requiring reasonable employer accommodations for disabled workers), it seems that there should be an increase in the employment rate for visually impaired people. Unfortunately, this has not been the case so far, but perhaps the situation will change as the current group of technologically competent visually impaired students reach adulthood. It may be that the best that schools can do is to prepare the visually impaired student to be an independent traveler, a self-advocate, an independent problem-solver with technological competency, and a life-long learner.

REFERENCES AND RECOMMENDED READING

Corn, A. (1985). An independence matrix for visually handicapped learners. *Education of the Visually Handicapped, 17,* 3–10.

Corn, A. (1989). Employing critical thinking strategies within a curriculum of critical things to think about for blind and visually impaired students. *Journal of Vision Rehabilitation, 3,* 17–36.

Corn, A. & Bishop, V. (1984). Acquisition of practical knowledge by blind and visually impaired students in grades 9–12. *Journal of Visual Impairment and Blindness, 78,* 552–556.

Harrell, R. & Strauss, F. (1980). Approaches to increasing assertive behavior and communication skills in blind and visually impaired persons. *Journal of Visual Impairment and Blindness, 74,* 794–798.

Hatlen, P. (1990). Meeting the unique needs of pupils with visual impairments. *RE:view, 22* (2), 79–82.

Hazecamp, J. (1986). The team approach to advocacy. In Scholl, G. (Ed.), *Foundations of education for blind and visually handicapped children and youth.* New York: American Foundation for the Blind.

Irwin, J. & Macdonnell, P. (1988). Access to transition services: Integral part of curriculum. *Journal of Visual Impairment and Blindness, 82,* 69–70.

Simpson, F. (1986). Transition to adulthood. In Scholl, G. (Ed.). *Foundations of education for blind and visually handicapped children and youth.* New York: American Foundation for the Blind.

Wolffe, K. (1985). Don't give those kids fish; Teach 'em how to fish! *Journal of Visual Impairment and Blindness, 79,* 470–472.

APPENDICES

Appendix A

LISTENING GAMES AND ACTIVITIES

There is a difference between hearing and listening: hearing is merely the physical function of the ears–the simple recording of sound. Listening is the brain's interpretation or understanding of the recorded sound. In simpler terms, hearing is what our ears do; listening is when our brain tells us what our ears hear and how to use the sound wisely. It is important to remember that the ability to learn by listening is a skill that should not be assumed; often, it must be taught. If mastered thoroughly in the primary and intermediate grades, the junior high and senior high school student will be armed with an indispensable learning technique. When a secondary level student needs remedial assistance in this area, it is necessary to evaluate his present level of listening ability, and then teach all the succeeding levels in approximate order. Some students are weaker at some levels than others; these pupils will require remedial help in only these areas. The format of this program is arranged in order of difficulty, and progresses from simple auditory discrimination ability to more complex analytical listening. The suggestions at any level should be adapted to the grade level or ability of the child, and progress should be periodically evaluated by the teacher. The child should move as quickly as possible from one level to another, so that he "learns to listen" effectively, early in his school years.

SIMPLE SOUND IDENTIFICATION

Activities

"What Can I Hear"

Child sits quietly at various given locations (classroom, outdoors, kitchen, etc.) and names the isolated sounds he hears. For example, in a classroom a child may hear such sounds as desks moving, children breathing or coughing, ventilator blowing, radiator steaming, books closing, windows rattling, chalk scratching on blackboard, etc. In a kitchen location, the child may hear pots and pans rattling, the oven and/or refrigerator opening and closing, stirring of a spoon, can opener, teakettle whistling, etc. The classroom teacher must adapt her expectations to her situation, as "city sounds" may be entirely different from "country sounds."

"What Is It"

A tape recording or record of isolated sounds is played. Child must correctly identify the sound, or its cause. Examples should be geared to the experience of the child, and limited to completely recognizable sounds. Each sound should be clear or distinct. They may progress from easily recognizable sounds to sounds which normally require visual clues for recognition. A suggested list of sounds might be as follows: telephone ringing, clock ticking, policeman's whistle, car horn, doorbell chimes, wind blowing, jet plane overhead, water pouring or coming from faucet. Sounds that normally require visual clues, but that should be auditorily recognizable may be as follows: dialing of a telephone, match striking, fire burning, chewing (as celery or raw carrots), walking or running of a person, infant "cooing" or babbling, truck going by, pages of a book being turned rapidly. The teacher will be able to add other sounds to her list from her experience or imagination. Do not include the spoken word or animal sounds, as this will be the next activity.

"Who Am I"

A tape recording or record of animal sounds is played, and the child simply identifies the animal. Some records are already available that may be used (see listing at the end of the chapter). Include animals other than the familiar dog and cat. Even though they may not be familiar, the lessen teaches the recognition of different animals by sound, as well as the discrimination of the sounds themselves.

"Good Morning, Miss Jones"

A child is placed with his back to the class; another child says "Good Morning, Miss Jones." The child who is "it" must identify the speaker from his voice. After some skill is gained in classmate identification using normal voice tones, the children may attempt to disguise their voices, making the game a little harder.

Many variations of the above activities will be apparent; the important factor involved is the simple auditory identification of isolated sound.

TONAL AND VOLUME DISCRIMINATION

Activities

"Near-Far"

Child must identify the sound simply as *near* or *far,* and need not identify the sound itself. Examples might be as follows: plane taking off nearby versus plane in the air, train whistle at a distance versus train whistle near the station, child walking in the hall versus child walking in the classroom, playground clamor versus classroom noises, telephone bell nearby versus telephone bell in another part of the house, dog barking next door versus dog barking in the kitchen for his supper.

"High-Low"

Child must identify as *high* pitch or *low* pitch the following suggested sounds: musical instrument tones–piano, horn, guitar; voice singing–soprano versus bass; male speaking voice versus female speaking voice; cat's meow versus large dog's bark; and small bell versus large bell.

"Loud-Soft"

Child must identify the sound as either *loud* or *soft.* Volume control may be utilized and the following suggested sounds may be presented: grandfather clock versus small watch, shout versus whisper, stamping feet versus tiptoeing, small bell versus large bell, book being dropped versus penny or needle being dropped, tapping on a desk versus pounding on a desk.

"Who Is Saying It"

Teacher reads a familiar story, short and simple of plot. Child must identify the character speaking by the pitch or dialect of the voice. The classic example, of course, is "The Three Bears" but even some stories from the child's own reader may be used. On an upper grade level, dialect or accent may be used to differentiate the character speaking.

IMITATION–REPRODUCING OF SOUND

Activities

"Do as I Do" (or **"Say"**)

Child must repeat, either verbally or physically, the sound or rhythm presented by the teacher. Drum beats, clapping rhythms, stamping sequences or rhythm-band instrument beats initiate this activity. Repetition of number sequences, progressing from three-number sets to five- or six-number sets (as, 1-4-8-5-2-9), with exact accuracy; repetition of nonsense syllables, in groups of three to five (mish, mash, mush, moosh; eena, deena, diner, duster; etc.); repeating of nonsense rhymes (some nursery rhymes, as Hey Diddle Diddle, or selections from Dr. Seuss books; limit to two lines), repeating of two-line rhymes, and progressing to four-line rhymes if the child has the ability to respond.

"Gossip"

A game wherein one child repeats a sentence to another, whispered, and that child repeats it to another, and so on. The object is to have the last child repeat the sentence *exactly* as the first child originated it. This game requires careful listening. The sentence need not make sense, or have a purpose, as the object of the game is accurate listening and accurate repetition.

RHYMING–SIMILARITIES OF SOUNDS

Activities

"One Like Mine"

Teacher says a word; the child must respond with a word that sounds the same, for example, ball-call, house-mouse, door-floor, etc. Follow-up activities involving "word families" may be indicated: "at" family–cat, bat, hat, fat, etc.

"Two Alike"

Teacher says three words, as "cat, bat, saw"; the child must select and restate the two words that sound alike.

"Poetry"

Simple selections are read aloud by the teacher; nursery rhymes and simple poems, with obvious rhyming words, are most desirable; the child must repeat the pair of rhymed words. Begin by emphasizing the rhymed words, using two lines at a time, and progress to two-line rhymes without emphasizing the pair of words. If the child's ability indicates it, four-line rhymes may be presented, using the same approach of emphasis and nonemphasis. A favorite selection of the author's, believed to be a nursery rhyme, is as follows:

Under a toadstool crept a wee elf,
Out of the rain to shelter himself.
"Oh me, oh my!" he loudly lamented.
And that's how umbrellas first were invented.

DISCRIMINATING DIFFERENCES IN SOUNDS

Activities

"One Out"

Teacher says three words; child must name the word that does not belong, or does *not* sound like the others, as "bag, rag, *back*." This activity involves the ability to hear a different sound, rather than to listen for sound-alikes.

"Change Me"

Teacher says two words, as "me, we"; child must indicate the *beginnings* are different; "get, guess"; child indicates that that ends are different; the child need not know the terms "initial, medial, or final," though they may be introduced to an older or above-average-ability child; the actual sounds need not be identified, as the purpose of the activity is listening for differences.

PHONICS

Most school systems already have some type of outlined program in this area, which may be injected or further reinforced at this point in developing good listening skills. However, this is the logical point in teaching listening skills to introduce actual letter sounds. For any teacher who does not have access to an outlined program in phonics, the following information may be helpful in planning a specific program of instruction to include in the teaching of listening skills.

Most research supports the viewpoint that some vowels usually occur before the majority of consonant sounds in normal patterns of speech development. However, the purpose of including phonics in the teaching of listening skills is auditory discrimination, not speech correction. It is helpful to know the normal sequence of consonantal development in speech as a basis to the phonics program, but it is not essential that the child be able to *make* the sound if he can auditorily discriminate and/or identify it. The fact that the average eight-year-old girl or nine-year-old boy should normally be able to articulate all speech sounds satisfactorily does not mean that the first-grader cannot be taught to discriminate auditorily sounds he may be unable to articulate successfully. Emphasis in phonics for the visually limited child should always be placed on the child's ability to *hear* the sound and identify it. It would be enough for a visually limited child in first grade to be able to point to a ruler, radio, or raisin as a means of indicating the initial "r" sound; he may be developmentally unable yet to articulate the sound himself.

It is the feeling and experience of the writer that most consonant sounds may be more successfully taught first, before actual teaching of vowel sounds, as there are fewer consonants with multiple sounds than vowels. A suggested order of presentation might be as follows: p, b, m (humming sound), w, h, t, d, n, g (as in girl), k, y, j (teach that g sometimes "borrows" this sound as well), c (teach that c has no real sound of its own, and must "borrow" the k sound or the s sound), s (snake sound), f (angry cat sound), v (vacuum cleaner sound), z (bumble bee sound sometimes "borrowed" by s), l (la-la, or singing sound), r (rooster sound); q is introduced as a combination of k and w; x need not be taught in isolation, but may be introduced in conjunction with, or as a preliminary to, vowel sounds (x is the equivalent of short e plus ks). Initial, final, and medial (in that order) positions in words should also be introduced; the child may be asked to identify beginning, ending, or middle positions in dictated words, or could name as many as possible that have the sound being studied and in the position under study.

Vowels may be introduced next, following the same procedure of auditory identification as with consonants. Vowel sounds should be limited, at first, to long, short, and that affected by r. Later, vowel-consonant combinations may be taught, and "word families" introduced (*at* family proceeds as: bat, cat, fat, hat, mat, pat, rat, sat; other families might be: -it, -et, -ot, -ut, -ate, -ame, -ime, -an, -un, -all, -ell, -ill, -ight, etc. The teacher will think of many more possibilities for families).

Blends and digraphs may be added next: "sh" (quiet sound), "ch" (train sound), th (voiced and voiceless), wh; bl, br, cl, cr, dr, fl, fr, gl, gr, pl, pr, sk, sl, sm, sn, sp, st, sw, tr. Again, begin with initial (beginning) position, and progress to final (end), where applicable, and medial (middle) positions. A review of word families, adding blends and digraphs, may be helpful reinforcement.

Following consonants, vowels, word families, blends and digraphs, the ensuing course of study might include endings, syllables, prefixes, suffixes, root words, and compound words, depending on the age and grade of the child. Keep foremost in mind that *listening* is the skill being taught, and activities should be oral insofar as possible; there will be great carry-over into the areas of reading and spelling, however, but methods of teaching should utilize the auditory approach more than the visual.

DISCRIMINATION INVOLVING EXTENDED ATTENTION SPAN

Activities

"What's New"

Teacher says two sentences; the second sentence should have one word changed. The child must identify and state the "new word." As skill is developed, the teacher may change two or even three words, but the child must still be able to identify the changes. Nonsense sentences, such as found in some of Dr. Seuss books are useful, as they involve little comprehensive clues; the child must listen for the sound change, rather than the meaning change. Original examples might be the following: "The fat cat met a sad cat. The fat cat met a sad rat." or "Sam sees a silly Billy Goat. Sam saw a silly Billy Goat."

At this point in the outline of teaching listening skills, the child should be able to identify and discriminate isolated sounds, either abstract or verbal, and should have developed some consistent accuracy in doing so. If he is weak in a particular area, it is wise to go back and reteach or reinforce that area until it is satisfactorily mastered. The following section is based, in part, on the preceding skills and begins to apply some of the simple discriminative abilities. Up to this point, little analytical thought or reasoning was required, over and above auditory discrimination. Now the child will be asked to use the skills already taught in a meaningful manner.

Purposeful listening can be sued to develop critical, analytical, and selective listening skills.

FOLLOWING DIRECTIONS

Activities

"Simon Says"

A game in which directions of simple types–stand up, sit down, go to the window, etc.–are given; the child is not expected to follow the command unless it is prefaced by "Simon Says."

"Bring Me"

A game in which the teacher asks the child to bring her various items; the child is to follow only those directives which are possible. For example, he *would* bring a particular book to the teacher, but would not bring the wall. This game requires some degree of analytical thinking as well as good listening.

"Do as I Say"

A simple game of following directions, wherein the teacher begins with single directions as "close the door," and increases the number of directions in one command, as "bring me your spelling book, open it to page 10, and point to the first word on the page." This game is good practice for the child who seems to have difficulty in following sets of either oral or written directions concerning his classwork. he child must listen to the full set of directions before beginning to execute any part of them; they are repeated only once.

WORD MEANINGS

(to develop analytical thinking in terms of single words)

Activities

"Riddles"

Simple riddles, either selected from some resource or teacher improvised, are given orally and the child must guess the answer. The riddles should proceed from simple to difficult, as "What animal has four legs, a fluffy tail, hops, and eats carrots? (rabbits)" to "What goes up the chimney down, but won't go down the chimney up? (umbrella)." Avoid puns or plays on words for the young child.

"I Am Thinking of"

A variation on the riddle technique. Separate the answers as to nouns, verbs, and describers, and use each set as separate games; the nouns will be the simplest and will be most like the riddles; the verbs will be a little more difficult and will encourage thought with regard to using action words that are not commonly overworked, as "I am thinking of a word which means to read and think at the same time (study)" or "I am thinking of a word which tells how a horse moves quickly (gallop)." The last group, describers, will develop use of descriptive words in creative writing and may be used in conjunction with study of adverbs and adjectives; "I am thinking of a word that tells how clothes feel when they come out of the washing machine (damp)" or "I am thinking of a word that tells how fast you get dressed on cold mornings (quickly)."

ANTONYMS, SYNONYMS, AND HOMONYMS

Activities

"Opposites"

The teacher dictates, one at a time, a list of words; the child must give, orally, the opposite. Begin with simple pairs, as black-white, and progress to more difficult pairs, as careless-careful.

"Likes"

Procedure the same as for "opposites," except that the required answer will be a word with a like meaning, as "silly-foolish," "needed-necessary." The child may respond with a word that was not the expected answer, but any reasonable synonym is acceptable.

"Sound Alikes"

Two activities may be used with regard to homonyms: a procedure similar to the one used for antonyms and synonyms may be first used, but the child, in replying, must give the different meanings for the pair of words given by the teacher. For example, the teacher says, "to, too, two" without spelling the words, and the child may respond by saying "one means going somewhere" (to), "one means the number" (two), and "the other one means also" (too). Usually the child's responses will be in terms of use, but this is acceptable, so long as the different meanings are expressed in some way. The second activity may be as follows: The teacher dictates a sentence containing a pair of homonyms; the child must identify orally the set of words, as "*Meet* me at the *meat* store." Most reading series contain a lesson on homonyms, and will list some of the more common ones; but be sure to include a few not commonly used, as "knight-night, bow-bough, taut-taught."

EMOTIONAL WORDS

Activities

"How Do You Feel?"

Teacher asks a question requiring a single word response involving emotion as applied to humans. For example, "How do you feel when it is your birthday?" (happy) or "How do you feel when something does not happen that you wanted very much to happen?" (disappointed). A variation may be the presentation of a story, where the child must supply each emotion word as it might apply. Animal stories are sometimes better for this purpose than human applications, as the human responds in various ways; an animal response is usually consistent. Some of the simple fairy tales may be used, as "The Three Little Pigs"–the feeling of the pigs when the wolf "huffs and puffs" may be elicited, as well as the feelings of the wolf as he is fooled by the third pig. Other stories serve this purpose equally as well, and may be used successfully, at the discretion of the teacher, and with regard to the grade level of the students.

ASSOCIATIONS AND ANALOGIES

Activities

"What Does Not Belong"

The teacher dictates three or four words with some relationships; included in the group of words is a word having no relationship with the others; the child must select the word that does not fit. Gear the selected words to the grade level of the child. Suggested groups might be the following: knife, fork, cow, spoon; car, truck, train, apple; bicycle, motorcycle, wagon, motorbike; apple, orange, banana, beets; pins, bottle, needle, thumbtack; etc.

"How Am I Related"

This activity involves rather highly developed critical thinking and should not be used with children who are not able to succeed in it. The teacher says three words the first two having a direct relationship, the third not related; the child must think of a word to match the third word, and having the same relationship presented in the first pair, as "bird-nest, person-(house), finger-ring, waist-(belt), cow-grass, bird-(worms or insects), etc. If the child experiences difficulty in this activity, discuss how the first two words are related, as "a cow eats grass, a bird eats . . . ; try to elicit the relationship from the child first, but assist him with clues if necessary until he gets the idea of the game.

SEQUENCE

Activities

"Tell Me Again"

The teacher reads a story to the child; simple short stories are best for a beginning; the child relates it back in sequential order. Gear the story to the age level of the child.

"What Happened Next"

This activity may be done with pictures and then with sentences written on individual cards. The set of pictures, as well as the sentence cards, should tell a story in sequence. If sentence cards are used, they may be taken from the child's own reading text. The child must arrange the pictures or sentence cards so that they tell a logical story in sequence.

FACT OR FICTION

Two approaches may be used to establish that some things are true and others are not true (could really happen, or are make-believe); various short stories, geared to the grade level, are read, and the child must decide if it could be true or if it is make-believe; elicit the child's reasons for his decision. The Paul Bunyon stories and many folk tales are excellent examples of fiction while simple biographical sketches or historically based stories are good examples of fact. A follow-up activity might be the child's telling of his own creative story, with his statement following of whether it was true (or could be true) or not true, and why. "Tall tales" can be used as an activity. The child makes up a "tall tale" and tells it; the parts of the story that make it a "tall tale" (or fiction) are explained by the child after he tells it. The technique of exaggeration in story-telling may be introduced, and the point made that some apparently factual presentations become untrue when exaggerated.

FACTUAL DETAILS

The general approach is one that is usually used as a study technique, both in classrooms and in textbooks. It is, of course, an important facet of analytical listening. The method is as follows: a story, or portion of a factual textbook (history, geography, etc.) is read; the teacher then asks the questions about the material presented. Answers require facts elicited from the material presented. If the child is unable to recall the facts asked for, the material may be read the second time, while the child listens particularly for the fact he did not recall. A variation of this activity is to present the list of questions orally prior to the reading of the material; the child is then alerted to listen for specific facts, and should be able to recall them with greater ease.

SELECTIVE LISTENING

A group of sentences are read aloud (usually only three or four sentences in the group); the group of sentences either tell a story or are related in thought. One sentence in the group is either unrelated or does not add a pertinent fact to the story–the child must select the sentence that does not belong. An example might be: "John went to the store. He took his wagon to carry the packages home. *The cookies were in the oven.* John was a good helper."

A related activity, but one that does not involve listening for meaning in itself, is listening amid distractions. Most children will, at some time, have to learn to study in situations that are not totally conducive to learning: television or radio sounds may be in the background, or normal household noises may be in evidence. In the classroom, the child often must be working to be able to concentrate on his own task without being disturbed by the surrounding noises or activities. Some instruction in this skill of selective listening is desirable. Techniques that might be used are as follows: A tape recording or record of general barnyard noise is played; the child must select the various recognizable animal sounds and identify the animals. The child may be asked to listen for a particular child's voice on the playground, amid the usual recess noise. The child could be asked to repeat a sentence the teacher dictates while the rest of the class tap their desks with their pencils. The distracting noises may be increased until the child is unable to hear what is being said. The point is, of course, that every attempt should be made by the child to eliminate unnecessary noise from his study area. It should be added that studying as well as listening is affected by distracting noise. This activity need not be overemphasized, but the point should be made that it is possible to select important sounds from extraneous noise.

INFORMATIVE LISTENING

A story, speaker, television, or radio program may be used for the basis of this activity. After the child has listened to the presentation, he is asked to relate the facts he learned, that is, the new information he gained. Oral reports may be made of group listening situations, or of assigned listening at home (usually television or radio). The introduction of paragraph form, with topic sentence, might be included here, as informative listening (and reading) is usually based on the selection of important facts. Topic sentences usually relate the main idea of the presentations, and should be listened for or observed. Study habit skills may be improved as this ability to listen informatively increases. Carry-over from the area of listening informatively to the field of reading informatively is usually positive.

RESEARCH TECHNIQUES

Although basic research techniques usually taught in the academic curriculums are not specifically adaptable to the area of listening, there is enough carry-over from listening skills to warrant the inclusion of this step in the listening program. The primary objective of teaching research techniques is to develop the child's ability to select and accumulate relative, pertinent information. The specific skill involved is the ability to identify main ideas. Enlarging upon this skill, the child should be able to select the pertinent data, restate it in his own words and make adequate notes that will recall the selected information. It will be immediately seen that some instruction in the use of note cards and outline form will be necessary. Included under the use of note cards should be concise restating of facts, single idea per card, reference given for each fact (bibliography form may be required teaching at this point), arrangement of cards in logical order after all information has been gathered, and establishing some creative and logical continuity in the finished written or oral report. Since this ability to use note cards is basic to activities on the secondary and higher education levels, it should be taught no later than the sixth grade, and preferably before.

Outline form should include the following points of instruction: use of numerical and alphabetical symbols for organizational purposes (when to use Roman, or

Arabic, numbers and parentheses, when to use capital or small letters, and parentheses, and the indented form of an outline); the consistent use of either sentence, phrase, or word form; and the reasons for the indented divisions (topics, sub-topics, etc.). The progression from note cards to outline form is a simple one, for the note cards may be organized into outline form prior to final writing or speaking.

The general approach in teaching research technique is usually applied to factual data (not fiction). The application should first be through the use of short informative presentations, either orally or read (paragraphs first, then chapters). The most difficult technique, requiring the most concentration, is the application of these skills using research texts or complete books. Usually, this last approach is reserved for secondary level research activities, however, the ability to use research books (encyclopedias, etc.) may be introduced in the intermediate grades. Although the child has probably been using encyclopedias of some kind since upper primary levels, the application in the intermediate grades will be more for research purposes than for simple informative reading. The skill of note-taking also begins here. Organized listing of the information develops naturally from the increased need for the child to record data in logical, sequential order.

EVALUATIVE LISTENING

This is a rather highly developed skill. Though it is usually not taught specifically, some techniques should be presented as early as the upper intermediate levels. The child should be encouraged to make his own judgments as to whether the speaker (or writer) has expressed an opinion or fact. The ability to do so involves abstract thinking and is difficult to teach; the more able the child, the easier he learns to do it. If the child can be encouraged to analyze his information in terms of opinion versus fact, he will learn to apply this skill in the area of writing. He should be made aware that facts must be backed-up by references or other facts, and that opinions should be so stated ("I think . . . , I believe. I have been led to believe . . . , it is felt . . . , etc.). The ability to evaluate opinion and fact while listening is a necessary prerequisite to intelligent class discussions and serves as a basis for accurate accumulation of information.

The last aspect of this program is creative expression. No specific approaches are presented, as the avenues are many (fictional creative writing, poetry, factual reporting involving personal viewpoints, class discussions, debates, etc.). Most secondary level English curriculums include a section or unit on creative expression, especially for those children who plan to continue their education beyond high school. The skill of verbal creation need not be limited to the bright child, however, for even the slow learner can express himself creatively with some guidance. The results will not be those expected of the gifted child, but the emotional involvement is often stronger. Any reasonable means of eliciting creative expression appropriate to the child's ability or grade level will satisfactorily fulfill the last aspect of this program.*

*From: Bishop, V. (1971). *Teaching the visually limited child.* Springfield, IL: Charles C Thomas.

Appendix B

TYPING LESSONS

The following adapted lessons may proceed at whatever speed the child is able to learn accurately. It may be necessary to blindfold the child during the instructional periods if he is unable to keep from looking at the keys. The use of a blindfold may be compared, for the child, to an airplane pilot who is flying at night–he relies on his radio (teacher's voice or taped/recorded lessons) and his instruments (fingers) to reach his destination (learning to type), because he is unable to see where he is going. The primary purpose of the instruction is, of course, to teach *touch* typing; no keyboard chart is used, and instructions are given orally. The teacher checks to be sure accuracy is in evidence. Speed is not encouraged, the child is told that speed will come by itself (as it will, when regular practice occurs). If the child has access to a typewriter at home, all the better, for he may have additional practice whenever he chooses. The parent must, however, be asked to supervise the practice, seeing that the child does not use his eyes to find the keys. A blindfold may be suggested for home practice as well.

It will be seen that these lessons have been prepared on the premise that the young student of typing desires immediate results. Thus, the keys are introduced in an order to facilitate almost immediate use in words and sentences. Capitalization and simple punctuation (periods and commas) are introduced early, as is spacing. Rows of keys are not memorized in order, rather position and proper finger of individual letters. "Home position" is taught before "upstairs," "downstairs," and "attic" keys. Immediate results are evident to the child himself, who is quickly able to type color and number words, names of the days and months, and, as early as possible, his own name. As soon as all the letters have been introduced, he is able to type spelling words, and sentences from his own textbooks. Numerals are introduced quite late in the lessons, as are the various symbols, because there is less need to use them in normal and routine classwork assignments.

It is expected that the child will move from lesson to lesson as quickly as he can do so with accuracy, although one lesson per week is usually the most he will be able to accomplish satisfactorily. After approximately fifteen lessons, the child has been introduced to all the letters; the remaining lessons may progress more slowly, and may be introduced only as needed, at the discretion of the teacher.

With reasonable practice, the young child may learn, in one year, to type well enough to do his homework assignments, still relatively slowly, but accurately. Speed will increase in direct proportion to the amount of typing he does and the accuracy with which it is done.

LESSON ONE

See that the child is seated comfortably in front of the typewriter, in a chair of proper size (so that his elbows are slightly below the level of the table; his feet may need to be placed on a box, so that they are not dangling). He should sit comfortably, but with his head erect.

Introduction of the parts of the typewriter should be in terms of usage. The exact names of the parts are not meant to be memorized, but the child should be able to refer to them correctly. Parts are introduced as needed, and the only parts necessary for operating the typewriter are presented in the first lesson. The child should be able to manipulate these parts satisfactorily, and may practice doing so several times prior to the introduction of finger position. He should feel or see what is happening as the working parts are introduced. A suggested presentation may be as follows: "This is where we place the paper. It must be straight for it to roll around correctly. Notice that we put the paper in with the wrong side facing us. That is because when it rolls around, the right side will come out first." (Demonstrate, and allow the child to insert the paper himself until he can do so correctly.) "If we happen to get the paper in crooked, we need not take it out again; we can use the *paper release* to straighten it." (Demonstrate, and allow the child to do it, lining up the top edge of the paper with the *paper bail.*) "Now we must get the carriage over as far as possible to the right. We do this so our paper is ready to type at the left-hand side. We will push the *carriage lever* gently as far as it will go, and let go of it." (Demonstrate, and let the child do it several times himself.) "Did you notice that the *platen*" (point to it) "turned a little all by itself when we pushed the *carriage* over? This is so we do not have to use our hands to roll the paper up a little when we are ready to type a new line. You can do it with your hands, if you need to" (demonstrate that the *platen* may be turned slowly, a line at a time, listening and feeling for the clicks; allow the child to do so) "but when we are busy typing, the typewriter does this for us each time we push the carriage over."

"This long bar at the bottom lets us skip a space between words. We will be using our thumbs to push it. Each time you push the *space bar,* you are skipping a space on the paper." (Demonstrate, spacing for most of a line; allow the child to do it.)

"Did you hear the little bell when we got almost to the end of the paper? that is a signal that we are at the end of the line; when you hear it, you will only have a very little bit of room left on your paper to type." (Demonstrate, if necessary.) "The bell is a warning that we are almost ready to type the next line."

"Now, let's find out where our fingers go. Close your eyes" (or use a blindfold) "and find the second row of *keys* from the bottom. Using your left hand, put your little finger on the first key, fourth finger on the next key, middle finger on the next key, and first finger on the fourth key; your thumb goes on the space bar." (Assist, if necessary.) "Now, using your right hand, put your thumb space bar and, on the same second row of keys, skip the two middle keys; put your first finger on the next key, middle finger on the next key, fourth finger on the next key, and little finger on the next key. Feel that there is one" (commonly only one, but, on some machines, to) "key left over. This is called your *home position.* There will always be two empty keys in the middle of the row. You will learn how to find all the other keys from this position." (Have the child remove his hands and replace them correctly until he is able to do so with a minimum of feeling around.)

(For the blind child, of course, the keys need not be covered or capped. However, the child with some vision may need to have them covered. Commercial caps are available, or the keys may simply be taped with adhesive tape. If the child has little vision, it may be sufficient to remind him to hold his head erect. He will not be able to see the letters, except at very close range. For the child with a good deal of vision, a blindfold may be used, or the keys may be covered. It is vitally important that the child does not attempt to find the keys visually; doing so establishes a bad habit that is difficult to break. *Touch typing* is, after all, the goal of the instruction.)

"The keys are not in A–B–C order, so we will learn where they are a few at a time. Today we will learn what some of the *home keys* are." (Begin from left to right, typing: asdfjkl only–omit the semicolon. The child should say the name of the key as he types it. Encourage individual finger stroke, not whole hand stroking. Fourth and little fingers will probably be weaker than the first and middle fingers.) "Type two lines of these keys, saying their names as you type each one." (Pause as the child does this.) "Now let's space between each letter." (Pause to allow the child to type two lines of the home keys, spacing between each letter.) "Now let's try something different: type two letters together, then space, then another two letters. Listen as I tell you which two letters to type." (Dictate jf kd ls; child should continue to name each letter as it is typed. One line of this is sufficient.)

"Now let's type some words. I shall help you spell them, but remember to spell them yourself again as you type them." (Dictate: as sad dad fad lad all lass fall; remind the child that there should be a space between each word; one or two lines of this exercise is sufficient.)

This is usually enough for the first lesson; practice lesson should ensue, until the letters and words presented in the first lesson are reasonably mastered as to position. It is important that the child repeat each letter as he types it, mentally reinforcing his tactile learning. This oral repetition need not be audible to the teacher as more letters are introduced (the child may say each letter to himself as he types it) but he should be *thinking* of what he is typing until the locating of position becomes almost a reflex action.

The remaining lessons will be written following a general presentation format. Always review the preceding lesson briefly prior to introducing new keys. Be sure, as new keys are introduced, that correct finger and "reach" relationship are established.

After approximately each five lessons, a blindfold "test" is given to be certain that the preceding lessons have been mastered.

Practice may be divided into sittings of time length convenient to both child and teacher. A suggested spacing of each lesson's practice material to cover a week's time (beginning with lesson six) might be as follows:

First Day: Introduction of new keys with practice; one line each of six selected words (three words for each new letter or key) using new keys.

Second Day: One line each of six additional selected words using the new letters or keys (three words from each new key set).

Third Day: Review practice, using six words selected from the group of words using both new letters or keys; one line of each word.

Fourth Day: Three selected sentences, two lines of each sentence.

Fifth Day: Three additional selected sentences; two lines of each sentence.

The imaginative teacher may wish to add or substitute words and original sentences that better suit the grade level or interests of the child, as long as the keys used are those known or under study.

LESSON TWO

Review the parts of the machine and operational procedure; one line each of: sad dad, lad lass; dad falls.

Introduce the letters g and h (g: index finger, left hand, moves one key toward the center of the row; h: index finger, right hand, moves one key toward the center of the row).

Practice new letters; one line each of: g h; h g.

Practice new words–"g" words: gas, gal, sag, lag, jag, glad, glass and "h" words: has, had, hall, hash, sash, dash. Type one line of each word.

Introduce the following first sentences: (one line of each "sentence"): dad has a glass jag a sad lad a gal has a sash (capitalization and punctuation have not been introduced yet).

LESSON THREE

Review the operational procedure and selected words from both preceding lessons (all letters in the "home row" have now been introduced).

Introduce the shift keys; note that the little fingers operate the shift keys in opposition to the hand used to type the letter (that is, right little finger operates the shift key for left hand keys; left little finger operates the shift key for right hand keys). Be sure the child understands: (a) the shift key enables a letter to be capitalized, (b) the shift key must be held down firmly until the letter has been typed, (c) the shift key must be completely released prior to the typing of the next letter, and (d) the remaining fingers must remain in the "home position" during the operation of the shift key, the little finger returning to its own position as soon as the shift key is released. Some practice of this operation is necessary to insure smooth function of capitalization.

Practice one lines each of several words; select single words from preceding lessons, but capitalize the initial letter. Proceed to a sentence, using known words from preceding lessons, capitalizing only the first letter of the first word (do not introduce the period as punctuation yet; single spacing between words–double spacing between sentences.

Sentences–type two lines of each sentence, repeating the sentence for a full line.
Dad has hash A sad lass lags

LESSON FOUR

Review two lines of a selected sentence from Lesson Three, applying capitalization and spacing as taught.

Introduce the semicolon (little finger, right hand, "home position"); establish that all punctuation immediately follows the last letter of a word, and a space *follows* the punctuation (it is not necessary to mention the double spacing after a period at this point in the instruction, as periods have not been introduced).

Practice one line each of selected sentences from any preceding lesson, substituting the semicolon at period position in the sentence. Single spacing between words and after the semicolons.

Suggested sentences: Gas has dash; A sad lad sags

LESSON FIVE

Review two lines, repeating the sentence, as many times as the line permits, of a selected sentence from any preceding lesson.

Introduce the period (fourth finger, right hand, "downstairs row," and slightly to the right). This finger is usually weak, and some amount of practice is necessary to develop accuracy and stroke. Emphasize that no space precedes a period, but double spacing follows a period.

Practice one line of two review sentences, substituting a period for the semicolon. Select sentences from those already used to minimize confusion; the procedure using the period is the object of this lesson.

Suggested sentences: Dad has a glass. Jag a sad lad. Dad has hash. A sad lass lags. Gas has dash. A sad lad sags.

Practice sessions for the week will utilize sentences from the above suggested list; two sentences per sitting are sufficient for practice purposes. Sittings should not be too long at this stage.

BLINDFOLD TEST

The blind child need not be blindfolded, but it is necessary to blindfold children with usable vision, to be sure touch has been established satisfactorily, and that visual clues as to key position are not in evidence.

Dictate five sentences (select three from those already used in preceding lessons, and two new or original ones) to be typed once, and one sentence per line.

Suggested "new" sentences might be: A glad lass has dash. A glass has a jag. All lads had falls. Dad has a fad.

No new letters are introduced at this sitting. If additional practice is needed, as evidenced by excessive errors during the test, any words or sentences from preceding lessons may be used.

Thus far, all of the "home" keys have been introduced (a, s, d, f, j, k, l, ;) as well as g, h, both shift keys for capitalization, and the period. The child should be thoroughly familiar with them, as well as with the general operation and procedure, before proceeding to the next lesson. Allow sufficient practice if needed, before going on.

Beginning with Lesson Six, practice sessions may be divided into sittings, with appropriate material used; refer to suggested lesson formats and sitting procedures, as outlined in Lesson One. Independence may be encouraged during practice sessions, but the instructor should be available to observe consistent errors (and correct them immediately) and to give any supervision needed. A child with vision sufficient to enable him to read large type, may have his lessons typed out in advance, with directions as to procedure (applicable only to practice sittings; teacher must be on hand for new key introduction). The blind, and/or severely visually limited might have the lesson and directions on tape; if this is done, earphones may be used, and sufficient time allowed for following the directions. It may be helpful to state, on the tape, when the recorder is to be shut off momentarily, so that the student may proceed with the instructed work. Some supervision is necessary, initially, if tapes are used, to familiarize the student with the general procedures.

LESSON SIX

Review one line of any sentence, using known letters, symbols, and procedures.

Introduce the letters i and e. Introduce a single letter at a time; at the discretion of the teacher, this lesson may be divided into two lessons, to teach i and e separately, as these vowels are commonly confused in typing. It is important that their position be learned accurately from the beginning i: middle finger, right hand, "upstairs row"; e: middle finger, left hand, "upstairs row," slightly to the left.

Practice the following i words: kid, did, lid, hid, is, his, dish, fish, said, laid, high (one line each of several selected words). Practice the following e words: fed, led, head, lead, dead, leaf, feed, feel, seek, keel, jade, fade, faded, sake (one line each of several selected words). Practice words using both i and e: (one line each of several selected words) lie, die, like, hike, aisle, field, alike, side, hide, like.

LESSON SEVEN

Review one line of any sentence.

Introduce the letters r and t (both are left hand, index finger, "upstairs row" keys; r reaches slightly to the left, t reaches slightly to the right).

Practice the following: (select several words for each letter, and for both together; one line each selected word) *r words:* are, ear, dear, fear, real, read, hear, gears, shark, hard, jar, far, lark, dark; *t words:* at, it, the, this, take, tale, tight, sight, fight, height, late, hate, gate, eight, kite, seat, eat, heat; practice words for *both r and t:* heart, there, their, tries, right, three, tree, dart.

Select two of the following sentences, type one line for each sentence. Tell a tall tale. I hate fights. The jar is tight. The shark is a fish. Sit at the eighth seat. Three trees are high. Take this reader. It is dark at eight.

LESSON EIGHT

Review one line of any selected sentence.

Introduce the letters y and u (both are index finger, right hand, "upstairs row keys; y reaches slightly to the left, u is nearly directly above).

Practice the following *y words:* (one line each of several selected words) they, yes, try, fly, fry, sky, say, day, lay, hay, yet, year, yell, tightly, eighty, really, ready, darkly, hardly; practice the following *u words:* rug, hug, jug, tug, dug, use, us, dust, just, rust, trust, thrust; words using *both y and u:* dusty, rusty, gusty, fussy, ruddy, huffy, stuffy.

Practice the following sentences: The sky is just dark. use just the right jug. They are trusty girls. I heard her yell. Dust the red rug lightly. They hay is hardly ready yet. The girls said they had eight tries. Trust us as dusters.

If original words or sentences, using the new keys, are more applicable, they may be substituted for this and any lesson following, as long as practice is achieved for the particular letters under current study.

BLINDFOLD REVIEW TEST

Dictate the following words, to be typed in one or two lines, single time each, single spacing between words. If the child cannot spell the words independently, the teacher may assist with spelling.

Tuesday Thursday Friday Saturday July August three eight red

Dictate two of the following sentences, to be typed once each, on separate lines.

Add it just right.
They said she says yes.
The red rug is the rug I like.
I hate fried fish; I like stuffed fish.
Gals like teas; lads like hikes.

No new letters are introduced at this sitting. Review practice may be needed; words and/or sentences may be given at the discretion of the teacher. It is important that the keys introduced thus far are very familiar, as the remaining letters will be added at a fairly rapid pace. Therefore, a pause for extended practice at this point may be helpful. The letters that have been introduced are the semicolon and period. Capitalization and spacing have also been introduced.

LESSON NINE

Review one line each of several selected words from the preceding four lessons.

Introduce the letters m and n (m: right hand, index finger, "downstairs row," slightly to the right; n: right hand, index finger, "downstairs row," slightly to the left).

Practice the following *m words:* (one line each of several selected words) made, make, May, him, jam, them, game, same; *n words:* neat, then, ten, ran, run, sun, nine, and, line, fine, Sunday, January, June; words using both m and n: mine, mean, name, meant.

Practice the following sentences (one line for each, several sentences):

Sister makes fine jam and jelly.
Father runs ten miles.
Games are fun; I like them.
They are singing in the rain.
The man made a fine jug.

LESSON TEN

Review one line each of several of the following words: January, May, June, July, August, Sunday, Tuesday, Thursday, Friday, Saturday, three, eight, nine, ten.

Introduce the letters v and b (v: left hand, index finger, "downstairs row," slightly to the right; b: left hand, index finger, "downstairs row," reach to the right).

Practice the following *v words:* very, live, give, five, eleven, seven, ever, every, never; *b words:* be, bean, bring, beat, February, bread, build, library; *v and b words:* brave, beaver, vibrate.

Practice the following sentences:

A brave beaver built a big dam.
I like liver and gravy.
Never bring jam in the library.
Save seven blue beans and eleven red beans.
Every light is very bright.

LESSON ELEVEN

Review the names of the known days, months, and numbers (Sunday, Tuesday, Thursday, Friday, Saturday, January, February, May, June, July, August, three, five, seven, eight, nine, ten, eleven (may be dictated by teacher and typed once; months on one line, days on the next line, numbers on the third line).

Introduce the letter c and the comma (c: left hand, middle finger, "downstairs row" slightly to the right; comma: right hand, middle finger, "downstairs row," slightly to the right).

Practice the following words: c–care, ice, came, each, reach, teach, beach, cherry, March, black; use of comma–choose two or three of the above words using c and type them in series; comma is placed immediately after each word, with a single space following the comma.

Practice the following sentences:

I like ice cream.
I saw Nancy, Dick, and Jack.
Use care in reading this sentence.
Each reach can teach us.
Cherries are red, green, and black.

LESSON TWELVE

Review the following: selected days, months, colors, and numbers; type each set in a series using commas to separate and type each set on a new line (suggested words known: January, February, March, May, June, July, August, December; Sunday, Tuesday, Thursday, Friday, Saturday; red, blue, green, black, gray; three, five, seven, eight, nine, ten, eleven).

Introduce the letters or and w (o: right hand, fourth finger, "upstairs row," almost directly above "l"); w: left hand, fourth finger, "upstairs now," almost directly above "s").

Practice the following *o words:* no, so, go, to, one, book, love, above, goat, boat, our, your; *w words:* we, why will, win, were, where, when, saw, few, knew; words using *both o and w:* who, two, how, now, know, slow, blow, brown, down, town, awoke, shower.

Practice the following sentences:

Carol ate a chocolate ice cream cone.
Write your letters carefully.
The wind is blowing harder.
They can read a few new books.
Yellow, orange, and brown are new colors.

LESSON THIRTEEN

Review all the days of the week; all months except April and September; all numbers to eleven except six; colors: red, yellow, blue, orange, black, green, brown, white, and gray.

Introduce the letters p and q (p: little finger, right hand, "upstairs row," above semicolon; q: little finger, left hand, "upstairs row," and above "a").

Practice the following *p words:* play, pretty, top, lip, puppy, pupil, type; *q words:* quick, quiet, quickly, quietly, antique, require, quotient.

Practice the following sentences:

Type the keys quickly.
We will play with the quiet puppy.
Teachers require quiet pupils.
Division problems have quotients.
Paul, Patty, and Peter are quiet pupils.

LESSON FOURTEEN

Review the days, months, numbers to eleven, except six, and colors (add purple and pink).

Introduce the letter x (fourth finger, left hand, "downstairs row," slightly to the right). This is sometimes a difficult "reach relationship" to establish; it may require some practice, and has been introduced singly for this reason.

Practice the following words: six, fox, foxes, box, boxes, axe, axes, ox, oxen, extra, example, except, tax, taxes, xylophone.

Practice the following sentences:

People pay taxes.
Quick foxes leap over boxes.
Woodsmen need axes to chop down trees.
Type this example quickly.
Six oxen jump quickly.

LESSON FIFTEEN

Review all of the days, all months, numbers to and including twenty; and colors as named.

Introduce the letter z (little finger, left hand, "downstairs row," slightly to the right). Again, this is a difficult "reach"; allow practice; introduce as separate lesson.

Practice the following words: dozen, size, zoo, haze, daze, zip, zipper, razor, buzz.

Practice the following sentences:

Zip up your zipper.
Bees buzz busily.
The pants were size six.
Zebras live in a zoo.
A dozen razors buzz loudly.

BLINDFOLD REVIEW TEST

Follow whatever procedure has been established for preceding test situations.

All letters have been introduced now, as well as the period, comma, semicolon, shift keys, space bar, and general operating procedures. This test will consist of three parts; the typing of the child's own name, the typing (from dictation, with assistance in spelling, if needed) of words, and the typing of several sentences.

Child's name: Repeat for a full line, single space between first and last name, double space after last name and before beginning first name again.

Dictated words: First line: Arithmetic, Reading, Spelling (repeat after double space). Second line: Writing, Science, Social Studies (repeat as above).

Select three of the following sentences; type each once per line.

Divisor, dividend, and quotient are division terms.
We may carry in addition; we may borrow in subtraction.
When we multiply, we are using a short way of adding.
Sixteen is a large size for clothing.
The quick brown fox jumps over the lazy dog. (This sentence contains all the letters of the alphabet, and may be used as a warm-up sentence for all future letters.)

After Lesson Fifteen, the lessons may take one of two directions: if learning to type is for purely communication purposes (i.e., the typewriter will be used for written communication, submitting assignments, etc.), the instruction can proceed, using the lessons in this program. Minor adjustments may have to be made, to allow for differences in typewriter design, but the basic premises are still useful in introducing the use of numbers, symbols, and machine function.

If, however, the need is for keyboarding skills, a different plan may need to be developed. The basic QWERTY keyboard has been introduced (i.e., the student should be able to locate all the letters by touch), but the various computer keyboard functions will differ. Numbers and symbols may be in similar locations as regular typewriter keyboards, but a number of new function keys will have to be learned. the instructor should consider the age of the student and his/her typing needs when deciding how much new information to present. If saving or retrieving files is required, those functions will obviously have to be taught (as well as "booting up" the computer and shutting it down). If formatting, selecting a font style or size, printing out materials, or accessing a particular program are required, then instruction in those functions will be required. The American Printing House for the Blind offers an instructional program specifically aimed at developing keyboarding skills: "Talking Typer" for Windows. this program includes instructional software, drills/practice exercises, and typing games, and can be used with children as young as six years of age.

The instructor must make a decision here about whether to continue with typing instruction or to move in the direction or computer orientation for keyboarding. If continuing typing instruction is indicated, go on to Lesson Sixteen; if emphasizing computer keyboarding, go to alternative instructions, either commercially available or instructor designed.

LESSON SIXTEEN

The *warm-up* usually consists of one of three lines, depending on the need of the child. Days, months, numbers, colors, child's name, or a sentence may be used, or a combination of any of these.

Introduce, discuss, and practice the setting of margins, form of and centering of titles and/or headings.

Since margin controls vary from machine to machine, the presentation of this technique is not explained in detail. The teacher should adapt her instruction to the machine being used, and should add that the child may have to locate margin controls himself on other machines. The child should be taught how to set the margin controls to allow adequate, but not excessive, marginal space (horizontally). some explanation should also be included with regard to the following: (a) top and bottom space allowances on the paper (a blind child may have to check periodically to be sure he still has sufficient space to continue typing; if no paper can be felt at the back of the roller, it is safe to assume that he has reached the limit of the paper); (b) controls for single, double, and triple spacing between lines (double spacing between lines is desirable for the visually limited child who plans to read his own work, as it is less crowded–large-type typewriters usually are readable with single line spacing, but it depends on the individual machine); and (c) paragraph indentation of five spaces–establish this procedure as a habit for all assignments involving paragraphs.

At this point, the child may be taught to center a title and to arrange a heading. In centering a title, the procedure may be presented as follows: locate the approximate center of the paper (horizontally, when in place in the machine); count the number of letters *and* spaces to be used in the title or heading; divide this number in half (extra letter may be added at the end); introduce the location of the "back space" key; back space half the total number of spaces and letters in the title or heading; type the required title or heading. Capitalize only major words of the title, not articles.

Headings are introduced similarly. If to be located at extreme left of paper, begin at the beginning of the line; if to be located at the extreme right of the paper, back space the total number of letters and spaces required in the longest line of the heading, centered, following the procedure for titles, but be sure to center every line, using the same center for each line.

Practice material may be selected from any of the child's texts or assignments.

Since all letters have now been introduced, procedures for this lesson and following lessons will vary, depending on the new material introduced. When new keys are presented, lesson format may be similar to that previously used; if new procedures are introduced, practice material may be as suggested, or selected from (or adapted to) the child's needs and/or assignments. The ensuing lessons may be presented as the need arises, at the discretion of the teacher, or as fast as can be assimilated by the child. Typing skill, at this point, however, should be adequate enough to encourage application; homework assignments, reports, spelling practice, etc. may serve the dual purpose of typing practice and academic application. Ensuing lessons need not proceed in the order indicated; deviation may be desirably presented prior to numbers, if columnar spelling drill is more applicable than the use of numbers in daily use). The teacher may feel free to adapt the remaining lessons to suit the needs of the pupil and the requirements of his typing skill. The general procedure is presented as a planned program, if no specific or individualized needs are pressing and urgent.

LESSON SEVENTEEN

Begin the lesson with a warm-up drill.

Introduce the colon, question mark, and virgule or slash line. These symbols may vary in location on different machines, but usually the colon is on the same key as the semicolon, using the shift key. Although the position of the question mark and slash mark vary, they are usually typed with the little finger, right hand. Particular finger position should be taught with regard to the machine being used.

Practice sentences should apply the symbols, and should teach their various uses. The use of the colon may tie-in with English grammar presentations; the question mark is consistent in it application; the slash mark may be postponed until numbers have been introduced, and its use in fractions presented, or, if presented now, the use of this symbol may also be tied in with grammar (and/or, etc.).

LESSON EIGHTEEN

Begin the lesson with a warm-up drill.

Introduce numbers. Point out that number one is typed as a small l, the remaining numbers proceed in order from two to nine, with zero following nine, on the "attic" row. Fourth finger, left hand types 2, middle finger left hand types 3, index finger left hand types 4 and 5, index finger right hand types 6 and 7, middle finger right hand types 8, fourth finger right hand types 9, little finger right hand types 0. Position location clues–3 and 8 are both middle finger keys; the index fingers both have two keys apiece; the remaining fingers are in order.

Practice typing dictated sets of numbers, dates, street addresses, and page numbers.

LESSON NINETEEN

Begin the lesson with a warm-up drill.

Introduce the symbols above the numbers; they are obtained by using shift keys. Encourage the association of the symbol with the corresponding number, especially the most commonly used ones (8 and ‘, 2 and “, 4 and $, 5 and %, 6 and –, 7 and &, 9 and (, 0 and), or as indicated on the individual machine; some machines may vary as to symbol location, but most machines follow the above arrangement).

Practice using material or sentences that apply the use of each symbol.

This lesson may be divided into left-hand symbols and right-hand symbols, or the symbols may be presented individually, if it seems advisable for the student. All symbols need not be presented at one sitting, or may even be presented only as needed in daily use. The teacher's discretion will be needed to decide which procedure is best for the individual student.

LESSON TWENTY

Begin the lesson with a warm-up drill.

Introduce any or all of the miscellaneous symbols found on the individual machine; this may include the asterisk, dash, plus sign, equal sign, fraction key (usually includes one-half and one-fourth), cent sign, @ symbol, and any others. Again, the introduction of these symbols may be geared to the needs of the individual, and may be presented all at once, or a few at a time. Progress of the pupil in developing usable skill, and his retentive powers with regard to “reach” positions, may be considered in deciding how many symbols to introduce at a time. Practice material will, of course, be in terms of the symbol or symbols presented, in applied situations.

LESSON TWENTY-ONE

Teach the setting of tabulator keys or controls, as applied in columnar arrangements for spelling or arithmetic. Outline form on the typewriter may be included in this lesson, as the tabulator controls may be utilized for outline form purposes as well.

LESSON TWENTY-TWO

Presentation or discussion of letter form, address form, catalogue ordering formats, etc.

LESSON TWENTY-THREE

Creative Writing

Assign a topic, on which the student may type an original composition. The final copy should be brief, but should demonstrate the application of "thinking while typing." The child should note that creative writing may be as easily done with a typewriter as with a pencil, should be thought out and arranged mentally prior to typing, and may be proofread more easily (both by himself, if sighted, and others who may be assisting in correcting or editing). Typing skills should, by this time, be such that individual letters are not being thought, but entire words. The fingers should be responding to thoughts in words and phrases, rather than in fragments of words or individual letters. Typing is now, or should be, an applied skill, to be used as much as possible to substitute for pencil writing whenever and wherever possible.

FINAL BLINDFOLD REVIEW TEST

Dictate the following, to be typed as accurately (both with regard to letters, form, and spacing) as possible.

1. A brief paragraph, dictated by the teacher, using relatively simple vocabulary (not to exceed ten lines, if possible). Material may be selected from a text, pleasure reading, or any reasonably simple source.
2. A short letter, either a friendly one or of the business type; it should include all parts of the basic letter form.
3. A brief outline, on a simple subject, preferably single-word headings; it should not exceed three main headings, if possible, with several subheadings under each main heading.
4. A short word list, approximately ten words, to be listed in two columns.
5. A brief creative paragraph on an assigned topic of interest.

This test, although fairly involved, may be administered in one sitting, or may be broken-down into five different sittings. If difficulty is experienced in any phase of the test, additional practice may be needed in that area.

In scoring errors on any test or assignment, consideration must be given for the age and ability of the child. The younger child may be slower to develop accuracy than the older one, just as the more intellectually gifted child may retain is knowledge longer. In general, however, five errors per assignment may be considered satisfactory achievement, as long as the errors are not consistently the same errors. Perfect performance should, of course, be greatly encouraged, but some mistakes are nearly unavoidable. Allow for a few, and score accordingly.

Appendix C

HANDWRITING GUIDE USING THE BRAILLE CELL FORMAT

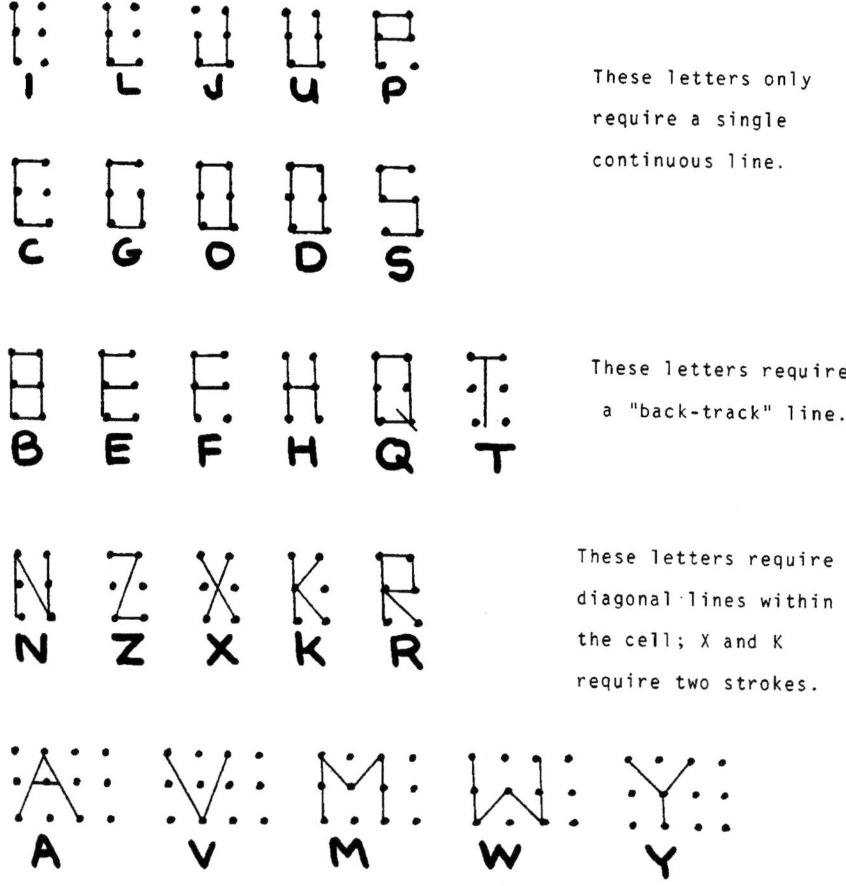

These letters all require part of a second cell to connect the diagonal lines properly.

Appendix D

MARKERS FOR AN EXEMPLARY GIFTED PROGRAM

An exemplary program for gifted students:

- Provides opportunities for the students to
  . . . think creatively; solve problems creatively;
  . . . think critically; acquire skills for analyzing and evaluating;
  . . . acquire knowledge at all levels of Bloom's Taxonomy (recall, comprehension, analysis, synthesis, application, evaluation);
  . . . develop research skills;
  . . . do independent study; and
  . . . develop leadership skills.

- Encourages each gifted student to develop his/her individual talents;

- Provides time *daily* for gifted students to interact with age peers *as well as* with gifted peers;

- Ensures that professionals (teachers, administrators, counselors) have received special training in how to work with gifted students, and understand their special characteristics, strengths, and needs;

- Involves parents in the program through seminars, inservices, or training sessions that help parents understand, nurture, and live with their gifted children; and

- Locates (and makes available) mentors in fields of individual students' areas of interest; makes every effort to provide real-world experience in those areas of interest for those gifted students who choose to explore vocational options or career opportunities.

Appendix E

ASSESSMENT INSTRUMENTS

Infants and Preschool Children

Basic School Skills Inventory. Hammill, D. & Leigh, J. (1983).	Pro-Ed
Battelle Developmental Inventory. Newborg, J., Stock, J., Wnek, L., Guidubaldi, J., & Svinicki, J. (1984). (For blind children, use with caution.)	DLM Teaching Resources
Bayley Scales of Infant Development: Infant Behavior Record. Bayley, N. (1969). (For blind children, use with caution.)	The Psychological Corporation
Boehm Test of Basic Concepts–Preschool Version. Boehm, A. (1986). (Only for children with sufficient vision.)	The Psychological Corporation
Brigance Diagnostic Inventory of Early Development, Brigance, A. (1978). (Use cautiously.)	Curriculum Associates
Checklist for Home Observation of Visually Impaired and Blind Infants and Preschoolers. (page 5)	In *Psychoeducational Assessment of Visually Impaired and Blind Students.* Sharon Bradley Johnson. (Pro-Ed, 1986).
Developmental Activities Screening Inventory II (DASI-II). Fewell, R. & Langley, M. (1984).	Pro-Ed
The Early Learning Accomplishment Profile for Developmentally Young Children (E-LAP). Glover, M., Preminger, J., & Sanford, A.	Kaplan Press
Growing Up: A Developmental Curriculum. Croft, N. & Robinson, L. (1984).	Parent Consultants

Hawaii Early Learning Profile (HELP). Feruno, S., O'Reilly, K., Inatsuka, T., Hosaka, C., Allman, T. & Zeisloft-Falbey, B. — VORT Corporation

Informal Assessment of Developmental Skills for Younger and Multihandicapped Children. Swallow, R., Mangold, S., & Mangold, P. (1978). (In Swallow, R., Mangold, S., & Mangold, P. (Eds.), *Informal Assessment of Developmental Skills for Visually Handicapped Students.*) — American Foundation for the Blind

Ordinal Scales of Psychological Development. Uzgiris, I. & Hunt, J. (1975). (Use caution with blind children.) — University of Illinois Press

Oregon Project for Visually Impaired and Blind Preschoolers (OR Project). Brown, D., Simmons, V., & Methvin, J. (1979). — Jackson County Educational Service District

Peabody Picture Vocabulary Test–Revised (PPVT-R). Dunn, L. & Dunn, L. (1981). (Only for children with sufficient vision.) — American Guidance Service, Inc.

Test of Language Development–2: Primary. Newcomer, P. & Hammill, D. (1977, 1982). — Pro-Ed

Wechsler Preschool and Primary Scale of Intelligence (WPPSI). Wechsler, D. (1964, 1967). (Use with caution.) — The Psychological Corporation

Children with Multiple Disabilities

Most of the infant and preschool instruments can also be used with severely delayed multiply disabled children who also have visual impairments. In addition, the following may be useful.

Behavior Rating Instrument for Autistic and Other Atypical Children (BRIAAC). Ruttenberg, B., Kalish, B., Wenar, C., & Wolf, E. — Stoelting Company

The *Behavioral State Analysis* approach (1988), developed by Doug Guess, Sally Roberts, et al.; Dept. of Special Education, 3103 East Haworth Hall, University of Kansas, Lawrence, KS 66045. (Described in the *Journal of Severely Handicapped* (1988), Vol. 13, No. 3, 163–174.)

Callier-Azusa Scale. Stillman, R. (Ed.). (1975). Forms G & H. (Especially useful with deaf-blind children.) — Callier Center for Communication Disorders

Selected checklists or scales from *Informal Assessment of Developmental Skills for Visually Handicapped Students.* Swallow, R., Mangold, S., & Mangold, P. (Eds). (1978). New York: American Foundation for the Blind.

Assessment of Spatial Reasoning and Fine Motor Skills. Swallow, R.

Body Image Screening Test for Blind Children. Cratty, B. & Sams, T.

A Checklist for Informal Evaluation of Prevocational Skills. Isaac, R.

Development of Piagetian Schemas During the Sensorimotor Period: Applications to Children's Toys for the Severely Handicapped. Poulsen, M. & Swallow, R. (1976).

Gross Motor Assessment. Swallow, R. (1978).

Orientation and Mobility Concept Assessment. Hutchinson, M.

Piagetian Right-Left Awareness Test. Laurendeau, M. & Pinard, A. (1970).

Pupil Behavior Rating Scale. High, C. (1978).

Vocational Skills Checklist (elementary levels). Teachers of the Visually Handicapped, San Mateo School District. (1978).

School-Aged Children

General:

Assessment Kit. Sewell, D. (1997). Volume 1: Informal Tools for Teacher Use Volume 2: Large Print Reading Assessments Volume 3: Braille Reading Assessments Volume 4: *Basic Reading Inventory.* Johns, J.	Texas School for the Blind and Visually Impaired

Cognitive:

Blind Learning Aptitude Test. Newland, T. (1971).	University of Illinois Press
Detroit Tests of Learning Aptitude, Revised (DTLA-2). Hammill, D. (1985). (Some subtests.)	Pro-Ed
Wechsler Adult Intelligence Scale, Revised (WAIS-R). Wechsler, D. (1981).	The Psychological Corporation
Wechsler Intelligence Scale for Children, Revised. (WISC-R). Wechsler, D. (1974).	The Psychological Corporation
Slosson Intelligence Test (SIT). Slosson, R. (1981, 1985). (Revised by Nicholson, C.)	Pro-Ed

Achievement:

Brigance Diagnostic Inventory of Basic Skills. Brigance, A. (1978).	Curriculum Associates, Inc. (In braille: APH)
Brigance Disagnostic Inventory of Essential Skills. Brigance, A. (1981).	Curriculum Associates, Inc.

Dolch Word Cards. Dolch, E. (1955). (In braille or large type.)	American Printing House for the Blind (APH)
Key Math Revised: A Diagnostic Inventory of Essential Math. Connolly, A. (1988).	American Guidance Service, Inc. (In braille from APH.)
Stanford Achievement Test and Tests of Academic Skills (An upward extension of the *Stanford Achievement Test.* Madden, R., Gardner, E., Rudman, H., Karlsen, B., & Merwin, J. (1973).	American Printing House for the Blind
Wide Range Achievement Test, Revised (WRAT-R). Jastak, S. & Wilkinson, G. (1984).	Pro-Ed (In braille/large type: APH)

Language Development:

Receptive and Expressive Language Assessment for the Visually Impaired (RELA).	Ingham Intermediate School District
Test of Adolescent Language (TOAL). Hammill, D., Brown, V., Larsen, S., & Wiederholt, J. (1980).	Pro-Ed
Test of Language Development–2 (Intermediate). (TOLD-2). Hammill, D. & Newcomer, P. (1982).	Pro-Ed

Concept Development:

Boehm Test of Basic Concepts, Revised (BTBC-R). Boehm, A. (1986). (For students with useful vision.)	The Psychological Corporation
Hill Performance Test of Selected Positional Concepts. Hill, E.	Stoelting Company
Tactile Test of Basic Concepts (TTBC). Caton, H. (1976).	American Printing House for the Blind

Perception:

Motor-free Visual Perception Test (MVPT). Colarusso, R. & Hammill, D. (1972).	Stoelting Company
Roughness Discrimination Test. Nolan, D. & Morris, M. (1965).	American Printing House for the Blind

Personality and Social/Personal:

Index of Personality Characteristics. Brown, L. & Coleman, M. (1988).	Pro-Ed

Myers-Briggs Type Indicator (MBTI). Myers, I. (1985).	Consulting Psychologists Press
Self-Esteem Index (SEI). Brown, L. & Alexander, J. (1990).	Pro-Ed
Walker-McConnell Scale of Social Competence and School Adjustment. Walker, H. & McConnell, S. (1988).	Pro-Ed

Behavior:

Behavior Rating Profile (BRP). Brown, L. & Hammill, D. (1983).	Pro-Ed
Burks Behavior Rating Scale. Burks, H. (1977).	Western Psychological Services
Pupil Behavior Rating Scale. High, C. (1978).	In *Informal Assessment of Developmental Skills for Visually Handicapped Students.* Swallow, R., Mangold, S., & Mangold, P. (Eds.). (1978).
Vineland Adaptive Behavior Scales: Expanded Form and *Classroom Edition.* Sparrow, S., Balla, D., & Cicchetti, D. (1984).	American Guidance Services, Inc.

Special Skills:

Braille Unit Recognition Battery: Diagnostic Test of Grade 2 Literary Braille. Caton, H., Duckworth, B., & Rankin, E. (1985).	American Printing House for
Braille Requisite Skills Inventory. Labossiere, S. & Rhodes, K. (1991).	Region 4 Education Service Center

Selected tests from: *Informal Assessment of Developmental Skills for Visually Handicapped Students.* Swallow, R., Mangold, S., & Mangold, P. (Eds.). (1978). American Foundation for the Blind.

Academic:

Braille Reading Readiness Skills. Mangold, S.

Diagnostic Assessment of Braille Reading Skills. Swallow, R.

Braille Writing. Swallow, R.

Assessment of Slate Skills. Mangold, P.

Assessment of Script Writing for the Blind. Swallow, R. & Mangold, S.

Assessment of Script Writing for Low Vision Students. Swallow, R.

Assessing Typing Skills of Visually Handicapped Students. Mangold, S. & Mangold, P.

Informal Assessment of Listening Skills. (Adapted from Jack Little.)

Model Assessment Items from Listening to Learn Program.

Optacon Reading, Stage 1 and *Optacon Reading, State 2.* (Developed by TSI.)

Orientation and Mobility:

Body-Image Screening Test for Blind Children. Cratty, B. & Sams, T.

Gross Motor Assessment. Swallow, R.

Assessment of Spatial Reasoning and Fine-Motor Skills. Swallow, R.

Orientation and Mobility Concept Assessment. Hutchinson, M.

Prevocational/Vocational:

A Checklist for Informal Evaluation of Prevocational Skills. Isaac, R. *Vocational Skills Checklist, Elementary and Secondary Levels.* Teachers of the Visually Handicapped, San Mataeo School District. (1978).	In *Informal Assessment of Developmental Skills for Visually Handicapped Students.* Swallow, R., Mangold, S., & Mangold, P. (Eds.). (1978).
Kuder Preference Record. Kuder, G. (1956). (Braille answer sheets from	Science Research Associates How Press)
Minnesota Rate of Manipulation Test. Betts, G. & Ziegler, W. (1967).	American Guidance Services
Pennsylvania Bi-Manual Work Sample. Roberts, J. (1969).	American Guidance Services
McCarron-Dial Work Evaluation System.	McCarron-Dial Systems

Functional Vision Evaluation

Functional Vision Inventory for Severely Handicapped Children. Langley, B. & Dubose, R.	Stoelting Company
Diagnostic Assessment Procedure (DAP). Barraga, N.	American Printing House for the Blind
Visual Efficiency Scale (VES). Barraga, N.	American Printing House for the Blind
Low Vision Manual. Levack, N.	TSBVI
Vision Screening Instruments (charts, cards, etc.)	Lighthouse, Inc. Bernell Corporation

Learning Media Assessment

Learning Media Assessment. Koenig, A. & Holbrook, C.	TSBVI
Basic Reading Inventory. (Pre-primer through Grade 8). Johns, J.	Kendall/Hunt Publishing Company

Family Assessment Instruments

Family Resource Scale. (1986). Dunst, C. & Leet, H. (Contact the Family, Infant and Preschool Program, Western Carolina Center, 300 Enola Road, Morganton, North Carolina 28655; also described in *Child: Care, Health and Development, 13,* 111–125).

Parent Needs Inventory. (Contact Parent Consultants.)

Family Needs Survey. (1990). Bailey, D. & Simeonsson, R. (Contact Frank Porter Graham child Development Center, Chapel Hill, NC.)

Family Needs Scale. (1988). Dunst, C., Cooper C., Weeldreyer, J., Snyder, K., & Chase, J. In Dunst, C., Trivette, C., & Deal, A. (Eds.), *Enabling and Empowering Families.* Cambridge, MA: Brookline Books.

For information on ecomapping. McWilliam, R. (2001). *Understanding the family ecology.* Project INTEGRATE. Frank Porter Graham Child Development Center, University of North Carolina at Chapel Hill.

School Assessment Instruments

Classroom Interaction Analysis. (1975). Bradfield, R. & Criner, J., In *Classroom interaction analysis.* San Raphael, CA: Academic Therapy.

Classroom Variables Analysis Form. (1982). Salend, S. & Viglianti, D. In Preparing secondary students for the mainstream. *Teaching Exceptional Children, 14,* (4), 137–140.

Social Climate Scales. Moos, R.

(1975). Assessment and impact of social climate. In McReynolds, P. (Ed.). *Advances in psychological assessment,* Vol. 3, 8–41. San Francisco: Jossey-Bass.

(1979). *Evaluating educational environments.* San Francisco: Jossey-Bass.

Teachers Interview/Classroom Observation Checklist for Visually Impaired and Blind Students. (1986). In Bradley-Johnson, S., *Psychoeducational assessment of visually impaired and blind students,* pp.9–10. Austin, TX: Pro-Ed.

Note: For addresses of sources, see Appendix F.

Appendix F

RESOURCES

Abacus Instruction: *Abacus Basic Competency*
Susan Millaway
EYE-DEAL Materials for the Visually Handicapped
2937 Clyston Road
Norristown, PA 19403

To buy an abacus: American Printing House for the Blind
1839 Frankfort Avenue
P.O. Box 6085
Louisville, KY 40206-0085
(502) 895-2405 1-800-223-1839

Braille Instruction: *Dot Codes* by Janet Wise and
Braille Codes & Calculations by Mary Ellen Pesavento
Exceptional Teaching Aids
20102 Woodbine Avenue
Castro Valley, CA 94546
(510) 582-4859 1-800-549-6999

(The above texts include literary braille, Nemeth Code, fingermath, and an introduction to music braille.)

New Programmed Instruction in Braille (2nd Ed.)
Ashcroft, S., Henderson, F., Sanford, L., & Koenig, A.
SCALARS Publishers–Dept. 5
P.O. Box 158123
Nashville, TN 37215
(615) 371-0205

The Computer Braille Code Made Easy by
Judy Dixon and Chris Gray
and
Just Enough to Know Better by Eileen Curran

National Braille Press
88 St. Stephen Street
Boston, MA 02115
(617) 266-6160

How to Read Braille by Bettye Krolick
Stipes Publishing Company
10–12 Chester Street
Champaign, IL 61820

Primer of Braille by Edward Jenkins
American Printing House for the Blind
1839 Frankfort Avenue
P.O. Box 6085
Louisville, KY 40206-0085
(502) 895-2405 1-800-223-1839
FAX 502-899-2274

Large Type and
Braille Music: Call 1-800-424-8567; ask for the Music Librarian
Music Section of the Library of Congress
Washington, DC 20542

Braille Music: National Braille Association
1290 University Avenue
Rochester, NY 14607
(716) 473-0900

Correspondence Courses: Hadley School for the Blind
700 Elm Street
Winnetka, IL 60093-0299
1-800-323-4238

(Courses for legally blind individuals; some courses for sighted parents of a blind or visually impaired child; a few courses for professionals and paraprofessionals.)

Early Childhood Publications: Blind Children's Center
4120 Marathon Street
P.O. Box 29159
Los Angeles, CA 90029-0159
(217) 664-2153 FAX 213-665-3828

Human Sexuality Models: Jim Jackson and Company
33 Richdale Avenue
Cambridge, MA 02140
(617) 864-9063

Adam & Eve Discovery Dolls
c/o Monique Felder
167–44 145 Avenue
Springfield Gardens, NY 11434
(718) 712-2057

Low Vision Devices:

C & E Optical, Inc.
10926 South Western Avenue
Chicago, IL 60643
(312) 881-8958 1-800-542-1071
FAX 312-881-4843

Designs for Vision, Inc.
760 Koehler Avenue
RanKonKoma, NY 11779
1-800-345-4009

Duffens Optical
3625 Willowbend Blvd.–Suie 110
Houston, TX 77054
(713) 663-3020 1-800-392-9774

Lighthouse, Inc.
Optical Aids Service
36–02 Northern Boulevard
Long Island City, NY 11101
1-800-453-4923 FAX 718-786-0437

LS & S Group
P.O. Box 673
Northbrook, IL 60065
(708) 498-9777 1-800-468-4789 (ordering)
FAX 708-498-1482

Parent Organizations:

National Association for Parents of the Visually Impaired, Inc. (NAPVI)
P.O. Box 317
Watertown, MA 02272-0317
1-800-562-6265 FAX 617-972-7444

American Council of Blind Parents
c/o American Council of the Blind
1153 15th St., NW
Washington, DC 20005
(202) 467-5081 1-800-424-8666

Professional Organizations:	Division of Visually Impaired (DVI) Council for Exceptional Children (CEC) 1110 North Glebe Road–Suite 300 Arlington, VA 22201 FAX 703-264-9494 (888) 232-7733 www.cec.sped.org
	Association for Education and Rehabilitation (AER) 1703 North Beauregard Street, Suite 440 Alexandria, VA 22311 (703) 671-4500 FAX 703-671-6391 www.aerbvi.org
Professional Publications:	American Foundation for the Blind 11 Penn Plaza–Suie 300 New York, NY 10001 (212) 502-7660 1-800-232-5463 FAX 212-502-7777
	American Printing House for the Blind 1839 Frankfort Avenue P.O. Box 6085 Louisville, KY 40206-0085 (502) 895-2405 1-800-223-1839 FAX 502-899-2274
	Texas School for the Blind and Visually Impaired (TSBVI) Business Office 1100 West 45th Street Austin, TX 78756-3494 (512) 454-8631 www.tsbvi.edu
Recorded Books:	Recording for the Blind 20 Roszel Road Princeton, NJ 08540 (609) 452-0606
	National Library Services for the Blind and Physically Handicapped Library of Congress 1291 Taylor Street N.W. Washington, DC 20542 (202) 287-5100 1-800-424-9100

(Call to locate your state's branch of this program.)

Science Materials:

Science Activities for the Visually Impaired (SAVI) and
Science Enrichment for Learners with Physical Handicaps (SELPH)
Center for Multisensory Learning
Hall of Science
University of California
Berkeley, CA 94720
(415) 642-8941

Science Products
Box 888
Southeastern, PA 19399
(610) 296-2111 1-800-888-7400

Social Studies Materials:

Materials Adaptations for Visually Impaired Students in Social Studies (MAVIS)
Social Science Education Consortium, Inc.
855 Broadway
Boulder, CO 80302
(303) 492-8154

Tangible Aids:

American Printing House for the Blind
1839 Frankfort Avenue
P.O. Box 6085
Louisville, KY 40206-0085
(502) 895-2405 1-800-223-1839
FAX 502-899-2274

Exceptional Teaching Aids
20102 Woodbine Avenue
Castro Valley, CA 94546
1-800-549-6999 FAX 510-582-5911

Independent Living Aids, Inc.
200 Robins Lane
Jericho, NY 11753-2341
1-800-537-2118

Lighthouse Low Vision Products
36–20 Northern Boulevard
Long Island City, NY 1101
1-800-453-4923 FAX 718-786-0437

Maxi Aids
42 Executive Boulevard
Farmindale, NY 11735
(631) 752-0738 1-800-281-3555

Royal National Institute for the Blind
224 Great Portland Street
London W1N 6AA
England
01-388-1266

Science Products
Box 888
Southeastern, PA 19399
(618) 296-2111 1-800-888-7400
FAX 215-296-0488

TACK-TILES
Los Olvidados, Ltd.
P.O. Box 475
Plaistow, NH 03865
(603) 382-1904 FAX 603-382-1748

Technology:		
	Zoom Text Xtra! Big Shot	Ai Aquared P.O. Box 669 Manchester Center, VT 05255-0669 (802) 362-1670 FAX 802-362-1670 www.aisquared.com
	Talking Typer Math Flash Learn Keys Termite Torpedo Book Port Braille 'n' Speak Scholar	American Printing House for the Blind 1830 Frankfort Avenue P.O. Box 6085 Louisville, KY 40206-0085 1-800-223-1839 www.aph.org
	Duxbury Translator Mac OS7–9 DOS Windows 95,98, ME, 2000, XP Megadots	Duxbury System, Inc. P.O. Box 1054 270 Littleton Road Westford, MA 01886-3523 (978) 692-3000 www.duxburysystems.com
	PAC Mate Jaws for Windows Open Book Connect Outloud Versapoint embosser Braille 'n' Speak	Freedom Scientific, Inc. 11800 31st Court N. St. Petersburg, FL 33716 1-800-444-4443 www.freedomscientific.com

	Type 'n' speak Braille Lite	
	Vocal Eyes Window Eyes	GW Micro 725 Airport North Office Park Ft. Wayne, IN 76825 (260) 489-3671 www.gwmicro.com
	Calculators CCTVs Software Embossers Variety of other technology	LS & S Group P.O. Box 673 Northbrook, IL 60065 1-800-468-4789 www.lssgroup.com
	Mountbatten Braille writer BrailleNote VoiceNote Traveller	Pulsedata Humanware, Texas Division Mesa Plaza Shopping Center 8022 Mesa Drive Austin, TX 78731 (512) 345-4123 www.pulsedata.com
	CCTVs	Optelec, US Inc. 6 Lyberty Way Westford, MA 01886 1-800-828-1056 www.optelec.com
	Orion Scientific Talking Calculator	Orbit Research 3422 Old Capitol Suite 585 Wilmington, DE 19808 1-88-60-ORBIT www.orbitreasearch.com
	Tiger Braille Embosser Accessible Graphing Calculator	ViewPlus 1853 SW Airport Avenue Corvallis, OR 97330 (866) 836-2184 www.viewplustech.com
Test Sources:		American Foundation for the Blind 11 Penn Plaza–Suite 300 New York, NY 1001 (212) 502-7660 1-800-232-5463 FAX 212-502-7777

American Guidance Service
4201 Woodland Road
P.O. Box 99
Circle Pines, MN 55014-1796
1-800-328-2560 FAX 612-786-9077

American Printing House for the Blind
1839 Frankfort Avenue
P.O. Box 6085
Louisville, KY 40206-0085
(502) 895-2405 1-800-223-1839

Bernell Corporation
750 Lincolnway East
P.O. Box 4637
South Bend, IN 46634

Callier Center for Communication Disorders
1966 Inwood Road
Dallas, TX 75235-7298

Curriculum Associates
5 Esquire Road
North Billerica, MA 01862-2589

DLM Teaching Resources
One DLM Park
Allen, TX 75002

Howe Press
Perkins School for the Blind
175 North Beacon Street
Watertown, MA 02172
(617) 924-3434

Ingham Intermediate School District
2630 West Howell Road
Mason, MI 48854
(517) 676-1051

Jackson County Educational Services District
101 North Grape Street
Medford, OR 97501
(503) 776-8550

Kaplan Companies
P.O. Box 609
Lewisville, NC 27023-0609
1-800-334-2014

Kendall/Hunt Publishing Company
1111 Purina Drive
Dubuque, IA 52001

Lighthouse, Inc.
Optical Aids Service
36–02 Northern Boulevard
Long Island City, NY 11101
1-800-453-4923 FAX 718-786-0437

McCarron-Dial Systems
P.O. Box 45628
Dallas, TX 75245
(214) 247-5945 FAX 214-634-9970

Parent Consultants
P.O. Box 12114
Ogden, UT 84412

Pro-Ed
8700 Shoal Creek Boulevard
Austin, TX 78757-6897
(512) 451-3246 FAX 512-451-8542

The Psychological Corporation
555 Academic Court
San Antonio, TX 78204-2498
1-800-228-0752 FAX 1-800-232-1223
(send orders to: P.O. Box 839954
San Antonio, TX 78283-3954)

Region 4 Education Service Center
7145 West Tidwell
P.O. Box 863
Houston, TX 77092-2096
(713) 744-6368 FAX 713-462-6827

Riverside Publishing Company
8420 Bryn Mawr Avenue
Chicago, IL 60631
1-800-767-8378 FAX 312-693-0325

Science Research Associates
259 East Erie Street
Chicago, IL 60611

Stoelting Company
620 Wheat Lane
Wood Dale, IL 60191
(708) 860-9700 FAX 708-860-9775

Texas School for the Blind and Visually Impaired
Business Office
1100 West 45th Street
Austin, TX 78756-3494
(512) 454-8631

University of Illinois Press
Box 5081–Station A
Gregory Drive
Champaign, IL 61820

VORT Corporation
P.O. Box 11132
Palo Alto, CA 94306

Western Psychological Services
12031 Wilshire Boulevard
Los Angeles, CA 90025-1251
1-800-648-8857 FAX 310-478-7838

Vision Screening Materials: Bernell Corporation
750 Lincolnway East
P.O. Box 4637
South Bend, IN 46634

Lighthouse, Inc.
36–20 Northern Boulevard
Long Island City, NY 11101
1-800-453-4923 FAX 718-786-0437

Nelson Canada (for STYCAR materials)
1120 Birchmount Road
Scarborough, Ontario M1K 5G4
Canada
(416) 752-9100 1-800-268-2222
FAX 416-752-9646

Prevent Blindness America
500 East Remington Road
Schaumburg, IL 60173-4557
1-800-331-2020

Vision Associates
7512 Dr. Phillips Boulevard–#50-316
Orlando, FL 32819
(407) 352-1200 FAX 407-352-5632

Other Miscellaneous Resources:

American Blind Bowling Association
315 North Main
Houston, PA 15342
(724) 745-5986

American Blind Lawyers Association
P.O. Box 1590
Indianola, MS 38751
(662) 887-5398

American Blind Skiing Foundation
610 South William Street
Mt. Prospect, IL 60058
(847) 255-1739

American Council of the Blind
1155 45th St., NW
Washington, DC 20005
(202) 467-5081 1-800-424-8666

Helen Keller National Center for Deaf-Blind Youths and Adults
111 Middle Neck Road
Sands Point, NY 11050-1299
(516) 944-8900

National Association of Blind Teachers
c/o American Council of the Blind
1155 15th St., NW
Washington, DC 20005
(202) 467-5081

National Federation of the Blind
1800 Johnson Street
Baltimore, MD 21230
(410) 659-9314

United States Association for Blind Athletes
33 North Institute Street
Colorado Springs, CO 80903
(719) 630-0422

Appendix G

A TIMELINE OF EVENTS RELATED TO THE EDUCATION OF CHILDREN WITH VISUAL IMPAIRMENT

1949 Denis Diderot, a respected French philosopher and physician, wrote a "letter on the Blind for the Use of Those Who See;" this letter was based on Diderot's discussions with, and observations of, capable, intelligent blind persons.

1783 Valentin Hauy established the first school for blind students in Paris; he used raised letters, read tactually, to teach his blind students to read.

1829 The first school for blind students was established in the United States; this was the New England Asylum for the Blind, later to be known as Perkins School for the Blind.

1834 Louis Braille perfected his literary raised-dot code of reading; this system was later to be called "braille."

1837 The first deaf-blind child was admitted to Perkins School for the Blind; this child was Laura Bridgman.

1860 The Missouri School for the Blind became the first residential school in the United States to use braille as a reading system.

1866 Samuel Gridley Howe, the first Superintendent at the Perkins School for the Blind, became concerned about segregated education for blind children.

1871 The American Association of Instructors of the Blind (AAIB) was formed.

1879 The Act to Promote the Education of the Blind was authorized to fund the American Printing House for the Blind; it is still authorized and funded today.

1887 Anne Sullivan, a graduate of the Perkins School for the Blind, began to teach Helen Keller.

1899 Connecticut enacted the first law requiring vision screening of school children.

1900 Day-school classes for blind children were established in Chicago public schools.

1907 The first issue of *The Outlook for the Blind* (a journal) was published; this professional journal became today's *Journal of Visual Impairment and Blindness.*

1909 Cleveland public schools organized braille reading classes for blind students.

1913 Boston and Cleveland started classes in the public schools for partially seeing students.

1915 The National Society for the Prevention of Blindess was founded.

1916 Braille was officially adopted in United States schools.

1918 The University of California offered the first university teacher preparation program for teachers of visually impaired students.

1921 The American Foundation for the Blind was founded.

1922 The Council for Exceptional Children was founded.

1925 Peabody College (Vanderbilt University) established the first summer program to prepare teachers of visually impaired children.

1928 Dog guides were introduced in the United States.

1929 The first dog guide school in the United States (Seeing Eye in Morristown, NJ) was established.

1930 Ophthalmologists agreed that vision was not harmed by use, thus eliminating the concept of "sight conservation;" it would be about 25 years before this term disappeared from educational jargon, however.

1932-1933 Standard English Braille was adopted by both American and British committees, and by the American Printing House for the Blind for textbook production.

1934 The American Medical Association defined "legal blindness" for the Social Security Act of 1935.

1935 Columbia University established the first year-round teacher preparation program in the area of visual impairment.

1935 The Library of Congress was funded to develop talking book machines.

1936 The American Printing House for the Blind produced the first recorded reading materials: "Talking Books."

1937 P.L. 75-37 provided special postage rates for blind persons mailing braille materials.

1943 The first textbook for teachers of partially seeing children was written: *Education and Health of the Partially Seeing Child,* by Winifred Hathaway.

1944 Richard Hoover developed the long-cane (a mobility device) at the Valley Forge Army Hospital; today, even school children learn to use a smaller version of the long-cane.

1947 The American Printing House for the Blind produced large print books for the first time.

1951 The Perkins braille writer was developed (and is still used today).

1953 The Nemeth Code of braille math was developed.

1954 *The Pinebrook Report* (a national report on the "state-of-the-art" in education for blind and visually impaired students) described educational services that included the full continuum: itinerant teachers serving regular schools, day classes, resource rooms, and residential schools. (This continuum is the basis of today's continuum of services in special education, described in P.L. 94-142.)

1954 The Supreme Court outlawed segregated education in its *Brown vs Topeka* decision.

1956 American Printing House materials became available to day school pupils.

1957 Peabody College (Vanderbilt University) expanded its teacher preparation program to a year-round basis.

1960 Boston College established the first university program to train Orientation and Mobility instructors.

1963 Natalie Barraga published her visual efficiency study, which was the foundation for the development of the *Program to Increase Visual Efficiency;* this now includes the *Diagnostic Assessment Procedure* (DAP) and the *Design for Instruction.* Dr. Barraga's concepts revolutionized educational ideas and practices for students with visual impairment.

1972 Head Start programs were required to include handicapped children.

1973 Section 504 of the Rehabilitation Act (P.L. 93-112) prohibited discrimination in programs receiving federal funds.

1975 P.L. 94-142 (The Education for All Handicapped Children Act) guaranteed a free and appropriate public school education for handicapped children, with additional special education, related services, and an individual education plan (IEP).

1974-1975 The first Closed Circuit Television (CCTV) became available, as did the first usable synthetic speech device; the first talking calculator became available, and used both audio and visual output.

1976 The Kurzweil Reader was invented (a prototype of the first print-to-speech translator/reader).

1978 Paperless braille appeared with the invention of the Versabraille.

1980 The National Association of Parents of Visually Impaired (NAPVI) was established.

1983 The first braille embosser was attached to a microcomputer.

1984 The Association for Education and Rehabilitation (AER) resulted from the merging of AEVH (Association of Educators of the Visually Handicapped, once American Association of Instructors of the Blind) and AAWB (American Association of Workers for the Blind–those who worked in a rehabilitation capacity, primarily with adults).

1986 P.L. 99-457 provided for special education for children from birth onward.

1990 The Americans With Disabilities Act (ADA, or P.L. 101-336) prohibited discrimination based on disability in employment, transportation, public accommodations/services, and telecommunications.

1990 P.L. 101-476 (Individuals with Disabilities Education Act, or IDEA), amendments to P.L. 94-142, changed the term "handicapped" to "disabled," mandated transition services for special needs students, and added assistive technology for students who needed such equipment/devices.

1991 Texas passed landmark legislation in the form of a "Braille Bill;" it required braille instruction for all functionally blind students, taught only by a certified teacher of visually impaired students, and required textbook publishers to provide their textbooks on diskette so that they could be translated electronically into braille.

1995 OSEP (the federal Office of Special Education Programs) issued a Policy Guidance statement to states, *reinforcing* appropriate placements, *requiring* the array of placement choices, and emphasizing the importance of literacy for blind and visually impaired students.

1995 The National Agenda was developed to focus on the needs of visually impaired students. Eight goals addressed: timely referrals, the role of parents, the need for professional personnel, teacher caseloads, the array of services, appropriate assessment, availability of instructional materials, and the expanded core curriculum.

1997 Public Law 105-17 (IDEA amendments of 1997) defined Orientation and Mobility instruction as a related service, reinforced the need for braille instruction and assistive technology, and reiterated the ongoing federal mandate for an available array (continuum) of service options.

1999 NASDE (National Association of State Directors of Special Education) disseminated guidelines that emphasized unique needs of students with visual impairments, and supported the need for choice in appropriate placements (i.e., continuum, or array).

GLOSSARY

Abacus–a manipulative-type math tool/device used by blind and visually impaired individuals in place of paper and pencil.

Accommodation–the automatic process of the visual system that allows the optical parts to adjust for near or distance vision; the lens changes shape and the eyes realign.

Achromatopsia–congenital lack of or reduced number of cones; reduced acuity and impaired color vision; photophobia.

Adventitious–acquired later.

Advocacy–the ability to stand up for one's own needs and rights, in a calm, informed, nonaggressive manner.

Albinism–pigmentary deficiency in the eyes (ocular albinism) or in the eyes, skin, and hair (oculocutaneous albinism); characteristics include reduced acuity, nystagmus, and photophobia.

Amblyopia–reduced visual acuity due to non-use, either because of different refractive errors in the two eyes or because of strabismus; in either case, the brain blocks out (or "suppresses') the image in one eye; over time, the suppression becomes a permanent loss; usually untreatable after age 8.

Angiography–a diagnostic procedure to examine vascular abnormalities in the eye.

Anoxia–oxygen deprivation; suffocation.

Aphakia–absence of the ocular lens.

Aqueous–clear fluid that fills the posterior and anterior chambers of the eye, from the front of the lens to the inner surface of the cornea; produced and drained at a constant, balanced rate.

Array–the continuum of placement choices mandated by federal law.

Articulation–the ability to form speech sounds.

Asphyxia–lack of oxygen.

Astigmatism–improperly curved cornea, resulting in a refractive error; corrected by a cylindrical lens.

Ataxia–shaky, clumsy, unsteady gait.

Athetosis–involuntary, slow, twisting muscle function; includes facial grimacing, drooling, and speech problems.

Basic concept–understanding of fundamental characteristics or properties of people and the environment.

Bifocal lenses–eyeglasses with a dual prescription, one for distance vision in the upper portion and one for near vision in the lower part.

Bioptics–small telescopes mounted (usually in the upper part) in a pair of glasses; can be monocular or binocular; used for viewing-as-needed, as in driving.

Blink reflex–automatic closing of the eyelids, either to protect the eye from an approaching object or to facilitate the flow of tears over the outer surface of the eye.

Bony orbit–the recessed cavity in the skull where the eye is located.

Braille–a system of raised dots used by blind persons as a literacy tool (for reading and writing).

Braillewriter–a mechanical writing device to produce braille.

Brain–the organ which controls all body systems in a living organism.

Brainstem–the oldest part of the brain evolutionarily; controls survival functions and determine alertness levels; includes the medulla, pons, and midbrain.

Canal of Schlemm–circular drainage canal behind the trabecular meshwork; drains aqueous fluid and transfers it to the venous system.

Cataract–clouding of the optical lens.

CAT scan (or CT scan)–computerized axial tomography; low-dose X-rays used to examine tissue layers.

CCTV–closed circuit television system used for spontaneous enlargement of materials (either print, pictures, or other materials which need to be made larger to be seen).

Cerebellum–part of the brain that controls posture and balance; coordinates muscle movements.

Cerebrum–the two brain "hemispheres" that process information; the part of the brain that "thinks."

CF–"count fingers;" the ability to tell how many fingers the examiner is holding up, at a specific distance.

Choroid–the vascular, nourishing, middle layer of the eye's outer wall.

Ciliary body–part of the uveal tract in the front, inner part of the eye; includes the ciliary muscle and ciliary processes.

Ciliary muscle–circular muscle part of the ciliary body that controls the shape of the lens by tensing or relaxing.

Ciliary processes–the part of the ciliary body that produces aqueous fluid.

Color blindness–the reduced ability to perceive color.

Communication disorder–combined expressive and receptive language disorders.

COMS–a certified orientation and mobility specialist.

Concave lens–spherical lens used to correct myopia; minus lens, curves inward.

Conductive hearing loss–hearing impairment resulting from a problem in the outer or middle ear.

Cones–retinal photoreceptor cell responsible for color perception and sharpest acuity; concentrated in the macula; sole type of photoreceptor cell in the fovea; operates best in the daylight and/or good lighting conditions.

Confrontation fields testing–a gross measure of peripheral vision, using a test object which approaches from the outer limits of the peripheral field towards the front or midline.

Congenital–present at birth.

Conjunctivitis–a group of eye diseases that infect or inflame the lining of the eyelids and/or outer tissue of the visible sclera.

Constriction–partial closing of an opening, such as the pupil of the eye; becoming smaller.

Contact lens–small soft or hard lens worn directly on the eye; covers the central portion of the cornea.

Convex lens–spherical lens used to correct hyperopia; plus lens, curves outward.

"CP"–cerebral palsy; a group of non-progressive symptoms of brain damage, characterized by poor muscle control; includes spasticity, athetosis, ataxia, or some combination thereof.

Core curriculum (Expanded Core Curriculum)–when applied to skills need by visually impaired students, includes the disability-related areas that must be specifically taught to these students because of their visual impairment.

Cornea–transparent front surface of the eye; curved to bend light rays as they enter the eye.

Corneal abrasion–a scratched cornea; the depth of the scratch determines the potential for scarring.

Corneal light reflex–the light reflection on the corneal surface.

Corneal transplant–the replacement of diseased or opaque corneal tissue with healthy corneal donor tissue.

Cortex–a thin layer of nerve cells which cover the cerebrum; the lobes are the first receptors of sensory information.

Criterion referenced–measurement term indicating that external criteria (rather than norms) have been established to indicate mastery.

Cylindrical lens–"slice" of a cylinder; used to correct astigmatism.

DAP–Diagnostic Assessment Procedure; a test of visual efficiency; items range from light perception to reading of regular size print; accompanied by an instructional program (Design for Instruction) to remediate deficits; both the DAP and the instructional program are part of the Program to Develop Visual Efficiency; a downward extension of activities is currently being planned.

Decibels–the unit of measuring hearing loss; measurement of sound intensity or loudness.

Diagnostic teaching–combined instruction and assessment to identify deficits in the learning process.

Dilation–enlarging of a hole, such as the pupil of the eye.

Diplegia–lower extremities more involved motorically than the upper extremities.

Disability-specific–related to a disability, either directly or indirectly.

Dvorine plates–test for color vision, utilizing dot designs of various colors.

Dyslexia–a severe form of learning disability where the individual cannot read the printed word.

Echolalia–the use of words for sound purposes only; usually repetitive but meaningless or irrelevant.

Ecomap–a graphic representation of a family's support systems, both psychological and material.

Educational blindness–a descriptive term indicating minimal functional vision; individual will probably use tactual and auditory senses for learning, and will likely read braille.

Enucleation–the eye has been surgically removed.

ERG–electroretinogram; clinical electrophysiological method of measuring retinal function.

Expressive language–speech; meaningful spoken language.

Extraocular muscles–the six external muscles of the eye which control its movements.

Eyelids–thin muscular tissues which cover the visible portion of the eye and serve to protect it from excess light or foreign objects; able to open or close to control light.

FAPE–free appropriate public education (with greatest emphasis on "appropriate").

Feinbloom Chart–a central-vision testing chart with numbers in sizes larger than those on the standard Snellen chart or any other standard vision testing chart); used to evaluate vision that is worse than 20/200.

Fixation–the ability to look at an object steadily for at least two seconds.

Following–the ability of the eyes to reposition and keep a stimulus in the central line of vision as the stimulus moves; "tracking."

Fovea–(also known as the "fovea centralis") the most specialized part of the retina; center of the macula which contains only cone photoreceptors; responsible for sharpest vision and color reception.

FVE–Functional Vision Evaluation; accumulation of information both test-oriented and observational, that determines how well vision is used in a variety of situations.

Glaucoma–an ocular condition when either too much aqueous is produced or the drainage system is blocked; pressure can build up within the eye, pushing outward against the cornea and inward against the retina and optic nerve; blindness can result if untreated.

Hemiplegia–poor coordination in the extremities on same sides of the body (e.g., both right arm and right leg).

HM–"hand movements;" the ability to tell that a hand is moving at a specified distance; usually represents minimal vision.

HOTV Chart–a distance-acuity test chart which uses irreversible letters.

House-Apple-Umbrella Chart–a distance acuity test chart which uses symbolic pictures of a house, an apple, and an umbrella as stimuli.

Hyaloid system–a vascular system within the eye during the embryonic period of development; nourishes the lens during the prenatal period; disappears before birth.

Hyperopia–farsightedness; caused by an eyeball that is too short; corrected by a spherical plus (convex) lens; nearpoint activities (e.g., reading) are affected in hyperopia; distance vision can also be affected if the condition is severe.

Hypertonia–tight muscle tone.

Hypotonia–low muscle tone.

IEP–Individual Education Plan; a specially designed instructional program for a disabled child (ages 3–21) that meets the individual needs of that child.

IFSP–Individual Family Service Plan; a specially designed instructional program for a disabled child and his/her family; applies to children from birth to 3 years of age.

Interdisciplinary team–special group of people with unique and shared expertise in assessment and programming for disabled children.

Iris–the visible, circular, colored part of the eye; the muscle that controls the amount of light entering the eye through the pupil.

Ishihara plates–a test for color vision using a set of dot designs in various colors.

Jaeger card–test of nearpoint vision using various sizes of print.

Lacrimal system–the tear system; composed of the lacrimal gland which produced tears, the puncta (openings through which the tears drain), and the lacrimal sac which collects the tears and passes them into the nose.

Lateral geniculate body–a kind of "sorting station" at the end of the optic tract, where electrical impulses are organized and re-routed through the optic radiations to the brain.

Learning–the acquisition of a new skill or knowledge which changes in individual's behavior or adds to the accumulation of information.

Least restrictive environment–legally, the placement that is closest to the child's home, with non-disabled peers; educationally, that placement which least restricts learning.

Legal blindness–20/200 central acuity in the better eye, corrected if applicable, or visual fields of 20° or less.

Lens–the small, transparent, round or ovate structure inside the eye, which is capable of altering its outer curvature to bend light rays in such a way as to focus them on the proper place in the retina.

Lighthouse cards/charts–tests of central acuity, at both nearpoint and distance; may be pictures, letters, or both.

Limbic system–a group of structures between the brainstem and cortex that regulate involuntary body functions (including pupillary reactions); includes the thalamus, hypothalamus, pituitary gland, hippocampus, and amygdala.

LMA–Learning Media Assessment; assessment procedure to establish best sensory learning channels and most efficient literacy medium.

Low vision–a severe visual impairment after correction, but potential exists for using available vision with or without optical or non-optical devices and/or modifications.

Low vision device–an optical (lens-based) or non-optical (other than the use of a lens or lens system) means of enhancing the visual abilities of a person with low vision.

LP–light perception; the ability to tell the presence or absence of light.

LProj.–light projection; the ability to point towards the source of light.

Macula–specialized portion of the retina where light rays focus most sharply; contains mostly cones; responsible for clear vision and color perception.

Macular degeneration–a gradual deterioration of the macular area of the retina; causes reduction in central acuity but usually leaves peripheral vision intact.

Magnifier–an optical device which enlarges an image, usually making a close image even larger.

Manipulatives–concrete, three-dimensional objects that are used to teach basic concepts in math and other subjects.

MAP–most appropriate placement, where the child's individual needs can best be met.

Mean–a measure of central tendency in statistics; the arithmetical average.

Median–a measure of central tendency in statistics; the middle score in a given group.

Mode–a measure of central tendency in statistics; the score achieved the most in a given group.

Monocular–an optical device used to bring distant objects closer; a "one-eye" telescope.

MVPT–Motor-Free Visual Perception Test; book of designs to test visual perception.

Myelin–the covering of nerves that acts as insulation, thus preventing "short circuits" between nerves.

Myopia–nearsightedness; caused by an eyeball that is too long; corrected by a spherical minus (concave) lens; distance vision is affected.

Natural environment–an environment that would be natural or normal for young non-disabled children; usually interpreted as the child's own home or neighborhood.

Nemeth Code–mathematical symbols which are part of the braille code; includes numerals and operational signs.

Nil–"nothing;" when used in an eye report, equal to total blindness.

Norm referenced–a measurement term that implies standardization, or the use of "norms" in assessment comparisons.

Null point–in nystagmus, the position of the head (turned or tilted) that minimizes the eye movements; the position of least hystagmus.

Nystagmus–an involuntary movement of the eyes, either side to side, or up and down.

Ocularist–one who makes artificial eyes.

OKN–optokinetic nystagmus; induced nystagmus, brought on by rotating a cylinder with black and white stripes; gives a gross measure of visual acuity.

Ophthalmologist–medical doctor who has specialized in defects and diseases of the eye; qualified to perform ocular surgery and prescribe medications for the eyes.

Ophthalmoscope–an instrument used to examine the retina.

Optic atrophy–malfunction of the optic nerve; acuities can range from mild losses to blindness.

Optic chiasm–cross-over point between the optic nerves and the optic tracts; nasal halves of retinal impulses cross and join with the opposite lateral halves of retinal impulses before continuing along the optic tracts.

Optic nerve–tubular collection of nerve bundles which transmit electrical impulses from the eye to the brain; technically includes only that portion from the retina to the optic chiasm.

Optic nerve hypoplasia–smaller than normal optic nerve, usually as a result of a central nervous system insult in the prenatal period.

Optic radiations–final routing of electrical impulses from the lateral geniculate bodies to the visual cortex.

Optic tract–portion of the visual pathway between the optic chiasm and lateral geniculate bodies; contain impulses from half of each eye (nasal half plus opposite lateral half).

Optical device (also known as a "low vision device")–any lens-based system of enhancing vision; usually used by individuals who have low vision.

Optical system–that part of the visual system which includes the eye and optic nerve; the part that receives light energy, changes it to electrical energy; and transmits the signals to the brain for processing.

Optician–professional who grinds lenses according to a prescription given by an ophthalmologist or optometrist, and fits them into eyeglass frames.

Optometrist–a nonmedical professional who can evaluate refractive errors and prescribe corrective lenses.

Orthoptist–special technician who conducts eye-muscle training under the supervision of an ophthalmologist.

Outcome-based instruction–the implementation of a set of goals and objectives that lead to long-term outcomes.

Perceptual system–that part of the visual system which makes sense of ("understands") the electrical impulses relayed by the optic nerve; includes the brain.

Peripheral vision–the vision resulting only from the activation of the photoreceptor rods; acuity is about 20/400; may be known as "side vision."

Phonics–a system of teaching word attack skills through the use of letter or letter-combination sounds.

Preferential looking/viewing–a means of evaluating visual acuity in young children by presenting patterned stimuli in one of two locations and recording which pattern the child prefers.

Prism lenses–special lenses (prisms) used to superimpose peripheral images on functional retinal area.

Prone–lying on the stomach.

Pupil–round opening in the center of the iris; visible "black" part in the center of the eye's colored portion.

Pupillary response–the automatic constriction of the pupil when sudden bright light is encountered.

Receptive language–language heard and understood.

Refraction–the bending of light rays as they pass through a transparent substance.

Refractive errors–improper focusing of light on the macula, caused by an eyeball that is too short or too long, or by an improperly curved cornea.

Reliability–measurement term meaning that a test will give essentially the same results; if used repeatedly on a given population.

Residential school–an educational setting where the students live and are instructed on the same campus.

Resource room–educational placement; for visually impaired students, the instructor is a certified TVI; the students are usually brought to a central location and enrolled in the regular grades; the resource room teacher is available as needed to *supplement* regular instruction (not a substitute for regular classes).

Retina–innermost layer of the wall of the eye; contains the photoreceptor cells (rods and cones) which receive light energy; convert it to electrical impulses, and transmit it to the optic nerve for relay to the brain.

Retinitis pigmentosa–a group of retinal diseases characterized by deteriorating retinal tissue; peripheral vision is usually lost first, and some types include central acuity losses as well.

Retinoblastoma–lethal eye tumor; treated with chemotherapy and/or surgery (enucleation).

Reverse telescope–telescopic device what has been turned around, thus optically making distance objects smaller but also widening the field of vision; because of the distortion of reality, only used for orientation purposes, not mobility.

RLF/ROP–originally called retrolental fibroplasia (RLF), now called retinopathy of prematurity (ROP); an ocular disease not uncommon in premature babies, but occasionally appears in full-term infants; the ocular vascular system develops improperly; exact cause still unknown.

Rods–type of retinal photoreceptor cells that operate under minimal lighting conditions; perceive shape and movement but no color.

Rubella (maternal)–measles contracted by a pregnant woman in the first trimester of pregnancy; can cause cataracts, hearing loss, heart disease ("rubella syndrome") in the fetus.

Sclera–tough, white, outer layer of the eye; protects the fragile inner contents of the eye.

Sensorineural hearing loss–hearing impairment resulting from a problem in the cochlea or auditory nerve.

Septo-optic dysplasia–severe form of optic nerve hypoplasia; usually characterized by brain abnormalities and/or endocrine problems.

Signature guide–a small device which enables a blind person to affix a signature on a line, within a predetermined space.

Slate and stylus–device for writing braille by hand; consists of a metal guide and a pointed writing instrument.

Snellen tests–charts and/or cards to assess central visual acuity at distance and/or nearpoint; includes the "illiterate" (or "tumbling") E chart, letter charts, and nearpoint cards.

Spasticity–involuntary tightening of the muscles.

Speech therapy–structured program of activities to remediate articulation, rhythm, or voice problems.

Spherical lens–round lens used to correct myopia (when it is ground into a concave, or minus, power) or hyperopia (when it is ground into a convex, or plus, power).

Standardization–measurement term indicating that a test instrument has been tried out on a large, representative sample of people, to establish validity; "norms" are generated and used as standards against which to compare each score.

Strabismus–ocular misalignment; includes esotropia, exotropia, hypertropia, hypotropia, and their corresponding -phorias.

Sty (hordeolum)–infected eyelash follicle.

STYCAR tests–a kit of vision screening materials that includes "rolling balls," toys, cards, and charts; manufactured in England.

Supine–lying on the back.

Suspensory ligaments–circle of fine, hair-like muscles (also called "zonules") attached to the outer edge of the lens and connected to the ciliary muscle; controls the shape of the lens.

Talking Books/Talking Book Machine–recorded books, either on "floppy" records or on tape; require a special record player, with a special slower speed, to play them.

Telescope–an optical device which brings distant objects closer by enlarging the image.

Tonometry–method to test intraocular pressure to identify glaucoma.

Toxoplasmosis–a disease that can affect many parts of the body, but when contracted by a pregnant woman, can cause an inflammation in the choroid and retina of the fetus; scar tissue formed as the inflammation heals can leave non-functional areas of the retina.

Trabecular meshwork–a sieve-like tissue that lines the angle formed by the junction of the iris and inner cornea; filters aqueous as it leaves the eye.

Transdisciplinary team–special group of people with expertise in assessment and programming for disabled children; team members release expertise to one or two service providers.

Transition–period of change in program plan; stage of moving from one phase of an educational program to another.

TVI–special teacher who is trained and certified in the special methods and curriculum for visually impaired children.

Ultrasonography–the use of high frequency sound waves to diagnose ocular tumors or lesions.

Uveal tract–includes the choroid, ciliary body, and iris; the vascular layer of the eye.

Validity–a measurement term; test measures what it *says* it measure.

Verbalism–in visually impaired children, the use of words without a clear understanding of their meanings.

VER/VEP–electrophysiological measurement of function of the visual cortex; visually evoked response/potential.

VI student–student whose vision is functionally impaired to such an extent that special instructional techniques are needed in school for optimum learning to take place.

Visual pathway–system which transmits impulses from the eye to the brain, including the optic nerves, optic chiasm, optic tracts, lateral geniculate bodies, and optic radiations.

Visual system–the combined optical and perceptual systems that result in "seeing."

Vitreous–clear, jelly-like substance inside the back two-thirds portion of the eye; maintains globe shape of the eyeball.

Zonules–(see suspensory ligaments).

INDEX